✪ W9-DFK-320

THE
Old Farmer's Almanac

CALCULATED ON A NEW AND IMPROVED PLAN FOR THE YEAR OF OUR LORD

2003

BEING 3RD AFTER LEAP YEAR AND (UNTIL JULY 4) 227TH YEAR OF AMERICAN INDEPENDENCE

Fitted for Boston and the New England states, with special corrections and calculations to answer for all the United States.

Containing, besides the large number of Astronomical Calculations and the Farmer's Calendar for every month in the year, a variety of

New, Useful, and Entertaining Matter.

Established in 1792

by Robert B. Thomas

There are loyal hearts, there are spirits brave,
There are souls that are pure and true;
Then give to the world the best you have,
And the best will come back to you.

–MADELINE BRIDGES [MARY AINGE DE VERE]

Cover T.M. registered in U.S. Patent Office

Copyright 2002 by Yankee Publishing Incorporated
ISSN 0078-4516

Library of Congress
Card No. 56-29681

Original wood engraving by Randy Miller

Address all editorial correspondence to: THE OLD FARMER'S ALMANAC, DUBLIN, NH 03444

Contents

The Old Farmer's Almanac • 2003

(c o n t i n u e d   o n   p a g e   4)

Discover more wit, wisdom, and weather at www.almanac.com.

Contents

(continued from page 2)

"Introducing my new Oreck XL². It's hotel strong, built to last twice as long, and still only 8 lbs. Try it free for 30 days!"

David Oreck
CHAIRMAN

Hi, I'm David Oreck. To prove to you that my new, 40th Anniversary 8-lb. Oreck XL² is one of the best investments you can make in home care appliances today—Take the Oreck Challenge.™ Try my Oreck XL² in your home for a full month, no charge and I'll give you my Oreck Cord Free Speed Iron™ as a gift! Imagine ironing without a cord. You'll cut ironing time in half. That's right, this $100 Cord Free Iron is free whether you keep my Oreck XL² or not.

I never put my name on anything that isn't the best. And my 40th Anniversary Oreck XL², with new 24-bar technology, is the best. It's built to last twice as long as my previous models which have lasted 25 years! Odds are you'd go through three other vacuums in the time you own one Oreck XL². And just wait until you see the beautiful job it does on carpets and bare floors. When you buy my Oreck XL² you get a complete system because I'll give you my Super Compact Canister with 8 attachments, absolutely free with purchase. It's a $165 value. Strong Enough To Pick Up A 16-lb. Bowling Ball.™ It's the perfect above-the-floor vacuum. Clean your home for 30 days on me. Then you decide.

BONUS GIFT

My $165 Super Compact Canister Vac is FREE with the purchase of an Oreck XL²! And my $100 Cord Free Speed Iron is yours FREE just for trying this remarkable vacuum!

1-800-388-4065
ext. BR314
or visit oreck.com

To Patrons

A pause before we proceed . . .

Traditionally, almanacs have been published and released in autumn, and this one has followed that tradition for 211 consecutive years. More recently, albeit for the past 33 years, new editions of this Almanac have gone on sale on the second Tuesday in September, faithfully, predictably, and (thankfully) without incident—until 2001. That year, our on-sale day for the 2002 issue was September 11, the day four hijacked planes changed course and altered history, a day that will be remembered forever as one of the saddest and most tragic this country has ever known. Alas, it is only now that we have the opportunity to suitably and publicly acknowledge the unfortunate circumstances that distinguish that date. One year hence, we pause to join with the rest of the world to honor the lives lost on that day and in the intervening days, and to salute the brave hearts who selflessly and courageously protect us, our country, and the freedoms and values we hold dear. We thank you. May God bless America.

As a calendar of celestial events, this Almanac chronicles the rhythm of the universe; since 1792, that has been our mission and our mandate. So it is with this issue that we endeavor (in the face of domestic and international affairs beyond our control or influence) to maintain that forward-moving momentum, offering in our inimitable fashion our predictions, forecasts, and features for 2003—in sum, a variety of new, useful, and entertaining matter.

Frequent patrons of this Almanac have come to appreciate and rely upon the consistency of its contents and the uniformity of its pages. Indeed, the pace of change herein would, when compared with the creeping advance of the proverbial snail, find the mollusk at a decided advantage. The calendar pages (44–71 in this issue) stand as the most enduring and proud evidence of that; they are *in essence* unchanged since this Almanac's debut. Further, since 1851, only minor modifications have been made to our cover.

We recognize, however, that this Almanac is *of* this world, not only *about* it; we are compelled to update our presentation every few . . . decades. So it is that some careful and measured changes appear in this edition.

The most visible changes are intended to answer the question most often put to us: "How do you decide what goes into the Almanac?" We attempt to solve that riddle with rubrics, or labels ("Astronomy," "Amusements," and "Anniversaries" among them), which convey the categories of our stories.

A word about our anniversary stories. These are sidelong glances at events, people, and situations that—despite their place in history (or, perhaps because of it)—haven't received the attention they deserve. An anniversary year is divisible by 10 or 5 (or better, 25), and there must be a good story lurking—with a humorous or quirky aspect that is of particular interest today.

Now, about our contributors. For each issue, we seek writers who not only have

Discover more wit, wisdom, and weather at www.almanac.com.

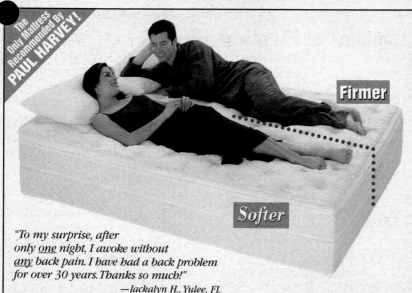

To Patrons (*continued from page 6*)

an interest but often expertise in specific topics; that's been the practice from the first. So it is that premiering here are modest biographies citing the professional credentials and career highlights of our contributors. These appear at the end of each article and, selectively, on page 34.

Last, you'll note that for centuries, this Almanac was limited in its coverage by the number of pages in each edition—but no longer, thanks to our Web site, www.almanac.com. Since its inception in 1996, almanac.com has enabled us to expand our content and make it available at any time.

Ah, time! Where does it go? As Benjamin Franklin opined, "Lost time is never found again," and who among us isn't often trying to "find the time" to do things? Here's a solution—a new feature on our Web site that enables you to create a personal home page and customize it with all sorts of timely Almanac data: local weather, tides, Moon and Sun rise and set times, daily wit and wisdom, and much more.

We expect that our founder, Robert B. Thomas, would look favorably upon these changes. He understood the importance of keeping up with the times—and of keeping track of time.

J. S., June 2002

However, it is by our works and not our words that we would be judged. These, we hope, will sustain us in the humble though proud station we have so long held in the name of

Your obedient servant,

Rob't B. Thomas.

Versatile <u>New</u> DR® FIELD and BRUSH MOWER...

cuts down and chops up tall, wiry field grasses —even 2"-thick hardwood saplings!

PLUS!

- **PERFECT FOR RECLAIMING** overgrown pastures, meadows, ditches, roadsides, fencelines, trails, pond edges, and woodlots of overgrown vegetation... <u>any</u> area too rough for ordinary mowers!

- **PIVOTING MOWER DECK** follows the ground without scalping. **MULCHING CHAMBER** shreds most vegetation into small pieces — so there's nothing to trip over or pick up like you get with hand-held brush cutters and sicklebar mowers.

  - **4-SPEEDS, POWER-REVERSE!** Your choice of engines from 9 to 17 HP with and without electric-starting!
    - **LIMITED-SLIP DIFFERENTIAL** for positive traction and easy turning.
    - **LOADED WITH NEW FEATURES** and options — built-in fuel gauge, hour meter, light, brakes, sealant-filled tires <u>and more</u>!

MADE IN USA
GSA Approved

The DR® CONVERTS in seconds without tools to a —

Pro-Style LAWN MOWER...

Powerful SNOW THROWER...

SNOW BLADE and more!

For Full Details of the New Multi-Purpose DR® FIELD and BRUSH MOWER

CALL TOLL-FREE
1-800-520-2525

PROUDLY Made in the U.S.A.

CONSUMER
TASTES & TRENDS

compiled by Christine Schultz

A Passion for Fashion

Anything Goes

"There are no fashion rules this season," says Lisa Herbert, executive vice president for Pantone, Inc., a leading color forecaster for the fashion and home industries. Individualism is in, with women choosing from a wide range of hip, bright colors: lollipop red, classic blue, sunset gold, and peppermint green. Also popular are sophisticated neutrals such as bleached sand and pussywillow gray.

TRENDS FOR WOMEN

■ Feminine styles are big, says Cynthia Leive, editor in chief of *Glamour* magazine—anything with small florals, lace, ruffles, tiered skirts, or embroidery. At the same time, there is also a strong move toward more masculine-styled pants, vests, and jackets. How to choose? Combine them both, says Leive.

TRENDS FOR MEN

■ The patriotic flag motif will continue to show up everywhere in menswear, from shirts and ties to swimsuits and headgear, forecasts the National Association of Men's Sportswear Buyers. Also watch for two conflicting trends: Business wear will become more conservative and serious, with the return of the diagonally striped tie, the trench coat, and tailored denim suits and blazers for young professionals. In contrast, men's leisure wear will take off into whimsy, with flowered sports shirts, brightly colored striped pants, handcrafted decorations on the back of jackets, and patterned shirts paired with patterned pants.

Style Makers

FOR HER

■ Hats are must-haves, from the high, furry beefeater to the flat leather beret.

■ Hardware is hot: chain belts, buckles on studded canvas, metal-laden leather suits.

■ As more people entertain at home, watch for the pajama look: evening

–photo courtesy Banana Republic

outfits with gold brocade and piping-trimmed pajama tops, gauzy nightgown-like dresses, baggy pajama-bottom pants.

FOR HIM

■ Distinction is in the details: a silk waistband in classic slacks, a zipper in place of buttons on a white shirt, a waterproof lining inside a camel-hair coat.

■ Men's handbags, popular in the 19?? (like the messenger bag shown), are back as essential accessories.

FOR BOTH

■ All denim styles are in, with a few new twists. Waistlines are rising and falling, and leg fit is shifting back and forth between baggy and tight. Fur (often faux) is found on collars, cuffs, and inside jean jackets. Neutral-colored or white denim is popular in warm months.

In	Out
FOR WOMEN:	**FOR WOMEN:**
■ Ruffled peasant blouses	■ Tight belly-revealing shirts
■ Big-tiered peasant skirts	■ Pencil-thin skirts
FOR MEN:	**FOR MEN:**
■ Mustaches	■ Goatees
■ Elegant attire	■ Grunge wear
■ Jeweled buttons and stiff, colored evening shirts with tuxedos	■ Traditional bow ties with tuxedos

The Home Front

The concepts of heritage and tradition will influence our color choices, predicts Leatrice Eiseman, director of Pantone's Color Institute. Early American–period colors that Pantone calls "emblematic" will dominate, notably colonial blues, burgundy reds, earth browns, and deep teals. The once-popular calming pastels will shift to darker hues. Many toys, plastic products, and accents, however, will tend toward bright reds, whites, and blues for added cheer.

The Tropical Look

■ In the quest for luxurious refuge at cheap prices, designers have hit upon the magic of mosquito netting. Draped over beds, couches, dining areas, baby bassinets—you name it—the see-through gauze gives ordinary items the exotic look of the romantic Caribbean or an African safari and adds the illusion of warmth in winter.

(continued)

Home, Sweet Second Home

■ More affluent baby boomers and childless couples are buying second homes. By 2010, 9.8 million people will own two homes, up from 5.5 million in 1990.

At Home in Canada

■ Color and comfort are key words, say the editors of Canada's decorating magazine *Style at Home*. Watch for . . .

■ 1960s-inspired geometric patterns in muted colors on draperies, rugs, upholstery, and home accessories.

■ Art deco furniture.

■ Gold tones and dark woods used with traditional-print wallpapers.

■ Curvy, playful designs in kitchen appliances and utensils.

■ Bold stripes.

■ Antique-style furniture upholstered in woven linens, bright corduroys, and multicolored velvet.

■ Cool contemporary wall colors like moonlit green, eclectic blue, and the new neutral: gray tinted with lilac.

In	Out
■ Minimalistic Zen touches	■ Western materialistic clutter
■ Multipurpose furniture (benches with hidden storage)	■ Overloaded bookshelves
■ 1960s "mod" styles, such as shag rugs and Charles Eames–era wallpaper	■ All-white rooms

In the Garden

Gardening appears to have become the darling of interior decorators," according to *Horticulture* magazine. Gardening implements are coming indoors: glass-covered birdbaths stand as side tables in living rooms; rakes and ladders rest in entryways; picket fences and trellises adorn bathrooms; and watering cans, pots, window boxes, and garden hats accent kitchens.

Hot Houseplants

■ Plants that bring good luck and prosperity—like the lucky bamboo and the money tree—will continue to gain popularity. Elegant orchids and other tropical plants will also find favor. Ferns, once popular in the '60s and '70s, will make a comeback (minus the macramé hangers).

14　　Air plant *(Tillandsia cyanea)*　　(continued)

Growing in Popularity

■ **Drought-resistant plants.** As we worry more about water availability, plants that aren't water hogs are getting noticed: purple coneflowers (*Echinacea*), wormwoods (*Artemisia*), black-eyed Susans (*Rudbeckia*), daylilies (*Hemerocallis*), junipers, rugosa roses, cedars, pines, and redbuds.

■ **The garden as a café.** Look for gardens designed as a series of rooms, with pathways leading from one to another. In the middle of it all (not just off the back door) is a secluded spot, with a stone or brick patio and a small round table and chairs reminiscent of a French café.

■ **Victorian classics with a new (and affordable) twist.** Garden ornaments popular 100 or more years ago are everywhere—gazing globes, garden statuary, birdbaths, obelisks, sundials, anything that looks like wrought iron—made from new-tech materials such as fiberglass, cast aluminum, freeze-resistant concrete, and weatherproof polyresin.

■ **A love affair with leaves.** Garden designers are smitten with plants that have showy, colorful leaves, mixing them right in with more-traditional garden plants. The attention is on begonias, caladiums, cannas, coleuses, colocasias, and plants with variegated foliage, especially multicolored hostas and grasses.

–Margo Letourneau

On the Farm

Fish, Not Beef

By 2010, fish farming will outstrip cattle farming, according to the Worldwatch Institute. It notes that beef production has stalled and that aquaculture has been the most actively growing worldwide source of food for over a decade.

Air, Not Grain

■ The World Future Society predicts that "future farmers could make more money from the air than from the land." This is because a quarter-acre of land that produces $100 worth of corn annually could bring $2,000 if leased to an electric company for turbine-generated wind energy.

Bar Codes, Not Bare Hands

■ With technology on smart farms doing everything from determining a cow's health by a bar-code tag attached to its ear to adjusting the feed mix based on the cow's needs, expect to see more professional managers than hands-on family farmers, predicts the World Future Society.

–photo: H. Armstrong Roberts

(continued)

Sky News and Views

Back to the Future

Scientists have recently learned that the most remote place on Earth gives the best view of the most remote time. Through telescopes at the South Pole, researchers from the National Science Foundation are observing the afterglow of the Big Bang and making discoveries about the birth and early development of the universe.

Star Parties

Star-watching parties are all the rage, reports *Sky & Telescope* magazine. The small, local parties of two decades ago have mushroomed into events that draw hundreds of amateur stargazers into the fellowship of dark skies and bright stars. To find a party near you, contact the Astronomical League, the world's largest federation of amateur astronomers, at www.astroleague.org.

A nursery of new stars.

—NASA

Look Out Below

Space rock hounds are searching Earth for pieces of meteors that fall from the sky. An estimated 20,000 space rocks strike Earth each year, according to a CNN report, and as of early 2002, 24 specimens had been determined to have come from Mars. The best places to find the iron-rich rarities are in deserts and Antarctica, where there is little if any grass, trees, or dirt. Some space rocks fetch out-of-this-world prices: Pieces of Mars can bring up to $3,000 per gram.

(continued)

Collectibles

Hello, Dollies

The Internet has brought down prices on limited-edition items by making them easier to get. As a result, Barbie dolls, Beanie Babies, and Hummel figurines have all plummeted in value and collectibility. But Barbie's two rivals— 1950s and '60s Chatty Cathy dolls and G. I. Joe action figures—are

—courtesy Mattel, Inc.

climbing in popularity. Adult males are buying G. I. Joes as much for themselves as for their kids.

Money in the Banks

■ Authentic antique cast-iron mechanical banks are hot, especially the Uncle Sam one that nods its head happily when a penny is put into its hand. Its value has jumped from a range of $300 to $500 in the 1970s to a range of $6,000 to $10,000 now, though you can sometimes find one at antique shows and toy fairs for around $2,000, according to *Kiplinger's* magazine.

The Industrial Sector

■ The value is rising on plain, old-fashioned stuff that you find at flea markets, says Terry Kovel, co-author with her husband of *Kovels' Antiques & Collectibles Price List*. "If there's any hot sector, it's 'age of industry' items that document a way of life that's gone and that don't have their own stores in cyberspace yet." Some examples:

■ Electric fans
■ Irons
■ Slide rules
■ Early manual or electric typewriters (IBM Selectrics can draw $100; early models can command $5,000.)

Food Fads

Going to the Grocery Store? Check These Out

■ More self-scan lanes for tech-savvy shoppers.

■ Ecofriendly food labels that sound good but are vague in meaning (like "bird-friendly," "cage-free," and "shade-grown").

■ Frozen "fix-it-fast meal kits," a food trend according to the *Chicago Tribune*. These offer the comfort of old-fashioned home cooking (meat loaf, casseroles, stews) with the convenience of takeout.

(continued)

■ Artisan cheeses, handmade chocolates, high-quality breads, and other small-batch foods—all selling fast.

■ Foods in shocking colors, such as sparkling-bright yogurt and neon-pink and neon-blue margarine. Kids want fun, and parents want happy kids, so colors are cool.

From Fine Vines . . .

■ Oenophiles—ahem, wine lovers—are applauding the exclusive and high-priced ($100 to $600 a bottle) vintages called cult wines. Usually cabernet sauvignons, these have an assertive, heavy fruit taste and are made in small batches by a few obsessive winemakers in their homes. Their time is ripe, according to the *New York Times:* Americans appreciate wine more than ever and are spending more on it.

Ever Wonder . . .

■ Who's drinking the most Slurpees these days? Canada's Winnipeg and Calgary are "the top two Slurpee-consuming cities in the world," reports *Maclean's* magazine.

The Fun Factor
Games We're Playing

ON THE DANCE FLOOR

■ Dance Dance Revolution, a Japanese invention that couples kids' passion for video games with their need for activity, is gaining popularity among U.S. teens in arcades. Players on a platform mimic dance moves on a screen in time with music, or perform tai chi–like arm movements to explode objects on-screen. It's one of the first video games to attract lots of female participants and to provide a workout for more body parts than just the thumbs.

ON THE SCREEN

■ Adult women are playing more video games and are now the fastest-growing market for Game Boys, according to the *New York Times.*

ON THE SNOW

■ The National Ski Area Association reports a rise in the age of snowboarders. Kids are grudgingly making room on the slopes for adults, whom they call "grays on trays."

ON THE ICE

■ Ringette, Canada's fast-paced version of ice hockey played with a straight stick and a rubber ring, has been popular in Ontario and Quebec for over a decade. *Canadian Living* magazine reports that the game has now caught on across the country as one of Canadian women's favorite activities. With over 50,000 participants, the trend is growing even more; boys now want to get in on the fun.

—Foto-Jorkka/Jorma Vainia

22

(continued on page 26)

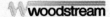

To Your Health

The Smell Will Tell

Watch for the subject of olfaction to explode, notes *The Scientist* journal, as more researchers try to determine how our sense of smell affects the biology of behavior. For example: Psychologist Rachel Herz, of Brown University, has found that women are influenced more by a man's body odor than any other physical feature.

The Big Story: Us

■ More than 54 million Americans are dieting, according to the *Journal of the American Medical Association*. OK, we're trying, but we've got to try harder: Up to 95 percent of those who lose weight can't keep it off. According to the Surgeon General, 61 percent of American adults are overweight, and 27 percent are obese.

Childhood obesity is also sky-rocketing, according to federal findings, with as many as one in seven children fitting into this category. "Many parents turn to weight-loss camps for kids, an industry that seems to be growing as fast as America's waistline," reports *Time* magazine.

—H. Armstrong Roberts

America's Fattest and Fittest Cities*

FAT	FIT
Houston	Colorado Springs
Chicago	Denver
Detroit	San Diego
Philadelphia	Seattle
Dallas	San Francisco

*According to *Men's Fitness* magazine

The Best Exercise Is . . .
Walking, say exercise researchers.

Pet News

Pets for the People

Sixty-two percent of American households share their space with at least one pet, according to research by the NPD Group for American Pet Products Manufacturers Association. Dogs and cats are still the most popular pets, but reptiles (including turtles, snakes, and iguanas)

You've got to feel it to believe it!™

AS LITTLE AS $33.00 MO AFTER HOME TRYOUT

RECOGNIZED BY NASA

LIMITED 20 YEAR WARRANTY

SPACE CERTIFIED TECHNOLOGY

Certified by the Space Foundation

FREE SAMPLE of TEMPUR® pressure-relieving material—the molecular heart of Tempur-Pedic's famous Weightless Sleep™ bed—is yours for the asking. You also get a free video and Free Home Tryout Certificate.

Soft...firm...everything in-between

Tempur-Pedic's Weightless Sleep bed actually molds itself to your body. Our sleep technology is recognized by NASA, raved about by the media, extolled worldwide by over 25,000 sleep clinics and health professionals.

Yet this miracle has to be *felt* to be believed.

While the thick, ornate pads that cover most mattresses are necessary to keep the hard steel springs inside, they create a hammock effect outside—and can actually *cause* pressure points. Inside our bed, billions of microporoscopic memory cells function as molecular springs that contour precisely to your every curve and angle.

Tempur-Pedic's Swedish scientists used NASA's early anti-G-force research to invent a new kind of viscoelastic bedding—TEMPUR pressure-relieving material—that *reacts* to body mass and temperature. It *self adjusts* to your exact shape and weight. And it's the reason why millions of Americans are falling in love with the first *really* new bed in 75 years: our high-tech Weightless Sleep marvel.

Small wonder, 3 out of 4 Tempur-Pedic owners go out of their way to recommend our Swedish Sleep System® to close friends and relatives. And 82% tell us it's the *best bed* they've ever had!

Please return the coupon at right, without the least obligation, for a FREE DEMONSTRATION KIT. Better yet, phone or send us a fax.

Tempur-Pedic beds, mattresses, overlays are priced from $532.

For demonstration kit, call toll-free

1-888-702-8557

or fax 1-859-514-4423

NAME

ADDRESS

CITY/STATE/ZIP

PHONE (OPTIONAL)

TEMPUR·PEDIC®
PRESSURE RELIEVING
SWEDISH MATTRESSES AND PILLOWS

Tempur-Pedic, Inc.,1713 Jaggie Fox Way, Lexington, KY 40511

are gaining: Some 4 million people reported having reptiles as pets in 2001.

Pets . . . as People?

We are treating our pets more like family:

—Index Stock

■ More than 50% of cat owners and nearly 40% of dog owners let their pet spend the night in bed with a family member.*

■ 78% of pet owners take their dog with them when they travel. (Only 15% take their cat.)**

■ 44% of travelers buy souvenirs for their pet while on vacation.‡

■ 66% of dog owners say they prepare special food for their pet.‡

■ 37% of pet owners talk to their pet on the phone or leave messages on the answering machine.‡

■ 75% of pet owners say they would go into debt to keep their pet healthy.‡ (That's why pet insurance is gaining in popularity, says *Kiplinger's* magazine.)

*NPD Group, for American Pet Products Manufacturers Association
**Travel Industry Association of America
‡American Animal Hospital Association

Demographica

Coming of Agelessness

The life expectancy of men and women is at a record high, according to the National Center for Health Statistics:

■ Women can expect to live 79.5 years.

■ Men can expect to live 74.1 years.

Expectations are rising: These days, about 50,000 Americans are 100 or older. By 2050, better health care will raise the number of centenarians to almost 1 million.

How Will We Spend All Our Time?
Learning.*

According to a survey by Hilton Hotels

—H. Armstrong Roberts

(continued)

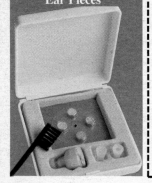

−H. Armstrong Roberts

Our Mood

The shift this year is *from* work and unchecked consumerism *to* family and spiritual values. The *Christian Science Monitor* calls it the "New American Hearth."

■ 67% of Americans polled by General Nutrition Centers put "enjoying life more" as their top New Year's resolution for 2002. "Spending more time with friends and family" came in second. (Losing weight and exercising usually top the list.)

■ The *New York Times* notes a "heightened interest in volunteer vacations," as more people seek to pack meaning into their time off.

■ 28 million Americans use the Internet to look for religious and spiritual information, according to a study by the Pew Internet & American Life Project. That's more than the number who bank, shop, date, or gamble on-line.

Northern Exposure

■ When asked* to name the most-important issues facing Canada at the beginning of 2002 . . .

■ **35% of Canadian women said "health/education."**

■ **32% of Canadian men said "unemployment/economy."**

When asked if, overall, they were more optimistic or more pessimistic about the future than they were a decade ago . . .

■ **37% said "more pessimistic."**

■ **30% said "more optimistic."**

*for a *Maclean's*/CBS News poll □ □

SO WHAT ELSE IS NEW?
For more statistics, data, and other colorful details on our life and times, go to
www.almanac.com and click on **Article Links 2003.**

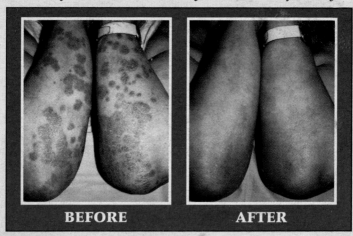

Accented With Sterling Silver and 24 Karat Gold.

It was the pride of the great American heartland. The machine of progress that kept the land cultivated and harvests bountiful. The John Deere Model B Tractor. The most popular tractor in John Deere history. Ruggedly built. Engineered with the finest features of its predecessors. And enhanced with innovations all its own.

Now, for the first time ever, comes a unique tribute to that workhorse of farmlands everywhere. A magnificent heirloom collector knife re-creating the vintage tractor in an intricate sculpture on the handle. Hand-painted in the trademark green enamel and precision-crafted with an authentic rubber tractor tire that actually turns. Emblazoned with the nostalgic John Deere emblem. And luxuriously accented in genuine sterling silver and 24 karat gold.

The John Deere moniker appears on the blade of stainless steel. And the minted medal of Franklin Mint Collector Knives is also set into the reverse of the handle. The entire edition is forever limited to just 45 casting days. Complete with its own padded and zippered case. Just $37.50. Available exclusively from The Franklin Mint, Franklin Center, PA 19091-0001.

JOHN DEERE
1948 MODEL B

JOHN DEERE
MOLINE, ILL.

▼ DETACH AND MAIL

- -

THE 2003 EDITION OF

The Old Farmer's Almanac

Established in 1792 and published every year thereafter

ROBERT B. THOMAS (1766–1846), *Founder*

YANKEE PUBLISHING INC.

EDITORIAL, ADVERTISING, AND PUBLISHING OFFICES

P.O. Box 520, Main Street, Dublin, NH 03444

Phone: 603-563-8111 • Fax: 603-563-8252

EDITOR IN CHIEF: Judson D. Hale Sr.
EDITOR *(13th since 1792)*: Janice Stillman
ART DIRECTOR: Margo Letourneau
SENIOR EDITOR: Mare-Anne Jarvela
COPY EDITOR: Ellen Bingham
SENIOR ASSOCIATE EDITOR: Heidi Stonehill
RESEARCH EDITORS: Joyce F. Monaco,
Martie Majoros
ASTROLOGER: Celeste Longacre
ASTRONOMER: George Greenstein
SOLAR PROGNOSTICATOR: Richard Head
WEATHER PROGNOSTICATOR: Michael A. Steinberg
WEATHER GRAPHICS AND CONSULTATION:
Accu-Weather, Inc.
CONTRIBUTING EDITORS: Bob Berman, *Astronomy;*
Castle Freeman Jr., *Farmer's Calendar*

PRODUCTION DIRECTOR: Susan Gross
PRODUCTION MANAGER: David Ziarnowski
SENIOR PRODUCTION ARTISTS: Lucille Rines,
Rachel Kipka, Nathaniel Stout
ADVERTISING PRODUCTION ARTIST: Janet Calhoun

WEB SITE: WWW.ALMANAC.COM

CREATIVE DIRECTOR, ON-LINE: Stephen O. Muskie
INTERNET EDITOR: Margaret Starvish
INTERNET PRODUCTION ARTIST: Lisa Traffie

CONTACT US

We welcome your questions and comments about articles in and topics for this periodical. Mail all editorial correspondence to Editor, The Old Farmer's Almanac, P.O. Box 520, Dublin, NH 03444-0520; fax us at 603-563-8252; or send e-mail to us at almanac@mail.ypi.com. The Old Farmer's Almanac can not accept responsibility for unsolicited manuscripts and will not return any manuscripts that do not include a stamped and addressed return envelope.

OUR CONTRIBUTORS

Bob Berman, our astronomy editor, is the director of Overlook Observatory in Woodstock and Storm King Observatory in Cornwall, both in New York. In 1976, he founded the Catskill Astronomical Society. Bob will go a long way for a good look at the sky: He has led many aurora and eclipse expeditions, venturing as far as the Arctic and Antarctic.

Castle Freeman Jr., who lives in southern Vermont, has been writing the Almanac's "Farmer's Calendar" essays for more than 20 years. The essays come out of his longtime interest in wildlife and the outdoors, gardening, history, and the life of rural New England. His latest book is *My Life and Adventures* (St. Martin's Press, 2002).

George Greenstein, Ph.D., who has been the Almanac's astronomer for more than 25 years, is the Sidney Dillon Professor of Astronomy at Amherst College in Amherst, Massachusetts. His research has centered on cosmology, pulsars, and other areas of theoretical astrophysics, and on the mysteries of quantum mechanics. He has written three books and many magazine articles on science for the general public.

Richard Head, Ph.D., a solar physicist and former NASA chief scientist, has been involved in the Almanac weather predictions since 1970. A firm believer that solar activity affects our weather patterns and our climate, he provides solar forecast data to be incorporated into our weather forecasts.

Celeste Longacre, our astrologer, often refers to astrology as "the world's second-oldest profession." A New Hampshire native, she has been a practicing astrologer for 25 years: "It is a study of timing, and timing is everything." Her book, *Love Signs* (Sweet Fern Publications, 1999), is available on her Web site, www.yourlovesigns.com.

Michael Steinberg, our meteorologist, has been forecasting weather for the Almanac since 1996. In addition to having college degrees in atmospheric science and meteorology, he brings a lifetime of experience to the task: He began making weather predictions when he attended the only high school in the world with weather teletypes and radar.

Amazing Diabetes Improvement

(SPECIAL) – Here's important news for anyone with diabetes. A remarkable book is now available that reveals medically tested principles that can help normalize blood sugar naturally...and greatly improve the complications associated with diabetes. People report **better vision, more energy, faster healing, regained feeling in their feet**, as well as a reduction of various risk factors associated with other diseases.

It's called the *"Diabetes Improvement Program"* and it was researched, developed and written by a leading nutrition specialist. It shows you exactly how nature can activate your body's built-in healers once you start eating the right combination of foods. It can work for both Type I and Type II diabetes and people report it has helped reduce their insulin resistance. It can give diabetics control of their lives and a feeling of satisfaction that comes from having normal blood sugar profiles.

The results speak for themselves. The *"Diabetes Improvement Program"* is based on research that many doctors may not be aware of yet. It tells you which delicious foods to eat and which to avoid. It also warns you of the potential danger of certain so-called "diabetes" diets. Diabetics have written letters to the publisher calling this book "very outstanding"..."a tremendous help"... and saying it made "a difference in my life." The *"Diabetes Improvement Program"* is based on documented scientific principles that can help:

- **Eliminate ketones and give you more abundant energy**
- **Make blood sugar levels go from High Risk to Normal**
- **Stimulate scratches and scrapes to heal faster**
- **Improve eyesight**
- **Improve your balance**
- **Help numb feet regain a level of feeling**
- **Reverse neuropathy and resultant heel ulcers**

Improvement may be seen in other areas as well, such as **lower blood pressure, lower cholesterol** and **reduced triglyceride levels**. There may also be a reduction of other risk factors associated with: **heart attacks, stroke, retinopathy, kidney damage**.

What's more, it may help improve **short term memory** and make you feel **more alert** and **no longer chronically tired**. Improvements of **double vision** or *diplopia* may also be experienced.

If you or someone you know have diabetes, this could be the most important book you'll ever read. As part of a special introductory offer, right now you can order a special press run of the *"Diabetes Improvement Program"* for only $12.95 plus $2.00 shipping. It comes with a 90 day money back guarantee. If you are not 100% satisfied, simply return it for a full refund...no questions asked.

Order an extra copy for family or friend and SAVE. You can order 2 for only $20 total.

HERE'S HOW TO ORDER:

Simply PRINT your name and address and the words "Diabetes Improvement" on a piece of paper and mail it along with a check or money order to: THE LEADER CO., INC., Publishing Division, Dept. DB684, P.O. Box 8347, Canton, Ohio 44711. VISA or MasterCard send card number and expiration date. Act now. Orders are fulfilled on a first come, first served basis.

©2002 The Leader Co., Inc.

Jesus

the World's Savior

"Never before in human experience has there been such a dire need for a competent ruler. We need one who would be able to lead the hate-infected nations of earth out of the cross-currents of selfishness and despair, into the wholesome atmosphere of trust and goodwill. Without this there can be no lasting peace on earth, and no security – either for individuals or for nations."

This quotation was taken from a booklet entitled,

"JESUS, THE WORLD'S SAVIOR"

You are invited to send for your FREE copy of this booklet. Send your request to:

**The Bible Answers
Box 60-Dept. F
General Post Office
New York, NY 10116
1-800-234-DAWN**

Visit us on the Web at:
www.dawnbible.com

THE 2003 EDITION OF

The Old Farmer's Almanac

Established in 1792 and published every year thereafter

ROBERT B. THOMAS (1766–1846), *Founder*

YANKEE PUBLISHING INC.
P.O. Box 520, Main Street, Dublin, NH 03444
Phone: 603-563-8111 • Fax: 603-563-8252

GROUP PUBLISHER: John Pierce
PUBLISHER *(23rd since 1792)*: Sherin Wight
ADVERTISING SALES COORDINATOR: Melissa Van Saun
DIRECT/RETAIL SALES MANAGER: Cindy Schlosser
DIRECT/RETAIL SALES ASSISTANT: Stacey Korpi
MAIL-ORDER MARKETING MANAGER: Susan Way
MAIL-ORDER/SUBSCRIPTION COORDINATOR: Priscilla Gagnon
MAIL-ORDER MARKETING ASSOCIATE: Beth Lorenz

ADVERTISING MARKETING REPRESENTATIVES
General and Mail-Order Advertising

Classified Advertising: Gallagher Group
Phone: 203-263-7171 • Fax: 203-263-7174

Midwest & South: Gallagher Group
Phone: 203-263-7171 • Fax: 203-263-7174

Northeast & West: Robert Bernbach
Phone: 914-769-0051 • Fax: 914-769-0691

FOR RETAIL SALES

Contact Cindy Schlosser, 800-729-9265, ext. 126,
or Stacey Korpi, ext. 160.

The Old Farmer's Almanac publications are available at special discounts for bulk purchases for sales promotions or premiums. Contact Mead/At-a-Glance, 800-333-1125.

SUBSCRIBE TO THIS ALMANAC

Subscription rate: 3 years, $15
Choose your region: • National • Western
• Southern • Canadian
Clearly indicate your region with your order.

Payment: Send check or money order (in U.S. funds drawn on a U.S. bank); we also accept Visa, Master-Card, American Express, and Discover/NOVUS
By mail: See address above
Phone: Toll-free at 800-895-9265, ext. 220
E-mail: customerservice@yankeepub.com

Jamie Trowbridge, *President;* Judson D. Hale Sr., John Pierce, *Senior Vice Presidents;* Jody Bugbee, Judson D. Hale Jr., Sherin Wight, *Vice Presidents;* Steve Brewer, *Treasurer.*

Thank you for buying this Almanac!
We hope you find it new, useful, and entertaining.
Thanks, too, to everyone who had a hand in its creation, including advertisers, distributors, and sales and delivery people.

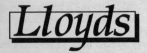

How to Use This Almanac

Anywhere in the United States

■ The calendar pages **(44–71)** are the heart of *The Old Farmer's Almanac.* They present astronomical data and sky sightings for the entire year and are what make this book a true almanac, a "calendar of the heavens." In essence, these pages are unchanged since 1792, when Robert B. Thomas published his first edition. The long columns of numbers and symbols reveal all of Nature's precision, rhythm, and glory —an astronomical look at the year 2003.

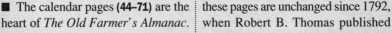

—Beth Krommes

Please note: All times given in this edition of the Almanac are for Boston, Massachusetts, and are in Eastern Standard Time (EST), except from 2:00 A.M., April 6, until 2:00 A.M., October 26, when Eastern Daylight Time (EDT) is given. Key Letters (A–E) are provided so that readers can calculate times for their own localities. The following four pages provide detailed explanations.

Seasons of the Year

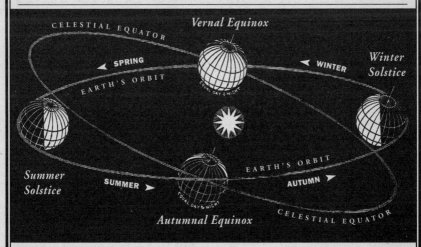

The seasons occur because Earth's axis is tilted with respect to its orbit of the Sun. Thus, the hemispheres take turns reaching their maximum tilt toward the Sun, which occurs at the solstices. The equinoxes mark the intersection of Earth's orbit with the plane of the celestial equator, when the hemispheres equally face the Sun.

■ *The Old Farmer's Almanac* Web site, **www.almanac.com,** provides a vast array of daily data: astronomical information, including Sun, Moon, and planet rise and set times, for many locations in the United States and Canada, as well as tide predictions for U.S. and Canadian coastlines. Also available are weather forecasts for anywhere in the United States and select locations around the world, plus U.S. and Canadian weather history since 1994. **(continued)**

The Left-Hand Calendar Pages

(Pages 44–70)

2002   NOVEMBER, The Eleventh Month

The combination of the clocks having "fallen back" to end Daylight Saving Time _____ *earlier each month suddenly brings Saturn out* _____ *piter up by 11:00 P.M. in midmonth. Saturn's rings* _____ *at a rare brilliance as it retrogrades back into Taurus. Meanwhile, Venus charges into the morning sky, rapidly rising ahead of the Sun and displaying its final lovely crescent profile (through binoculars) until the year 2004. On the 17th, the East Coast could experience a fantastic Leonid meteor shower. Predictions suggest that more than 25,000 meteors per hour will be visible.*

● New Moon	4th day	15th hour	34th minute
☽ First Quarter	11th day	15th hour	52nd minute
○ Full Moon	19th day	20th hour	34th minute
☾ Last ...er	...ay	10...ur	...ute

Times are given in Eastern Standard Time.

For an explanation of this page, see page 40; for values of Key Letters, see page 226.

Day of Year	Day of Month	Day of Week	☀ Rises h. m.	Key	☀ Sets h. m.	Key	Length of Day h. m.	Sun Fast m.	Declination of Sun °	High Tide Boston Light—A.M. **Bold**—P.M.	☽ Rises h. m.	Key	☽ Sets h. m.	Key	☽ Place	☽ Age
305	1	Fr.	6 17	D	4 38	B	10 21	32	14 s. 31	7¼ **8**	1⅛56	C	3⅞17	D	LEO	26
306	2	Sa.	6 19	D	4 36	B	10 17	32	14 50	8½ **8¾**	3 13	D	3 44	C	VIR	27

1 Use these two Key Letter columns to calculate the sunrise/sunset times for your locale. Each sunrise/sunset time is assigned a Key Letter whose value is given in minutes in the **Time Corrections table on page 226.** Find your city, or the city nearest you, in the table, and add or subtract those minutes to Boston's sunrise or sunset time.

E X A M P L E :

■ To find the time of sunrise in Denver, Colorado, on November 1, 2002:

Sunrise, Boston, with Key Letter D (above)	6:17 A.M. EST
Value of Key Letter D for Denver (p. 227)	+ 11 minutes
Sunrise, Denver	6:28 A.M. MST

2 This column shows how long the Sun is above the horizon in Boston. To determine your city's length of day, find the sunrise/sunset Key Letter values for your city **on page 226.** Add or subtract the sunset value to Boston's length of day. Then sim-

ply *reverse* the sunrise sign (from minus to plus, or plus to minus) and add (or subtract) this value to the result of the first step.

E X A M P L E :

■ To find the length of day in Richmond, Virginia, on November 1, 2002:

Length of day, Boston (above)	10:21
Sunset Key Letter B (p. 229)	+ 32 minutes
	10:53
Reverse sunrise Key Letter D (p. 229, +17 to –17)	– 17 minutes
Length of day, Richmond (10 hr., 36 min.)	10:36

3 The Sun Fast column is designed to change sundial time to clock time in Boston. A sundial reads natural, or Sun, time, which is neither Standard nor Daylight time except by coincidence. From a sundial reading, subtract the minutes given in the Sun Fast column to get Boston clock time, and use Key Letter C in the table **on page 226** to convert the time to your city.

EXAMPLE:

■ To change sundial time to clock time in Boston, or Salem, Oregon, on November 1, 2002:

Sundial reading, Nov. 1 (Boston or Salem)	12:00 noon
Subtract Sun Fast (p. 40)	– 32 minutes
Clock time, Boston	11:28 A.M. EST
Use Key Letter C for Salem (p. 229)	+ 27 minutes
Clock time, Salem	11:55 A.M. PST

4 This column gives the degrees and minutes of the Sun from the celestial equator at noon EST or EDT.

5 The High Tide column gives the times of daily high tides in Boston. For example, on November 1, the first high tide occurs at 7:30 A.M. and the second occurs at 8:00 P.M. (A dash under High Tide indicates that high water occurs on or after midnight and so is recorded on the next day.) Figures for calculating high tide times and heights for localities other than Boston are given in the **Tide Corrections table on page 232.**

6 Use these two Key Letter columns to calculate the moonrise/moonset times for localities other than Boston. (A dash indicates that moonrise/moonset occurs on or after midnight and so is recorded on the next day.) Use the same procedure as explained in #1 for calculating your moonrise/moonset time, then factor in an additional correction based on longitude (see table below). For the longitude of your city, **see page 226.**

Longitude of city	Correction minutes
58° – 76°	0
77° – 89°	+1
90° – 102°	+2
103° – 115°	+3
116° – 127°	+4
128° – 141°	+5
142° – 155°	+6

EXAMPLE:

■ To determine the time of moonrise in Lansing, Michigan, on November 1, 2002:

Moonrise, Boston, with Key Letter C (p. 40)	1:56 A.M. EST
Value of Key Letter C for Lansing (p. 228)	+ 53 minutes
Correction for Lansing longitude 84° 33'	+ 1 minute
Moonrise, Lansing	2:50 A.M. EST

Use the same procedure to determine the time of moonset.

–Beth Krommes-

7 The Moon's place is its *astronomical,* or *actual,* placement in the heavens. (This should not be confused with the Moon's *astrological* place in the zodiac, as explained **on page 223.**) All calculations in this Almanac are based on astronomy, not astrology, except for the information **on pages 222, 223, and 224.**

In addition to the 12 constellations of the astronomical zodiac, five other abbreviations may appear in this column: Auriga **(AUR),** a northern constellation between Perseus and Gemini; Cetus **(CET),** which lies south of the zodiac, just south of Pisces and Aries; Ophiuchus **(OPH),** a constellation primarily north of the zodiac but with a small corner between Scorpius and Sagittarius; Orion **(ORI),** a constellation whose northern limit first reaches the zodiac between Taurus and Gemini; and Sextans **(SEX),** which lies south of the zodiac except for a corner that just touches it near Leo.

8 The last column gives the Moon's age, which is the number of days since the previous new Moon. (The average length of the lunar month is 29.53 days.)

(c o n t i n u e d)

The Right-Hand Calendar Pages

(Pages 45–71)

■ Throughout the **Right-Hand Calendar Pages** are groups of symbols that represent notable celestial events. The symbols and names of the principal planets and aspects are:

☉	**Sun**	♆	**Neptune**
○●☾	**Moon**	♇	**Pluto**
☿	**Mercury**	☌	**Conjunction (on the same celestial longitude)**
♀	**Venus**		
⊕	**Earth**		
♂	**Mars**	☊	**Ascending node**
♃	**Jupiter**	☋	**Descending node**
♄	**Saturn**	☍	**Opposition (180 degrees apart)**
♅	**Uranus**		

For example, ☌♂☾ next to November 2, 2002 (see opposite page), means that a conjunction (☌) of Mars (♂) and the Moon (☾) occurs on that date, when they are aligned along the same celestial longitude and appear to be closest together in the sky.

–Beth Krommes

The Seasons of 2002–2003

Fall 2002	**Sept. 23, 12:55 A.M. EDT**
Winter 2002	**Dec. 21, 8:14 P.M. EST**
Spring 2003	**Mar. 20, 8:00 P.M. EST**
Summer 2003	**June 21, 3:10 P.M. EDT**
Fall 2003	**Sept. 23, 6:47 A.M. EDT**
Winter 2003	**Dec. 22, 2:04 A.M. EST**

Earth at Perihelion and Aphelion 2003

■ Earth will be at perihelion on January 3, 2003, when it will be 91,402,145 miles from the Sun. Earth will be at aphelion on July 4, 2003, when it will be 94,502,872 miles from the Sun.

Movable Feasts and Fasts for 2003

Septuagesima Sunday	**Feb. 16**
Shrove Tuesday	**Mar. 4**
Ash Wednesday	**Mar. 5**
Palm Sunday	**Apr. 13**
Good Friday	**Apr. 18**
Easter	**Apr. 20**
Rogation Sunday	**May 25**
Ascension Day	**May 29**
Whitsunday-Pentecost	**June 8**
Trinity Sunday	**June 15**
Corpus Christi	**June 19**
First Sunday in Advent	**Nov. 30**

Chronological Cycles for 2003

Dominical Letter	**E**
Epact	**27**
Golden Number (Lunar Cycle)	**9**
Roman Indiction	**11**
Solar Cycle	**24**
Year of Julian Period	**6716**

Era	Year	Begins
Byzantine	**7512**	**Sept. 14**
Jewish (A.M.)*	**5764**	**Sept. 26**
Chinese (Lunar) [Year of the Sheep]	**4701**	**Feb. 1**
Roman (A.U.C.)	**2756**	**Jan. 14**
Nabonassar	**2752**	**Apr. 23**
Japanese	**2663**	**Jan. 1**
Grecian (Seleucidae)	**2315**	**Sept. 14 (or Oct. 14)**
Indian (Saka)	**1925**	**Mar. 22**
Diocletian	**1720**	**Sept. 12**
Islamic (Hegira)*	**1424**	**Mar. 4**

***Year begins at sunset.**

Sample Right-Hand Calendar Page (from November 2002, page 45)

■ Day of the month.

■ Day of the week.

■ Conjunction of Mars and the Moon.

■ The bold letter in this column is the Dominical Letter, a traditional ecclesiastical designation for Sunday. The letter for 2002 is F, because the first Sunday of the year falls on the sixth day of January. The letter for 2003 is E, the first Sunday falling on January 5.

■ 24th Sunday after Pentecost. (Sundays and special holy days generally appear in this typeface.)

■ St. Martin. (Religious feasts appear in this typeface.)

■ Veterans Day. (Civil holidays appear in this typeface.)

■ Folklore and legend.

■ Noteworthy historical events.

■ The Moon is on the celestial equator.

■ First high tide at Boston is 9.7 feet; second high tide is 9.2 feet.

■ Proverbs, poems, and adages appear in this typeface.

■ Weather prediction rhyme. **(For detailed regional forecasts, see pages 140–155.)**

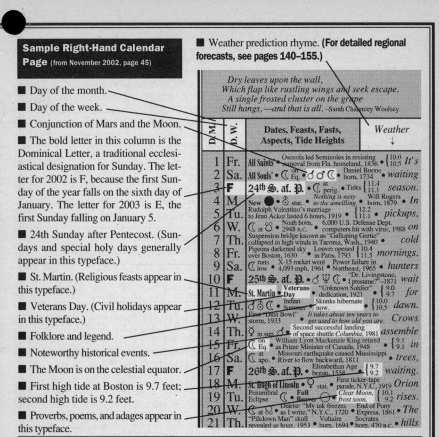

Dry leaves upon the wall,
Which flap like rustling wings and seek escape,
A single frosted cluster on the grape
Still hangs,—and that is all. –Sarah Chauncey Woolsey

D. M.	D. W.	Dates, Feasts, Fasts, Aspects, Tide Heights	*Weather* ↓
1	Fr.	All Saints • Osceola led Seminoles in resisting removal from Fla. homeland, 1836 • {10.0 / 10.5	*It's*
2	Sa.	All Souls' • ☾ on Eq. • ☌ ♂ ☾ • Daniel Boone born, 1734 •	*waiting*
3	**F**	24th 𝕾. af. 𝕻. • ☾ at perig. • Tides {11.4 / 11.1	*season.*
4	M.	New ● • ♅ stat. • *Nothing is easy to the unwilling* • Will Rogers born, 1879 •	*In*
5	Tu.	Rudolph Valentino's marriage to Jean Acker lasted 6 hours, 1919 • {12.2 / 11.1 •	*pickups,*
6	W.	☾ at ☋ • Noah born, 2948 B.C. • 6,000 U.S. Defense Dept. computers hit with virus, 1988	*on*
7	Th.	Suspension bridge known as "Galloping Gertie" collapsed in high winds in Tacoma, Wash., 1940 •	*cold*
8	Fr.	Pigeons darkened sky over Boston, 1630 • Louvre opened in Paris, 1793 {10.4 / 11.5	*mornings,*
9	Sa.	☾ runs low • X-15 rocket went 4,093 mph, 1961 • Power failure in Northeast, 1965 •	*hunters*
10	**F**	25th 𝕾. af. 𝕻. • ☌ ♆ ☾ • "Dr. Livingstone, I presume?"–1871	*wait*
11	M.	St. Martin • **Veterans Day** • "Unknown Soldier" dedication, 1921 • {9.0 / 9.7	*for*
12	Tu.	☌ ♅ ☾ • Indian Summer • Skunks hibernate now. • {10.0 / 10.5	*dawn.*
13	W.	First "Dust Bowl" storm, 1933 • *It takes about ten years to get used to how old you are.*	*Crows*
14	Th.	☿ in sup. ☌ • Second successful landing of space shuttle *Columbia*, 1981	*assemble*
15	Fr.	☾ on Eq. • William Lyon Mackenzie King retired as Prime Minister of Canada, 1948 • {9.1 / 9.1	*in*
16	Sa.	☾ at apo. • Missouri earthquake caused Mississippi River to flow backward, 1811 •	*trees,*
17	**F**	26th 𝕾. af. 𝕻. • Elizabethan Age began, 1558 • {9.7 / 9.2	*waiting.*
18	M.	St. Hugh of Lincoln • ♀ stat. • First ticker-tape parade, N.Y.C., 1919	*Orion*
19	Tu.	Penumbral Eclipse ☾ • Full Beaver ○ • *Clear Moon, frost soon.* {10.1 / 9.2	*rises.*
20	W.	☾ at ☊ • Diarist: "My ink freezes as I write," N.Y.C., 1720 • End of Pony Express, 1861 •	*The*
21	Th.	"Piltdown Man" skull revealed as hoax, 1953 • Voltaire born, 1694 • Socrates born, 470 B.C. •	*hills*

For an explanation of terms used in the Almanac, see the glossaries on pages 74, 80, and 88.

Predicting Earthquakes

■ Note the dates, in the **Right-Hand Calendar Pages,** when the Moon rides high or runs low. The date of the high begins the most likely five-day period of earthquakes in the Northern Hemisphere; the date of the low indicates a similar five-day period in the Southern Hemisphere. Also noted each month are the days when the Moon is on the celestial equator, indicating the most likely two-day earthquake periods in both hemispheres.

Forecasting the Almanac Weather

■ We derive our weather forecasts from a secret formula devised by the founder of this Almanac in 1792, enhanced by the most-modern scientific calculations based on so-

–Beth Krommes

lar activity and current meteorological data. We believe that nothing in the universe occurs haphazardly but that there is a cause-and-effect pattern to all phenomena, thus making long-range weather forecasts possible. However, neither we nor anyone else has as yet gained sufficient insight into the mysteries of the universe to predict the weather with anything resembling total accuracy.

2002 NOVEMBER, The Eleventh Month

The combination of the clocks having "fallen back" to end Daylight Saving Time and the planets rising two hours earlier each month suddenly brings Saturn out right after nightfall and brilliant Jupiter up by 11:00 P.M. in midmonth. Saturn's rings are now wide open, giving the planet a rare brilliance as it retrogrades back into Taurus. Meanwhile, Venus charges into the morning sky, rapidly rising ahead of the Sun and displaying its final lovely crescent profile (through binoculars) until the year 2004. On the 17th, the East Coast could experience a fantastic Leonid meteor shower. Predictions suggest that more than 25,000 meteors per hour will be visible.

●	New Moon	4th day	15th hour	34th minute
☽	First Quarter	11th day	15th hour	52nd minute
○	Full Moon	19th day	20th hour	34th minute
☾	Last Quarter	27th day	10th hour	46th minute

Times are given in Eastern Standard Time.

For an explanation of this page, see page 40; for values of Key Letters, see page 226.

Day of Year	Day of Month	Day of Week	☼ Rises h. m.	Key	☼ Sets h. m.	Key	Length of Day h. m.	Sun Fast m.	Declination of Sun ° '	High Tide Boston Light—A.M. Bold—P.M.		☽ Rises h. m.	Key	☽ Sets h. m.	Key	☽ Place	☽ Age
305	1	Fr.	6 17	D	4 38	B	10 21	32	14 s. 31	7½	**8**	1 P.M. 56	C	3 P.M. 17	D	LEO	26
306	2	Sa.	6 19	D	4 36	B	10 17	32	14 50	8½	**8¾**	3 13	D	3 44	C	VIR	27
307	3	**F**	6 20	D	4 35	B	10 15	32	15 09	9¼	**9¾**	4 31	D	4 11	C	VIR	28
308	4	M.	6 21	D	4 34	B	10 13	32	15 28	10¼	**10¾**	5 51	E	4 41	B	VIR	0
309	5	Tu.	6 22	D	4 33	B	10 11	32	15 46	11	**11½**	7 11	E	5 16	B	LIB	1
310	6	W.	6 24	D	4 32	B	10 08	32	16 05	11¾	—	8 31	E	5 57	A	LIB	2
311	7	Th.	6 25	D	4 30	B	10 05	32	16 22	12½	**12½**	9 45	E	6 45	A	OPH	3
312	8	Fr.	6 26	D	4 29	A	10 03	32	16 40	1¼	**1½**	10 52	E	7 42	A	SAG	4
313	9	Sa.	6 27	D	4 28	A	10 01	32	16 57	2¼	**2¼**	11 A.M. 47	E	8 45	B	SAG	5
314	10	**F**	6 29	D	4 27	A	9 58	32	17 14	3¼	**3¼**	12 P.M. 32	E	9 50	B	SAG	6
315	11	M.	6 30	D	4 26	A	9 56	32	17 30	4¼	**4¼**	1 08	E	10 56	B	CAP	7
316	12	Tu.	6 31	D	4 25	A	9 54	32	17 46	5¼	**5¼**	1 37	E	11 P.M. 59	C	CAP	8
317	13	W.	6 32	D	4 24	A	9 52	31	18 02	6¼	**6½**	2 02	D	—	–	AQU	9
318	14	Th.	6 34	D	4 23	A	9 49	31	18 18	7	**7¼**	2 24	D	1 A.M. 01	C	AQU	10
319	15	Fr.	6 35	D	4 22	A	9 47	31	18 34	8	**8¼**	2 44	D	2 02	D	PSC	11
320	16	Sa.	6 36	D	4 21	A	9 45	31	18 49	8¾	**9**	3 04	C	3 02	D	CET	12
321	17	**F**	6 37	D	4 21	A	9 44	31	19 04	9¼	**9¾**	3 25	C	4 02	D	PSC	13
322	18	M.	6 39	D	4 20	A	9 41	31	19 18	10	**10½**	3 48	B	5 03	E	ARI	14
323	19	Tu.	6 40	D	4 19	A	9 39	30	19 32	10½	**11**	4 15	B	6 05	E	ARI	15
324	20	W.	6 41	D	4 18	A	9 37	30	19 45	11	**11¾**	4 46	A	7 09	E	TAU	16
325	21	Th.	6 42	D	4 18	A	9 36	30	19 59	11¾	—	5 23	A	8 12	E	TAU	17
326	22	Fr.	6 43	D	4 17	A	9 34	30	20 11	12¼	**12¼**	6 09	A	9 14	E	TAU	18
327	23	Sa.	6 45	D	4 16	A	9 31	29	20 24	1	**1**	7 03	A	10 11	E	GEM	19
328	24	**F**	6 46	D	4 16	A	9 30	29	20 37	1¾	**1¾**	8 06	A	11 01	E	GEM	20
329	25	M.	6 47	D	4 15	A	9 28	29	20 48	2½	**2½**	9 14	B	11 A.M. 44	E	CAN	21
330	26	Tu.	6 48	D	4 15	A	9 27	29	21 00	3¼	**3½**	10 26	B	12 P.M. 20	E	CAN	22
331	27	W.	6 49	E	4 14	A	9 25	28	21 11	4¼	**4½**	11 P.M. 38	C	12 51	D	LEO	23
332	28	Th.	6 50	E	4 14	A	9 24	28	21 21	5¼	**5½**	—	–	1 19	D	LEO	24
333	29	Fr.	6 51	E	4 13	A	9 22	28	21 32	6¼	**6½**	12 A.M. 52	D	1 45	D	VIR	25
334	30	Sa.	6 53	E	4 13	A	9 20	27	21 s. 41	7	**7½**	2 A.M. 07	D	2 P.M. 10	C	VIR	26

NOVEMBER hath 30 days. 2002

Dry leaves upon the wall,
Which flap like rustling wings and seek escape,
A single frosted cluster on the grape
Still hangs,—and that is all. –Sarah Chauncey Woolsey

D. M.	D. W.	Dates, Feasts, Fasts, Aspects, Tide Heights	Weather ↓
1	Fr.	All Saints' • Osceola led Seminoles in resisting removal from Fla. homeland, 1836 • {10.0 / 10.5	*It's*
2	Sa.	All Souls' • ☾ on Eq. • ☌ ♂ ☾ • Daniel Boone born, 1734 •	*waiting*
3	F	24th S. af. P. • ☾ at perig. • Tides {11.4 / 11.1	*season.*
4	M.	New ● • ♅ stat. • *Nothing is easy to the unwilling.* • Will Rogers born, 1879 •	*In*
5	Tu.	Rudolph Valentino's marriage to Jean Acker lasted 6 hours, 1919 • {12.2 / 11.1 •	*pickups,*
6	W.	☾ at ☋ • Noah born, 2948 B.C. • 6,000 U.S. Defense Dept. computers hit with virus, 1988	*on*
7	Th.	Suspension bridge known as "Galloping Gertie" collapsed in high winds in Tacoma, Wash., 1940 •	*cold*
8	Fr.	Pigeons darkened sky over Boston, 1630 • Louvre opened in Paris, 1793 {10.4 / 11.5	*mornings,*
9	Sa.	☾ runs low • X-15 rocket went 4,093 mph, 1961 • Power failure in Northeast, 1965 •	*hunters*
10	F	25th S. af. P. • ☌ ♆ ☾ • "Dr. Livingstone, I presume?"–1871	*wait*
11	M.	St. Martin • Veterans Day • "Unknown Soldier" dedication, 1921 • {9.0 / 9.7	*for*
12	Tu.	☌ ♅ ☾ • Indian Summer • Skunks hibernate now. • {10.0 / 10.5	*dawn.*
13	W.	First "Dust Bowl" storm, 1933 • *It takes about ten years to get used to how old you are.*	*Crows*
14	Th.	☿ in sup. ☌ • Second successful landing of space shuttle *Columbia,* 1981	*assemble*
15	Fr.	☾ on Eq. • William Lyon Mackenzie King retired as Prime Minister of Canada, 1948 • {9.1 / 9.1	*in*
16	Sa.	☾ at apo. • Missouri earthquake caused Mississippi River to flow backward, 1811 •	*trees,*
17	F	26th S. af. P. • Elizabethan Age began, 1558 • {9.7 / 9.2	*waiting.*
18	M.	St. Hugh of Lincoln • ♀ stat. • First ticker-tape parade, N.Y.C., 1919	*Orion*
19	Tu.	Penumbral Eclipse ☾ • Full Beaver ○ • *Clear Moon, frost soon.* {10.1 / 9.2	*rises.*
20	W.	☾ at ☊ • Diarist: "My ink freezes as I write," N.Y.C., 1720 • End of Pony Express, 1861 •	*The*
21	Th.	"Piltdown Man" skull revealed as hoax, 1953 • Voltaire born, 1694 • Socrates born, 470 B.C. •	*hills*
22	Fr.	☌ ♄ ☾ • *Everyone is crazy but me and thee, and sometimes I suspect thee a little.* {9.1 / 10.2	*wait*
23	Sa.	St. Clement • ☾ rides high • Doctors banned from prescribing beer, 1921 •	*for*
24	F	27th S. af. P. • "Battle above the Clouds" Lookout Mt., Tenn., 1863 •	*snow.*
25	M.	Prune grapevines now. • A meal of soup, steak, coffee, and half a pie cost 12¢, 1834 •	*We*
26	Tu.	☌ ♃ ♅ • Queen Elizabeth II announced she would pay taxes, 1992 •	*gather*
27	W.	James Agee born, 1909 • Meteor hit Lake Michigan, 1919 • Shakespeare married, 1582	*around*
28	Th.	Thanksgiving • Washington Irving died, 1859 • William Blake born, 1757 •	*a*
29	Fr.	☾ on Eq. • *Mules make a great fuss of their ancestors having been horses.* • {9.7 / 9.9	*table,*
30	Sa.	First day of Chanukah • Mark Twain born, 1835 • {10.3 / 10.1	*waiting.*

Do your duty in all things. You cannot do more.
You should never wish to do less. –Gen. Robert E. Lee

Farmer's Calendar

■ One of the less satisfactory points about owning cats is their insatiable and sadistic predation. Any cat worth its hire will catch, kill, and tear to pieces a toll of victims to make Genghis Khan look like a summer afternoon. Now, for the owner of one of these engines of destruction, finding the hindquarters of a mouse on the kitchen counter, a little more in the hall, the rest in the parlor, is a lousy way to start the day. It's enough to make you take up dogs. Fortunately, with cats, as with much else, age seems to change things.

In the middle of the night, I'm awakened by the unmistakable sound of our middle cat's having caught a mouse: a long, penetrating *meeee-oww-wow-wow,* having an oddly guttural or muffled timbre, as though you tried to sing with your mouth full of peas; then a scurrying and a patter of footfalls, followed by the same cry—announcing the near approach of one mouse's hideous demise.

And yet, in the morning, peace and calm. There's the cat, asleep in her chair. There's the mouse, her last night's prey, very much alive, watching her from under the stove. On my coming into the kitchen, he exits under the pantry door, fit as a flea.

What's here? What else but *catch-and-release mousing,* a kind of feline dry-fly refinement, in which all the joy is in the style and rigor of the pursuit. It's a mature sport, reflective and quite bloodless. This cat is 12 years old, after all. In her slashing salad days, she'd have made that rodent smart, but now she's a philosopher.

DECEMBER, The Twelfth Month

The year ends with uncommon splendor. Venus has a superb, don't-miss conjunction with the crescent Moon and Mars on the 1st, an awesome predawn coming-together of our three nearest cosmic neighbors. Simply dazzling, Venus achieves its greatest brilliancy on the 6th and floats near dim Mars all month. The Geminid meteor shower, this year's richest, peaks on the 13th and 14th. A gibbous Moon will diminish the show for those unwilling to wait until the Moon sets around 2:00 A.M. Saturn is out all night and reaches an extraordinary opposition on the 17th, high up and at its brightest since 1973. Winter arrives with the solstice on the 21st. Jupiter is brilliant and rises by 8:00 P.M. on the 23rd.

●	New Moon	4th day	2nd hour	34th minute
☽	First Quarter	11th day	10th hour	49th minute
○	Full Moon	19th day	14th hour	10th minute
☾	Last Quarter	26th day	19th hour	31st minute

Times are given in Eastern Standard Time.

For an explanation of this page, see page 40; for values of Key Letters, see page 226.

Day of Year	Day of Month	Day of Week	☼ Rises h. m.	Key	☼ Sets h. m.	Key	Length of Day h. m.	Sun Fast m.	Declination of Sun ° '	High Tide Boston Light—A.M.	**Bold—P.M.**	☽ Rises h. m.	Key	☽ Sets h. m.	Key	☽ Place	☽ Age
335	1	**F**	6 54	E	4 13	A	9 19	27	21s. 51	8	**8½**	3 A.M. 23	E	2 P.M. 38	B	VIR	27
336	2	M.	6 55	E	4 12	A	9 17	26	22 00	9	**9½**	4 41	E	3 09	B	LIB	28
337	3	Tu.	6 56	E	4 12	A	9 16	26	22 08	9¾	**10½**	6 00	E	3 46	B	LIB	29
338	4	W.	6 57	E	4 12	A	9 15	26	22 17	10½	**11¼**	7 18	E	4 30	A	OPH	0
339	5	Th.	6 58	E	4 12	A	9 14	25	22 25	11½	—	8 31	E	5 24	A	OPH	1
340	6	Fr.	6 59	E	4 12	A	9 13	25	22 32	12¼	**12¼**	9 33	E	6 25	B	SAG	2
341	7	Sa.	7 00	E	4 12	A	9 12	24	22 38	1	**1**	10 24	E	7 32	B	SAG	3
342	8	**F**	7 01	E	4 11	A	9 10	24	22 45	1¾	**2**	11 05	E	8 39	B	CAP	4
343	9	M.	7 02	E	4 11	A	9 09	24	22 51	2¾	**2¾**	11 A.M. 38	E	9 46	B	CAP	5
344	10	Tu.	7 03	E	4 12	A	9 09	23	22 56	3½	**3¾**	12 P.M. 05	D	10 49	C	AQU	6
345	11	W.	7 03	E	4 12	A	9 09	23	23 02	4½	**4¾**	12 28	D	11 P.M. 51	C	AQU	7
346	12	Th.	7 04	E	4 12	A	9 08	22	23 06	5½	**5¾**	12 49	D	—	–	AQU	8
347	13	Fr.	7 05	E	4 12	A	9 07	22	23 10	6¼	**6½**	1 09	C	12 A.M. 51	D	CET	9
348	14	Sa.	7 06	E	4 12	A	9 06	21	23 14	7	**7½**	1 30	C	1 51	D	PSC	10
349	15	**F**	7 06	E	4 12	A	9 06	21	23 17	8	**8¼**	1 52	B	2 52	D	PSC	11
350	16	M.	7 07	E	4 13	A	9 06	20	23 19	8½	**9¼**	2 16	B	3 53	E	ARI	12
351	17	Tu.	7 08	E	4 13	A	9 05	20	23 22	9¼	**10**	2 46	A	4 57	E	TAU	13
352	18	W.	7 08	E	4 13	A	9 05	19	23 24	10	**10½**	3 21	A	6 01	E	TAU	14
353	19	Th.	7 09	E	4 14	A	9 05	19	23 25	10¾	**11¼**	4 04	A	7 04	E	TAU	15
354	20	Fr.	7 10	E	4 14	A	9 04	18	23 26	11¼	**12**	4 57	A	8 04	E	GEM	16
355	21	Sa.	7 11	E	4 15	A	9 04	18	23 26	**12**	—	5 58	A	8 58	E	GEM	17
356	22	**F**	7 11	E	4 15	A	9 04	17	23 26	12¾	**12¾**	7 05	B	9 44	E	LEO	18
357	23	M.	7 11	E	4 16	A	9 05	17	23 25	1½	**1½**	8 17	B	10 22	E	LEO	19
358	24	Tu.	7 11	E	4 16	A	9 05	16	23 24	2¼	**2¼**	9 29	C	10 55	D	LEO	20
359	25	W.	7 12	E	4 17	A	9 05	16	23 23	3	**3¼**	10 42	D	11 23	D	LEO	21
360	26	Th.	7 12	E	4 17	A	9 05	15	23 22	3¾	**4¼**	11 P.M. 54	D	11 A.M. 49	D	VIR	22
361	27	Fr.	7 12	E	4 18	A	9 06	15	23 19	4¾	**5¼**	—	–	12 P.M. 13	C	VIR	23
362	28	Sa.	7 13	E	4 19	A	9 06	14	23 16	5¾	**6¼**	1 A.M. 07	D	12 39	C	VIR	24
363	29	**F**	7 13	E	4 20	A	9 07	14	23 13	6¾	**7¼**	2 22	E	1 08	B	VIR	25
364	30	M.	7 13	E	4 20	A	9 07	13	23 09	7¾	**8¼**	3 38	E	1 40	B	LIB	26
365	31	Tu.	7 13	E	4 21	A	9 08	13	23s. 04	8½	**9¼**	4 A.M. 54	E	2 P.M. 20	B	SCO	27

DECEMBER hath 31 days. 2002

The hills look gaunt in russet garb:
Against the sky the leafless woods
Are dark, and in their solitudes
The chill wind pierces like a barb. –Clinton Scollard

D. M.	D. W.	Dates, Feasts, Fasts, Aspects, Tide Heights	*Weather* ↓
1	**F**	1st S. in Advent • ☌ ♂ ☾ • ☌ ♀ ☾ •	*Deck*
2	M.	St. Viviana • ☾ at perig. • Charles Dickens gave first American reading, Boston, 1867	*the*
3	Tu.	☾ at ☋ • Heavy fog enveloped London, causing 106 deaths, 1962 • { 11.9 10.5	*halls*
4	W.	New ● • Eclipse ☉ • ♃ stat. • National Grange founded, 1867	*with*
5	Th.	Gypsies banned, England, 1537 • Ty Cobb died, 1951 • Strom Thurmond born, 1902	*plastic*
6	Fr.	St. Nicholas • ☾ runs low • ♀ Gr. Bril. • { 10.3 11.7	*sheeting:*
7	Sa.	St. Ambrose • **National Pearl Harbor Remembrance Day** • Willa Cather born, 1873	*First*
8	**F**	2nd S. in Advent • ☌ ♆ ☾ • Eli Whitney born, 1765 •	*it*
9	M.	☌ ♅ ☾ • ☌ ♇ ☉ • Marco Polo died, 1324 • { 9.3 10.1 •	*rains*
10	Tu.	St. Eulalia • *You cannot open a book without learning something.* • Tides { 9.0 9.5	*and*
11	W.	A monument to the boll weevil, which had forced farmers to diversify, erected in Enterprise, Ala., 1919	*now*
12	Th.	"The Katzenjammer Kids" first appeared, 1897 • *Depend not on fortune but on conduct.* •	*it's*
13	Fr.	St. Lucy • ☾ at apo. • ☾ on Eq. • 35°F in Miami, Fla., 1962 •	*sleeting.*
14	Sa.	Prince Albert died, 1861 • Charlie Rich born, 1932 • South Pole discovered, 1911	*Southern*
15	**F**	3rd S. in Advent • Gustave Eiffel born, 1832 { 9.2 8.6	*breezes,*
16	M.	30-ft.-high ice jam backed up Ohio River for 100 miles, 1917 • Beethoven born, 1770 • { 9.5 8.6	*warm*
17	Tu.	♄ at ☍ • Wrights in flight, 1903 • Lazarus died for the second time, A.D. 63 • { 9.8 8.8	*but*
18	W.	Ember Day • ☾ at ☊ • N.H. passed act to mark horse thieves' faces with ink, 1792	*fleeting;*
19	Th.	St. Timothy • **Full Long Nights** ○ • ☌ ♄ ☾ •	*showers*
20	Fr.	Ember Day • Cold front caused quick drop from 40° to 0°F in central Illinois, 1836 • Halcyon Days	*soak*
21	Sa.	**Winter Solstice** • ☾ rides high • Ember Day • Tides { 10.5 — •	*our*
22	**F**	4th S. in Adv. • Bluebeard the pirate strangled, 1440 •	*season's*
23	M.	☌ ♃ ☾ • Van Gogh cut off part of his ear, 1888 • { 9.1 10.5 •	*greetings.*
24	Tu.	"Silent Night" composed, 1818 • *There are no miracles to the man who does not believe in them.*	*Santa*
25	W.	Christmas Day • 62°F Burlington, Vt., 1964 • { 9.3 10.2 •	*has*
26	Th.	St. Stephen • **Boxing Day (Canada)** • ☿ Gr. Elong. (20° E.) • Tides { 9.5 9.9	*to*
27	Fr.	St. John • ☾ on Eq. • Beware the Pogonip. • Tides { 9.8 9.7 •	*water-*
28	Sa.	Holy Innocents • Creosote bush in Mojave Desert reported to be 11,700 years old, 1984 •	*ski,*
29	**F**	1st S. af. Ch. • ☾ at perig. • ☌ ♂ ☾ •	*splashing*
30	M.	☌ ♀ ☾ • Albatrosses nest now. • Union of Soviet Socialist Republics formed, 1922	*into*
31	Tu.	St. Sylvester • ☾ at ☋ • *A closed mouth gathers no foot.* • { 11.2 9.7	*'003!*

Farmer's Calendar

■ There is really only one weather story in the news these days. It runs on the obituary page. Winter has died. Whether by the hand of man or from natural causes, winter has met with its end at last; it will be seen no more. Melting polar ice, receding glaciers, softening permafrost, thinning mountain snowpack, warmer seas here, colder seas there, southern species wandering north, northern species moving farther north, hotter summers, shorter winters—the vital signs are flat. It's time to give winter a shave, fold his hands on his breast, lay him out in the black wagon, and haul him up to Boot Hill. The old boy has croaked.

And the odd thing is, we mourn. You'd think we'd be dancing in the streets. In the north, unless you happen to live by winter tourism, you've spent your life dreading winter, enduring it, or recovering from it. Now it's gone. Are we glad? We are not. We're full of foreboding, regret, and a kind of vague guilt. Nobody takes the news of the death of winter to be good news. It's as though we were subjects of a cruel king who has died without a visible successor. We don't know what comes next.

Well, let us not worry ourselves too much. Recall the famous line of Mark Twain: "Reports of my death are greatly exaggerated." As I write this, it is snowing so hard that the big maple trees beside the road, 50 feet off, are only fitfully visible. The forecast is for ten below tomorrow, when the usual big freeze follows the passing storm. It looks like winter may be around for a while yet.

2003 JANUARY, The First Month

The year opens with Venus already blazing at its highest and brightest of 2003. This predawn lighthouse floats to the left of dim orange Mars all month and is readily seen hovering above Mercury after the 20th. Meanwhile, Saturn, in Taurus on the 9th, is nicely up in the east at nightfall, at its brightest of the entire year (magnitude –0.5) and telescopically wondrous throughout the night. Jupiter, in Cancer, is dazzling as it rises by 8:00 P.M. and dominates the sky most of the night throughout the month. The Moon meets Saturn on the 15th and Jupiter on the 19th. Earth's closest Sun-approach (perihelion) is at midnight, January 3–4.

●	New Moon	2nd day	15th hour	23rd minute
☽	First Quarter	10th day	8th hour	15th minute
○	Full Moon	18th day	5th hour	48th minute
☾	Last Quarter	25th day	3rd hour	33rd minute

Times are given in Eastern Standard Time.

For an explanation of this page, see page 40; for values of Key Letters, see page 226.

Day of Year	Day of Month	Day of Week	☼ Rises h. m.	Key	☼ Sets h. m.	Key	Length of Day h. m.	Sun Fast m.	Declination of Sun ° '	High Tide Boston Light—A.M.	Bold—P.M.	☽ Rises h. m.	Key	☽ Sets h. m.	Key	☽ Place	☽ Age
1	1	W.	7 13	E	4 22	A	9 09	12	22 s. 59	9½	**10¼**	6 A.M. 08	E	3 P.M. 08	A	OPH	28
2	2	Th.	7 14	E	4 23	A	9 09	12	22 54	10¼	**11**	7 15	E	4 06	A	SAG	0
3	3	Fr.	7 14	E	4 24	A	9 10	11	22 49	11¼	**12**	8 12	E	5 10	B	SAG	1
4	4	Sa.	7 14	E	4 25	A	9 11	11	22 43	**12**	—	8 58	E	6 19	B	CAP	2
5	5	**E**	7 14	E	4 26	A	9 12	11	22 36	12¾	**12¾**	9 35	E	7 27	B	CAP	3
6	6	M.	7 13	E	4 27	A	9 14	10	22 29	1½	**1½**	10 05	E	8 34	B	AQU	4
7	7	Tu.	7 13	E	4 28	A	9 15	10	22 21	2¼	**2¼**	10 30	D	9 37	C	AQU	5
8	8	W.	7 13	E	4 29	A	9 16	9	22 13	3	**3¼**	10 52	D	10 39	D	AQU	6
9	9	Th.	7 13	E	4 30	A	9 17	9	22 05	3¾	**4**	11 12	D	11 P.M. 39	D	PSC	7
10	10	Fr.	7 13	E	4 31	A	9 18	8	21 57	4½	**5**	11 33	C	—	–	PSC	8
11	11	Sa.	7 12	E	4 32	A	9 20	8	21 48	5½	**5¾**	11 A.M. 54	B	12 A.M. 39	E	PSC	9
12	12	**E**	7 12	E	4 33	A	9 21	8	21 38	6¼	**6¾**	12 P.M. 17	B	1 40	E	ARI	10
13	13	M.	7 12	E	4 34	A	9 22	7	21 28	7	**7¾**	12 44	B	2 42	E	TAU	11
14	14	Tu.	7 11	E	4 35	A	9 24	7	21 17	8	**8½**	1 17	A	3 46	E	TAU	12
15	15	W.	7 11	E	4 37	A	9 26	6	21 06	8¾	**9½**	1 57	A	4 50	E	TAU	13
16	16	Th.	7 11	E	4 38	A	9 27	6	20 55	9½	**10¼**	2 46	A	5 52	E	GEM	14
17	17	Fr.	7 10	E	4 39	A	9 29	6	20 44	10¼	**11**	3 44	A	6 49	E	GEM	15
18	18	Sa.	7 09	E	4 40	A	9 31	5	20 31	11	**11½**	4 51	B	7 38	E	GEM	16
19	19	**E**	7 09	E	4 41	A	9 32	5	20 19	11¾	—	6 03	B	8 20	E	CAN	17
20	20	M.	7 08	E	4 43	A	9 35	5	20 06	12¼	**12½**	7 17	C	8 56	E	LEO	18
21	21	Tu.	7 08	E	4 44	A	9 36	5	19 53	1	**1¼**	8 32	C	9 26	D	LEO	19
22	22	W.	7 07	E	4 45	A	9 38	4	19 39	1¾	**2**	9 45	D	9 53	D	VIR	20
23	23	Th.	7 06	D	4 46	A	9 40	4	19 25	2½	**2¾**	10 P.M. 58	D	10 18	C	VIR	21
24	24	Fr.	7 05	D	4 48	A	9 43	4	19 11	3½	**3¾**	—	–	10 43	C	VIR	22
25	25	Sa.	7 05	D	4 49	A	9 44	3	18 56	4¼	**4¾**	12 A.M. 12	E	11 10	B	VIR	23
26	26	**E**	7 04	D	4 50	A	9 46	3	18 41	5¼	**5¾**	1 26	E	11 A.M. 41	B	LIB	24
27	27	M.	7 03	D	4 51	A	9 48	3	18 26	6¼	**7**	2 41	E	12 P.M. 17	A	SCO	25
28	28	Tu.	7 02	D	4 53	A	9 51	3	18 11	7¼	**8**	3 54	E	1 00	A	OPH	26
29	29	W.	7 01	D	4 54	A	9 53	3	17 55	8¼	**9**	5 02	E	1 53	A	SAG	27
30	30	Th.	7 00	D	4 55	A	9 55	2	17 38	9¼	**10**	6 01	E	2 54	A	SAG	28
31	31	Fr.	6 59	D	4 57	A	9 58	2	17 s. 22	10¼	**10¾**	6 A.M. 51	E	4 P.M. 00	B	SAG	29

JANUARY hath 31 days. 2003

Oh, what a goodly and glorious show;
The stately trees have decked themselves with white,
And stand transfigured in a robe of light;
Wearing for each lost leaf a flake of snow. –Richard Wilton

D. M.	D. W.	Dates, Feasts, Fasts, Aspects, Tide Heights	*Weather* ↓
1	W.	New Year's Day • **Circumcision** • Tides {11.3 / 9.6} •	*Rain*
2	Th.	**St. Basil** • New ● • ☾ runs low • ☿ stat. • {11.4 / 9.7} •	*and*
3	Fr.	☌☿☾ • Alaska became 49th state, 1959 • Tides {11.3 / 9.6} •	*snow*
4	Sa.	**St. Elizabeth Ann Seton** • ☌♆☾ • ⊕ at perihelion	*and*
5	**E**	Twelfth Night • ☌♅☾ • New Hampshire became first state to adopt a constitution, 1776	*wintry*
6	M.	**Epiphany** • First commercial flight around the world, 1942 • {9.4 / 10.4}	*glow;*
7	Tu.	Distaff Day • *Make today yesterday's pupil.* • Tides {9.2 / 9.9} •	*get*
8	W.	George Washington delivered the first State of the Union Address, 1790 • {9.0 / 9.3} •	*ready*
9	Th.	☾ on Eq. • Jean Pierre Blanchard made the first North American balloon flight, 1793 {8.9 / 8.8}	*for*
10	Fr.	☾ at apo. • ♀ Gr. Elong. (47° W.) • Rod Stewart born, 1945 • Tides {8.8 / 8.4} •	*a*
11	Sa.	☿ in inf. ☌ • Amelia Earhart began flight from Hawaii to U.S. mainland, 1935	*Northeast*
12	**E**	**1st S. af. Ep.** • *Batman* TV series debuted, 1966 • {8.8 / 8.0}	*blow!*
13	M.	**St. Hilary** • Plough Monday • First Frisbee, 1957 • {9.0 / 8.0}	*Bright*
14	Tu.	☾ at ☊ • Marilyn Monroe married Joe DiMaggio, 1954 • Tides {9.2 / 8.1}	*but*
15	W.	☌♄☾ • Margaret O'Brien born, 1937 • Tides {9.6 / 8.3}	*shivery—*
16	Th.	Ivan the Terrible crowned as first Russian czar, 1547 • 13" snow in N.Y.C., 1879 • {9.9 / 8.6}	*all*
17	Fr.	☾ rides high • Benjamin Franklin born, 1706 • Operation *Desert Storm* launched, 1991	*your*
18	Sa.	**Full Wolf** ○ • *Live with wolves, howl like a wolf.* • A. A. Milne born, 1882 •	*mail*
19	**E**	**2nd S. af. Ep.** • ☌♃☾ • Tides {10.9 / —}	*comes*
20	M.	**Martin Luther King Jr.'s Birthday (observed)** • André Ampère born, 1775 •	*splashial*
21	Tu.	First nuclear submarine, U.S.S. *Nautilus*, launched, 1954 • Tides {9.7 / 11.0}	*delivery.*
22	W.	**St. Vincent** • ☿ stat. • Lyndon B. Johnson died, 1973	*Mountains*
23	Th.	☾ on Eq. • ☾ at perig. • Bathyscaphe dove a record-breaking 35,800 feet, 1960	*whiter,*
24	Fr.	Typewriter ribbon patented by Jacob L. Wortman, 1888 • Tides {10.2 / 10.0} •	*skiers*
25	Sa.	**Conversion of Paul** • *Guiding Light* debuted on radio, 1937 •	*cheer—*
26	**E**	**3rd S. af. Ep.** • Midwest blizzard formed drifts up to 15 feet high, 1978	*south*
27	M.	**Sts. Timothy & Titus** • ☾ at ☋ • ☌♂☾	*is brighter,*
28	Tu.	**St. Thomas Aquinas** • ☌♀☾ • Space shuttle *Challenger* exploded, 1986 •	
29	W.	Oprah Winfrey born, 1954 • *Fine words butter no parsnips.* • Tides {10.6 / 9.0}	*skies*
30	Th.	☾ runs low • ☌☿☾ • ☌♆☉ • {10.7 / 9.2} •	*are*
31	Fr.	*Do business but be not a slave to it.* • Racoons mate now. • Tides {10.8 / 9.3} •	*clear.*

Farmer's Calendar

■ A big storm arrived yesterday, a nor'easter, one of your real snow machines. It began about noon, slowed for an hour, then got going properly. Snow fell all afternoon, all evening, all night. Next morning, there was two feet of new snow—or as close to two feet as doesn't matter. People appeared in the roads, going about their business. At first they seemed to go gingerly, diffidently. They looked around them with a kind of awed curiosity.

A winter storm marches over an area like a vast white army, and when it has passed on, whoever is left alive looks cautiously about him to see what the invaders have wrought. You find your surroundings changed, stripped. The roadsides are gone. In their place are snowbanks high enough that you can't see over them. If you could see over them, you'd find little to look at, for the woods are so choked with snow as to be impenetrable. Fences and walls are minor humps in the landscape; parked automobiles, major humps. Houses are buried to their windows.

It seems impossible that the world should recover. The first efforts of your neighbors, your own first efforts, to make a way through the snow seem antlike, pathetic. Here a man flounders about with his puny shovel. There a tiny, ineffectual fountain of snow shows where another is using his snowblower to move an unprofitable quantity of the stuff an insignificant distance.

Still, it's not so bad. All that new snow is kind of pretty. A good thing, too, for you've got lots of it.

2003 FEBRUARY, The Second Month

This is a wonderful planet-month. Jupiter reaches opposition on Groundhog Day. Out all night, its brilliant magnitude of –2.6 lets it easily outshine every star and planet until the predawn rising of Venus, which starts the month at magnitude –4.3, down from its year opener. Saturn remains prominent from dusk until after midnight and closely meets the Moon on the 11th. Shortly before dawn, a diagonal string of planets illuminates the east, with Mars in Ophiuchus standing above Venus in Sagittarius, which, in turn, is above Mercury, whose brightest showing is from the 1st to the 20th. The Moon joins this insomniac's party the final three days of the month.

● New Moon	1st day	5th hour	48th minute
☽ First Quarter	9th day	6th hour	11th minute
○ Full Moon	16th day	18th hour	51st minute
☾ Last Quarter	23rd day	11th hour	46th minute

Times are given in Eastern Standard Time.

For an explanation of this page, see page 40; for values of Key Letters, see page 226.

Day of Year	Day of Month	Day of Week	☀ Rises h. m.	Key	☀ Sets h. m.	Key	Length of Day h. m.	Sun Fast m.	Declination of Sun ° '	High Tide Boston Light—A.M. Bold—P.M.	☽ Rises h. m.	Key	☽ Sets h. m.	Key	Place	Age
32	1	Sa.	6 58	D	4 58	A	10 00	2	17s.05	11 11½	7ᴬ31	E	5ᴮM09	B	CAP	0
33	2	**E**	6 57	D	4 59	A	10 02	2	16 47	11¾ —	8 03	E	6 17	B	CAP	1
34	3	M.	6 56	D	5 00	A	10 04	2	16 30	12¼ 12½	8 30	D	7 22	C	AQU	2
35	4	Tu.	6 55	D	5 02	A	10 07	2	16 12	1 1¼	8 54	D	8 25	D	AQU	3
36	5	W.	6 54	D	5 03	A	10 09	2	15 54	1¾ 1¾	9 15	D	9 26	D	PSC	4
37	6	Th.	6 53	D	5 04	A	10 11	2	15 36	2¼ 2½	9 35	C	10 27	D	CET	5
38	7	Fr.	6 51	D	5 06	A	10 15	2	15 17	3 3¼	9 56	C	11ᴮM27	D	PSC	6
39	8	Sa.	6 50	D	5 07	B	10 17	1	14 58	3¾ 4¼	10 18	B	—	—	ARI	7
40	9	**E**	6 49	D	5 08	B	10 19	1	14 39	4½ 5	10 43	B	12ᴬM29	E	ARI	8
41	10	M.	6 48	D	5 10	B	10 22	1	14 20	5½ 6	11 13	B	1 31	E	TAU	9
42	11	Tu.	6 47	D	5 11	B	10 24	1	14 00	6¼ 7	11ᴬM49	A	2 34	E	TAU	10
43	12	W.	6 45	D	5 12	B	10 27	1	13 40	7¼ 8	12ᴮM33	A	3 36	E	TAU	11
44	13	Th.	6 44	D	5 14	B	10 30	1	13 20	8 8¾	1 27	A	4 35	E	GEM	12
45	14	Fr.	6 43	D	5 15	B	10 32	1	13 00	9 9¾	2 30	B	5 28	E	GEM	13
46	15	Sa.	6 41	D	5 16	B	10 35	1	12 39	9¾ 10½	3 41	B	6 14	E	CAN	14
47	16	**E**	6 40	D	5 17	B	10 37	1	12 18	10½ 11¼	4 56	C	6 52	E	LEO	15
48	17	M.	6 38	D	5 19	B	10 41	2	11 57	11¼ 11¾	6 13	C	7 25	E	LEO	16
49	18	Tu.	6 37	D	5 20	B	10 43	2	11 36	12	7 29	D	7 53	D	LEO	17
50	19	W.	6 36	D	5 21	B	10 45	2	11 15	12½ 1	8 45	D	8 20	D	VIR	18
51	20	Th.	6 34	D	5 22	B	10 48	2	10 53	1¼ 1¾	10 01	E	8 46	C	VIR	19
52	21	Fr.	6 33	D	5 24	B	10 51	2	10 32	2¼ 2½	11ᴮM17	E	9 12	B	VIR	20
53	22	Sa.	6 31	D	5 25	B	10 54	2	10 10	3 3½	—	—	9 42	B	LIB	21
54	23	**E**	6 30	D	5 26	B	10 56	2	9 48	4 4½	12ᴬM32	E	10 17	A	LIB	22
55	24	M.	6 28	D	5 27	B	10 59	2	9 26	5 5½	1 46	E	10 58	A	OPH	23
56	25	Tu.	6 26	D	5 29	B	11 03	2	9 04	6 6¾	2 55	E	11ᴬM47	A	SAG	24
57	26	W.	6 25	D	5 30	B	11 05	3	8 41	7 8	3 57	E	12ᴮM45	A	SAG	25
58	27	Th.	6 23	D	5 31	B	11 08	3	8 19	8¼ 9	4 48	E	1 49	A	SAG	26
59	28	Fr.	6 22	D	5 32	B	11 10	3	7s.56	9¼ 9¾	5ᴬM30	E	2ᴮM56	B	CAP	27

FEBRUARY hath 28 days. 2003

Come when the rains
Have glazed the snow, and clothed the trees with ice,
While the slant sun of February pours
Into the bowers a flood of light. –William Cullen Bryant

D. M.	D. W.	Dates, Feasts, Fasts, Aspects, Tide Heights	Weather ↓
1	Sa.	St. Brigid • Chinese New Year • New ● • Tides {10.8 9.5 •	*It's*
2	**E**	4th S. af. Ep. • Candlemas • Groundhog Day	*glacial:*
3	M.	☿ Gr. Elong. (25° W.) • Norman Rockwell born, 1894 • Tides {9.5 10.5	*Snow*
4	Tu.	*Do nothing in great haste, except catching fleas and running from a mad dog.* • {9.5 10.2	*forts*
5	W.	St. Agatha • ☾ on Eq. • Walt Disney's *Peter Pan* premiered, 1953 {9.4 9.8	*are*
6	Th.	Sun-Maid raisins trademark registered, 1917 • Tides {9.3 9.3 •	*palatial.*
7	Fr.	☾ at apo. • Laura Ingalls Wilder born, 1867 • {9.1 8.8	*Miserable—*
8	Sa.	Former president Warren G. Harding had the first radio installed in the White House, 1922 • {9.0 8.3 •	*a*
9	**E**	5th S. af. Ep. • U.S. Weather Bureau established, 1870 •	*blizzard*
10	M.	☾ at ☊ • Edmund Halley became second Astronomer Royal of England, 1720	*makes*
11	Tu.	☌♄☾ • Thomas Alva Edison born, 1847 • Tides {8.8 7.7 •	*roads*
12	W.	Abraham Lincoln born, 1809 • *Tears and laughter are the language of the heart.* •	*hardly*
13	Th.	☾ rides high • Strauss's *Blue Danube* premiered in Vienna, 1867 • {9.4 8.2	*visible!*
14	Fr.	St. Valentine • Sts. Cyril & Methodius • {9.9 8.7 •	*Trade*
15	Sa.	☌♃☾ • The National Flag of Canada inaugurated, 1965 • {10.4 9.2	*your*
16	**E**	Septuagesima • Full Snow ○ • Winter's back breaks.	*parka*
17	M.	George Washington's Birthday (observed) • ☌♅☉ • Tides {11.2 10.2	*for*
18	Tu.	*Adventures of Huckleberry Finn* published in the U.S., 1885 • Pluto discovered, 1930 •	*a*
19	W.	☾ on Eq. • ☾ at perig. • Grandpa Jones died, 1998 {10.6 11.3	*sweater;*
20	Th.	☌☿♆ • The Metropolitan Museum of Art opened in New York City, 1872 •	*build*
21	Fr.	*The highest branch is not the safest roost.* • Richard Nixon visited China, 1972 • {10.9 10.5	*an*
22	Sa.	♄ stat. • George Washington born, 1732 • F. W. Woolworth Co. opened, 1879	*ark,*
23	**E**	Sexagesima • ☾ at ☋ • Tootsie Roll introduced by Leo Hirshfield, 1896	*a*
24	M.	American painter Winslow Homer born, 1836 • Tides {10.3 8.8	*week that's*
25	Tu.	☌♂☾ • First trained monkey act in the U.S., 1751 • {10.1 8.6 •	*wetter.*
26	W.	☾ runs low • New York City's World Trade Center bombed, 1993 {10.0 8.6	*Flop-flip!*
27	Th.	☌♀☾ • Annual Mardi Gras celebration began in New Orleans, 1827 {10.1 8.8	*Mixed*
28	Fr.	☌♆☾ • First televised basketball game, 1940 • Tides {10.2 9.1	*precip!*

The best and most beautiful things in the world cannot be seen or even touched. They must be felt with the heart.
–Helen Keller, American author, educator, and lecturer

Farmer's Calendar

■ Crouched over the feeder, packing in the birdseed with both hands, a gray squirrel stuffs itself. Its soft gray coat is rich, its lavish tail full and billowy. Clearly, this squirrel is in its prime—and why wouldn't it be, with plenty of tasty and nourishing food thoughtfully provided by me?

I never grudge the squirrel its seed, however. For me, the northern gray squirrel *(Sciurus carolinensis)*, now generally regarded as a nuisance, is one of the great American animal stories. Early in the 19th century, these squirrels were legendary for their mass migrations. Like European lemmings, gray squirrels would descend on a vicinity by the million, consuming crops as well as forest mast. It was debated how, in these movements, they managed to cross rivers. "It is believed by many people," wrote John James Audubon in 1845, "that they carry a piece of bark to the shore and seat themselves on this substitute for a boat, hoist their broad tails as a sail, and float safely to the opposite shore."

"This we suspect to be apocryphal," noted Audubon. He went on to record a multitude of gray squirrels crossing the Hudson River in 1808. They didn't sail; they swam, and not very well.

Now the gray squirrel is in reduced circumstances. The forests are farmland and towns. The squirrels' prodigious migrations are forgotten. Still, things could be worse. In city parks, the handout peanuts are plentiful. And there is always another sentimental fool with a bird feeder that needs lightening.

2003 MARCH, The Third Month

Venus now noticeably loses some of its predawn dazzle and passes almost directly in front of distant Neptune on the 12th and green Uranus on the 28th. Both conjunctions are very low and require a telescope or binoculars. In the evening sky, much less challenging, those same binoculars easily show Jupiter next to Cancer's famous "beehive" star cluster during the final week of March. That period also allows the brightest asteroid, Vesta, to be marginally glimpsed by the naked eye in dark skies without moonlight interference. Vesta reaches opposition on the 26th. Spring arrives with the vernal equinox at exactly 8:00 P.M. *EST on the 20th.*

●	New Moon	2nd day	21st hour	35th minute
☽	First Quarter	11th day	2nd hour	15th minute
○	Full Moon	18th day	5th hour	34th minute
☾	Last Quarter	24th day	20th hour	51st minute

Times are given in Eastern Standard Time.

For an explanation of this page, see page 40; for values of Key Letters, see page 226.

Day of Year	Day of Month	Day of Week	☼ Rises h. m.	Key	☼ Sets h. m.	Key	Length of Day h. m.	Sun Fast m.	Declination of Sun ° '	High Tide Boston Light—A.M.	**Bold—P.M.**	☽ Rises h. m.	Key	☽ Sets h. m.	Key	☽ Place	☽ Age
60	1	Sa.	6 20	D	5 34	B	11 14	3	7 S. 34	10	**10½**	6 A.M. 04	E	4 P.M. 03	B	CAP	28
61	2	**E**	6 19	D	5 35	B	11 16	3	7 11	10¾	**11¼**	6 32	E	5 09	C	AQU	0
62	3	M.	6 17	D	5 36	B	11 19	3	6 48	11½	**12**	6 57	D	6 13	C	AQU	1
63	4	Tu.	6 15	D	5 37	B	11 22	4	6 25	**12**	—	7 18	D	7 15	D	PSC	2
64	5	W.	6 14	D	5 39	B	11 25	4	6 02	12½	**12¾**	7 39	C	8 16	D	CET	3
65	6	Th.	6 12	D	5 40	B	11 28	4	5 38	1	**1½**	7 59	C	9 16	E	PSC	4
66	7	Fr.	6 10	D	5 41	B	11 31	4	5 15	1¾	**2**	8 20	B	10 17	E	PSC	5
67	8	Sa.	6 09	D	5 42	B	11 33	5	4 52	2¼	**2¾**	8 44	B	11 P.M. 19	E	ARI	6
68	9	**E**	6 07	D	5 43	B	11 36	5	4 28	3	**3½**	9 11	A	—	–	TAU	7
69	10	M.	6 05	D	5 44	B	11 39	5	4 05	3¾	**4½**	9 43	A	12 A.M. 22	E	TAU	8
70	11	Tu.	6 04	D	5 46	B	11 42	5	3 41	4½	**5¼**	10 23	A	1 24	E	TAU	9
71	12	W.	6 02	C	5 47	B	11 45	6	3 18	5½	**6¼**	11 A.M. 12	A	2 23	E	GEM	10
72	13	Th.	6 00	C	5 48	B	11 48	6	2 54	6½	**7¼**	12 P.M. 10	A	3 17	E	GEM	11
73	14	Fr.	5 59	C	5 49	B	11 50	6	2 30	7½	**8¼**	1 16	B	4 05	E	CAN	12
74	15	Sa.	5 57	C	5 50	B	11 53	6	2 07	8½	**9**	2 29	B	4 46	E	CAN	13
75	16	**E**	5 55	C	5 51	B	11 56	7	1 43	9¼	**9¾**	3 45	C	5 21	E	LEO	14
76	17	M.	5 53	C	5 53	B	12 00	7	1 19	10¼	**10¾**	5 03	D	5 51	D	LEO	15
77	18	Tu.	5 52	C	5 54	B	12 02	7	0 55	11	**11½**	6 21	D	6 19	D	VIR	16
78	19	W.	5 50	C	5 55	B	12 05	8	0 32	11¾	—	7 39	E	6 45	C	VIR	17
79	20	Th.	5 48	C	5 56	C	12 08	8	0 S. 08	12¼	**12½**	8 58	E	7 12	C	VIR	18
80	21	Fr.	5 46	C	5 57	C	12 11	8	0 N. 16	1	**1½**	10 17	E	7 41	B	LIB	19
81	22	Sa.	5 45	C	5 58	C	12 13	8	0 39	1¾	**2¼**	11 P.M. 35	E	8 15	A	LIB	20
82	23	**E**	5 43	C	5 59	C	12 16	9	1 03	2½	**3¼**	—	–	8 54	A	OPH	21
83	24	M.	5 41	C	6 01	C	12 20	9	1 27	3½	**4¼**	12 A.M. 48	E	9 42	A	SAG	22
84	25	Tu.	5 39	C	6 02	C	12 23	9	1 50	4½	**5½**	1 53	E	10 38	A	SAG	23
85	26	W.	5 38	C	6 03	C	12 25	10	2 14	5¾	**6½**	2 48	E	11 A.M. 41	A	SAG	24
86	27	Th.	5 36	C	6 04	C	12 28	10	2 37	6¾	**7¾**	3 32	E	12 P.M. 47	B	CAP	25
87	28	Fr.	5 34	C	6 05	C	12 31	10	3 01	8	**8¾**	4 08	E	1 54	B	CAP	26
88	29	Sa.	5 33	C	6 06	C	12 33	11	3 24	9	**9½**	4 37	E	3 00	C	AQU	27
89	30	**E**	5 31	C	6 07	C	12 36	11	3 47	9¾	**10¼**	5 02	D	4 04	C	AQU	28
90	31	M.	5 29	C	6 09	C	12 40	11	4 N. 11	10½	**10¾**	5 A.M. 23	D	5 P.M. 06	D	AQU	29

MARCH hath 31 days. 2003

March is a boisterous fellow,
And undeterred by fear,
With many pranks proclaims himself
The tomboy of the year! –Unknown

D. M.	D. W.	Dates, Feasts, Fasts, Aspects, Tide Heights	Weather ↓
1	Sa.	St. David • ☌☿☾ • *One swallow does not make a spring.* • {10.3 9.3	Our
2	E	Quinquagesima • New ● • Tides {10.4 9.5	focus
3	M.	St. Chad • "The Star-Spangled Banner" became U.S. national anthem, 1931 •	is on
4	Tu.	Shrove Tuesday • ☌☿♅ • Swan Lake debuted, 1877	crocuses—
5	W.	Ash Wednesday • Islamic New Year • ☾ on Eq. •	all
6	Th.	*Only believe half of what you hear. Then get it in writing.* • Tides {9.7 9.6 •	we
7	Fr.	St. Perpetua • ☾ at apo. • Joseph Maurice Ravel born, 1875 •	hear
8	Sa.	First U.S. combat troops arrived in Vietnam, 1968 • President Jimmy Carter began Middle East peace mission, 1979	is
9	E	1st S. in Lent • ☾ at ☊ • Tides {9.2 8.4 •	snow
10	M.	Pure Monday • First telephone call, by Alexander Graham Bell, 1876	cusses!
11	Tu.	☌♄☾ • Lawrence Welk born, 1903 • Tides {8.9 7.8 •	Pleasin'
12	W.	Ember Day • ☌♀♆ • President FDR began fireside chats on radio, 1933	for
13	Th.	☾ rides high • Earmuffs patented by Chester Greenwood, 1877 • Tides {9.0 8.0 •	the
14	Fr.	☌♃☾ • Ember Day • First National Wildlife Refuge, 1903	season—
15	Sa.	Ember Day • Beware the Ides of March. • Dr. Benjamin Spock died, 1998 •	strap
16	E	2nd S. in Lent • Sunday of Orthodoxy • {10.5 9.8	your
17	M.	St. Patrick • Rubber bands patented by Stephen Perry, 1845 • {11.1 10.5 •	skis
18	Tu.	Full Worm ○ • Soviet cosmonaut Alexei Leonov became first spacewalker, 1965 • {11.4 11.1	on!
19	W.	St. Joseph • ☾ on Eq. • ☾ at perig. • *Do not tie dogs with sausages.* •	The
20	Th.	Vernal Equinox • The first Farm Bureau in U.S. formed in Binghamton, New York, 1911	equinox
21	Fr.	☿ in sup. ☌ • Alcatraz prison closed, 1963 • Tides {11.7 11.1 •	brings
22	Sa.	☾ at ☋ • William Shatner born, 1931 • Tides {11.6 10.5 •	wind
23	E	3rd S. in Lent • ♇ stat. • Tides {11.3 9.9 •	and
24	M.	Senator Robert Kennedy was first to reach summit of Mt. Kennedy in Yukon Territory, 1965 •	cloud
25	Tu.	Annunciation • ☾ runs low • ☌♂☾ • Tides {10.3 8.8	and
26	W.	*If it takes two to make a bargain, it should take two to break it.* • Tides {9.9 8.6	geese
27	Th.	☌♆☾ • Patty Smith Hill born, 1868 • Seattle Metropolitans won Stanley Cup, 1917	in
28	Fr.	☌♀♅ • Nuclear power accident at Three Mile Island, 1979 • {9.7 8.9	flocks,
29	Sa.	☌♅☾ • ☌♀☾ • First show of Ringling Bros. and Barnum & Bailey circus, 1919	their
30	E	4th S. in Lent • Game show *Jeopardy* premiered, 1964 •	voices
31	M.	*So many mists in March you see, So many frosts in May will be.* • Tides {10.0 9.7 •	loud.

Farmer's Calendar

■ Town Meeting time again: time once more to kindle the flame of local democracy, time for the sovereign people to gather for the momentous task of exercising self-government by determining who among them shall serve in the year ahead as Town Tree Warden, Town Fence Viewer, Town Inspector of Wood, Town Weigher of Shingles, Town Weigher of Coal.

Now, it may be true that in your town the contests for some of these offices are less than hard-fought. It may be that some of your fellow townspeople have no clear idea what it is these officers do. The officers themselves may not, in every case, be fully informed of the precise nature of their authority, or fully impressed with its solemnity. Once installed in office, they may find their duties leave them time for other pursuits. Nevertheless, the importance of these officers is not measured by the work they do; it is an importance in principle.

America's most astute visitor, Alexis de Tocqueville, observed 175 years ago that the genius of the New England township was to achieve freedom, not by lessening the power of government but by dispersing it among many individuals, hence the quaint multiplicity of minor magistrates in small-town New England. There, Tocqueville wrote, "authority is great and the official is small." Vestigial township authorities like the Inspector of Wood are an example of Tocqueville's principle. It's a good principle. It's also quite up to date. Should the accredited officer show up at your place one fine day wishing to view your fence, don't deny him.

Jupiter and Saturn are both high up at nightfall and vanish in the west between midnight (Saturn) and 3:00 A.M. (Jupiter). Jupiter remains close to the lovely "beehive" star cluster the first week of the month, and Saturn meets the Moon on the 7th. Mercury has its best evening showing of the year from the 1st to the 20th. Brightest during April's first few days, Mercury looks like a ruddy "star" 10 to 15 degrees above the western horizon in evening twilight. The last quarter Moon is in conjunction with Mars and Neptune. Telescope owners under dark skies should easily see Saturn pass near the famous Crab Nebula, an exploded-star remnant, during April's final week.

●	New Moon	1st day	14th hour	19th minute
☽	First Quarter	9th day	19th hour	40th minute
○	Full Moon	16th day	15th hour	36th minute
☾	Last Quarter	23rd day	8th hour	18th minute

After 2:00 A.M. on April 6, Eastern Daylight Time (EDT) is given.

For an explanation of this page, see page 40; for values of Key Letters, see page 226.

Day of Year	Day of Month	Day of Week	☼ Rises h. m.	Key	☼ Sets h. m.	Key	Length of Day h. m.	Sun Fast m.	Declination of Sun ° '	High Tide Boston Light—A.M. Bold—P.M.	☽ Rises h. m.	Key	☽ Sets h. m.	Key	☽ Place	☽ Age
91	1	Tu.	5 27	B	6 10	C	12 43	11	4 N.34	11 11½	5ᴬᴹ44	C	6ᴾᴹ07	D	CET	0
92	2	W.	5 26	B	6 11	C	12 45	12	4 57	11¾ 12	6 04	C	7 07	E	PSC	1
93	3	Th.	5 24	B	6 12	C	12 48	12	5 20	12¼ —	6 24	B	8 08	E	PSC	2
94	4	Fr.	5 22	B	6 13	C	12 51	12	5 43	12½ 1	6 47	B	9 10	E	ARI	3
95	5	Sa.	5 21	B	6 14	D	12 53	13	6 06	1 1½	7 12	B	10ᴾᴹ13	E	TAU	4
96	6	**E**	6 19	B	7 15	D	12 56	13	6 29	1¾ 3¼	8 42	A	—	–	TAU	5
97	7	M.	6 17	B	7 16	D	12 59	13	6 51	3½ 4	9 19	A	12ᴬᴹ14	E	TAU	6
98	8	Tu.	6 15	B	7 18	D	13 03	13	7 14	4¼ 4¾	10 03	A	1 14	E	GEM	7
99	9	W.	6 14	B	7 19	D	13 05	14	7 36	5 5¾	10 56	A	2 10	E	GEM	8
100	10	Th.	6 12	B	7 20	D	13 08	14	7 59	6 6¾	11ᴬᴹ57	A	2 59	E	GEM	9
101	11	Fr.	6 10	B	7 21	D	13 11	14	8 21	7 7¾	1ᴾᴹ06	B	3 42	E	CAN	10
102	12	Sa.	6 09	B	7 22	D	13 13	15	8 43	8 8½	2 19	B	4 18	E	LEO	11
103	13	**E**	6 07	B	7 23	D	13 16	15	9 05	9 9½	3 34	C	4 49	E	LEO	12
104	14	M.	6 06	B	7 24	D	13 18	15	9 26	9¾ 10¼	4 51	D	5 17	D	LEO	13
105	15	Tu.	6 04	B	7 25	D	13 21	15	9 48	10¾ 11	6 09	D	5 43	D	VIR	14
106	16	W.	6 02	B	7 27	D	13 25	16	10 09	11½ 12	7 29	E	6 09	C	VIR	15
107	17	Th.	6 01	B	7 28	D	13 27	16	10 30	12½ —	8 51	E	6 37	B	VIR	16
108	18	Fr.	5 59	B	7 29	D	13 30	16	10 51	12¾ 1¼	10 12	E	7 09	B	LIB	17
109	19	Sa.	5 58	B	7 30	D	13 32	16	11 12	1½ 2¼	11ᴾᴹ31	E	7 47	A	OPH	18
110	20	**E**	5 56	B	7 31	D	13 35	17	11 33	2¼ 3	—	–	8 33	A	OPH	19
111	21	M.	5 54	B	7 32	D	13 38	17	11 53	3¼ 4	12ᴬᴹ43	E	9 28	A	SAG	20
112	22	Tu.	5 53	B	7 33	D	13 40	17	12 13	4¼ 5	1 43	E	10 30	A	SAG	21
113	23	W.	5 51	B	7 34	D	13 43	17	12 33	5¼ 6	2 32	E	11ᴬᴹ37	B	CAP	22
114	24	Th.	5 50	B	7 36	D	13 46	17	12 53	6¼ 7¼	3 11	E	12ᴾᴹ45	B	CAP	23
115	25	Fr.	5 48	B	7 37	D	13 49	17	13 13	7½ 8¼	3 42	E	1 52	B	AQU	24
116	26	Sa.	5 47	B	7 38	D	13 51	18	13 32	8½ 9¼	4 08	D	2 56	C	AQU	25
117	27	**E**	5 46	B	7 39	D	13 53	18	13 51	9½ 10	4 30	D	3 59	D	AQU	26
118	28	M.	5 44	B	7 40	D	13 56	18	14 10	10¼ 10¾	4 50	C	5 00	D	PSC	27
119	29	Tu.	5 43	B	7 41	D	13 58	18	14 29	11 11¼	5 10	C	6 00	D	CET	28
120	30	W.	5 41	B	7 42	D	14 01	18	14 N.48	11¾ 11¾	5ᴬᴹ30	C	7ᴾᴹ01	E	PSC	29

APRIL hath 30 days. 2003

It's the Sun like watermelon,
And the sidewalks overlaid
With a glaze of yellow yellow
Like a jar of marmalade. –Marcia Masters

D. M.	D. W.	Dates, Feasts, Fasts, Aspects, Tide Heights	Weather ↓
1	Tu.	All Fools' • New ● • ☾ on Eq. • *The doors of wisdom are never shut.*	Take
2	W.	Charles Martin Hall patented an inexpensive way to make aluminum, 1889 • {9.9 / 10.0 •	it
3	Th.	St. Richard of Chichester • ☾ at apo. • Tides {9.7 / — •	to
4	Fr.	Susanna Madora Salter became first woman mayor in U.S., 1887 • ♃ stat. • {10.0 / 9.4	the
5	Sa.	☾ at ☊ • *My Fair Lady* won an Academy Award for Best Picture, 1965 •	bank—
6	E	5th S. in Lent • Daylight Saving Time begins, 2:00 A.M. •	it's
7	M.	☌♄☾ • Dancer Irene Castle born, 1893 • Tides {9.5 / 8.5 •	dank.
8	Tu.	Hank Aaron broke Babe Ruth's record by hitting a 715th home run, 1974 • {9.3 / 8.2	We're
9	W.	☾ rides high • Civil War ends, 1865 • First tax-supported U.S. public library, 1833	finally
10	Th.	Walter Hunt patented the first safety pin, 1849 • William Booth born, 1829 • {9.1 / 8.1	sun-
11	Fr.	☌♃☾ • Up to 51 tornadoes hit the Midwest, 1965 • {9.3 / 8.4 •	shinily!
12	Sa.	"Aquarius/Let the Sunshine In" by the 5th Dimension topped charts and stayed there for six weeks, 1969 •	Still
13	E	Palm Sunday • Thomas Jefferson born, 1743 •	mopping
14	M.	President Lincoln assassinated, 1865 • Katharine Hepburn became first to win three Best Actress Oscars, 1969	up,
15	Tu.	☾ on Eq. • R.M.S. *Titanic* sank in early morning after striking iceberg the evening before, 1912 •	but
16	W.	Full Pink ○ • ☿ Gr. Elong. (20° E.) • Tides {11.3 / 11.8 •	jonquils
17	Th.	First day of Passover • ☾ at perig. • William Holden born, 1918 •	are
18	Fr.	Good Friday • ☾ at ☋ • Tides {12.1 / 11.2	popping
19	Sa.	Charles Darwin died, 1882 • *April snow stays no longer than water on the trout's back.* •	up.
20	E	Easter • Pierre Trudeau became 15th prime minister of Canada, 1968 • {11.9 / 10.4	We'll
21	M.	World record: 2,664-pound great white shark caught, 1959 • Tides {11.4 / 9.8 •	put
22	Tu.	☾ runs low • Germans released chlorine gas, WWI, 1915 • Tides {10.8 / 9.3 •	our
23	W.	☌♂☾ • ☌♆☾ • Shirley Temple born, 1928 •	money
24	Th.	Robert B. Thomas born, 1766 • *What soap is to the body, laughter is to the soul.* • {9.8 / 8.8	on
25	Fr.	☌♅☾ • Morris S. Frank was the first to be presented with a seeing eye dog, 1928	sunny,
26	Sa.	☿ stat. • An F5 tornado hit Andover, Kansas, killing 13 in a trailer park, 1991 • {9.4 / 9.1	but
27	E.	1st S. af. Easter • Orthodox Easter • {9.4 / 9.4	wise
28	M.	St. George • ☾ on Eq. • ☌♀☾ • {9.5 / 9.7	investors
29	Tu.	St. Mark • ABC's *Wide World of Sports* premiered, 1961 • {9.5 / 9.9	buy
30	W.	Adolf Hitler committed suicide, 1945 • Tides {9.5 / 10.0	sou'westers.

Life happened because I turned the pages. –Alberto Manguel, Canadian author

Farmer's Calendar

■ In the world of outdoor work and its tools, there is no more pleasing form than that of an ordinary axe handle. That long, shallow S, with its straight top and recurved handle, has a grace that no other implement equals. The fit of the axe handle's delicate curve with the job it has to do seems a thing of perfection. It's surprising, then, to read in a recent book by a Maine author that the axe handle's utilitarian beauty is an illusion.

Until about 1840, according to D. Cook in *The Axe Book,* the common, single-bit axe invariably had a straight handle. S-curved handles began to be used for single-bit axes around that time (double-bit axes, of course, still have straight handles) and eventually superseded the straight. The reason is unclear, for the curved handle is inferior to the straight in every practical way. Because curved axe handles are sawn out partly across the grain of the wood, they break more easily than straight handles, which are full-grained all through. For the same reason, despite the apparent suppleness of the S curve, a curved handle is less limber than a straight one and so more tiring to use.

The ascendancy of the curved axe handle, it seems, is partly due to the imperatives of manufacture. Single-bit axe heads were made with handle openings that would accept only curved handles, and replacing a handle is cheaper than buying a new axe. And then there is the look of the thing. The curved handle is beautiful; the straight one, not. Beauty wins, always, even here.

2003 MAY, The Fifth Month

May is an exciting month. Mars busts through zero magnitude as it explosively brightens and rises by 2:00 A.M. Saturn crosses into Orion's raised arm at midmonth and lurks low in the west at nightfall. Mercury passes in front of the Sun on the 7th. This transit, visible at sunrise, can be seen from the eastern half of North America, the first time in many years; eye protection is essential. The 15th brings a total lunar eclipse to North America, the first of two this year. The Moon enters penumbra at 6:05 P.M., reaches totality at 9:06 P.M. (when it will appear coppery red), and leaves penumbra at 11:15 P.M.

●	New Moon	1st day	8th hour	15th minute
☽	First Quarter	9th day	7th hour	53rd minute
○	Full Moon	15th day	23rd hour	36th minute
☾	Last Quarter	22nd day	20th hour	31st minute
●	New Moon	31st day	0 hour	20th minute

Times are given in Eastern Daylight Time.

For an explanation of this page, see page 40; for values of Key Letters, see page 226.

Day of Year	Day of Month	Day of Week	☼ Rises h. m.	Key	☼ Sets h. m.	Key	Length of Day h. m.	Sun Fast m.	Declination of Sun ° '	High Tide Boston Light—A.M. Bold—P.M.		☽ Rises h. m.	Key	☽ Sets h. m.	Key	☽ Place	☽ Age
121	1	Th.	5 40	B	7 43	D	14 03	18	15 N.06	12¼	—	5 A.M. 51	B	8 P.M. 02	E	ARI	0
122	2	Fr.	5 39	B	7 45	D	14 06	19	15 24	12½	1	6 16	B	9 05	E	ARI	1
123	3	Sa.	5 37	B	7 46	D	14 09	19	15 42	1	1½	6 44	A	10 07	E	TAU	2
124	4	E	5 36	A	7 47	D	14 11	19	15 59	1½	2¼	7 18	A	11 P.M. 08	E	TAU	3
125	5	M.	5 35	A	7 48	D	14 13	19	16 16	2¼	3	7 59	A	—	–	TAU	4
126	6	Tu.	5 33	A	7 49	D	14 16	19	16 33	3	3¾	8 49	A	12 A.M. 05	E	GEM	5
127	7	W.	5 32	A	7 50	D	14 18	19	16 50	3¾	4½	9 47	A	12 56	E	GEM	6
128	8	Th.	5 31	A	7 51	D	14 20	19	17 06	4½	5¼	10 A.M. 52	B	1 40	E	CAN	7
129	9	Fr.	5 30	A	7 52	D	14 22	19	17 22	5½	6¼	12 P.M. 01	B	2 17	E	CAN	8
130	10	Sa.	5 29	A	7 53	D	14 24	19	17 38	6½	7	1 13	C	2 49	E	LEO	9
131	11	E	5 27	A	7 54	D	14 27	19	17 54	7½	8	2 27	C	3 17	D	LEO	10
132	12	M.	5 26	A	7 55	D	14 29	19	18 10	8½	9	3 42	D	3 42	D	VIR	11
133	13	Tu.	5 25	A	7 56	D	14 31	19	18 24	9¼	9¾	4 59	E	4 08	C	VIR	12
134	14	W.	5 24	A	7 58	D	14 34	19	18 39	10¼	10½	6 19	E	4 34	C	VIR	13
135	15	Th.	5 23	A	7 59	E	14 36	19	18 53	11¼	11½	7 41	E	5 03	B	LIB	14
136	16	Fr.	5 22	A	8 00	E	14 38	19	19 07	12	—	9 03	E	5 38	B	LIB	15
137	17	Sa.	5 21	A	8 01	E	14 40	19	19 21	12¼	1	10 21	E	6 20	A	OPH	16
138	18	E	5 20	A	8 02	E	14 42	19	19 34	1¼	1¾	11 P.M. 29	E	7 12	A	SAG	17
139	19	M.	5 19	A	8 03	E	14 44	19	19 47	2	2¾	—	–	8 13	A	SAG	18
140	20	Tu.	5 18	A	8 04	E	14 46	19	20 00	3	3¾	12 A.M. 26	E	9 21	A	SAG	19
141	21	W.	5 18	A	8 05	E	14 47	19	20 12	4	4¾	1 10	E	10 32	B	CAP	20
142	22	Th.	5 17	A	8 06	E	14 49	19	20 24	5	5¾	1 44	E	11 A.M. 41	B	CAP	21
143	23	Fr.	5 16	A	8 06	E	14 50	19	20 36	6	6¾	2 12	E	12 P.M. 47	C	AQU	22
144	24	Sa.	5 15	A	8 07	E	14 52	19	20 47	7	7¾	2 36	D	1 51	C	AQU	23
145	25	E	5 14	A	8 08	E	14 54	19	20 58	8	8½	2 56	D	2 52	D	PSC	24
146	26	M.	5 14	A	8 09	E	14 55	19	21 08	9	9¼	3 16	C	3 53	D	CET	25
147	27	Tu.	5 13	A	8 10	E	14 57	19	21 18	9¾	10	3 36	C	4 53	E	PSC	26
148	28	W.	5 12	A	8 11	E	14 59	18	21 28	10½	10¾	3 57	B	5 55	E	CET	27
149	29	Th.	5 12	A	8 12	E	15 00	18	21 37	11¼	11¼	4 20	B	6 57	E	ARI	28
150	30	Fr.	5 11	A	8 13	E	15 02	18	21 46	12	12	4 47	A	8 00	E	TAU	29
151	31	Sa.	5 10	A	8 13	E	15 03	18	21 N.55	12½	—	5 A.M. 19	A	9 P.M. 02	E	TAU	0

MAY hath 31 days. 2003

The birds around me hopped and played,
Their thoughts I cannot measure;
But the least motion which they made
It seemed a thrill of pleasure. –William Wordsworth

D. M.	D. W.	Dates, Feasts, Fasts, Aspects, Tide Heights	Weather ↓
1	Th.	May Day • New ● • ☾ at apo. • Tides {9.5 — •	*Rotten*
2	Fr.	St. Athanasius • ☾ at ☊ • Northern Dancer won the Kentucky Derby, 1964	*luck,*
3	Sa.	Sts. Philip & James • Invention of the Holy Cross • Tides {10.1 9.2	*it's*
4	E	2nd S. af. Easter • Audrey Hepburn born, 1929 •	*raining*
5	M.	☌♄☾ • Chanel No. 5 introduced, 1921 • Tides {9.9 8.8 •	*buckets.*
6	Tu.	☾ rides high • First postage stamps issued, 1840 • Tides {9.8 8.6	*Foggy,*
7	W.	☿ in inf. ☌ • R.M.S. *Lusitania* sunk by German sub, killing 1,198 in 1915	*boggy,*
8	Th.	St. Julian of Norwich • ☌♃☾ • V-E Day, 1945 •	*smells*
9	Fr.	First American cartoon debuted in *The Pennsylvania Gazette*, 1754 • Tides {9.5 8.7 •	*wet-*
10	Sa.	Adler Planetarium, first in U.S., opened, 1930 • *When the old dog barks, it is time to watch.*	*doggy.*
11	E	3rd S. af. Easter • Siam was renamed Thailand, 1949 • **Three**	*Not*
12	M.	☾ on Eq. • The Manitoba Act was passed, making Manitoba a Canadian province, 1840 • **Chilly**	*as*
13	Tu.	☌♂♆ • Stevie Wonder born, 1950 • Tides {10.4 11.1 • **Saints**	*cold,*
14	W.	St. Matthias • Olympic games held for first time in U.S., 1904 • George Lucas born, 1944	*but*
15	Th.	Full Flower ○ • Eclipse ☾ • ☾ at perig. • ♆ stat. •	*we're*
16	Fr.	☾ at ☋ • Marie Antoinette married future King Louis XVI of France, 1770 •	*growing*
17	Sa.	First U.S. cross-country helicopter flight ended, 1942 • N.Y. Stock Exchange started, 1792	*mold.*
18	E	4th S. af. Easter • India became world's sixth nuclear power, 1974	*We*
19	M.	St. Dunstan • **Victoria Day (Canada)** • ☾ runs low • ☿ stat. •	*regret*
20	Tu.	*It is better to conceal one's knowledge than to reveal one's ignorance.* • Tides {11.4 9.8 •	*to*
21	W.	☌♂☾ • Baltimore Light became first nuclear-powered lighthouse, 1964	*mention*
22	Th.	☌♅☾ • First permanent IMAX theater opened in Toronto, 1971 •	*another*
23	Fr.	North-West Mounted Police (now called Royal Canadian Mounted Police) formed, 1873	*drenchin'.*
24	Sa.	First telegraph message received in Baltimore, 1844 • Tides {9.3 9.1 •	*Sunny*
25	E	Rogation S. • ☾ on Eq. • First Catholic priest ordained in U.S., 1793	*at*
26	M.	St. Bede • **Memorial Day** • Sally K. Ride born, 1951 • Tides {9.0 9.5	*last!*
27	Tu.	☌☿♀ • German battleship *Bismarck* sunk, 1941 • Tides {9.0 9.7 •	*Look*
28	W.	☾ at apo. • Golden Gate Bridge opened to vehicles, 1937 • Tides {9.0 9.9	*fast!*
29	Th.	Ascension • ☌☿☾ • *A little wind kindles, too much puts out the fire.* •	*It*
30	Fr.	☾ at ☊ • Benny Goodman born, 1909 • Tides {9.0 10.1 •	*won't*
31	Sa.	Visit. of Mary • New ● • Eclipse ☉ • {9.0 — •	*last.*

Farmer's Calendar

■ As his admirers will remember, Detective Sherlock Holmes once remarked to Dr. Watson on the importance of observing people's dogs. "A dog reflects the family life," Holmes declared. "Whoever saw a frisky dog in a gloomy family, or a sad dog in a happy one? Snarling people have snarling dogs, dangerous people have dangerous ones."

"Surely, Holmes," Watson objected, "this is a little far-fetched."

So it is. I'm with Watson here. I'd better be, because from the dogs in my own life, the inferences to be drawn from Holmes's premise are dire. This household consists of two supposed adults, three cats, and two dogs—dachshunds. The last are the subject for today. They are loud, disorderly, ill-tempered, and excitable. They bark constantly at nothing, they growl, they snap. They are not friendly. People, besides their owners, they can do without—children especially, embarrassingly, they detest. Cats they chase. Other dogs they hate and attempt to devour.

What would Holmes make of these two? What would he make of their masters? Disorderly we may be, comparatively. But loud? Ill-tempered? Excitable? Never. Holmes has got it wrong, in our case, I'd say. But what if he hasn't? What if he's right? Maybe we *are* loud, excitable, and so on—and don't know it. Dangerous people have dangerous dogs. Are we dangerous? Surely not. But consider the dachshunds. Together, they don't weigh 30 pounds. If we're harmless, maybe it's only because, like them, we're feeble.

Jupiter, near the crescent Moon on the 5th, gets lower in the west and is now visible only before midnight. The Moon is at perigee on the 12th. Mercury and Venus come strikingly close together on the 20th but are a difficult sight a few degrees above the eastern horizon in predawn twilight. Saturn is totally gone, invisibly entering Gemini before passing behind the Sun on the 24th. The big story is Mars, now brilliant (and 500 times brighter than Uranus, which floats just above the red planet). Rising soon after midnight, Mars is near the Moon on the 19th. Summer begins with the solstice on the 21st at 3:10 in the afternoon.

☽ First Quarter	7th day	16th hour	28th minute
○ Full Moon	14th day	7th hour	16th minute
☾ Last Quarter	21st day	10th hour	45th minute
● New Moon	29th day	14th hour	39th minute

Times are given in Eastern Daylight Time.

For an explanation of this page, see page 40; for values of Key Letters, see page 226.

Day of Year	Day of Month	Day of Week	☀ Rises h. m.	Key	☀ Sets h. m.	Key	Length of Day h. m.	Sun Fast m.	Declination of Sun ° '	High Tide Boston Light—A.M. Bold—P.M.	☽ Rises h. m.	Key	☽ Sets h. m.	Key	Place	☽ Age
152	1	E	5 10	A	8 14	E	15 04	18	22 N.04	12½ **1¼**	5 ᴹ58	A	10 ᴿ00	E	TAU	1
153	2	M.	5 10	A	8 15	E	15 05	18	22 12	1¼ **1¾**	6 45	A	10 54	E	GEM	2
154	3	Tu.	5 10	A	8 16	E	15 06	18	22 19	1¾ **2½**	7 41	A	11 ᴿ40	E	GEM	3
155	4	W.	5 09	A	8 16	E	15 07	17	22 27	2½ **3¼**	8 43	B	—	–	CAN	4
156	5	Th.	5 08	A	8 17	E	15 09	17	22 33	3¼ **4**	9 51	B	12 ᴬ19	E	CAN	5
157	6	Fr.	5 08	A	8 18	E	15 10	17	22 39	4¼ **4¾**	11 ᴬ01	C	12 51	E	LEO	6
158	7	Sa.	5 08	A	8 18	E	15 10	17	22 45	5 **5¾**	12 ᴾᴹ12	C	1 20	D	LEO	7
159	8	E	5 08	A	8 19	E	15 11	17	22 51	6 **6½**	1 24	D	1 45	D	VIR	8
160	9	M.	5 08	A	8 20	E	15 12	17	22 57	7 **7½**	2 37	D	2 09	D	VIR	9
161	10	Tu.	5 07	A	8 20	E	15 13	16	23 01	8 **8½**	3 53	E	2 34	C	VIR	10
162	11	W.	5 07	A	8 21	E	15 14	16	23 06	9 **9¼**	5 12	E	3 00	B	VIR	11
163	12	Th.	5 07	A	8 21	E	15 14	16	23 09	10 **10¼**	6 33	E	3 31	B	LIB	12
164	13	Fr.	5 07	A	8 22	E	15 15	16	23 13	10¾ **11**	7 53	E	4 09	A	SCO	13
165	14	Sa.	5 07	A	8 22	E	15 15	16	23 16	11¾ **12**	9 07	E	4 55	A	OPH	14
166	15	E	5 07	A	8 23	E	15 16	15	23 18	12¾ **—**	10 11	E	5 53	A	SAG	15
167	16	M.	5 07	A	8 23	E	15 16	15	23 21	12¾ **1½**	11 02	E	6 59	A	SAG	16
168	17	Tu.	5 07	A	8 23	E	15 16	15	23 23	1¾ **2½**	11 ᴾᴹ41	E	8 11	B	CAP	17
169	18	W.	5 07	A	8 24	E	15 17	15	23 24	2¾ **3½**	—	–	9 23	B	CAP	18
170	19	Th.	5 07	A	8 24	E	15 17	14	23 26	3½ **4¼**	12 ᴬ13	D	10 33	C	AQU	19
171	20	Fr.	5 07	A	8 24	E	15 17	14	23 26	4½ **5¼**	12 39	D	11 ᴬ39	E	AQU	20
172	21	Sa.	5 07	A	8 24	E	15 17	14	23 26	5½ **6**	1 01	D	12 ᴾᴹ42	E	PSC	21
173	22	E	5 08	A	8 25	E	15 17	14	23 26	6¼ **7**	1 21	D	1 44	D	CET	22
174	23	M.	5 08	A	8 25	E	15 17	14	23 25	7¼ **7¾**	1 41	C	2 44	D	PSC	23
175	24	Tu.	5 08	A	8 25	E	15 17	13	23 24	8¼ **8½**	2 01	B	3 45	E	PSC	24
176	25	W.	5 08	A	8 25	E	15 17	13	23 23	9 **9¼**	2 24	B	4 47	E	ARI	25
177	26	Th.	5 09	A	8 25	E	15 16	13	23 22	10 **10**	2 49	B	5 50	E	TAU	26
178	27	Fr.	5 09	A	8 25	E	15 16	13	23 19	10¾ **10¾**	3 19	A	6 53	E	TAU	27
179	28	Sa.	5 10	A	8 25	E	15 15	13	23 17	11½ **11½**	3 56	A	7 53	E	TAU	28
180	29	E	5 10	A	8 25	E	15 15	12	23 14	12 **—**	4 41	A	8 49	E	GEM	0
181	30	M.	5 10	A	8 25	E	15 15	12	23 N.10	12 **12¾**	5 ᴬᴹ34	A	9 ᴿ38	E	GEM	1

JUNE hath 30 days. 2003

I meant to do my work to-day—
But a brown bird sang in the apple-tree
And a butterfly flitted across the field,
And all the leaves were calling me. –Richard Le Gallienne

D. M.	D. W.	Dates, Feasts, Fasts, Aspects, Tide Heights	*Weather* ↓
1	**E**	1st S. af. Asc. • ☌♄☾ • Alanis Morissette born, 1974 •	*Not*
2	M.	☾ rides high • Grover Cleveland married, 1886 • Tides {10.1 8.9 •	*half*
3	Tu.	☿ Gr. Elong. (24° W.) • *He surely is in want of another's patience who has none of his own.* •	*bad*
4	W.	Henry Ford took his first car, the quadricycle, for a test drive, 1896 • Tides {10.1 8.8	*for*
5	Th.	St. Boniface • Orthodox Ascension • ☌♃☾ •	*Dad*
6	Fr.	Shavuot • D Day, 1944 • Josephine Peary was first woman to join polar expedition, 1891	*and*
7	Sa.	♅ stat. • Louis XIV crowned King of France, 1654 • Daniel Boone first saw Ky., 1769	*grad.*
8	**E**	Whit S. • Pentecost • Barbara Bush born, 1925 •	*Father*
9	M.	☾ on Eq. • ♇ at ☍ • Michael J. Fox born, 1961 • Tides {9.8 10.3 •	*of*
10	Tu.	*Love is the reward of love.* • Italy declared war on France and Great Britain, 1940 •	*the*
11	W.	St. Barnabas • Ember Day • Jacques-Yves Cousteau born, 1910 •	*bride*
12	Th.	☾ at ☋ • ☾ at perig. • George H. W. Bush born, 1929 {10.2 11.8	*should*
13	Fr.	Ember Day • Boxer Rebellion began in China, 1900 • Tides {10.3 12.0 •	*march*
14	Sa.	Full Strawberry ○ • Ember Day • Donald Trump born, 1946 • {10.3 12.1	*her*
15	**E**	Trinity • Orthodox Pentecost • ☾ runs low • {10.3 —	*inside*
16	M.	Cosmonaut Valentina Tereshkova orbited Earth in *Vostok 6*, becoming first woman in space, 1963 •	*lest*
17	Tu.	☌♆☾ • Republican Party's first national convention, 1856 • {11.6 10.0	*showers*
18	W.	War of 1812 began • Paul McCartney born, 1942 • {11.2 9.7 •	*interrupt*
19	Th.	Corpus Christi • ☌♅☾ • ☌♂☾ • Tides {10.6 9.5	*the*
20	Fr.	☌♂♅ • ☌☿♀ • F5 tornado hit Fargo, N.Dak., killing ten, 1957	*nup-*
21	Sa.	Summer Solstice • John Archer became first to receive Bachelor of Medicine degree in U.S., 1768	*tials!*
22	**E**	2nd S. af. P. • Orthodox All Saints' • ☾ on Eq.	*Lower*
23	M.	St. Alban • *A wise man gathers from the past what is to come.* • {8.8 9.3 •	*neck-*
24	Tu.	Nativ. John the Baptist • Midsummer Day • ☾ at apo. •	*lines,*
25	W.	Sitting Bull defeated General Custer at the Battle of Little Bighorn, 1876 • {8.5 9.6 •	*higher*
26	Th.	☾ at ☊ • First boardwalk in the world opened in Atlantic City, 1870 {8.5 9.7	*degrees;*
27	Fr.	Illinois became first state to require seat belts for automobiles, 1955 • {8.6 9.9	*raindrops*
28	Sa.	St. Irenaeus • Gilda Radner born, 1946 • Tides {8.7 10.1 •	*rustle in*
29	**E**	3rd S. af. P. • New ● • Mesa Verde National Park established, 1906	*the*
30	M.	Sts. Peter & Paul • ☾ rides high • First Corvette rolled off assembly line, 1953	*trees.*

The trouble with facts is that there are so many of them.
–Samuel McChord Crothers, American writer

Farmer's Calendar

■ Nature is the classic and furnishes the classic's unfailing satisfaction, the quality of being known but also new.

Last year around this time, I was walking along an old logging road pretty far back in the woods. The track was maybe 15 feet across, grown up in long, rough grass, with thick fir woods on both sides. It's very quiet out there: You might hear an airplane overhead, you might hear a chickadee or other little bird of the dark brushwoods, but even *they* seem to whisper. My own footfalls were the only real sound to be heard, when, in an instant, the path before, beside, and behind me seemed to explode into a chaos of rustling, scrabbling, flapping, and cheeping. I had walked into a mother partridge and her brood of unfledged young.

I never saw any of the chicks. They scattered to all sides, hidden under the grass and in the shadows. The mother was on the ground, too, ten feet ahead of me, flopping about, dragging one wing, then the other, and all the while keeping up a piteous clamor of peeps, cries, and whimpers, designed to lead me after her so her brood could get away. It's what a mother partridge does. It's what she knows. It's her form.

I have seen the same performance 50 times, and each time I'm charmed and, somehow, reassured. It's that grateful response on the part of the onlooker that belongs to the classic and is available nowhere else. J. S. Bach supplies it, so does Shakespeare—so does this common woodland chicken.

JULY, The Seventh Month

Earth's aphelion (farthest point from the Sun) arrives on the 4th, with the Sun now at its dimmest of the year. In fact, everything but Mars seems to be reaching a choreographed nadir. Jupiter, near the crescent Moon on the 2nd, crosses into Leo and drops so low into evening twilight that its lovely conjunction with Mercury on the 25th will be a challenge to see. Saturn is lost in solar glare until the end of the month. Venus's long performance as a morning star sputters to a close. But Mars makes up for it all: Near the Moon on the 17th and brighter than magnitude –1.0, it rises by 11:00 P.M. and overwhelms the dim stars of Aquarius, its home until December.

☽	First Quarter	6th day	22nd hour	32nd minute
○	Full Moon	13th day	15th hour	21st minute
☾	Last Quarter	21st day	3rd hour	1st minute
●	New Moon	29th day	2nd hour	53rd minute

Times are given in Eastern Daylight Time.

For an explanation of this page, see page 40; for values of Key Letters, see page 226.

Day of Year	Day of Month	Day of Week	☼ Rises h. m.	Key	☼ Sets h. m.	Key	Length of Day h. m.	Sun Fast m.	Declination of Sun ° '	High Tide Boston Light—A.M.	**Bold—P.M.**	☽ Rises h. m.	Key	☽ Sets h. m.	Key	☽ Place	☽ Age
182	1	Tu.	5 11	A	8 25	E	15 14	12	23 N. 06	12¾	**1½**	6 A.M. 36	B	10 P.M. 19	E	CAN	2
183	2	W.	5 11	A	8 25	E	15 14	12	23 02	1½	**2¼**	7 43	B	10 54	E	CAN	3
184	3	Th.	5 12	A	8 25	E	15 13	12	22 57	2¼	**3**	8 53	B	11 24	E	LEO	4
185	4	Fr.	5 13	A	8 24	E	15 11	11	22 52	3	**3¾**	10 03	C	11 P.M. 49	D	LEO	5
186	5	Sa.	5 13	A	8 24	E	15 11	11	22 47	3¾	**4½**	11 A.M. 14	D	—	–	LEO	6
187	6	**E**	5 14	A	8 24	E	15 10	11	22 41	4¾	**5¼**	12 P.M. 26	D	12 A.M. 14	C	VIR	7
188	7	M.	5 14	A	8 23	E	15 09	11	22 35	5½	**6**	1 39	E	12 37	C	VIR	8
189	8	Tu.	5 15	A	8 23	E	15 08	11	22 28	6½	**7**	2 54	E	1 02	B	VIR	9
190	9	W.	5 16	A	8 23	E	15 07	11	22 21	7½	**8**	4 11	E	1 30	B	LIB	10
191	10	Th.	5 16	A	8 22	E	15 06	10	22 13	8½	**9**	5 29	E	2 03	B	SCO	11
192	11	Fr.	5 17	A	8 22	E	15 05	10	22 05	9¾	**10**	6 45	E	2 44	A	OPH	12
193	12	Sa.	5 18	A	8 21	E	15 03	10	21 57	10½	**10¾**	7 53	E	3 36	A	SAG	13
194	13	**E**	5 19	A	8 21	E	15 02	10	21 49	11½	**11¾**	8 50	E	4 38	A	SAG	14
195	14	M.	5 20	A	8 20	E	15 00	10	21 40	**12½**	—	9 35	E	5 48	A	SAG	15
196	15	Tu.	5 20	A	8 19	E	14 59	10	21 31	12½	**1¼**	10 10	E	7 01	B	CAP	16
197	16	W.	5 21	A	8 19	E	14 58	10	21 21	1½	**2¼**	10 39	E	8 13	B	AQU	17
198	17	Th.	5 22	A	8 18	E	14 56	10	21 11	2¼	**3**	11 03	D	9 22	C	AQU	18
199	18	Fr.	5 23	A	8 17	E	14 54	9	21 01	3	**3¾**	11 24	D	10 28	D	AQU	19
200	19	Sa.	5 24	A	8 17	E	14 53	9	20 50	4	**4½**	11 P.M. 44	C	11 A.M. 31	D	PSC	20
201	20	**E**	5 25	A	8 16	E	14 51	9	20 39	4¾	**5¼**	—	–	12 P.M. 33	D	PSC	21
202	21	M.	5 26	A	8 15	E	14 49	9	20 28	5¾	**6**	12 A.M. 05	B	1 34	E	PSC	22
203	22	Tu.	5 27	A	8 14	E	14 47	9	20 15	6½	**7**	12 26	A	2 36	E	ARI	23
204	23	W.	5 28	A	8 13	E	14 45	9	20 04	7½	**7¾**	12 50	A	3 39	E	ARI	24
205	24	Th.	5 28	A	8 12	E	14 44	9	19 51	8½	**8½**	1 18	A	4 41	E	TAU	25
206	25	Fr.	5 29	A	8 11	E	14 42	9	19 38	9¼	**9½**	1 53	A	5 43	E	TAU	26
207	26	Sa.	5 30	A	8 10	D	14 40	9	19 25	10	**10¼**	2 34	A	6 41	E	TAU	27
208	27	**E**	5 31	A	8 09	D	14 38	9	19 12	11	**11**	3 25	A	7 33	E	GEM	28
209	28	M.	5 32	A	8 08	D	14 36	9	18 58	11¾	**11¾**	4 24	A	8 17	E	GEM	29
210	29	Tu.	5 33	A	8 07	D	14 34	9	18 44	**12¼**	—	5 31	B	8 55	E	CAN	0
211	30	W.	5 34	A	8 06	D	14 32	9	18 29	12½	**1**	6 41	B	9 26	E	LEO	1
212	31	Th.	5 35	A	8 05	D	14 30	9	18 N. 14	1¼	**1¾**	7 A.M. 53	C	9 P.M. 53	D	LEO	2

JULY hath 31 days. 2003

Come ye into the summer woods;
There entereth no annoy;
All greenly wave the chestnut leaves,
And the earth is full of joy. –Mary Howitt

D. M.	D. W.	Dates, Feasts, Fasts, Aspects, Tide Heights	*Weather* ↓
1	Tu.	**Canada Day** • First U.S. zoo opened in Philadelphia, 1874 • Tides {10.3 9.0	*Red,*
2	W.	☌♃☾ • Alligator fell from sky during thunderstorm in Charleston, S.C., 1843	*white,*
3	Th.	**St. Thomas** • Dog Days begin. • *Every dog has its day.* • {10.4 9.3 •	*blue,*
4	Fr.	**Independence Day** • ⊕ at aphelion • Tides {10.4 9.5 •	*and*
5	Sa.	☿ in sup. ☌ • P. T. Barnum born, 1810 • {10.3 9.7 •	*Hades-hot*
6	**E**	**4th S. af. P.** • ☾ on Eq. • Roy Rogers died, 1998 • {10.1 10.0	*for*
7	M.	*The sun does not shine on both sides of the hedge at once.* • Tides {9.9 10.3	*summer*
8	Tu.	☌♀♄ • Vermont became first American colony to abolish slavery, 1777 •	*sailor*
9	W.	☾ at ☋ • Corncob pipe patented by Henry Tibbe, 1878 • Tides {9.6 11.0	*and*
10	Th.	☾ at perig. • George Hodgson won two Olympic gold medals for swimming, 1912	*sunshine*
11	Fr.	U.S. space station *Skylab* returned to Earth, 1979 • Tides {9.6 11.5 •	*patriot.*
12	Sa.	R. Buckminster Fuller born, 1895 • Cornscateous air is everywhere. • {9.7 11.6	*It's*
13	**E**	**5th S. af. P.** • **Full Buck** ○ • ☾ runs low •	*perishing:*
14	M.	**Bastille Day** • Edward Whymper was first to summit the Matterhorn, 1865 • {9.9 —	*Rain*
15	Tu.	**St. Swithin** • ☌♆☾ • Tides {11.5 9.9 •	*would*
16	W.	☌♅☾ • Dr. Emily Howard Stowe became first woman licensed to practice medicine in Canada, 1880	*be*
17	Th.	☌♂☾ • Spain ceded Florida to U.S., 1821 • Tides {10.9 9.8	*worth*
18	Fr.	*Lightning in summer indicates good healthy weather.* • {10.4 9.6	*cherishing.*
19	Sa.	☾ on Eq. • Bloomers introduced to first Woman's Rights Convention, 1848 •	*Best*
20	**E**	**6th S. af. P.** • British Columbia joined the Canadian Confederation, 1871 •	*way*
21	M.	Jesse James's gang robbed its first train, 1873 • Ernest Hemingway born, 1899 • {8.9 9.2	*to*
22	Tu.	**St. Mary Magdalene** • ☾ at apo. • Gregor Mendel born, 1822 •	*beat*
23	W.	☾ at ☊ • George Lee "Sparky" Anderson inducted into National Baseball Hall of Fame, 2000	*the*
24	Th.	Hulda Crooks climbed Mt. Fuji at age 91, 1987 • Tennessee readmitted to Union after Civil War, 1866	*heat*
25	Fr.	**Sts. James & Christopher** • ☌☿♃ • Tides {8.2 9.5 •	*is*
26	Sa.	**St. Anne** • ☌♄☾ • Benjamin Franklin became the first Postmaster General, 1775	*get*
27	**E**	**7th S. af. P.** • ☾ rides high • Peggy Fleming born, 1948	*outdoors*
28	M.	Johann Sebastian Bach died, 1750 • Lee Majors married Farrah Fawcett, 1973 • {8.8 10.4 •	*and*
29	Tu.	**St. Martha** • **New** ● • *Live and learn.* • Tides {9.1 — •	*grill*
30	W.	☌☿☾ • ☌♃☾ • ♂ stat. • *Mister Roberts* premiered, 1955	*some*
31	Th.	**St. Ignatius of Loyola** • U.S. probe *Ranger 7* relayed first Moon close-ups, 1964	*meat.*

Farmer's Calendar

■ As a gardener, I reckon I have paid my dues. Each summer for 30 years, I have worked to make my tiny patch of earth produce vegetables. Nobody can say I have slacked. Therefore, I decided to take a year off from gardening. It happened that I was away from home at planting time, so the year seemed the right one to give gardening a season of fallow.

I confess to being apprehensive at neglecting the garden. Not from any practical cause: The garden would be unharmed, I knew. It wasn't the earth I feared for; it was myself. Can you simply omit any task you have performed unfailingly for so long? Superstition says no. Am I to put myself above superstition? Simply not to have a garden. Is it safe? Who knows what the consequences might be?

The consequences were other than I'd feared. They were good. May, then June passed free of tilling, mulching, thinning, weeding, staking, hoeing. The grass I'd sown on the garden to beat the weeds grew tall and waved in the breeze, transforming my lumpy and confined patch into a kind of dollhouse Kansas. No Garden Police knocked on my door. No famine visited my hearth.

On the contrary, the season was one of unexampled bounty. My generous neighbors saw my ungardened plight and rode to the rescue. They piled tomatoes upon peas, carrots upon squash. My cup ran over. I got more produce by doing nothing than I was used to getting in return for my sweat. I've considered making my retirement perpetual—but surely that would be pushing too far.

AUGUST, The Eighth Month

Venus and Jupiter closely, but invisibly, bunch behind the Sun as they meet on the 22nd, going in opposite directions. Venus transitions from a morning star to an evening star while Jupiter does the converse, a role reversal that will produce brilliance by year's end. Other wimpy events include Neptune's opposition on the 4th, the Perseid meteor shower's washout by a full Moon on the 11th, and Uranus's opposition on the 24th, when in dark skies it can be dimly glimpsed above Mars by the naked eye. However, kneel before the great Martian opposition on the 28th, when the red planet comes nearer and gets brighter than it has been in thousands of years!

☽	First Quarter	5th day	3rd hour	28th minute
○	Full Moon	12th day	0 hour	48th minute
☾	Last Quarter	19th day	20th hour	48th minute
●	New Moon	27th day	13th hour	26th minute

Times are given in Eastern Daylight Time.

For an explanation of this page, see page 40; for values of Key Letters, see page 226.

Day of Year	Day of Month	Day of Week	☼ Rises h. m.	Key	☼ Sets h. m.	Key	Length of Day h. m.	Sun Fast m.	Declination of Sun ° '	High Tide Boston Light—A.M.	Bold—P.M.	☽ Rises h. m.	Key	☽ Sets h. m.	Key	☽ Place	☽ Age
213	1	Fr.	5 36	A	8 04	D	14 28	9	17N. 59	1¾	**2½**	9 A.M. 05	D	10 P.M. 18	D	LEO	3
214	2	Sa.	5 37	A	8 03	D	14 26	9	17 44	2¾	**3¼**	10 17	D	10 42	C	VIR	4
215	3	**E**	5 38	A	8 02	D	14 24	9	17 29	3½	**4**	11 A.M. 30	D	11 06	B	VIR	5
216	4	M.	5 39	A	8 01	D	14 22	9	17 13	4¼	**4¾**	12 P.M. 43	E	11 P.M. 32	B	VIR	6
217	5	Tu.	5 40	A	7 59	D	14 19	10	16 57	5¼	**5¾**	1 59	E	—	–	LIB	7
218	6	W.	5 41	A	7 58	D	14 17	10	16 41	6¼	**6¾**	3 16	E	12 A.M. 03	B	LIB	8
219	7	Th.	5 43	A	7 57	D	14 14	10	16 24	7¼	**7¾**	4 31	E	12 40	A	OPH	9
220	8	Fr.	5 44	A	7 55	D	14 11	10	16 07	8½	**8¾**	5 40	E	1 26	A	SAG	10
221	9	Sa.	5 45	A	7 54	D	14 09	10	15 50	9½	**9¾**	6 40	E	2 23	A	SAG	11
222	10	**E**	5 46	A	7 53	D	14 07	10	15 32	10½	**10¾**	7 28	E	3 29	A	SAG	12
223	11	M.	5 47	A	7 51	D	14 04	10	15 15	11¼	**11½**	8 07	E	4 40	B	CAP	13
224	12	Tu.	5 48	A	7 50	D	14 02	10	14 57	**12¼**	—	8 38	E	5 53	B	CAP	14
225	13	W.	5 49	A	7 49	D	14 00	11	14 39	12¼	**1**	9 04	D	7 04	C	AQU	15
226	14	Th.	5 50	A	7 47	D	13 57	11	14 20	1¼	**1¾**	9 26	D	8 12	C	AQU	16
227	15	Fr.	5 51	B	7 46	D	13 55	11	14 02	2	**2½**	9 47	C	9 17	D	PSC	17
228	16	Sa.	5 52	B	7 44	D	13 52	11	13 43	2¾	**3**	10 07	C	10 20	D	CET	18
229	17	**E**	5 53	B	7 43	D	13 50	11	13 24	3½	**3¾**	10 28	B	11 A.M. 22	D	PSC	19
230	18	M.	5 54	B	7 41	D	13 47	12	13 05	4¼	**4½**	10 51	B	12 P.M. 24	E	ARI	20
231	19	Tu.	5 55	B	7 40	D	13 45	12	12 45	5	**5¼**	11 17	B	1 26	E	ARI	21
232	20	W.	5 56	B	7 38	D	13 42	12	12 26	5¾	**6**	11 P.M. 49	A	2 29	E	TAU	22
233	21	Th.	5 57	B	7 37	D	13 40	12	12 06	6¾	**7**	—	–	3 31	E	TAU	23
234	22	Fr.	5 58	B	7 35	D	13 37	13	11 45	7¾	**8**	12 A.M. 27	A	4 30	E	TAU	24
235	23	Sa.	5 59	B	7 34	D	13 35	13	11 25	8¾	**8¾**	1 14	A	5 24	E	GEM	25
236	24	**E**	6 01	B	7 32	D	13 31	13	11 05	9½	**9¾**	2 09	A	6 12	E	GEM	26
237	25	M.	6 02	B	7 30	D	13 28	13	10 44	10¼	**10½**	3 13	B	6 52	E	CAN	27
238	26	Tu.	6 03	B	7 29	D	13 26	14	10 23	11	**11¼**	4 23	B	7 26	E	CAN	28
239	27	W.	6 04	B	7 27	D	13 23	14	10 02	11¾	**12**	5 36	C	7 55	D	LEO	0
240	28	Th.	6 05	B	7 25	D	13 20	14	9 41	**12½**	—	6 50	C	8 21	D	LEO	1
241	29	Fr.	6 06	B	7 24	D	13 18	14	9 20	12¾	**1¼**	8 04	D	8 45	D	VIR	2
242	30	Sa.	6 07	B	7 22	D	13 15	15	8 58	1½	**2**	9 18	D	9 09	C	VIR	3
243	31	**E**	6 08	B	7 20	D	13 12	15	8N. 37	2¼	**2¾**	10 A.M. 33	E	9 P.M. 35	B	VIR	4

AUGUST hath 31 days. 2003

His labor is a chant,
His idleness a tune;
Oh, for a bee's experience
Of clovers and of noon! –Emily Dickinson

D. M.	D. W.	Dates, Feasts, Fasts, Aspects, Tide Heights	Weather ↓
1	Fr.	**Lammas Day** • William Clark (of Lewis and Clark fame) born, 1770 •	*Delugin's*
2	Sa.	☾ on Eq. • Iraq invaded Kuwait, 1990 • First federal oleomargarine law passed in U.S., 1886 •	*of*
3	E	**8th S. af. P.** • First intercollegiate boat race, 1852 •	*grandeur!*
4	M.	♆ at ☍ • Hans Christian Andersen died, 1875 • {10.2 / 10.6	*Worthy*
5	Tu.	Sir Alec Guinness died, 2000 • *Ideas never work unless you do.* • Tides {9.8 / 10.7	*of*
6	W.	**Transfiguration** • ☾ at ☋ • ☾ at perig. •	*applause.*
7	Th.	**Name of Jesus** • *The Don Messer Show* premiered on CBC, 1959 •	*Thunder-*
8	Fr.	**St. Dominic** • Fifteen robbers stole 2.6 million pounds in Britain's "Great Train Robbery," 1963	*claps*
9	Sa.	☾ runs low • Richard M. Nixon resigned as President of the U.S., 1974 • {9.2 / 11.0	*and*
10	E	**9th S. af. P.** • Missouri became the 24th state, 1821 • {9.4 / 11.1	*willi-*
11	M.	**St. Clare** • Dog Days end. • ☌♆☾ • Tides {9.6 / 11.2	*waws!*
12	Tu.	**Full Sturgeon** ○ • ☌♅☾ • Tides {9.8 / —	*Mercy, it's*
13	W.	☌♂☾ • Walt Disney's *Bambi* premiered, 1942 • {11.1 / 9.9	*Perseids*
14	Th.	☿ Gr. Elong. (27° E.) • Oliver B. Shallenberger received patent for an electric meter, 1888 •	*time.*
15	Fr.	**Assumption** • ☾ on Eq. • Rose Marie born, 1923 • {10.5 / 9.8	*Damper*
16	Sa.	*The lives of swine are short and sorry— Pig today and pork tomorry.* • Tides {10.1 / 9.7	*for*
17	E	**10th S. af. P.** • Cat Nights begin. • Tides {9.6 / 9.6	*campers*
18	M.	♀ in sup. ☌ • Genghis Khan died, 1227 • Tides {9.1 / 9.4 •	*and*
19	Tu.	☾ at ☊ • ☾ at apo. • Strong earthquake in Turkey killed 2,520 in 1966	*cooler,*
20	W.	The Plant Quarantine Act took effect, 1912 • *Insist on yourself, never imitate.* •	*too.*
21	Th.	Arthur R. Eldred became the first Eagle Scout, the highest rank in the Boy Scouts of America, 1912	*Perfect*
22	Fr.	☌♃☉ • Schooner *America* won international yacht race, 1851 • {7.9 / 9.1 •	*for*
23	Sa.	☾ rides high • ☌♄☾ • U.S. *Lunar Orbiter 1* took photo of Earth from Moon's orbit, 1966	*a*
24	E	**11th S. af. P.** • ♅ at ☍ • {8.3 / 9.8 •	*barbecue!*
25	M.	**St. Bartholomew** • National Park Service established, 1916 • {8.7 / 10.2	*Thor*
26	Tu.	Bill 101 took effect in Quebec, 1977 • First televised major-league baseball game, 1939	*hammers*
27	W.	New ● • ☿ stat. • Tides {9.6 / 10.9	*windjammers:*
28	Th.	**St. Augustine of Hippo** • ☌☿☾ • ♂ at ☍ •	*Stay*
29	Fr.	**St. John the Baptist** • ☾ on Eq. • Tides {11.1 / 10.5 •	*in*
30	Sa.	♇ stat. • *Never offer your hen for sale on a rainy day.* • Tides {11.1 / 10.8 •	*port,*
31	E	**12th S. af. P.** • ☾ at perig. • Tides {11.0 / 11.0	*sport!*

Farmer's Calendar

■ The best monsters are not monsters at all but harmless things exaggerated. They are the common, familiar creatures of every day imagined as larger, more powerful, somehow more alive than they are in life. Their scariness comes from their familiarity as much as from their power. Grass snakes, garden toads, caterpillars, water bugs: Give them a good set of dentures and make them the size of a pickup truck, and you have your dragon, right enough.

The less malign a creature is in real life, the better a monster it can make. Even plants furnish material. One of the most famous monsters of antiquity was Hydra, a river serpent in Greek myth that had the interesting quality of instantly growing a new head when one of its many heads was cut off. A fairly exotic specimen, you say? Not at all. I've got one of them growing in front of my woodshed. It's a burdock *(Arctium)*, a husky, big-leaved, hairy weed armed with spiny burs. It comes up on the same spot summer after summer and will grow to my height if I let it. I don't let it. I chop it down. The burdock grows right back; in fact, it seems to return with added vigor after it's been destroyed. Put an animal's engine on this thing, give it speed, and there's your Hydra, right enough.

Perhaps the perennial appeal of these old monsters is that their common-life analogues make them just scary enough. The myth makers wanted their monsters scary but not too scary, so they built them out of well-known parts. After all, what's really scary is what you *don't* know.

Mars rocks. Its historic superclose approach during the last days of August ensures a dazzling all-night dominance of the heavens throughout September. On the 1st, Mars shines at an amazing magnitude of –2.9, three times brighter than Jupiter and ten times brighter than anything in the midnight sky. But don't blink: Earth speeds so quickly past Mars that the red planet dramatically loses half its light during September. Meanwhile, Jupiter emerges in the predawn east and conspicuously hovers above Mercury after the 21st; the two are strikingly joined by the Moon on the 24th. Fall begins with the autumnal equinox on the 23rd, at 6:47 A.M.

☽	First Quarter	3rd day	8th hour	34th minute
○	Full Moon	10th day	12th hour	36th minute
☾	Last Quarter	18th day	15th hour	3rd minute
●	New Moon	25th day	23rd hour	9th minute

Times are given in Eastern Daylight Time.

For an explanation of this page, see page 40; for values of Key Letters, see page 226.

Day of Year	Day of Month	Day of Week	☀ Rises h. m.	Key	☀ Sets h. m.	Key	Length of Day h. m.	Sun Fast m.	Declination of Sun ° ′	High Tide Boston Light—A.M. Bold—P.M.		☽ Rises h. m.	Key	☽ Sets h. m.	Key	☽ Place	☽ Age
244	1	M.	6 09	B	7 19	D	13 10	15	8 N. 15	3¼	3½	11ᴹ 49	E	10ᴾᴹ 05	B	LIB	5
245	2	Tu.	6 10	B	7 17	D	13 07	16	7 53	4	4½	1ᴹ 06	E	10 40	A	LIB	6
246	3	W.	6 11	B	7 15	D	13 04	16	7 31	5	5¼	2 22	E	11ᴾᴹ 23	A	LIB	7
247	4	Th.	6 12	B	7 14	D	13 02	16	7 09	6	6¼	3 33	E	—	–	OPH	8
248	5	Fr.	6 13	B	7 12	D	12 59	17	6 47	7¼	7½	4 35	E	12ᴬᴹ 15	A	SAG	9
249	6	Sa.	6 14	B	7 10	D	12 56	17	6 25	8¼	8½	5 26	E	1 17	A	SAG	10
250	7	**E**	6 15	B	7 09	D	12 54	17	6 02	9¼	9½	6 06	E	2 26	B	CAP	11
251	8	M.	6 16	B	7 07	D	12 51	18	5 40	10¼	10½	6 39	E	3 37	B	CAP	12
252	9	Tu.	6 17	B	7 05	C	12 48	18	5 17	11	11¼	7 06	D	4 48	B	AQU	13
253	10	W.	6 18	B	7 03	C	12 45	18	4 55	11¾	—	7 29	D	5 56	C	AQU	14
254	11	Th.	6 20	B	7 02	C	12 42	19	4 32	12	12½	7 50	D	7 02	D	AQU	15
255	12	Fr.	6 21	B	7 00	C	12 39	19	4 09	12¾	1¼	8 10	C	8 06	D	CET	16
256	13	Sa.	6 22	B	6 58	C	12 36	19	3 46	1½	1¾	8 31	B	9 09	E	PSC	17
257	14	**E**	6 23	B	6 56	C	12 33	20	3 23	2¼	2½	8 53	B	10 11	E	PSC	18
258	15	M.	6 24	B	6 54	C	12 30	20	3 00	2¾	3	9 17	B	11ᴬᴹ 14	E	ARI	19
259	16	Tu.	6 25	B	6 53	C	12 28	20	2 37	3½	3¾	9 46	A	12ᴾᴹ 17	E	TAU	20
260	17	W.	6 26	B	6 51	C	12 25	21	2 14	4¼	4½	10 21	A	1 19	E	TAU	21
261	18	Th.	6 27	B	6 49	C	12 22	21	1 51	5¼	5½	11 04	A	2 19	E	TAU	22
262	19	Fr.	6 28	B	6 47	C	12 19	22	1 27	6¼	6¼	11ᴾᴹ 55	A	3 15	E	GEM	23
263	20	Sa.	6 29	C	6 46	C	12 17	22	1 04	7	7¼	—	–	4 04	E	GEM	24
264	21	**E**	6 30	C	6 44	C	12 14	22	0 41	8	8¼	12ᴬᴹ 55	B	4 47	E	GEM	25
265	22	M.	6 31	C	6 42	C	12 11	23	0 N. 17	9	9	2 02	B	5 23	E	CAN	26
266	23	Tu.	6 32	C	6 40	C	12 08	23	0 s. 06	9¾	10	3 13	B	5 54	E	LEO	27
267	24	W.	6 33	C	6 39	C	12 06	23	0 29	10½	10¾	4 27	C	6 21	D	LEO	28
268	25	Th.	6 34	C	6 37	C	12 03	24	0 53	11¼	11½	5 41	D	6 46	D	LEO	0
269	26	Fr.	6 35	C	6 35	C	12 00	24	1 16	12	—	6 57	D	7 10	C	VIR	1
270	27	Sa.	6 37	C	6 33	C	11 56	24	1 39	12¼	12¾	8 14	E	7 36	B	VIR	2
271	28	**E**	6 38	C	6 32	B	11 54	25	2 03	1¼	1½	9 33	E	8 05	B	VIR	3
272	29	M.	6 39	C	6 30	B	11 51	25	2 26	2	2¼	10ᴬᴹ 52	E	8 38	B	LIB	4
273	30	Tu.	6 40	C	6 28	B	11 48	25	2 s. 49	2¾	3	12ᴾᴹ 11	E	9ᴬᴹ 19	A	SCO	5

SEPTEMBER hath 30 days. 2003

"Take the fruit I give you," says the bending tree,
"Nothing but a burden is it all to me.
Lighten ye my branches; let them toss in air!
Only leave me freedom next year's load to bear." –Lucy Larcom

D. M.	D. W.	Dates, Feasts, Fasts, Aspects, Tide Heights	*Weather* ↓
1	M.	**Labor Day** • First female telephone operator (Emma Nut), 1878 • {10.6 / 11.0	*Thunder-*
2	Tu.	☾ at ☋ • Cleveland Amory born, 1917 • Tides {10.1 / 10.9 •	*storms*
3	W.	**St. Gregory the Great** • First professional football game played, 1895 •	*and*
4	Th.	*As long as the Sun shines, one does not ask for the Moon.* • {9.2 / 10.6	*schoolkids*
5	Fr.	☾ runs low • First standardized naval uniforms adopted for U.S., 1776 •	*mutter.*
6	Sa.	Most Canadian highway signs converted to metric, 1977 • Tides {9.0 / 10.4 •	*Sweet*
7	**E.**	**13th S. af. P.** • ☌ ♆ ☾ • Maurice Duplessis died, 1959 •	*as*
8	M.	*Star Trek* series premiered, 1966 • *Still waters run deep.* • Tides {9.4 / 10.6	*butter.*
9	Tu.	**St. Omer** • ☌ ♂ ☾ • ☌ ♅ ☾ • Tides {9.7 / 10.7 •	*A*
10	W.	**Full Harvest** ○ • ☿ in inf. ☌ • Charles Kuralt born, 1934	*soaking,*
11	Th.	**Sts. Protus & Hyacinth** • Terrorist attacks on America, 2001 •	*and*
12	Fr.	☾ on Eq. • John F. Kennedy married Jacqueline Bouvier, 1953 • Tides {10.4 / 10.0	*we're*
13	Sa.	Hurricane San Felipe (the second) hit Puerto Rico, 1928 • Tides {10.1 / 10.0 •	*not*
14	**E**	**14th S. af. P.** • **Holy Cross** • Tides {9.8 / 9.9	*joking!*
15	M.	☾ at ☊ • Bomb killed four girls in a Birmingham, Ala., church used for civil rights meetings, 1963	*Be*
16	Tu.	☾ at apo. • William Durant incorporates General Motors, 1908 •	*prepared*
17	W.	Ember Day • Vanessa Williams became the first African American "Miss America," 1983 •	*to*
18	Th.	*September dries up ditches or breaks down bridges.* • Tides {8.2 / 9.0 •	*swelter,*
19	Fr.	Ember Day • ☌ ♄ ☾ • ☿ stat. • Tides {8.0 / 8.9 •	*then*
20	Sa.	**St. Eustace** • Ember Day • ☾ rides high • Dr. Joyce Brothers born, 1928	*run*
21	**E**	**15th S. af. P.** • Frank Church replied, "Yes, Virginia, there *is* a Santa Claus," 1897	
22	M.	Turner Broadcasting System announced plans to merge with Time Warner, 1995 •	*for shelter!*
23	Tu.	Harvest Home • **Autumnal Equinox** • Tides {9.1 / 10.3 •	*Summer*
24	W.	☌ ♃ ☾ • ☌ ☿ ☾ • Muppet-creator Jim Henson born, 1936 •	*lingers,*
25	Th.	New ● • First transatlantic telephone cable began operation, 1956 • {10.3 / 11.1 •	*but*
26	Fr.	☾ on Eq. • ☿ Gr. Elong. (18° W.) • Olivia Newton-John born, 1948 • {10.9 / —	*we*
27	Sa.	**St. Vincent de Paul** • **Rosh Hashanah** • Tides {11.3 / 11.4 •	*feel*
28	**E**	**16th S. af. P.** • ☾ at perig. • Tides {11.2 / 11.6	*fall's*
29	M.	**St. Michael** • ☾ at ☋ • ♂ stat. • Tides {11.0 / 11.7	*frosty*
30	Tu.	**St. Sophia** • Woodchucks hibernate now. • Tides {10.6 / 11.5 •	*fingers.*

Wonders will never cease. –Sir Henry Bate Dudley, English clergyman and writer

Farmer's Calendar

■ Machines have all the fun, don't they? So many of the tasks that people have been relieved of by technology afforded, in spite of their tedium and difficulty, a kind of tactile, sensory pleasure. Think of the kitchen. Mixing, beating, kneading, grinding, cutting, chopping, grating, and a dozen other little jobs that could be enjoyable, at least sometimes and in small doses, have been taken over by hardware. With computers, machinery even begins to appropriate the fun of discovery, inference, association. Soon there won't be much left for humans to do but pay the electric bill.

Outdoors, gas-engine hydraulic wedges now split a lot more firewood than axe-swinging householders. The splitters do a better job, too. They split tough wood easily that you scarcely can, and they do it quickly. It almost doesn't make sense *not* to use one. But if you do, you miss out on another small, purely physical pleasure. Splitting firewood with an axe has its fun side. Of course, to enjoy it, you have to take your time, you have to get a kind of rhythm or tempo going between the wood, the axe, and you. If you're going to enjoy the work, you have to lose yourself in the heft, the movements, the back-and-forth of it. In short: You have to become a machine yourself, at least for a time.

Here, then, is the joke: The fun you relinquish to the machine in giving it your work to do is, in its essence, mechanical fun. It looks like, one way or another, a machine is going to do this job. The machine can be a machine. Or the machine can be you.

Though still the sky's brightest "star," Mars's brilliance is again cut in half between the 1st and the 31st as it floats among the pathetically dim stars of Aquarius, visible from dusk until 2:30 A.M. The Moon keeps Mars company on the 5th and 6th, and the red planet dangles below green Uranus most closely from the 10th to the 20th, with the intriguingly green seventh planet easily viewable through binoculars. Meanwhile, Venus grudgingly starts to appear extremely low above the southwestern horizon at dusk and presents a close, prominent skyline conjunction with the slender crescent Moon on the 26th.

☽	First Quarter	2nd day	15th hour	9th minute
○	Full Moon	10th day	3rd hour	27th minute
☾	Last Quarter	18th day	8th hour	31st minute
●	New Moon	25th day	8th hour	50th minute
☽	First Quarter	31st day	23rd hour	25th minute

After 2:00 P.M. on October 26, Eastern Standard Time (EST) is given.

For an explanation of this page, see page 40; for values of Key Letters, see page 226.

Day of Year	Day of Month	Day of Week	☀ Rises h. m.	Key	☀ Sets h. m.	Key	Length of Day h. m.	Sun Fast m.	Declination of Sun °	High Tide Boston Light—A.M. Bold—P.M.		☽ Rises h. m.	Key	☽ Sets h. m.	Key	☽ Place	☽ Age
274	1	W.	6 41	C	6 26	B	11 45	26	3 s.13	3¾	4	1 ᴹ 25	E	10 ᴾ 10	A	OPH	6
275	2	Th.	6 42	C	6 25	B	11 43	26	3 36	4¾	5	2 31	E	11 ᴾ 10	A	SAG	7
276	3	Fr.	6 43	C	6 23	B	11 40	26	3 59	5¾	6	3 25	E	—	—	SAG	8
277	4	Sa.	6 44	C	6 21	B	11 37	27	4 22	7	7¼	4 08	E	12 ᴬ 17	B	CAP	9
278	5	**E**	6 45	C	6 19	B	11 34	27	4 45	8	8¼	4 43	E	1 27	B	CAP	10
279	6	M.	6 46	C	6 18	B	11 32	27	5 08	9	9½	5 10	E	2 37	B	AQU	11
280	7	Tu.	6 48	C	6 16	B	11 28	28	5 31	10	10¼	5 34	D	3 45	C	AQU	12
281	8	W.	6 49	C	6 14	B	11 25	28	5 54	10¾	11	5 55	D	4 51	D	AQU	13
282	9	Th.	6 50	C	6 13	B	11 23	28	6 17	11½	11¾	6 15	C	5 55	D	PSC	14
283	10	Fr.	6 51	C	6 11	B	11 20	28	6 40	12	—	6 35	B	6 58	D	PSC	15
284	11	Sa.	6 52	C	6 09	B	11 17	29	7 03	12½	12¾	6 56	B	8 00	E	PSC	16
285	12	**E**	6 53	C	6 08	B	11 15	29	7 25	1	1¼	7 19	B	9 03	E	ARI	17
286	13	M.	6 54	C	6 06	B	11 12	29	7 48	1¾	1¾	7 46	B	10 06	E	ARI	18
287	14	Tu.	6 55	D	6 04	B	11 09	29	8 10	2¼	2½	8 19	A	11 ᴹ 09	E	TAU	19
288	15	W.	6 57	D	6 03	B	11 06	30	8 33	3	3¼	8 58	A	12 ᴾ 10	E	TAU	20
289	16	Th.	6 58	D	6 01	B	11 03	30	8 55	3¾	4	9 45	A	1 07	E	TAU	21
290	17	Fr.	6 59	D	6 00	B	11 01	30	9 17	4¾	4¾	10 40	A	1 58	E	GEM	22
291	18	Sa.	7 00	D	5 58	B	10 58	30	9 39	5½	5¾	11 ᴹ 43	A	2 43	E	GEM	23
292	19	**E**	7 01	D	5 56	B	10 55	30	10 00	6½	6¾	—	—	3 20	E	CAN	24
293	20	M.	7 03	D	5 55	B	10 52	31	10 22	7½	7½	12 ᴹ 51	B	3 52	E	LEO	25
294	21	Tu.	7 04	D	5 53	B	10 49	31	10 43	8¼	8½	2 02	B	4 20	D	LEO	26
295	22	W.	7 05	D	5 52	B	10 47	31	11 05	9	9½	3 15	C	4 45	D	LEO	27
296	23	Th.	7 06	D	5 50	B	10 44	31	11 26	10	10¼	4 30	D	5 10	C	VIR	28
297	24	Fr.	7 07	D	5 49	B	10 42	31	11 47	10¾	11	5 46	D	5 34	C	VIR	29
298	25	Sa.	7 09	D	5 48	B	10 39	31	12 07	11½	12	7 05	E	6 02	B	VIR	0
299	26	**E**	6 10	D	4 46	D	10 36	32	12 28	11¼	11¾	7 26	E	5 33	B	LIB	1
300	27	M.	6 11	D	4 45	D	10 34	32	12 48	12	—	8 49	E	6 12	A	LIB	2
301	28	Tu.	6 12	D	4 43	D	10 31	32	13 08	12¾	12¾	10 09	E	7 00	A	LIB	3
302	29	W.	6 13	D	4 42	B	10 29	32	13 28	1½	1¾	11 ᴹ 21	E	7 59	A	SAG	4
303	30	Th.	6 15	D	4 41	B	10 26	32	13 48	2½	2¾	12 ᴹ 21	E	9 06	A	SAG	5
304	31	Fr.	6 16	D	4 39	B	10 23	32	14 s.07	3½	3¾	1 ᴹ 09	E	10 ᴾ 17	B	SAG	6

OCTOBER hath 31 days. 2003

Listen! the wind is rising,
and the air is wild with leaves,
We have had our summer evenings,
now for October eves! –Humbert Wolfe

D. M.	D. W.	Dates, Feasts, Fasts, Aspects, Tide Heights	Weather ↓
1	W.	St. Gregory • Maria Mitchell discovered comet Mitchell 1847VI, 1847 • { 10.0 / 11.1	*Red*
2	Th.	Gene Autry died, 1998 • "Peanuts" cartoon debuted, 1950 • Tides { 9.5 / 10.7	*are*
3	Fr.	☾ runs low • First Canadian troops left for Britain to fight in World War I, 1914 • { 9.1 / 10.3	*the*
4	Sa.	St. Francis of Assisi • ☌ ♆ ☾ • Anne Rice born, 1941 •	*apples*
5	E	17th S. af. P. • World Series first broadcast on radio, 1921 •	*we're*
6	M.	Yom Kippur • ☌ ♂ ☾ • ☌ ♅ ☾ • { 9.3 / 10.1	*picking*
7	Tu.	*Pride in prosperity turns to misery in adversity.* • James Whitcomb Riley born, 1849	*for*
8	W.	Faith Ringgold born, 1930 • *The Adventures of Ozzie and Harriet* debuted, 1944 •	*pies,*
9	Th.	☾ on Eq. • The Washington Monument opened to the public, 1888 • { 10.0 / 10.1	*yellow*
10	Fr.	Full Hunter's ○ • The Red Baron first appeared in "Peanuts" comic strip, 1965 •	*the*
11	Sa.	Succoth • *Saturday Night Live* premiered, 1975 • Tides { 9.9 / 10.2 •	*light*
12	E	18th S. af. P. • ☾ at ☊ • Tides { 9.7 / 10.1	*slanting*
13	M.	Columbus Day • Thanksgiving Day (Canada) • ☾ at apo. • { 9.4 / 10.0	*down*
14	Tu.	*Winnie-the-Pooh* published, 1926 • First televised wedding, 1928 • Tides { 9.1 / 9.8	*from*
15	W.	Hurricane Hazel, Category 4, hit the Carolinas, 1954 • P. G. Wodehouse born, 1881 •	*the*
16	Th.	Angela Lansbury born, 1925 • Cape Breton Island was re-annexed to Nova Scotia, 1820	*skies;*
17	Fr.	St. Ignatius of Antioch • ☾ rides high • ☌ ♄ ☾ •	*rain*
18	Sa.	St. Luke • Mason-Dixon Line, border of Md. and Pa., settled, 1767 • { 8.0 / 9.0	*brings*
19	E	19th S. af. P. • Queen Elizabeth II went to U.S. football game, 1957 •	*a*
20	M.	*When spiders' webs in air do fly, The spell will soon be very dry.* • Tides { 8.4 / 9.4	*shower*
21	Tu.	☌ ♃ ☾ • U.S.S. *Constitution* launched in Boston, Mass., 1797 • { 8.9 / 9.8 •	*of*
22	W.	♆ stat. • André-Jacques Garnerin performed the first parachute jump, 1797	*auburns*
23	Th.	☾ on Eq. • Charles Chaplin married Mildred Harris, 1918 • Tides { 10.3 / 10.7	*and*
24	Fr.	Nylons went on sale for first time, 1939 • Gene Roddenberry died, 1991 •	*maizes—*
25	Sa.	New ● • ☿ in sup. ☌ • ♄ stat. • { 11.6 / 11.1	*orange*
26	E	☾ at perig. • **Daylight Saving Time ends, 2:00 A.M.** • Tides { 12.0 / 11.1	*are*
27	M.	First day of Ramadan • Jascha Heifetz's American debut, 1917 •	*pumpkins*
28	Tu.	Sts. Simon & Jude • Bill Gates born, 1955 • Tides { 10.8 / 12.1 •	*and*
29	W.	*Men and pyramids are not made to stand on their heads.* • Tides { 10.4 / 11.7 •	*Home-*
30	Th.	☾ runs low • Elton John appeared in a performance for the Queen of England, 1972	*coming*
31	Fr.	All Hallows Eve • St. Wolfgang • Tides { 9.5 / 10.6 •	*blazes.*

Farmer's Calendar

■ Lying on the brick hearth, a leaf the color of a lemon. It's a thing out of its place, a bit of outdoor nature strayed where it doesn't belong. Probably it came down the chimney. In October, the leaves turn, then they fall. For a week, they fill the day, dropping through the light-filled air on every side, like a million weary butterflies. They blanket the lawn, they cover the road, they drift and bank up against the house like snow. Inevitably, a couple of leaves in their descent hit the chimney, slip down the flue into the fireplace, and come out into the room.

This one came off a beech tree. See it as a tiny part of the autumn scramble for shelter. As the nights get longer and the frosts deeper, everything that can moves into the house: not only its owners but also mice, squirrels, insects, cats, dogs—even the trees send their emissaries. They come into the house as the animals in Genesis went on board the ark. They seek preservation. And they find it. With damp and frost, the other leaves that lie so deep over the outdoors quickly fade and disappear. Not this one. Its yellow will lose a shade or two of its brightness, but its color will last.

There ought to be a quaint rural custom of preserving autumn leaves that have found their way indoors by circuitous paths. Treat them as a saving remnant of the vegetable year. Keep them through the winter, and then, in April or May, when their next generation is beginning to green on the boughs, open a window and pitch them out. Let them go. Give them back.

Mars keeps leaking brilliance but remains the brightest "star" during the night's first half, after slowly improving Venus sets in evening twilight. Jupiter, coming up two hours earlier each month, now rules as the "brilliance champion" after it rises at 1:00 A.M. Saturn, very bright in Gemini and a better telescopic target than Mars, is conveniently up by 9:00 P.M. The erratic midmonth Leonid meteors are greatly diminished by bright moonlight. The rare spectacle of two North American lunar eclipses in the same year culminates on the 8th. The beginning of penumbra will be visible in eastern North America; the end will be visible throughout North America. Look for a short Moon-reddening totality after sunset.

○ Full Moon	8th day	20th hour	13th minute
☾ Last Quarter	16th day	23rd hour	15th minute
● New Moon	23rd day	17th hour	59th minute
☽ First Quarter	30th day	12th hour	16th minute

Times are given in Eastern Standard Time.

For an explanation of this page, see page 40; for values of Key Letters, see page 226.

Day of Year	Day of Month	Day of Week	☀ Rises h. m.	Key	☀ Sets h. m.	Key	Length of Day h. m.	Sun Fast m.	Declination of Sun ° '	High Tide Boston Light—A.M. Bold—P.M.	☽ Rises h. m.	Key	☽ Sets h. m.	Key	☽ Place	☽ Age
305	1	Sa.	6 17	D	4 38	B	10 21	32	14 s. 27	4½ 4¾	1 ᴘ 46 M	E	11 ᴘ 28	B	CAP	7
306	2	**E**	6 18	D	4 37	B	10 19	32	14 46	5¾ 6	2 16	E	—	—	CAP	8
307	3	M.	6 20	D	4 35	B	10 15	32	15 05	6¾ 7	2 40	D	12 ᴀ 37 M	C	AQU	9
308	4	Tu.	6 21	D	4 34	B	10 13	32	15 23	7¾ 8	3 01	D	1 43	C	AQU	10
309	5	W.	6 22	D	4 33	B	10 11	32	15 42	8½ 9	3 21	C	2 47	D	PSC	11
310	6	Th.	6 23	D	4 32	B	10 09	32	16 00	9¼ 9¾	3 41	C	3 50	D	PSC	12
311	7	Fr.	6 25	D	4 31	B	10 06	32	16 18	10 10½	4 01	B	4 52	E	PSC	13
312	8	Sa.	6 26	D	4 30	A	10 04	32	16 35	10½ 11	4 23	B	5 54	E	ARI	14
313	9	**E**	6 27	D	4 28	A	10 01	32	16 53	11¼ 11¾	4 49	A	6 57	E	ARI	15
314	10	M.	6 28	D	4 27	A	9 59	32	17 10	11¾ —	5 19	A	8 00	E	TAU	16
315	11	Tu.	6 30	D	4 26	A	9 56	32	17 26	12¼ 12¼	5 56	A	9 02	E	TAU	17
316	12	W.	6 31	D	4 25	A	9 54	32	17 42	1 1	6 40	A	10 00	E	TAU	18
317	13	Th.	6 32	D	4 24	A	9 52	31	17 58	1¾ 1¾	7 32	A	10 54	E	GEM	19
318	14	Fr.	6 33	D	4 23	A	9 50	31	18 14	2¼ 2½	8 31	B	11 ᴀ 40 M	E	GEM	20
319	15	Sa.	6 35	D	4 23	A	9 48	31	18 30	3¼ 3¼	9 36	B	12 ᴘ 19 M	E	CAN	21
320	16	**E**	6 36	D	4 22	A	9 46	31	18 45	4 4	10 44	B	12 52	E	CAN	22
321	17	M.	6 37	D	4 21	A	9 44	31	19 00	4¾ 5	11 ᴘ 54 M	C	1 21	D	LEO	23
322	18	Tu.	6 38	D	4 20	A	9 42	31	19 15	5¾ 6	—	—	1 46	D	LEO	24
323	19	W.	6 40	D	4 19	A	9 39	30	19 29	6¾ 7	1 ᴀ 05 M	C	2 09	D	VIR	25
324	20	Th.	6 41	D	4 18	A	9 37	30	19 42	7½ 8	2 18	D	2 33	C	VIR	26
325	21	Fr.	6 42	D	4 18	A	9 36	30	19 55	8¼ 8¾	3 34	D	2 58	C	VIR	27
326	22	Sa.	6 43	D	4 17	A	9 34	30	20 08	9¼ 9¾	4 53	E	3 27	B	VIR	28
327	23	**E**	6 44	D	4 16	A	9 32	29	20 21	10 10½	6 16	E	4 02	B	LIB	0
328	24	M.	6 45	D	4 16	A	9 31	29	20 33	10¾ 11½	7 39	E	4 46	A	LIB	1
329	25	Tu.	6 47	D	4 15	A	9 28	29	20 45	11¾ —	8 59	E	5 41	A	OPH	2
330	26	W.	6 48	D	4 15	A	9 27	29	20 57	12½ 12½	10 07	E	6 47	A	SAG	3
331	27	Th.	6 49	E	4 14	A	9 25	28	21 08	1¼ 1½	11 03	E	8 00	B	SAG	4
332	28	Fr.	6 50	E	4 14	A	9 24	28	21 19	2¼ 2½	11 ᴀ 45 M	E	9 14	B	CAP	5
333	29	Sa.	6 51	E	4 13	A	9 22	28	21 29	3¼ 3½	12 ᴘ 18 M	E	10 26	C	CAP	6
334	30	**E**	6 52	E	4 13	A	9 21	27	21 s. 39	4¼ 4½	12 ᴘ 45 M	D	11 ᴘ 34 M	C	AQU	7

NOVEMBER hath 30 days. 2003

What moistens the lip
and what brightens the eye?
What calls back the past,
like the rich pumpkin pie? –J. G. Whittier

D. M.	D. W.	Dates, Feasts, Fasts, Aspects, Tide Heights	*Weather* ↓
1	Sa.	All Saints' • Sadie Hawkins Day • ☌ ♆ ☾ • Tides { 9.2 10.1	*A*
2	E	21st S. af. P. • ☌ ♅ ☾ • Tides { 9.1 9.8 •	*scoop*
3	M.	All Souls' • ☌ ♂ ☾ • First national auto show, held in New York City, 1900 •	*of*
4	Tu.	Election Day • James Ritty received a patent for a cash register, 1879 •	*vanilla*
5	W.	☾ on Eq. • Bryan Adams born, 1959 • Tides { 9.6 9.6 •	*on*
6	Th.	*The barber shows you the mirror, but it's too late to raise a squawk.* • { 9.9 9.6	*northern*
7	Fr.	Last spike of the transcontinental Canadian Pacific Railway driven at Craigellachie, B.C., 1885	*hills*
8	Sa.	Full Beaver ○ • Eclipse ☾ • ♅ stat. • Tides { 10.1 9.4	*gives*
9	E	22nd S. af. P. • ☾ at ☊ • Sally Tompkins born, 1833	*the*
10	M.	☾ at apo. • S.S. *Edmund Fitzgerald* sank in storm, entire crew of 29 lost, 1975 •	*snow-*
11	Tu.	St. Martin • Veterans Day • Indian Summer • Tides { 9.1 10.0	*blower*
12	W.	Largest iceberg on record (208x60 miles) discovered by U.S.S. *Glacier*, 1956 •	*salesman*
13	Th.	☾ rides high • ☌ ♄ ☾ • Tides { 8.6 9.6 •	*thrills.*
14	Fr.	First performance of a Western theatrical production in North America, 1606 • { 8.4 9.4 •	*The*
15	Sa.	Explorer Zebulon Pike spotted a mountain he called Grand Peak, later renamed Pikes Peak, 1806	*sight*
16	E	23rd S. af. P. • Skunks hibernate now. • Tides { 8.3 9.2 •	*of*
17	M.	St. Hugh of Lincoln • Computer mouse patented, 1970 • { 8.4 9.2	*white,*
18	Tu.	☌ ♃ ☾ • Captain Nathaniel B. Palmer discovered Antarctica, 1820 •	*however*
19	W.	*If there be ice in November that will bear a duck, There will be nothing thereafter but sleet and muck.*	*meager,*
20	Th.	☾ on Eq. • First nighttime photograph taken from airplane, 1925 { 10.0 10.0	*makes*
21	Fr.	North Carolina became the 12th state, 1789 • Tides { 10.8 10.3 •	*the*
22	Sa.	Statue of Liberty began role as first U.S. lighthouse to use electricity, 1886 • { 11.5 10.6	*skiers*
23	E	24th S. af. P. • New ● • Eclipse ⊙ •	*eager*
24	M.	St. Clement • ☌ ☿ ☾ • Tides { 12.3 10.7 •	*beavers.*
25	Tu.	☌ ♀ ☾ • Ireland voted to legalize divorce, 1995 •	*Snowmobilers*
26	W.	☾ runs low • Archaeologist Howard Carter opened second doorway to tomb of Tutankhamen, 1922	*sing*
27	Th.	Thanksgiving • CARE organization founded, 1945 • { 10.2 11.7	*Hosanna*
28	Fr.	☌ ♆ ☾ • Ferdinand Magellan reached Pacific through newly discovered strait, 1520 •	*for*
29	Sa.	☌ ♅ ☾ • Former Beatle George Harrison died, 2001 • Tides { 9.5 10.5	*frozen*
30	E	1st S. in Advent • Lucy Maud Montgomery born in P.E.I., 1874	*manna.*

Happy is said to be the family which can eat onions together. –Charles Dudley Warner, American author

Farmer's Calendar

■ The news has no mercy. The more of it there is, the worse it gets. The morning paper, the local six-o'clock broadcast, which only a few years ago you could safely sleep through, now scare you out of your wits. What does the news tell you? It tells you that you're never out of danger. The world in all its aspects is either actively malign or lethally indifferent; either way, its course with you will be measured in degrees of calamity. Not only in its content does the news appall. Even more alarming is its method: a kind of cinema gone mad, a St. Vitus's Dance of obsessive, repetitive images and words, all run at top speed, that would be terrifying if they were used to document the manufacture of oatmeal.

It wasn't always so. I have before me *The Vermont Phoenix* for Thursday, November 18, 1911. Published in Brattleboro, Vermont, the *Phoenix* took seriously its mission to give readers news of local importance. "Mr. and Mrs. A. F. Cheney have returned from their visit in Springfield, Mass.," I read. "J. A. Veinot is building a henhouse for F. W. Smith." "Charles Alexander has returned from his vacation." So it goes, for 17 column inches.

Certainly it's restful. Certainly the contrast it offers with the murder, mayhem, and misfortune of journalism today is striking. Do you like it? Don't be too sure. Perhaps we get what we want. The placid annals of our grandparents' time may be for us like so much of the real life of another age: great stuff if you can stay awake.

2003 DECEMBER, The Twelfth Month

Mercury is readily seen below Venus during the first half of the month, and Venus finally gets conspicuously high at dusk beginning midmonth. The Geminid meteors on the 13th, like all other major showers this year, are washed out by a bright Moon. Mars enters Pisces and dims to below zero magnitude. Starring roles now go to brilliant Jupiter, which rises by midnight, and especially to Saturn, which rises soon after nightfall and reaches opposition on the final night of the year. Sitting atop the zodiac with rings wide open, Saturn won't offer such optimal viewing conditions for another 28 years. Winter begins with the solstice on the 22nd at 2:04 A.M.

○	Full Moon	8th day	15th hour	37th minute
☾	Last Quarter	16th day	12th hour	42nd minute
●	New Moon	23rd day	4th hour	43rd minute
☽	First Quarter	30th day	5th hour	3rd minute

Times are given in Eastern Standard Time.

For an explanation of this page, see page 40; for values of Key Letters, see page 226.

Day of Year	Day of Month	Day of Week	☼ Rises h. m.	Key	☼ Sets h. m.	Key	Length of Day h. m.	Sun Fast m.	Declination of Sun ° '	High Tide Boston Light—A.M.	Bold—P.M.	☽ Rises h. m.	Key	☽ Sets h. m.	Key	☽ Place	☽ Age
335	1	M.	6 53	E	4 13	A	9 20	27	21s.48	5¼	**5½**	1 P.M. 07	D	—	–	AQU	8
336	2	Tu.	6 54	E	4 12	A	9 18	27	21 57	6¼	**6½**	1 28	C	12 A.M. 40	C	PSC	9
337	3	W.	6 55	E	4 12	A	9 17	26	22 06	7¼	**7½**	1 47	C	1 43	D	CET	10
338	4	Th.	6 56	E	4 12	A	9 16	26	22 15	8	**8½**	2 07	B	2 44	E	PSC	11
339	5	Fr.	6 57	E	4 12	A	9 15	25	22 23	8¾	**9¼**	2 28	B	3 46	E	ARI	12
340	6	Sa.	6 58	E	4 12	A	9 14	25	22 30	9½	**10**	2 52	B	4 48	E	ARI	13
341	7	**E**	6 59	E	4 12	A	9 13	25	22 37	10	**10¾**	3 21	A	5 51	E	TAU	14
342	8	M.	7 00	E	4 11	A	9 11	24	22 43	10¾	**11¼**	3 55	A	6 54	E	TAU	15
343	9	Tu.	7 01	E	4 11	A	9 10	24	22 49	11¼	**12**	4 37	A	7 54	E	TAU	16
344	10	W.	7 02	E	4 12	A	9 10	23	22 55	**12**	—	5 27	A	8 50	E	GEM	17
345	11	Th.	7 03	E	4 12	A	9 09	23	23 01	12½	**12½**	6 24	A	9 38	E	GEM	18
346	12	Fr.	7 04	E	4 12	A	9 08	22	23 05	1¼	**1¼**	7 28	A	10 20	E	CAN	19
347	13	Sa.	7 05	E	4 12	A	9 07	22	23 09	2	**2**	8 34	B	10 54	E	CAN	20
348	14	**E**	7 05	E	4 12	A	9 07	21	23 13	2¾	**2¾**	9 42	B	11 24	E	LEO	21
349	15	M.	7 06	E	4 12	A	9 06	21	23 16	3½	**3½**	10 P.M. 50	C	11 A.M. 49	D	LEO	22
350	16	Tu.	7 07	E	4 13	A	9 06	20	23 19	4¼	**4½**	—	–	12 P.M. 12	D	LEO	23
351	17	W.	7 08	E	4 13	A	9 05	20	23 21	5¼	**5½**	12 A.M. 00	D	12 34	D	VIR	24
352	18	Th.	7 08	E	4 13	A	9 05	19	23 23	6	**6½**	1 11	D	12 58	C	VIR	25
353	19	Fr.	7 09	E	4 14	A	9 05	19	23 25	7	**7½**	2 26	E	1 23	B	VIR	26
354	20	Sa.	7 09	E	4 14	A	9 05	18	23 26	7¾	**8½**	3 44	E	1 54	B	LIB	27
355	21	**E**	7 10	E	4 14	A	9 04	18	23 26	8¾	**9½**	5 06	E	2 32	A	OPH	28
356	22	M.	7 10	E	4 15	A	9 05	17	23 26	9¾	**10¼**	6 27	E	3 21	A	OPH	29
357	23	Tu.	7 11	E	4 16	A	9 05	17	23 26	10½	**11¼**	7 43	E	4 22	A	SAG	0
358	24	W.	7 11	E	4 16	A	9 05	16	23 25	11½	—	8 47	E	5 34	A	SAG	1
359	25	Th.	7 12	E	4 17	A	9 05	16	23 24	12¼	**12¼**	9 37	E	6 50	B	CAP	2
360	26	Fr.	7 12	E	4 17	A	9 05	15	23 22	1	**1¼**	10 15	E	8 06	B	CAP	3
361	27	Sa.	7 12	E	4 18	A	9 06	15	23 20	2	**2**	10 45	E	9 19	C	AQU	4
362	28	**E**	7 13	E	4 19	A	9 06	14	23 17	2¾	**3**	11 10	D	10 27	D	AQU	5
363	29	M.	7 13	E	4 19	A	9 06	14	23 13	3¾	**4**	11 32	C	11 P.M. 32	D	AQU	6
364	30	Tu.	7 13	E	4 20	A	9 07	13	23 10	4½	**5**	11 A.M. 52	C	—	–	CET	7
365	31	W.	7 13	E	4 21	A	9 08	13	23s.05	5½	**6**	12 P.M. 12	C	12 A.M. 35	D	PSC	8

Granny's come to our house,
And ho! my lawzy-daisy!
All the childern round the place
Is ist a-runnin' crazy! –James Whitcomb Riley

D. M.	D. W.	Dates, Feasts, Fasts, Aspects, Tide Heights	Weather ↓
1	M.	☌ ♂ ☾ • The Christmas Club savings account began, 1909 • {9.2 / 9.4	*There's*
2	Tu.	St. Viviana • ☾ on Eq. • First controlled, self-sustained nuclear chain reaction, 1946 •	*a*
3	W.	Oberlin Collegiate Institute became first coeducational college in U.S., 1833 • {9.3 / 9.0	*run on*
4	Th.	Cardinal de Richelieu died, 1642 • Marcel Marceau appeared on television, 1955	*winter*
5	Fr.	Phi Beta Kappa founded at the College of William and Mary, 1776 •	*underwear.*
6	Sa.	St. Nicholas • ☾ at ☊ • Agnes Moorehead born, 1906 • {9.8 / 8.9	*We*
7	E	**2nd S. in Advent** • ☾ at apo. • Tides {10.0 / 8.9	*need*
8	M.	St. Ambrose • Full Cold ○ • *A full Moon eats clouds.* • {10.0 / 8.8	*some*
9	Tu.	☿ Gr. Elong. (21° E.) • Christmas seals sold for first time, 1907 • {10.1 / 8.8 •	*like*
10	W.	St. Eulalia • ☾ rides high • ☌ ♄ ☾ • {10.0 / —	*reindeer*
11	Th.	Joe DiMaggio announced his retirement from baseball, 1951 • Tides {8.7 / 10.0 •	*on*
12	Fr.	☌ ♇ ☉ • Father Edward Flanagan founded a home for boys in Omaha, Nebr., 1917 •	*the*
13	Sa.	St. Lucy • Anthony B. Heinsbergen born, 1894 •	*tundra wear!*
14	E	**3rd S. in Advent** • Halcyon Days • Tides {8.6 / 9.6 •	*A*
15	M.	☌ ♃ ☾ • *Superman* movie premiered, 1978 • Tides {8.7 / 9.5 •	*teaser,*
16	Tu.	Beware the Pogonip. • *The wise man sits on the hole in his carpet.* • Tides {8.9 / 9.4	*then*
17	W.	Ember Day • ☾ on Eq. • ☿ stat. • Termination of Project Blue Book, 1969	*back*
18	Th.	Ty Cobb born, 1886 • John William Draper took first photo of the Moon, 1839 • Tides {9.8 / 9.4	*in*
19	Fr.	The National Hockey League played its first games, 1917 • Ember Day • Tides {10.4 / 9.6	*the*
20	Sa.	Ember Day • First day of Chanukah • ☾ at ☋ •	*freezer.*
21	E	**4th S. in Advent** • Tides {11.5 / 10.0 •	*Bearable*
22	M.	Winter Solstice • ☾ at perig. • *An early winter, a surly winter.* • {11.9 / 10.2	*for*
23	Tu.	New ● • "Account of a Visit from St. Nicholas" published, 1823 •	*caroling.*
24	W.	☾ runs low • First great fire of San Francisco, 1849 • Tides {12.1 / —	*Flurries,*
25	Th.	**Christmas Day** • ☌ ♆ ☾ • ☌ ♀ ☾ •	*floods,*
26	Fr.	Boxing Day (Canada) • First day of Kwanzaa • ☿ in inf. ☌ • {10.1 / 11.5	*and*
27	Sa.	St. John • ☌ ♅ ☾ • Radio City Music Hall opened in New York City, 1932	*muddy*
28	E	**1st S. af. Ch.** • Woodrow Wilson born, 1856 •	*floors—*
29	M.	Holy Innocents • *He only truly lives who lives in peace.* • {9.4 / 9.6	*hurry up,*
30	Tu.	☾ on Eq. • ☌ ♂ ☾ • ☌ ♀ ♆ • {9.2 / 9.1 •	*2004!*
31	W.	St. Sylvester • ♄ at ☍ • Ottawa selected by Queen Victoria as capital of Province of Canada, 1857	

Farmer's Calendar

■ *December 2.* A gray, still day at winter's doorstep. Took the dogs to the little wooded pond at the top of the hill. Nobody around. We followed the dirt road that runs alongside the water to its end—about a half-mile. Both dogs do the whole trip with their noses intently in the dirt. They quarter avidly back and forth across the road. It's not recreation for them but serious business. It's what they do.

Recent temperatures in the 20s have begun to freeze the pond over. A windowpane of ice now seems to go clear across. You couldn't walk on it, but it will support a small stone. I pick one up and shy it sidearm out over the pond as though I were aiming to make it skip on the water. The stone lands and slides freely over the ice toward the middle of the pond. As it slides, it makes—or the ice beneath it makes—a peculiar quavering, whistling sound, resonant and surprisingly loud, almost like the noise of an enormous musical saw.

What makes that noise? I imagine it's from waves induced in the thin ice by the stone's passing across it, the sound amplified by the little air space between the ice and the water below, or by the water itself. The new-frozen pond becomes a sound chamber, a giant cello. It's an effect that is evident only briefly. Another few cold days and the ice will get thicker. The pond will fall silent. I try another stone. *Whoo-oo-oo-uh,* goes the pond. The dogs hear it. They look up, but it doesn't hold their interest. They're impatient. They feel it's time to get moving.

Holidays and Observances, 2003

A selected list of commemorative days, with federal holidays denoted by *.

Jan. 1	New Year's Day*
Jan. 17	Benjamin Franklin's Birthday
Jan. 20	Martin Luther King Jr.'s Birthday (observed)*
Feb. 2	Groundhog Day; Guadalupe-Hidalgo Treaty Day (N.Mex.)
Feb. 12	Abraham Lincoln's Birthday
Feb. 14	St. Valentine's Day
Feb. 15	Susan B. Anthony's Birthday (Fla., Wis.)
Feb. 17	George Washington's Birthday (observed)*
Mar. 2	Texas Independence Day
Mar. 4	Town Meeting Day (Vt.); Mardi Gras (Baldwin & Mobile Counties, Ala.; La.)
Mar. 15	Andrew Jackson Day (Tenn.)
Mar. 17	St. Patrick's Day; Evacuation Day (Suffolk Co., Mass.)
Mar. 31	Seward's Day (Alaska)
Apr. 2	Pascua Florida Day
Apr. 13	Thomas Jefferson's Birthday
Apr. 21	Patriots Day (Maine, Mass.); San Jacinto Day (Tex.)
Apr. 25	National Arbor Day
May 1	May Day
May 8	Truman Day (Mo.)
May 11	Mother's Day
May 17	Armed Forces Day
May 19	Victoria Day (Canada)
May 22	National Maritime Day
May 26	Memorial Day (observed)*
June 5	World Environment Day
June 11	King Kamehameha I Day (Hawaii)
June 14	Flag Day
June 15	Father's Day
June 17	Bunker Hill Day (Suffolk Co., Mass.)
June 19	Emancipation Day (Tex.)
June 20	West Virginia Day
July 1	Canada Day
July 4	Independence Day*
July 24	Pioneer Day (Utah)
Aug. 4	Colorado Day
Aug. 11	Victory Day (R.I.)
Aug. 16	Bennington Battle Day (Vt.)
Aug. 19	National Aviation Day
Aug. 26	Women's Equality Day
Sept. 1	Labor Day*
Sept. 7	Grandparents Day
Sept. 9	Admission Day (Calif.)
Sept. 17	Citizenship Day
Oct. 6	Child Health Day
Oct. 9	Leif Eriksson Day
Oct. 13	Columbus Day (observed)*; Thanksgiving Day (Canada); Native Americans Day (S.Dak.)
Oct. 18	Alaska Day
Oct. 24	United Nations Day
Oct. 31	Halloween; Nevada Day
Nov. 4	Election Day; Will Rogers Day (Okla.)
Nov. 11	Veterans Day*
Nov. 19	Discovery Day (Puerto Rico)
Nov. 27	Thanksgiving Day*
Nov. 28	Acadian Day (La.)
Nov. 30	John F. Kennedy Day (Mass.)
Dec. 7	National Pearl Harbor Remembrance Day
Dec. 15	Bill of Rights Day
Dec. 17	Wright Brothers Day
Dec. 25	Christmas Day*
Dec. 26	Boxing Day (Canada); First day of Kwanzaa

Religious Observances

Epiphany	Jan. 6	Orthodox Easter	Apr. 27
Ash Wednesday	Mar. 5	Whitsunday-Pentecost	June 8
Islamic New Year	Mar. 5	Rosh Hashanah	Sept. 27
Palm Sunday	Apr. 13	Yom Kippur	Oct. 6
First day of Passover	Apr. 17	First day of Ramadan	Oct. 27
Good Friday	Apr. 18	First day of Chanukah	Dec. 20
Easter	Apr. 20	Christmas Day	Dec. 25

Glossary of Almanac Oddities

Many readers have expressed puzzlement over the rather obscure notations that appear on our **Right-Hand Calendar Pages (45–71).** These "oddities" have long been fixtures in the Almanac, and we are pleased to provide some definitions. (Once explained, it may seem that they are not so odd after all!)

Ember Days (Movable)

The Almanac traditionally marks the four periods formerly observed by the Roman Catholic and Anglican churches for prayer, fasting, and the ordination of clergy. These Ember Days are the Wednesdays, Fridays, and Saturdays that follow in succession after (1) the First Sunday in Lent; (2) Whitsunday-Pentecost; (3) the Feast of the Holy Cross, September 14; and (4) the Feast of St. Lucy, December 13. The word *ember* is perhaps a corruption of the Latin *quatuor tempora,* "four times."

Folklore has it that the weather on each of the three days foretells the weather for three successive months; that is, for September's Ember Days, Wednesday forecasts weather for October, Friday for November, and Saturday for December.

Plough Monday (January)

The first Monday after Epiphany and Plough Sunday, so called because it was the end of the Christmas holidays, when men returned to their plough, or daily work. It was customary for farm laborers to draw a plough

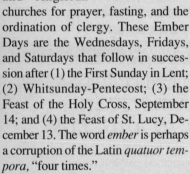

through the village, soliciting money for a "plough-light," which was kept burning in the parish church all year. In some areas, the custom of blessing the plough is maintained.

Three Chilly Saints (May)

Mamertus, Pancras, and Gervais, three early Christian saints, whose feast days occur on May 11, 12, and 13, respectively. Because these days are traditionally cold (an old French saying goes: "St. Mamertus, St. Pancras, and St. Gervais do not pass without a frost"), they have come to be known as the Three Chilly Saints.

Midsummer Day (June 24)

Although it occurs near the summer solstice, to the farmer it is the midpoint of the growing season, halfway between planting and harvest and an occasion for festivity. The English church considered it a "Quarter Day," one of the four major divisions of the liturgical year. It also marks the feast day of St. John the Baptist.

Cornscateous Air (July)

A term first used by the old almanac makers to signify warm, damp air.

(continued on page 76)

Though it signals ideal climatic conditions for growing corn, it also poses a danger to those affected by asthma, pneumonia, and other respiratory problems.

Dog Days (July–August)

The hottest and most unhealthy days of the year. Also known as "Canicular Days," the name derives from the Dog Star, Sirius. The Almanac lists the traditional timing of Dog Days: The 40 days beginning July 3 and ending August 11, coinciding with the heliacal (at sunrise) rising of Sirius.

Cat Nights Begin (August)

The term harks back to the days when people believed in witches. An old Irish legend has it that a witch could turn herself into a cat eight times and then regain herself, but on the ninth time—August 17—she couldn't change back; hence, the saying: "A cat has nine lives." Because August is a "yowly" time for cats, this may have prompted the speculation about witches on the prowl in the first place.

Harvest Home (September)

In Europe and Britain, the conclusion of the harvest each autumn was once marked by great festivals of fun, feasting, and thanksgiving known as "Harvest Home." It was also a time to hold elections, pay workers, and collect rents. These festivals usually took place around the time of the autumnal equinox. Certain ethnic groups in this country, particularly the Pennsylvania Dutch, have kept the tradition alive.

St. Luke's Little Summer (October)

A spell of warm weather occurring about the time of the saint's feast day, October 18. This period is sometimes referred to as Indian summer.

Indian Summer (November)

A period of warm weather following a cold spell or a hard frost. Although there are differing dates for the time of occurrence, for more than 200 years the Almanac has adhered to the saying, "If All Saints' brings out winter, St. Martin's brings out Indian summer." Accordingly, Indian summer can occur between St. Martin's Day (November 11) and November 20. As for the origin of the term, some say it comes from the early Native Americans, who believed that the condition was caused by a warm wind sent from the court of their southwestern god, Cautantowwit.

Halcyon Days (December)

A period (about 14 days) of calm weather, following the blustery winds of autumn's end. The ancient Greeks and Romans believed them to occur around the time of the winter solstice, when the halcyon, or kingfisher, was brooding. In a nest floating on the sea, the bird was said to have charmed the wind and waves so that the waters were especially calm during this period.

Beware the Pogonip (December)

The word *pogonip* is a meteorological term used to describe an uncommon occurrence—frozen fog. The word was coined by Native Americans to describe the frozen fogs of fine ice needles that occur in the mountain valleys of the western United States. According to Indian tradition, breathing the fog is injurious to the lungs. □ □

Black Listed Cancer Treatment Could Save Your Life

Baltimore, MD— As unbelievable as it seems the key to stopping many cancers has been around for over 30 years. Yet it has been banned. Blocked. And kept out of your medicine cabinet by the very agency designed to protect your health—the FDA.

In 1966, the senior oncologist at St. Vincent's Hospital in New York rocked the medical world when he developed a serum that **"shrank cancer tumors in 45 minutes!"** 90 minutes later they were gone... Headlines hit every major paper around the world. Time and again this life saving treatment worked miracles, but the FDA ignored the research and hope he brought and shut him down.

You read that right. He was not only shut down—but also forced out of the country where others benefited from his discovery. How many other treatments have they been allowed to hide?

Decades ago, European research scientist Dr. Johanna Budwig, a six-time Nobel Award nominee, discovered a totally natural formula that not only protects against the development of cancer, but has helped people all over the world diagnosed with incurable cancer—now lead normal lives.

After 30 years of study, Dr. Budwig discovered that the blood of seriously ill cancer patients was deficient in certain substances and nutrients. Yet, healthy blood always contained these ingredients. It was the lack of these nutrients that allowed cancer cells to grow wild and out of control.

By simply eating a combination of two natural and delicious foods (found on page 134) not only can cancer be prevented—but in case after case it was actually healed! "Symptoms of cancer, liver dysfunction, and diabetes were completely alleviated." Remarkably, what Dr. Budwig discovered was a totally natural way for eradicating cancer.

However, when she went to publish these results so that everyone could benefit—**she was blocked by manufacturers with heavy financial stakes!** For over 10 years now her methods have proved effective—yet she is denied publication—blocked by the giants who don't want you to read her words.

What's more, the world is full of expert minds like Dr. Budwig who have pursued cancer remedies and come up with remarkable natural formulas and diets that work for hundreds and thousands of patients. *How to Fight Cancer and Win* author William Fischer has studied these methods and revealed their secrets for you—so that you or someone you love may be spared the horrors of conventional cancer treatments.

As early as 1947, Virginia Livingston, M.D., isolated a cancer-causing microbe. She noted that every cancer sample analyzed (whether human or other animal) contained it.

This microbe—a bacteria that is actually in each of us from birth to death—multiplies and promotes cancer when the immune system is weakened by disease, stress, or poor nutrition. Worst of all, the microbes secrete a special hormone protector that short-circuits our body's immune system—allowing the microbes to grow undetected for years. No wonder so many patients are riddled with cancer by the time it is detected. But there is hope even for them...

Turn to page 82 of *How to Fight Cancer and Win* for the delicious diet that can help stop the formation of cancer cells and shrink tumors.

They walked away from traditional cancer treatments...and were healed! Throughout the pages of *How to Fight Cancer and Win* you'll meet real people who were diagnosed with cancer—suffered through harsh conventional treatments—turned their backs on so called modern medicine—only to be miraculously healed by natural means! Here is just a sampling of what others have to say about the book.

"We purchased *How to Fight Cancer and Win*, and immediately my husband started following the recommended diet for his just diagnosed colon cancer. He refused the surgery that our doctors advised. Since following the regime recommended in the book he has had no problems at all, cancer-wise. If not cured, we believe the cancer has to be in remission."—*Thelma B.*

"I bought *How to Fight Cancer and Win* and this has to be the greatest book I've ever read. I have had astounding results from the easy to understand knowledge found in this book. My whole life has improved drastically and I have done so much for many others. The information goes far beyond the health thinking of today."—*Hugh M.*

"I can't find adequate words to describe my appreciation of your work in providing *How to Fight Cancer and Win*. You had to do an enormous amount of research to bring this vast and most important knowledge to your readers.

My doctor found two tumors on my prostate with a high P.S.A. He scheduled a time to surgically remove the prostate, but I canceled the appointment. Instead I went on the diet discussed in the book combined with another supplement. Over the months my P.S.A. has lowered until the last reading was one point two." —*Duncan M.*

"In my 55 years as a Country Family Physician, I have never read a more 'down to earth,' practical resume of cancer prevention and treatments, than in this book. It needs to be studied worldwide for the prevention of cancer by all researchers who are looking for a cure."—*Edward S., MD*

"As a cancer patient who has been battling lymphatic cancer on and off for almost three years now, I was very pleased to stumble across *How to fight Cancer and Win*. The book was inspiring, well-written and packed with useful information for any cancer patient looking to maximize his or her chances for recovery."—*Romany S.*

"I've been incorporating Dr. Budwig's natural remedy into my diet and have told others about it. Your book is very informative and has information I've never heard about before (and I've read many books on the cancer and nutrition link). Thanks for the wonderful information."—*Molly G.*

Don't waste another minute. Claim your book today and you will be one of the lucky few who no longer have to wait for cures that get pushed "underground" by big business and money hungry giants.

To get your copy of *How to Fight Cancer and Win* call **1-888-821-3609 and ask for code 9098** to order by credit card. Or write "Fight Cancer—Dept. P680C901 on a plain piece of paper with your name, address, phone number (in case we have a question about your order) and a check for $19.95 plus $4.00 shipping and mail to: **Agora Health Books, Dept. P680C901, P.O. Box 977, Frederick, MD 21705-9838**

If you are not completely satisfied, return the book within one year for a complete and total refund—no questions asked. This will probably be the most important information you and your loved ones receive—so order.

©2002 Agora Health Books, LLC

We're looking for people to—

Write Children's Books

By Kristi Holl

I f you've ever dreamed of writing for children, here's your chance to test that dream. . . and find out if you have the aptitude to make it a reality. If you do, we'll teach you how to crack one of today's most rewarding markets for new writers.

The $2 billion children's market

The tremendous recent success of children's books has made the general public aware of what we've known for years: There's a huge market out there. And there's a growing need for new writers trained to create the nearly $2 billion of children's books purchased every year. . . plus the stories and articles needed by more than 600 publishers of magazines for and about children and teenagers.

Who are these needed writers? They're ordinary people like you and me.

"But am I good enough?"

Fifteen years ago, I was where you may be now. My occasional thoughts of writing had been pushed down by self-doubt, and I didn't know where to turn for help. Then, on an impulse, I sent for the Institute's free writing aptitude test and it turned out to be the spark I needed. I took their course and my wonderful author-instructor helped me to discover, step-by-step, that my everyday life—probably not much different from yours—was an endless creative resource for my writing!

The promise that paid off

The Institute made the same promise to me that they'll make to you, if you demonstrate basic writing aptitude: *You will complete at least one manuscript suitable to submit to editors by the time you finish the course.*

I really didn't expect to be pub-

lished before I finished the course, but I was. I sold three stories. And I soon discovered that that was not unusual at the Institute. Now, as a graduate and a nationally published author of 24 children's books, and more than 100 stories and articles, I'm teaching: I'm passing along what I've learned to would-be writers like you.

One-on-one training with your own instructor

My fellow instructors—all of them professional writers or editors—work with their students the same way I

Kristi Holl, a graduate of our course, has published 24 books and more than 100 stories and articles. She is now an instructor at the Institute.

work with mine: When you've completed an assignment on your own schedule, at your own pace, you send it to me. I read it and reread it to make sure I get everything out of it that you've put into it. Then I edit it line-by-line and send you a detailed letter explaining my edits. I point out your strengths and show you how to shore up your weaknesses. Between your pushing and my pulling, you learn how to write—and how to market what you write.

I am the living proof

What I got from my instructor at the Institute changed me from a "wannabe" into a nationally published writer. While there's no guarantee that every student will have the same success, we're showered with letters like these from current and former students.

"Since graduating from your course," says Heather Klassen, Edmonds, WA, "I've sold 125 stories to magazines for children and teenagers."

"Before this, I didn't know if my work was typical or bland, or if there was even a spark of life in it," writes Kate Spanks, Maple Ridge, BC. "I now have over 30 articles published. . . ."

". . .a little bird. . .has just been given freedom"

This course has helped me more than I can say," says Jody Drueding, Boston, MA. "It's as if a little bird that was locked up inside of me has just been given the freedom of the garden."

". . .I was attracted by the fact that you require an aptitude test," says Nikki Arko, Raton, NM. "Other schools sign you up as long as you have the money to pay, regardless of talent or potential."

"I'd take the course again in a heartbeat!"

"My most recent success has been the publication of the novel I started for my last Institute assignment," writes Jennifer Jones, Homer, NY. "Thank you for giving me the life I longed for."

"I'd take the course again in a heartbeat!", says Tonya Tingey, Woodruff, UT. "It made my dream a reality."

Don't let your dream die— send for your free test today!

If life as a successful writer is your dream, here's your chance to test that dream. We've developed a revealing aptitude test based on our 32 years of experience. Just fill out and mail the coupon below to receive your free test and a 32-page introduction to our course, *Writing for Children and Teenagers,* and 80 of our instructors.

There is no obligation.

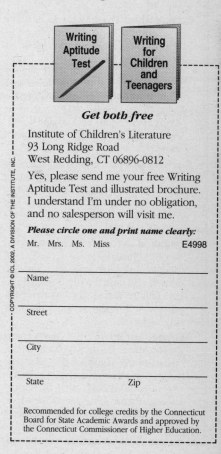

Writing Aptitude Test

Writing for Children and Teenagers

Get both free

Institute of Children's Literature
93 Long Ridge Road
West Redding, CT 06896-0812

Yes, please send me your free Writing Aptitude Test and illustrated brochure. I understand I'm under no obligation, and no salesperson will visit me.

Please circle one and print name clearly:

Mr. Mrs. Ms. Miss   E4998

Name

Street

City

State   Zip

Recommended for college credits by the Connecticut Board for State Academic Awards and approved by the Connecticut Commissioner of Higher Education.

— COPYRIGHT © ICL 2002, A DIVISION OF THE INSTITUTE, INC.

Astronomical Glossary

Aphelion (Aph.): The point in a planet's orbit that is farthest from the Sun.

Apogee (Apo.): The point in the Moon's orbit that is farthest from Earth.

Celestial Equator (Eq.): The circle around the celestial sphere that is halfway between the celestial poles. It can be thought of as the plane of Earth's equator projected out onto the sphere.

Celestial Sphere: An imaginary sphere projected into space that represents the entire sky, with an observer on Earth at its center. All celestial bodies other than Earth are imagined as being on its inside surface.

Conjunction: The time at which two or more celestial bodies appear closest in the sky. (Dates for conjunction are given in the Right-Hand Calendar Pages 45–71; sky sightings of closely aligned bodies are given in the descriptive text at the top of the Left-Hand Calendar Pages 44–70.) **Inferior (Inf.):** Mercury or Venus is between the Sun and Earth. **Superior (Sup.):** The Sun is between a planet and Earth.

Declination: The celestial latitude of an object in the sky, measured in degrees north or south of the celestial equator; analogous to latitude on Earth. The Almanac gives the Sun's declination at noon PST or PDT.

Dominical Letter: A letter from A to G, denoting Sundays in the ecclesiastical calendar for a given year, determined by the date on which the first Sunday falls. If it falls on Jan. 1, the letter [for the year] is A; if it falls on Jan. 2, the letter is B; and so on.

Eclipse, Lunar: The full Moon enters the shadow of Earth, which cuts off all or part of the Moon's light. **Total:** The Moon passes completely through the umbra (central dark part) of Earth's shadow. **Partial:** Only part of the Moon passes through the umbra. **Penumbral:** The Moon passes through only the penumbra (area of partial darkness surrounding the umbra).

Eclipse, Solar: Earth enters the shadow of the new Moon, which cuts off all or part of the Sun's light. **Total:** Earth passes through the umbra (central dark part) of the Moon's shadow, resulting in totality for observers within a narrow band on Earth. **Annular:** The Moon appears silhouetted against the Sun, with a ring of sunlight showing around it. **Partial:** The Moon blocks only part of the Sun.

Ecliptic: The apparent annual path of the Sun around the celestial sphere. The plane of the ecliptic is tipped 23½° from the celestial equator.

Elongation: The difference in degrees between the celestial longitudes of a planet and the Sun. **Greatest Elongation (Gr. Elong.):** The greatest apparent distance of a planet from the Sun, as seen from Earth.

Epact: A number from 1 to 30 that indicates the Moon's age on Jan. 1 at Greenwich, England; used for determining the date of Easter.

Equinox: When the Sun crosses the celestial equator. This occurs two times each year: **Vernal** around March 21 and **Autumnal** around September 23.

Evening Star: A planet that is above the western horizon at sunset and less than 180° east of the Sun in right ascension.

Golden Number: A number in the 19-year cycle of the Moon, used for determining the date of Easter. (The Moon repeats its phases approximately every 19 years.) Add 1 to any given year and divide the result by 19; the remainder is the Golden Number. If there is no remainder, the Golden Number is 19.

Julian Period: A period of 7,980 years beginning Jan. 1, 4713 B.C. Devised in 1583 by Joseph Scaliger, it provides a chronological basis for the study of ancient history. To find the Julian year, add 4,713 to any year. **(continued on page 82)**

Moon on Equator: The Moon is on the celestial equator.

Moon Rides High/Runs Low: The Moon is highest above or farthest below the celestial equator.

Moonrise/Moonset: The Moon's rising above or descending below the horizon.

Moon's Phases: The continually changing appearance of the Moon, caused by the different angles at which it is illuminated by the Sun. **First Quarter:** The right half of the Moon is illuminated, as seen from the Northern Hemisphere. **Full:** The Sun and the Moon are in opposition; the entire disk of the Moon is illuminated as viewed from Earth. **Last Quarter:** The left half of the Moon is illuminated, as seen from the Northern Hemisphere. **New:** The Sun and the Moon are in conjunction; the entire disk of the Moon is darkened as viewed from Earth.

Moon's Place, Astronomical: The actual position of the Moon within the constellations on the celestial sphere. **Astrological:** The astrological position of the Moon within the zodiac according to calculations made over 2,000 years ago. Because of precession of the equinoxes and other factors, this is not the Moon's actual position in the sky.

Morning Star: A planet that is above the eastern horizon at sunrise and less than 180° west of the Sun in right ascension.

Node, Ascending/Descending: Either of the two points where a body's orbit intersects the ecliptic. The body is moving from south to north of the ecliptic at the ascending node, and from north to south at the descending node.

Occultation (Occn.): The eclipse of a star or planet by the Moon or another planet.

Opposition: The Moon or a planet appears on the opposite side of the sky from the Sun (elongation 180°).

Perigee (Perig.): The point in the Moon's orbit that is closest to Earth.

Perihelion (Perih.): The point in a planet's orbit that is closest to the Sun.

Precession: The slowly changing position of the stars and equinoxes in the sky resulting from variations in the orientation of Earth's axis.

Right Ascension (R.A.): The celestial longitude of an object in the sky, measured eastward along the celestial equator in hours of time from the vernal equinox; analogous to longitude on Earth.

Roman Indiction: A number in a 15-year cycle, established Jan. 1, A.D. 313, as a fiscal term. Add 3 to any given year in the Christian era and divide by 15; the remainder is the Roman Indiction. If there is no remainder, it is 15.

Solar Cycle: A period of 28 years in the Julian calendar, at the end of which the days of the month return to the same days of the week.

Solstice, Summer: The Sun reaches its greatest declination (23½°) north of the celestial equator. **Winter:** The Sun reaches its greatest declination (23½°) south of the celestial equator.

Stationary (Stat.): The apparent halted movement, as it reaches opposition, of a planet against the background of the stars, shortly before it appears to move backward (retrograde motion).

Sun Fast/Slow: When a sundial reading is behind (slow) or ahead of (fast) clock time.

Sunrise/Sunset: The visible rising and setting of the Sun's upper limb across the unobstructed horizon of an observer whose eyes are 15 feet above ground level.

Twilight: The interval of time following sunset and preceding sunrise, during which the sky is partially illuminated. The three ranges of twilight are **civil** (from sunset/sunrise to when the Sun is 6° below the horizon), **nautical** (greater than 6° and ending at 12°), and **astronomical** (greater than 12° and ending at 18°—full darkness). (See page 88 to calculate twilight times in your area.) □ □

Why wait ten months?

Now you can have rich, dark compost *in just 14 days!*

With the amazing ComposTumbler, you'll have bushels of crumbly, ready-to-use compost — *in just 14 days!* (And, in the ten months it takes to make compost the old way, your ComposTumbler can produce *hundreds of pounds* of rich food for your garden!)

Say good-bye to that messy, open compost pile (and to the flies, pests, and odors that come along with it!) Bid a happy farewell to the strain of trying to turn over heavy, wet piles with a pitchfork.

Compost the Better Way

Compost-making with the ComposTumbler is neat, quick and easy!

Gather up leaves, old weeds, kitchen scraps, lawn clippings, etc. and toss them into the roomy 18-bushel drum. Then, once each day, give the ComposTumbler's *gear-driven* handle a few easy spins.

The ComposTumbler's Magic

Inside the ComposTumbler, carefully positioned mixing fins blend materials, pushing fresh mixture to the core where the temperatures are the hottest (up to 160°) and the composting bacteria most active.

After just 14 days, open the door, and you'll find an abundance of dark, sweet-smelling "garden gold" — ready to enrich and feed your garden!

NEW SMALLER SIZE!

Now there are 2 sizes. The 18-bushel original ComposTumbler and the NEW 9.5-bushel Compact ComposTumbler. Try either size risk-free for 30 days!

See for yourself! Try the ComposTumbler risk-free with our 30-Day Home Trial!

Call Toll-Free 1-800-880-2345

NOW ON SALE— SAVE UP TO $115!

ComposTumbler®

The choice of more than 250,000 gardeners

❑ YES! Please rush FREE information on the ComposTumbler, including special savings and 30-Day Home Trial.

Name _____

Address _____

City _____

State _____ ZIP _____

MAIL TO: **ComposTumbler**
30 Wright Ave., **Dept. 42013C**
Lititz (Lancaster Co.), PA 17543

© 2002 PBM Group

Bright Stars, 2003

Transit Times

■ This table shows the time (EST or EDT) and altitude of a star as it transits the meridian (i.e., reaches its highest elevation while passing over the horizon's south point) at Boston on the dates shown. The transit time on any other date differs from that of the nearest date listed by approximately four minutes per day. To find the time of a star's transit for your location, convert its time at Boston using Key Letter C.*

Star	Constellation	Magnitude	Time of Transit (EST/EDT) Boldface—P.M. Lightface—A.M.						Altitude (degrees)
			Jan. 1	Mar. 1	May 1	July 1	Sept. 1	Nov. 1	
Altair	Aquila	0.8	**12:50**	8:58	5:59	1:59	**9:51**	**4:51**	56.3
Deneb	Cygnus	1.3	**1:41**	9:49	6:49	2:50	**10:42**	**5:42**	92.8
Fomalhaut	Psc. Aus.	1.2	**3:56**	**12:04**	9:04	5:04	1:00	**7:57**	17.8
Algol	Perseus	2.2	**8:07**	**4:15**	**1:15**	9:15	5:11	12:11	88.5
Aldebaran	Taurus	0.9	**9:34**	**5:42**	**2:42**	10:42	6:38	1:39	64.1
Rigel	Orion	0.1	**10:12**	**6:20**	**3:20**	11:21	7:17	2:17	39.4
Capella	Auriga	0.1	**10:14**	**6:22**	**3:22**	11:22	7:19	2:19	93.6
Bellatrix	Orion	1.6	**10:23**	**6:31**	**3:31**	11:31	7:28	2:28	54.0
Betelgeuse	Orion	var. 0.4	**10:53**	**7:01**	**4:01**	**12:01**	7:57	2:58	55.0
Sirius	Can. Maj.	−1.4	**11:43**	**7:51**	**4:51**	**12:51**	8:47	3:47	31.0
Procyon	Can. Min.	0.4	12:40	**8:44**	**5:45**	**1:45**	9:41	4:41	52.9
Pollux	Gemini	1.2	12:46	**8:50**	**5:51**	**1:51**	9:47	4:47	75.7
Regulus	Leo	1.4	3:09	**11:13**	**8:14**	**4:14**	**12:10**	7:10	59.7
Spica	Virgo	var. 1.0	6:26	2:34	**11:30**	**7:30**	**3:26**	10:26	36.6
Arcturus	Bootes	−0.1	7:16	3:24	12:21	**8:21**	**4:17**	11:17	66.9
Antares	Scorpius	var. 0.9	9:29	5:37	2:37	**10:34**	**6:30**	**1:30**	21.3
Vega	Lyra	0	11:37	7:45	4:45	**12:41**	**8:37**	**3:38**	86.4

Risings and Settings

■ To find the time of a star's rising at Boston on any date, subtract the interval shown at right from the star's transit time on that date; add the interval to find the star's setting time. To find the rising and setting times for your city, convert the Boston transit times above using the Key Letter* shown at right before applying the interval. The directions in which the stars rise and set, shown for Boston, are generally useful throughout the United States. Deneb, Algol, Capella, and Vega are circumpolar stars—they never set but appear to circle the celestial north pole.

Star	Interval (h. m.)	Rising Key	Dir.	Setting Key	Dir.
Altair	6:36	B	EbN	E	WbN
Fomalhaut	3:59	E	SE	D	SW
Aldebaran	7:06	B	ENE	D	WNW
Rigel	5:33	D	EbS	B	WbS
Bellatrix	6:27	B	EbN	D	WbN
Betelgeuse	6:31	B	EbN	D	WbN
Sirius	5:00	D	ESE	B	WSW
Procyon	6:23	B	EbN	D	WbN
Pollux	8:01	A	NE	E	NW
Regulus	6:49	B	EbN	D	WbN
Spica	5:23	D	EbS	B	WbS
Arcturus	7:19	A	ENE	E	WNW
Antares	4:17	E	SEbE	A	SWbW

*The values of Key Letters are given in the Time Corrections table (page 226).

—Beth Krommes

Learn. Earn.

The top ten reasons why training at home is the smart way to learn new career skills.

1 You can choose from over 60 Specialized Associate Degree and Career Diploma programs in today's hottest fields.

2 All study materials, equipment, and tools are included and are shipped right to your door.

3 You study at your own pace, in your own place, eliminating the need to ever commute to classes.

4 You'll have round-the-clock access to helpful, experienced instructors by phone or e-mail.

5 You take your exams when you decide you're ready — by mail, telephone, or online.

6 Education Direct is nationally accredited by the Accrediting Commission of the Distance Education and Training Council, and licensed by the Pennsylvania State Board of Private Licensed Schools.

7 You'll earn continuing education units (CEUs) approved by the International Association for Continuing Education and Training.

8 Over 12 million students from the U.S. and abroad have chosen Education Direct training programs.

9 Over half of the Fortune 500 companies use the simple, step-by-step Education Direct method to train their employees.

10 Your program can help you begin a new career, advance in your current one, or even open your own business, where you can make more money doing work you love!

313A

Eclipses, 2003

■ There will be four eclipses in 2003, two of the Sun and two of the Moon. Solar eclipses are visible only in certain areas and require eye protection to be viewed safely. Lunar eclipses are technically visible from the entire night side of Earth, but during a penumbral eclipse, the dimming of the Moon's illumination is slight.

1 **Penumbral eclipse of the Moon, May 15–16.** The beginning of the umbral phase will be visible in eastern North America; the end will be visible in North America except for the extreme northwestern part. The Moon enters penumbra at 9:05 P.M. EDT (6:05 P.M. PDT) on the 15th and leaves at 2:15 A.M. EDT on the 16th (11:15 P.M. PDT on the 15th).

2 **Annular eclipse of the Sun, May 30.** This partial eclipse will be visible in eastern Alaska and the extreme northwestern part of Canada. The annular eclipse will begin at 6:46 P.M. PDT and end at 11:30 P.M. PDT and will not be visible in eastern North America.

3 **Penumbral eclipse of the Moon, November 8.** The beginning of the penumbral phase will be visible in eastern North America; the end will be visible throughout North America. The Moon enters penumbra at 5:15 P.M. EST (not visible PST) and leaves penumbra at 11:22 P.M. EST (8:22 P.M. PST).

4 **Total eclipse of the Sun, November 23.** This eclipse will not be visible in the United States or Canada.

Full-Moon Dates

	2003	2004	2005	2006	2007
Jan.	18	7	25	14	3
Feb.	16	6	23	12	2
Mar.	18	6	25	14	3
Apr.	16	5	24	13	2
May	15	4	23	13	2 & 31
June	14	3	22	11	30
July	13	2 & 31	21	10	29
Aug.	12	29	19	9	28
Sept.	10	28	17	7	26
Oct.	10	27	17	6	26
Nov.	8	26	15	5	24
Dec.	8	26	15	4	23

Principal Meteor Showers

Shower	Best Viewing	Point of Origin	Date of Maximum*	Peak Rate (/hr.)**	Associated Comet
Quadrantid	Predawn	N	Jan. 4	80	—
Lyrid	Predawn	S	Apr. 22	12	Thatcher
Eta Aquarid	Predawn	SE	May 4	20	Halley
Delta Aquarid	Predawn	S	July 30	10	—
Perseid	Predawn	NE	Aug. 11–13	75	Swift-Tuttle
Draconid	Late evening	NW	Oct. 9	6	Giacobini-Zinner
Orionid	Predawn	S	Oct. 21–22	25	Halley
Taurid	Midnight	S	Nov. 9	6	Encke
Leonid	Predawn	S	Nov. 18	20	Tempel-Tuttle
Andromedid	Late evening	S	Nov. 25–27	5	Biela
Geminid	All night	NE	Dec. 13–14	65	—
Ursid	Predawn	N	Dec. 22	12	Tuttle

*Date of actual maximum occurrence may vary by one or two days in either direction.
**Approximate.

The Twilight Zone

How to determine the length of twilight and the times of dawn and dark.

■ Twilight is the period of time between dawn and sunrise, and again between sunset and dark. Both dawn and dark are defined as moments when the Sun is 18 degrees below the horizon. The latitude of a place and the time of year determine the length of twilight. To find the latitude of your city or the city nearest you, consult the **Time Corrections table, page 226.** Use that figure in the chart below with the appropriate date, and you will have the length of twilight in your area.

Latitude	Length of Twilight (hours and minutes)								
	Jan. 1 to Apr. 10	Apr. 11 to May 2	May 3 to May 14	May 15 to May 25	May 26 to July 22	July 23 to Aug. 3	Aug. 4 to Aug. 14	Aug. 15 to Sept. 5	Sept. 6 to Dec. 31
25° N to 30° N	1 20	1 23	1 26	1 29	1 32	1 29	1 26	1 23	1 20
31° N to 36° N	1 26	1 28	1 34	1 38	1 43	1 38	1 34	1 28	1 26
37° N to 42° N	1 33	1 39	1 47	1 52	1 59	1 52	1 47	1 39	1 33
43° N to 47° N	1 42	1 51	2 02	2 13	2 27	2 13	2 02	1 51	1 42
48° N to 49° N	1 50	2 04	2 22	2 42	—	2 42	2 22	2 04	1 50

■ To determine when dawn will break and when dark will descend, apply the length of twilight to the times of sunrise and sunset. Follow the instructions given in **How to Use This Almanac, page 39,** to determine sunrise/sunset times for your locality. Subtract the length of twilight from the time of sunrise for dawn. Add the length of twilight to the time of sunset for dark. (See examples at right.)

	Boston, Mass. (latitude 42° 22')	Oshkosh, Wis. (latitude 44° 1')
Sunrise, August 1	5:36 A.M.	5:40 A.M.
Length of twilight	–1:52	–2:13
Dawn breaks	3:44 A.M. EDT	3:27 A.M. CDT
Sunset, August 1	8:04 P.M.	8:16 P.M.
Length of twilight	+1:52	+2:13
Dark descends	9:56 P.M. EDT	10:29 P.M. CDT

Tidal Glossary

Apogean Tide: A monthly tide of decreased range that occurs when the Moon is at apogee (farthest from Earth).

Diurnal Tide: A tide with one high water and one low water in a tidal day of approximately 24 hours.

Mean Lower Low Water: The arithmetic mean of the lesser of a daily pair of low waters, observed over a specific 19-year cycle called the National Tidal Datum Epoch.

Neap Tide: A tide of decreased range that occurs twice a month, when the Moon is in quadrature (during its first and last quarters, when the Sun and the Moon are at right angles to each other relative to Earth).

Perigean Tide: A monthly tide of increased range that occurs when the Moon is at perigee (closest to Earth).

Semidiurnal Tide: A tide with one high water and one low water every half day. East

Coast tides, for example, are semidiurnal, with two highs and two lows during a tidal day of approximately 24 hours.

Spring Tide: A tide of increased range that occurs at times of syzygy each month. Named not for the season of spring but from the German *springen* ("to leap up"), a spring tide also brings a lower low water.

Syzygy: The nearly straight-line configuration that occurs twice a month, when the Sun and the Moon are in conjunction (on the same side of Earth at the new Moon) and when they are in opposition (on opposite sides of Earth at the full Moon). In both cases, the gravitational effects of the Sun and the Moon reinforce each other, and tidal range is increased.

Vanishing Tide: A mixed tide of considerable inequality in the two highs and two lows, so that the lower high (or higher low) may become indistinct or appear to vanish.

The Visible Planets, 2003

■ Listed here for Boston are the times (EST/EDT) of the visible rising and setting of the planets Venus, Mars, Jupiter, and Saturn on the 1st, 11th, and 21st of each month. The approximate times of their visible rising and setting on other days can be found by interpolation. The capital letters that appear beside the times are Key Letters and are used to convert the times to other localities **(see pages 40 and 226)**. For definitions of morning and evening stars, see the **Glossary on page 80.**

—Illustrations by Beth Krommes

Venus has an insignificant year. Our sister planet is usually highest as an evening star in spring or a morning star in autumn. In 2003, its morning and evening appearances occur at the wrong seasons. Venus opens the year as a dazzling morning star, slowly fading and sinking closer to the horizon each dawn. Still noteworthy until March, it fizzles away in June. Passing behind the Sun on August 18, it slowly emerges in the west as a low evening star at dusk but is not eye-catching until late October. Venus grows higher and brighter in December.

Mars has its best appearance in thousands of years! Starting 2003 as an inconspicuous "star" in the predawn east and remaining a morning star through spring, the red planet explosively brightens 70-fold to reach an astonishing brilliance in late August. It then far outshines everything in the night sky and appears larger than at any time in history. Dazzling from July through September and out most of the night, Mars floats below faint Uranus in Aquarius, helping binocular owners locate the strange green planet.

		Boldface—P.M.		Lightface—A.M.		
Jan.........1 rise	3:26 D	July ....1 rise	4:15 A	Jan.........1 rise	3:13 D	July ....1 **rise 11:28** D
Jan.......11 rise	3:36 D	July .....11 rise	4:28 A	Jan.......11 rise	3:07 D	July .....11 **rise 10:58** D
Jan.......21 rise	3:47 E	July .....21 rise	4:46 A	Jan.......21 rise	3:01 E	July .....21 **rise 10:26** D
Feb. ....1 rise	4:01 E	Aug. ....1 rise	5:10 A	Feb. ....1 rise	2:53 E	Aug. ......1 **rise** 9:46 D
Feb. .....11 rise	4:12 E	Aug. ....11 rise	5:34 A	Feb. .....11 rise	2:45 E	Aug. ....11 **rise** 9:06 D
Feb. .....21 rise	4:20 E	Aug. ....21 **set** **7:44** D		Feb. .....21 rise	2:37 E	Aug. ....21 **rise** 8:23 D
Mar. ......1 rise	4:23 D	Sept. ......1 **set** **7:33** D		Mar. ......1 rise	2:29 E	Sept. ......1 set 5:39 B
Mar. ....11 rise	4:23 D	Sept. .....11 **set** **7:21** C		Mar. ....11 rise	2:18 E	Sept. .....11 set 4:49 B
Mar. ....21 rise	4:20 D	Sept. .....21 **set** **7:09** C		Mar. ....21 rise	2:05 E	Sept. .....21 set 4:04 B
Apr........1 rise	4:12 D	Oct. ....1 **set** **6:56** B		Apr........1 rise	1:50 E	Oct. ....1 set 3:22 B
Apr......11 rise	5:03 C	Oct. .....11 **set** **6:45** B		Apr......11 rise	2:34 E	Oct. .....11 set 2:51 B
Apr......21 rise	4:52 C	Oct. .....21 **set** **6:37** B		Apr......21 rise	2:16 E	Oct. .....21 set 2:26 B
May.......1 rise	4:40 B	Nov. ......1 **set** **5:32** A		May.......1 rise	1:57 E	Nov. ......1 set 1:04 B
May.....11 rise	4:28 B	Nov. ....11 **set** **5:33** A		May.....11 rise	1:37 D	Nov. ....11 set 12:47 B
May.....21 rise	4:18 B	Nov. ....21 **set** **5:40** A		May.....21 rise	1:15 D	Nov. ....21 set 12:34 B
June.......1 rise	4:10 A	Dec.........1 **set** **5:54** A		June.......1 rise 12:47 D		Dec.........1 set 12:22 B
June.....11 rise	4:07 A	Dec.......11 **set** **6:13** A		June.....11 rise 12:23 D		Dec.......11 set 12:11 C
June.....21 rise	4:08 A	Dec.....21 **set** **6:36** A		June.....21 **rise 11:56** D		Dec.......21 set 12:03 C
		Dec.....31 **set** **7:01** A				Dec.......31 **set 11:54** C

Mercury darts in and out of the Sun's glare but is easy to see when its orbit makes a high angle with the horizon; when it is near its orbit's "edge," which separates it from the Sun; and when it is on the far side of the Sun, where its phase is nearly "full," boosting its brightness. In 2003, those conditions mesh in the evening sky about a half hour after sunset from April 1 to 20 and, to a lesser extent, from November 27 to December 15. As a morning star just before dawn, the small orange world is best this year from September 26 to October 12.

DO NOT CONFUSE 1) Mercury with Jupiter from September 21 to October 6. Jupiter is brighter and higher, while Mercury is somewhat orange. 2) Saturn with Gemini's major stars Castor and Pollux. Saturn is distinctly brighter. 3) Mercury with Venus from the end of the third week of May to late June when Venus is brighter. Note: 2003 presents amazingly few conjunctions of planets with bright stars or other planets, keeping potential confusion to a minimum.

Jupiter has a magnificent "bookend" year, at its best during the cold months of 2003. With a February 2 opposition in Cancer, the giant world brilliantly dominates the heavens and is out most or all of the night during the first three months of the year. During spring and early summer, it fades and can be seen only in the evening sky before midnight. Passing into Leo before slipping behind the Sun on August 22, it emerges in the predawn east in October and is once again prominent before midnight starting in November.

Saturn enjoys its best year in the half-century span of 1974 to 2030. High overhead in Taurus with its rings wide open, Saturn is very bright as the year opens. It remains well placed through April, slides through Orion in May, and enters its new home of Gemini in June. The magnificent world starts getting high enough to be noticeable again in August and begins rising before midnight in October. By mid-November, it rises before 9 P.M. and reaches another fine pinnacle in December with its opposition on the 31st.

		Boldface—P.M.		Lightface—A.M.			
Jan.........1 **rise**	**7:11** A	July ....1 **set 10:33** D	Jan.........1 set 6:07 E	July ....1 rise 4:50 A
Jan.......11 **rise**	**6:26** A	July .....11 **set 9:59** D	Jan.......11 set 5:25 E	July .....11 rise 4:17 A
Jan.......21 **rise**	**5:41** A	July .....21 **set 9:25** D	Jan.......21 set 4:43 E	July .....21 rise 3:43 A
Feb........1 **rise**	**4:50** A	Aug. ......1 **set 8:48** D	Feb........1 set 3:57 E	Aug. ......1 rise 3:06 A
Feb......11 set	6:31 D	Aug. ....11 **set 8:14** D	Feb......11 set 3:17 E	Aug. ....11 rise 2:32 A
Feb......21 set	5:48 D	Aug. ....21 **set 7:40** D	Feb......21 set 2:37 E	Aug. ....21 rise 1:57 A
Mar. ......1 set	5:14 E	Sept.......1 rise 5:30 B	Mar. ......1 set 2:06 E	Sept.......1 rise 1:19 A
Mar. ....11 set	4:32 E	Sept.....11 rise 5:02 B	Mar. ....11 set 1:28 E	Sept.....11 rise 12:43 A
Mar. ....21 set	3:51 E	Sept.....21 rise 4:33 B	Mar. ....21 set 12:51 E	Sept.....21 rise 12:07 A
Apr........1 set	3:07 E	Oct. ....1 rise 4:04 B	Apr........1 set 12:10 E	Oct. ....1 **rise 11:27** A
Apr......11 set	3:28 E	Oct. .....11 rise 3:35 B	Apr......11 set 12:31 E	Oct. .....11 **rise 10:49** A
Apr......21 set	2:49 E	Oct. .....21 rise 3:05 B	Apr......21 **set 11:56** E	Oct. .....21 **rise 10:10** A
May......1 set	2:12 E	Nov. ......1 rise 1:32 B	May.......1 **set 11:21** E	Nov. ......1 rise 8:27 A
May.....11 set	1:35 E	Nov. .....11 rise 1:00 B	May.....11 **set 10:47** E	Nov. .....11 **rise** 7:47 A
May.....21 set	1:00 E	Nov. .....21 rise 12:28 B	May.....21 **set 10:13** E	Nov. .....21 **rise** 7:05 A
June.......1 set	12:17 E	Dec........1 **rise 11:51** B	June.......1 set 9:35 E	Dec........1 **rise** 6:23 A
June.....11 **set 11:42**	D	Dec.......11 **rise 11:16** B	June.....11 set 9:02 E	Dec.......11 **rise** 5:41 A
June.....21 **set 11:07**	D	Dec.......21 **rise 10:39** B	June.....21 set 8:28 E	Dec.......21 **rise** 4:58 A
		Dec.......31 **rise 10:01** B		Dec.......31 **rise** 4:15 A

RED ALERT:

Mars to

—NASA/GSFC

Dust off that old telescope; Mars is coming close in 2003. Very close. More than merely the summer's brightest "star," the red planet will appear larger than anyone has ever seen it since the telescope was invented in 1608.

Although Earth and Mars meet every

In August, Mars will pass Earth at its absolutely minimum distance and display its polar cap, visible at the top.

26 months, those get-togethers happen at widely varying gaps between our two orbits: This is why Mars varies in its appar-

BY BOB BERMAN

THE VIEW?
THE EYES HAVE IT

ent size and brightness more than any other planet. Last spring, for example, Mars was no brighter than the stars of the Big Dipper, its disk the same apparent width as distant, tiny-seeming Uranus.

Size *does* matter. We can see more detail on objects that appear large in our sky, like the Moon. Last year, when Mars was distant, it appeared only as big as a 25-cent coin a mile away. At such times,

The first step is to find Mars, a no-brainer: Just look south around midnight during August and September. You won't have to search; as the brightest thing in the sky, distinctively yellow-orange in color, Mars will readily catch your eye. (No, Mars is not red. Never has been.

Skim By Earth

only tremendous magnification can reveal detail, but the more telescopic power that is used, the more our own intervening atmosphere's blurriness is amplified. Bottom line: Forget about seeing Martian features when the red planet is farther than 60 million miles away, no matter how good your telescope is.

On an average biennial meeting with Earth, Mars comes about as close as 45 million miles—nothing exciting. During really close visits every 15 years or so, Mars may venture as near as 38 million miles. That's when astronomers take dramatic photos that grace the pages of countless textbooks. But this August, Mars skims by at its absolutely minimum distance of 34.6 million miles and will grow big enough to easily display surface features without excessive blur-inducing magnification. It will then float within the constellation Aquarius, about halfway up the sky for U.S. observers, a little lower for Canadians and most Europeans.

The golden color you see in the sky—that's its true color.)

If all you've got for viewing is the naked eye, watch Mars dramatically brighten as it rushes straight toward you during the first half of the year. From May through July, Mars draws a million miles nearer each day! The final week of August brings a decisive climax, with the closest point being reached on the 27th. Then, and through September, Mars is out all night and is able to grab attention even in big cities. This isn't a subtle aurora; no need to get out to the countryside to see it better.

If you have a telescope, use a magnification of around 150x and wait patiently for moments when the atmosphere isn't wiggling. Suddenly, a stark-white polar cap or dusky marking will appear. Don't expect too much; Mars is challenging, and your instrument isn't the Space Telescope. Still, it's a thrill to view the only planet whose surface features show up from your backyard.

The big Martian disk will not last long. Our planet rushes past it for just a quick hello; by autumn, Mars will have lost half its light. We have waited hundreds of years, and this historic celestial event will pass quickly, so we should savor this opportunity.

Martian Chronicles

No other planet shares with Mars its uneasy aura of mystery and intrigue. Its eerie reputation can be traced back to the ancient Babylonians, who interpreted the planet's orange-red color as bad news. To them, planets were gods, so they believed that a red one represented fire, fury, and blood—a warlike connection. Now, despite knowing that the rusty color simply comes from rust itself (iron oxides on the surface), we're left with a legacy of militaristic Martian language, like *martial arts* and *court martial*.

Only a century ago, some observers imagined seeing canals on Mars, indicating intelligent life. This inspired endless *War of the Worlds* nightmare scenarios featuring alien invasions.

Even in our modern era, much mystery remains, as conspiracy advocates focus on a curious development: More than half of our space probes to Mars have blown up or vanished—though Mars is closer and thus potentially easier to reach than the other planets (a space probe needs just five months to get to Mars compared with four years to get to Saturn). Of the 30-plus U.S. and Russian spacecraft launched to Mars since 1960, 19 have exploded,

crashed, or malfunctioned. Conspiracy-lovers have pounded on that slim success rate, contending that malevolent Martians do not like our snooping.

Of course, this doesn't explain why some of our craft have been successful. The twin *Viking* probes of 1976 and the *Mars Pathfinder* and *Global Surveyor* missions of the 1990s worked flawlessly, and the recent 2001 *Mars Odyssey* still sends back orbital data. For example, the infamous "face on Mars" is clearly seen as a rocky hillside. Probes reveal a sandy, dusty, hostile landscape that probably had rushing water on it billions of years ago and perhaps more recently.

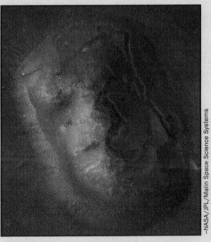

–NASA/JPL/Malin Space Science Systems

Shadows in a rocky hillside create the illusion of eyes, a nose, and a mouth in the "face on Mars."

Got the Urge for Going?

Utopians have been perennially obsessed with the red planet as a possible refuge for human colonists. It's viewed as a virgin land that beckons

adventurers with offers of a new beginning, the final frontier, the Alaska of the solar system. Such dreams derive from Mars's status as the most Earth-like world of our known planets: Mercury and Venus are true hells, more torrid than roaring fireplaces. The planets from Jupiter outward have no solid surface at all until you get to the maybe-planet Pluto, an eternally frozen ice ball.

That leaves Mars. Alas, Mars may be the most terrestrial world, but it's far from visitor-friendly:

■ **The air on Mars is as thin as Earth's at 55,000 feet, where the Concorde flies.**

■ **What little air there is consists almost entirely of carbon dioxide, the gas we exhale.**

■ **Temperatures typically hover at a nasty −80°F (−62°C).**

■ **Human colonies on Mars would be enclosed in synthetic bubbles; daily life would unfold in an artificial environment.**

According to NASA's best estimates, any hands-on Martian endeavors lie 20 to 30 years in the future. So for now, our dreams of traveling to Mars will continue. But—count on it—someday we *will* make that trip. □□

Bob Berman, the host of *Skywindow* on National Public Radio, is the author of *Cosmic Adventure* (HarperTrade, 2000) and *Secrets of the Night Sky* (HarperCollins, 1996). His next book, *Strange Universe* (Henry Holt and Company), is due out soon.

EARTH-TO-MARS EXPRESS
To learn more about Mars, go to **www .almanac.com** and click on **Article Links 2003.**

SCIATICA RELIEF!

If you want to get relief from Sciatica and have suffered symptoms such as: pain in the buttocks, pain in lower back, pain shooting down one or both legs, or numbness in your legs or feet, you should get a copy of the new book, *The Sciatica Relief Handbook*. The book covers the latest natural, alternative and medical solutions to sciatica. The book reveals how virtually everyone can put an end to sciatica symptoms thanks to new understandings of this problem.

Over 165 million people experience sciatica and lower back discomfort. Many people are needlessly suffering because they are not aware of new ways to put an end to this problem. This book is of vital importance to every person suffering from sciatica or lower back pain.

The book tells you what causes sciatica symptoms, how to alleviate the symptoms and how to prevent and protect yourself from future sciatica and lower back problems. You'll learn about new natural remedies and treatments and find out how and why they work—without unnecessary drugs or surgery.

You'll discover: ● how a simple exercise brings dramatic relief ● specific pressure points that soothe the sciatic nerve ● vital tips to prevent possible serious problems ● what you must know about the mineral potassium ● how certain foods promote healing of the sciatic nerve.

The book explains all about the sciatic nerve, the various ways it may become inflamed and cause pain, how to find out specifically what causes distress (you may be surprised), and what to do and what not to do to prevent flare-ups.

Get all the facts. Put an end to sciatica and lower back pain once and for all. *The Sciatica Relief Handbook* is available for only $14.95 *(plus $3 P&H)*. To order, send your name and address with check or money order to United Research Publishers, Dept. OFK-04; 132 N. El Camino Real #T; Encinitas CA 92024. For VISA or MasterCard, send card number and expiration date. You may return the book within 90 days for a refund if not satisfied.

www.unitedresearchpubs.com

IRRITABLE BOWEL SYNDROME
NATURAL FREEDOM FROM SYMPTOMS

If you suffer from Irritable Bowel Syndrome (IBS) and experience constipation, bloating, diarrhea, gas, stomach cramps, heartburn, pain and discomfort, you should know about a new book, *The Irritable Bowel Syndrome & Gastrointestinal Solutions Handbook*.

This book gives you facts on new up-to-date, all-natural, and alternative ways to stop IBS and gastrointestinal problems. You'll learn all about these new measures and how to beat these problems once and for all—without drugs or surgery.

You'll discover what you can do to avoid Irritable Bowel, colon and digestive problems, what foods promote healing and what to avoid, a safe, natural gel readily available at health food stores that flushes out toxins and clears inflammation, what you should know about peppermint oil and gluten—and why IBS is so often misdiagnosed by doctors. The book reveals simple, natural remedies that are helping thousands overcome IBS every day.

Here's what satisfied readers of the book report: Mrs. Castor said, "after 2 years of searching for relief I ordered your book and finally found relief." Mr. Allen wrote that, thanks to the book, he has been free from IBS symptoms for six months. Mr. Swanson said his wife has been bothered by IBS for years. "She followed your simple tips in the book and is much improved. Our doctor wants a copy."

Many people are putting up with IBS, stomach and digestive problems because they are unaware of new, natural treatments revealed in this book.

Get all the facts. This book is available for only $14.95 *(plus $3 P&H)*. To order, send your name and address with a check or money order to: United Research Publishers, Dept. OFS-08; 132 N. El Camino Real #T; Encinitas CA 92024. For MasterCard or VISA send card number and expiration date. You may return the book within 90 days for a refund if not completely satisfied.

www.unitedresearchpubs.com

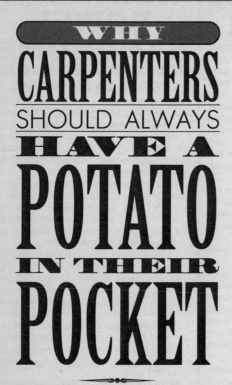

WHY CARPENTERS SHOULD ALWAYS HAVE A POTATO IN THEIR POCKET

FOOD REMEDIES FOR SOME OF LIFE'S LITTLE MALADIES

by Steve Calechman

Most people think of a potato as a satisfying and nutritious, yet unexciting, side dish. Rarely does one of its more powerful qualities ever get mentioned: for instance, that it's a remedy for splinters.

It's true. Potatoes can help to extract buried splinters. And the potato isn't the only food that has medicinal effects. Cabbages, onions, and beef are not only good for you, but they can make you feel good—or, at least, better—if you get burned, bitten, or bruised. So read on and remember: Next time you need relief, check the kitchen pantry before you rummage through your medicine chest.

A SPUD FOR
SPLINTERS

Carpenters, woodworkers, and handypersons, listen up! Your hammer and nails are important, but don't forget to put a potato on your tool belt. It can help pull out splinters that are embedded too deep in your skin to extricate with a needle and tweezers, says Konrad Kail, a naturopathic physician in Phoenix, Arizona. Peel and wash a thumb-size piece of a white or red potato, and grate it. (Don't use a sweet potato; it contains too much sugar and is too moist to attract liquid.) Place the potato gratings into a piece of gauze bandage. Wrap the gauze so the potato bits won't fall out, and tape it to the area over the splinter. Leave it on for at least a few hours, or overnight if possible, so the potato has the chance to dry. As it dries, it draws fluid to it,

Kail says. In fact, the potato doesn't draw out a sliver of wood; it attracts body fluids, and that moisture carries the splinter to the surface, making it easier to remove.

Grated carrot can be mixed in with the potato, because it has the same drawing effects, and its beta-carotene helps heal skin and wounds, says Kail.

CABBAGE FOR
BURNS

When short-order cooks singe their skin, they grab a couple of cabbage leaves—and so should you. "Cabbage is high in glutamine, which helps new cells grow and protects against infection," says Thom Kruzel, a naturopathic physician at Southwest College

of Naturopathic Medicine & Health Sciences in Tempe, Arizona. Take one or two leaves, put them into a blender, add enough water to moisten the leaves, and grind them up. The grinding will extract the juice that contains the glutamine. Put that paste directly onto the burned area, cover it with a piece of gauze, and secure it with tape. Or wrap the paste in gauze, tie it off, and secure it to the burned area with tape. If you choose the latter method, squeeze some of the cabbage juice through the gauze onto the affected area. Leave the cabbage on for 30 minutes to an hour, Kruzel says.

If you don't have a blender, soften the leaves in a pan or bowl of hot water; this has the same effect as grinding them. Then tear the leaves into small pieces, wrap them in a piece of gauze, and apply it to the burned area, giving a squeeze to release some of the juice. Leave the cabbage in place for 30 minutes to an hour.

AN ONION FOR
INSECT BITES

Whether you're a postal letter carrier or a weekend gardener, you're bound to get a few bug bites. You could resign yourself to getting bitten and just toughing it out. Or you could have an onion nearby. "Onions have antimicrobial properties, which reduce infection, and they contain flavonoids, which promote healing," says Richard Maurer, a naturopathic physician in Portland, Oregon. Onions also contain sulfur compounds, which break down the venom and pull

out the toxin, thereby reducing inflammation, says Jared Zeff, a naturopathic physician also in Portland. Put a slice of onion over the bite and leave it on for 30 minutes to an hour. You could also grate the onion to release more of the juice.  "In that case, put the juice onto the affected area, tape a piece of gauze over it, and leave it on for 15 minutes," Maurer says. The stronger the onion is, the more effective it will be. Yellow and red onions are best. Sweet onions, such as Vidalias, contain less sulfur and antimicrobials.

BEEF FOR
BRUISES

Hollywood movies aren't always 100 percent accurate, but they get it right when they show a boxer holding a piece of steak against his black eye after a fight. By applying a raw beefsteak to a bruise, you can reduce  inflammation. Leave it on for an hour; as the meat deteriorates, it releases protease, which destroys the blood clot and helps speed up healing, says Kruzel.　*(continued)*

No beef? Put a piece of pine-apple over the bruise, wrap the area with a gauze bandage, and leave it on for an hour. Pineapple contains bromelain, a collection of enzymes that breaks down protein and de-stroys the clot, Kruzel says.

OATMEAL FOR
ITCHING

Campers, hikers, and lovers of na-ture, here's a tip: Have some oat-meal handy if a walk in the woods leaves you scratching. "Oatmeal has a calming effect on the skin and can help with most kinds of itching," says Maurer.

For a general treatment at home, put a fistful of rolled oats into a thin sock or a piece of gauze, tie it off, and let it float in a bathtub of lukewarm water like a tea bag. Every so often, squeeze the bag, so that the oatmeal's white, milky substance (cellulose) gets into the water. That's the active ingredient that helps with the itching. Then get into the tub and soak for 15 to 20 minutes.

For localized itching on the trail or at home, you can make an oat-meal bag as above, run warm wa-ter through it, and squeeze the milky substance onto the affected area, leaving it on until it dries, advises Kruzel. □ □

Steve Calechman frequently writes on natural health subjects for *Men's Health* and other magazines.

GOT HEARTBURN OR HICCUPS?
Relief is just a swallow away: Go to **www.almanac.com** and click on **Article Links 2003**.

Get Out Your Camera...

... and show us how you use *The Old Farmer's Almanac*. Send us your picture with the Almanac:

- **checking the weather**
- **setting seeds or plants in your garden**
- **cooking up a winning recipe**
- **scanning the sky for a peak at a planet**
- **reading and relaxing in your easy chair**
- **or . . . surprise us!**

☞ We'll put your picture on our Web site, **www.almanac.com,** and let the world know how truly "new, useful, and entertaining" this Almanac is. Mail pictures, with the name(s) of the peo-ple photographed, to The Old Farmer's Almanac, P.O. Box 520, Dublin, NH 03444; or e-mail scans to **almanac@yankeepub.com** (subject: Photos). Submission conveys permission to use. To ensure return, include a self-addressed, stamped envelope. Thanks! And remember to smile!

Long-term care coverage
Who needs it; how to find the right policy

Shop Smart

Americans are living longer than ever and are now facing the important decision of whether to purchase long-term care insurance. Most people buy this coverage to protect assets, preserve independence and provide quality care. A growing number of younger people are buying it to help their aging parents.

In general, long-term care protection makes sense for those with assets of at least $75,000 (excluding your home and car) and an annual income of at least $25,000 to $35,000.

With over 100 policies on the market—each with different benefits, premiums, exclusions and application requirements—it pays to comparison shop. According to respected *Money Magazine* financial editor, Jean Chatzky, "Your best bet is to get quotes from at least three companies."[1] In addition, you should consider a policy with at least a three-year term—the average time people need care.

Look for a daily benefit that would cover the average daily nursing-facility cost in your area. The national average is $125 ($46,000 per year), but in some areas it can run twice as much.[2]

Look for an elimination period (the time before your benefits begin) of 90 days. Remember, this is catastrophic coverage. Most people who need the insurance can afford the cost of care for three months. Plus, this approach lowers your cost—in some cases, by as much as 30% per year. Equally important, insist on insurers rated "A" or better by A.M. Best and "strong" by Standard & Poor's and Moody's.

If you'd like to receive three quotes with just one call, Long-Term Care Quote will provide them—free of charge. The company—which has been recommended in *Consumers Digest*, *Kiplinger's* and on NBC's *The Early Today Show*—will ask for basic information on your age, health and location, then shop up to 17 top-rated carriers on your behalf. You'll get details and quotes on the three most suitable policies for you, plus a copy of *The Consumer's Guide to Long-Term Care Insurance*.

To request your free Information Kit and personalized quotes, either write to Long-Term Care Quote, 600 W. Ray Road, Bldg. D4, Chandler, AZ 85225, visit www.LongTermCareQuote.com or call 1-800-587-3279.

Please provide date of birth on written requests. [1] *USA Weekend*, 05/15/98; [2] Health Insurance Association of America, 2000; Writing agent Robert W. Davis, CA License #0B78024. All inquiries kept strictly confidential.

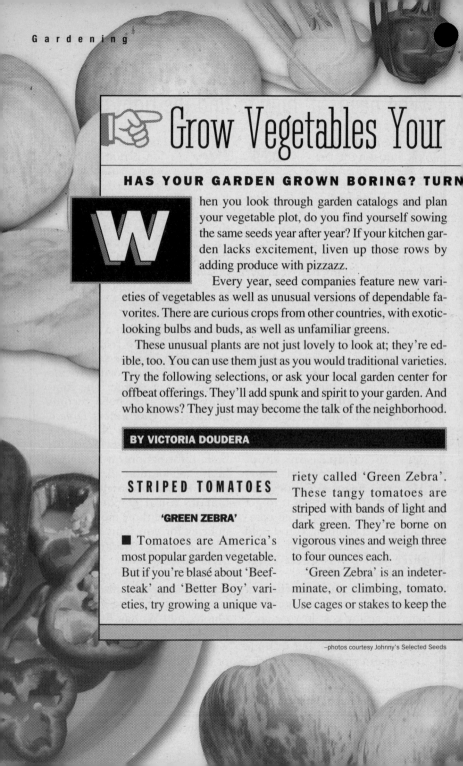

☞ Grow Vegetables Your

HAS YOUR GARDEN GROWN BORING? TURN

When you look through garden catalogs and plan your vegetable plot, do you find yourself sowing the same seeds year after year? If your kitchen garden lacks excitement, liven up those rows by adding produce with pizzazz.

Every year, seed companies feature new varieties of vegetables as well as unusual versions of dependable favorites. There are curious crops from other countries, with exotic-looking bulbs and buds, as well as unfamiliar greens.

These unusual plants are not just lovely to look at; they're edible, too. You can use them just as you would traditional varieties. Try the following selections, or ask your local garden center for offbeat offerings. They'll add spunk and spirit to your garden. And who knows? They just may become the talk of the neighborhood.

BY VICTORIA DOUDERA

STRIPED TOMATOES

'GREEN ZEBRA'

■ Tomatoes are America's most popular garden vegetable. But if you're blasé about 'Beefsteak' and 'Better Boy' varieties, try growing a unique variety called 'Green Zebra'. These tangy tomatoes are striped with bands of light and dark green. They're borne on vigorous vines and weigh three to four ounces each.

'Green Zebra' is an indeterminate, or climbing, tomato. Use cages or stakes to keep the

–photos courtesy Johnny's Selected Seeds

Neighbors Won't Recognize

EADS WITH THESE ODD VARIETIES.

plants from taking over your garden and to keep fruit off the soil. Be sure not to damage the roots when you insert stakes.

PICK AND EAT. 'Green Zebra' is ripe just as the green fruit starts getting a yellow blush, accentuating the dark-green stripes. Pick the tomatoes as they ripen, using a slight twist of the wrist or sharp scissors to cut the stem.

Enjoy these tomatoes in salads—alone or mixed with red, yellow, orange, and pink varieties.

STRIPED TOMATOES

WHITE EGGPLANTS

'SNOWY', 'WHITE EGG', 'OSTEREI'

■ Picture an eggplant, and a dark-purple vegetable will probably come to mind. Yet "egg" plant is so named because some early types were white. Today,

WHITE EGGPLANTS

(c o n t i n u e d)

authentic-looking versions of the fruit have a gourmet mystique.

PICK AND EAT. Test the ripeness of eggplants by pressing down on the flesh with your thumb. If the skin of the fruit presses in but bounces back out, it's ripe. If you can't press it in, it's not ready yet. If it gives under thumb pressure and does not bounce back, it's overripe. Clip the fruit stem with sharp shears, and pick the fruits regularly to keep production high.

White eggplant has a mild, non-bitter taste. It's great grilled, as an accompaniment to spicy sauces, and in classic dishes like ratatouille and eggplant parmigiana.

YELLOW CUCUMBERS

YELLOW CUCUMBERS

'LEMON APPLE', 'LEMON'

■ Here's a weird but wonderful variation on a classic summer vegetable. Strong vines bear round or lemon-shaped yellow fruits with a mild, pleasant cucumber flavor. Although they seem new and refreshing, these are actually heirloom varieties that your great-grandmother may have planted.

PICK AND EAT. Lemon cucumbers are ready about 60 days after seeding, and you can expect up to a six-week harvest period. Pick the cucumbers regularly, every other day, during this time. They're ready when they are young and firm but filled out, and when they have a bright, lemon-yellow hue. Remove overripe or damaged fruits to encourage the plant to continue production.

Slice and enjoy these sunny cukes in salads, in tea sandwiches, or with a zippy yogurt dip.

COCOA-COLORED PEPPERS

'SWEET CHOCOLATE', 'PEPPOURRI CHOCOLATE', 'CHOCOLATE BEAUTY HYBRID'

■ These rich-brown bell peppers are prized not only for their unusual color but also for their shiny, smooth skin and fresh, crisp flavor.

(c o n t i n u e d)

COCOA-COLORED PEPPERS

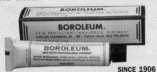

PICK AND EAT. These beauties will start off green and ripen gradually to a rich chocolate color. Pick them when they are fully mature—about three inches by six inches—and you just may get a pound or two per plant.

Enjoy all these varieties cooked or raw; either way, they'll keep their brown color.

PURPLE KOHLRABI

'EARLY PURPLE VIENNA', 'PURPLE VIENNA', 'KOLIBRI'

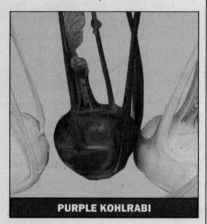
PURPLE KOHLRABI

■ Kohlrabi is the strangest-looking veggie around—a swollen, above-the-ground bulb-shaped plant with stems and leaves that shoot out like skinny arms and legs. It's popular in Asia and central Europe, especially in Germany, where it's dished up with a flavorful cream sauce. (The German word *kohlrabi* means "cabbage turnip.") The purple varieties boast firm flesh with a fruity taste, which admirers have likened to radishes, artichokes, cabbages, and, yes, turnips.

PICK AND EAT. Kohlrabi should be picked when the fruits are golf-ball size, about two inches in diameter. In addition to the bulbous fruit, the leaves (first remove the tough ribs) and the stems are edible.

Steam or sauté the leaves; the stems can be eaten raw or prepared in recipes calling for turnips. Use young purple kohlrabi raw in dips and salads.

MINIATURE CABBAGES

'BABY HEAD', 'ARROWHEAD'

■ These diminutive cabbages are about half the girth of a normal cabbage, thus taking up less space in the garden.

PICK AND EAT. Pick miniature cabbages when they have made a small rounded head about the size of a softball.

Cabbage is a versatile veggie. Mini varieties are delicious raw in salads. Chop it up as well for soups, main dishes such as corned beef and cabbage, and coleslaw.

MINIATURE CABBAGES

(c o n t i n u e d)

Now Get 200 U.S. Postage Stamps – up to 100 years old! *Only $2*

200 historic United States postage stamps are yours for only $2.

Hard to find and worth much more, this collection is a real value. Each cancelled stamp tells a piece of America's story – the Presidents, patriots and places that make our country the greatest.

These stamps are history you hold in your hands, and up to 100 years old!

Send today and also receive special collector's information and pricelists along with other interesting offers on approval. Your satisfaction is guaranteed.

Giant Grabbag of U.S. Stamps

☑**Yes!** Please send me the Giant Grabbag of postally used United States stamps. Enclosed is $2. My satisfaction is guaranteed. Limit one.

Name _____

Address_____

City/State/Zip_____

Please send $2 with coupon to:
Mystic Stamp Company, Dept. 5A440
9700 Mill Street, Camden, NY 13316

HOW TO GROW STRANGE VEGGIES

	WHEN TO START SEEDS	HOW TO SOW	WHEN TO TRANSPLANT
HEAT-LOVING PLANTS			
STRIPED TOMATOES: 'Green Zebra'	Indoors, 6 weeks before the last expected frost	In flats or peat pots, ¼ inch deep; repot into 2- to 3-inch pots when the first true leaves develop	When seedlings are 4 to 6 inches tall and danger of frost has passed
WHITE EGGPLANTS: 'Snowy' 'White Egg' 'Osterei'	Indoors, 8 weeks before the last expected frost; seeds germinate best at about 80°F; will sprout in about a week at this temperature	In flats or peat pots, about ¼ inch deep	When soil is warm and danger of frost has passed
YELLOW CUCUMBERS: 'Lemon Apple' 'Lemon'	Indoors, 5 weeks before the last expected frost	In individual peat pots, about 1 inch deep	When soil is warm and danger of frost has passed
COCOA-COLORED PEPPERS: 'Sweet Chocolate' 'Peppourri Chocolate' 'Chocolate Beauty Hybrid'	Indoors, 8 weeks before the last expected frost	In individual peat pots, about ¼ inch deep	When soil is warm and danger of frost has passed
COOL-SEASON PLANTS			
PURPLE KOHLRABI: 'Early Purple Vienna' 'Purple Vienna' 'Kolibri'	Indoors in midspring for earliest crop	In flats or individual peat pots, ¼ to ½ inch deep	In late spring, when soil is tillable and plants are 4 to 6 weeks old
MINIATURE CABBAGES: 'Baby Head' 'Arrowhead'	Indoors in midspring for earliest crop	In flats or individual peat pots, ½ inch deep	In late spring, when soil is tillable and plants are 4 to 6 weeks old

(Follow the directions on the seed packets if you wish to sow seeds directly into your garden.)

GENERAL ADVICE	SPACE BETWEEN PLANTS	HOW TO FERTILIZE	WHEN TO WATER
For strong and sturdy stems, transplant these tomatoes a little deeper than most, so that the soil comes up to the first set of true leaves	14 inches	With fish emulsion, chicken manure, or a balanced fertilizer when transplanted, when fruits have begun to set, and every 3 weeks thereafter	Evenly and deeply; fairly frequent soakings are ideal
Mulch with black plastic to keep the soil around the plants warm	18 to 24 inches	With fish emulsion, liquid kelp, or a balanced, soluble fertilizer throughout the growing season	Moderately; don't let plants dry out
Use caution when transplanting, as cucumbers do not like having their roots disturbed	24 inches	With a balanced, soluble fertilizer throughout the growing season	Amply, or their flavor may get bitter
Pick the first peppers promptly to encourage more production	12 to 18 inches	With a soluble fertilizer high in phosphorus throughout the growing season	Deeply, as needed throughout the growing season
Provide rich soil with plenty of organic matter	4 inches, to keep fruits golf-ball size	With a balanced, soluble mixture regularly	Deeply, as needed throughout the growing season
Germinate seeds in temperatures above 75°F; after seeds sprout, a temperature of about 60° is fine until transplant time	8 inches, to maintain compact size	With a balanced, soluble mixture often— cabbages are heavy feeders	Regularly and evenly throughout the growing season

(c o n t i n u e d)

GET GROWING!

CONSULT YOUR LOCAL NURSERY, OR CONTACT THESE SOURCES
FOR STRANGE-VEGGIE SEEDS:

■ For 'Snowy' and 'White Egg' eggplants; 'Lemon' cucumber:

W. ATLEE BURPEE & CO.
300 Park Ave., Warminster, PA 18974
800-888-1447
www.burpee.com

■ For 'Osterei' eggplant; 'Lemon' cucumber; 'Sweet Chocolate' pepper:

THE COOK'S GARDEN
P.O. Box 5010, Hodges, SC 29653-5010
800-457-9703
www.cooksgarden.com

■ For 'Green Zebra' tomato; 'Snowy' eggplant; 'Sweet Chocolate' pepper; 'Kolibri' kohlrabi; 'Arrowhead' cabbage:

JOHNNY'S SELECTED SEEDS
184 Foss Hill Rd., RR 1 Box 2580
Albion, ME 04910-9731
207-437-4301
www.johnnyseeds.com

■ For 'Chocolate Beauty Hybrid' pepper; 'Purple Vienna' kohlrabi:

LINDENBERG SEEDS
803 Princess Ave.
Brandon, MB R7A 0P5
204-727-0575
www.lindenbergseeds.mb.ca

■ For 'Peppourri Chocolate' pepper:

OTIS S. TWILLEY SEED CO.
121 Gary Rd., Hodges, SC 29653
800-622-7333
www.twilleyseed.com

■ For 'Chocolate Beauty Hybrid' pepper; 'Baby Head' cabbage:

SBE SEEDS
3421 Bream St., Gautier, MS 39553
800-336-2064
www.seedman.com

■ For 'Early Purple Vienna' kohlrabi:

STOKES
P.O. Box 548, Buffalo, NY 14240-0548
Canadian address:
P.O. Box 10, 39 James St.
St. Catharines, ON L2R 6R6

800-396-9238
www.stokeseeds.com

■ For 'Lemon Apple' cucumber; 'Early Purple Vienna' kohlrabi:

THE VICTORY SEED COMPANY
P.O. Box 192, Molalla, OR 97038
503-829-3126
www.victoryseeds.com

GROUND RULES
To learn more about starting seedlings, hardening off your plants, and prepping your soil, go to www.almanac.com and click on **Article Links 2003.**

Frosts and Growing Seasons

Courtesy of National Climatic Center

■ Dates given are normal averages for a light freeze (32°F); local weather and topography may cause considerable variations. The possibility of frost occurring after the spring dates and before the fall dates is 50 percent. The classification of freeze temperatures is usually based on their effect on plants, with the following commonly accepted categories: **Light freeze:** 29° to 32°F—tender plants killed. **Moderate freeze:** 25° to 28°F—widely destructive effect on most vegetation. **Severe freeze:** 24°F and colder—heavy damage to most plants.

City	State	Growing Season (days)	Last Spring Frost	First Fall Frost	City	State	Growing Season (days)	Last Spring Frost	First Fall Frost
Mobile	AL	272	Feb. 27	Nov. 26	North Platte	NE	136	May 11	Sept. 24
Juneau	AK	133	May 16	Sept. 26	Las Vegas	NV	259	Mar. 7	Nov. 21
Phoenix	AZ	308	Feb. 5	Dec. 15	Concord	NH	121	May 23	Sept. 22
Tucson	AZ	273	Feb. 28	Nov. 29	Newark	NJ	219	Apr. 4	Nov. 10
Pine Bluff	AR	234	Mar. 19	Nov. 8	Carlsbad	NM	223	Mar. 29	Nov. 7
Eureka	CA	324	Jan. 30	Dec. 15	Los Alamos	NM	157	May 8	Oct. 13
Sacramento	CA	289	Feb. 14	Dec. 1	Albany	NY	144	May 7	Sept. 29
San Francisco	CA	*	*	*	Syracuse	NY	170	Apr. 28	Oct. 16
Denver	CO	157	May 3	Oct. 8	Fayetteville	NC	212	Apr. 2	Oct. 31
Hartford	CT	167	Apr. 25	Oct. 10	Bismarck	ND	129	May 14	Sept. 20
Wilmington	DE	198	Apr. 13	Oct. 29	Akron	OH	168	May 3	Oct. 18
Miami	FL	*	*	*	Cincinnati	OH	195	Apr. 14	Oct. 27
Tampa	FL	338	Jan. 28	Jan. 3	Lawton	OK	217	Apr. 1	Nov. 5
Athens	GA	224	Mar. 28	Nov. 8	Tulsa	OK	218	Mar. 30	Nov. 4
Savannah	GA	250	Mar. 10	Nov. 15	Pendleton	OR	188	Apr. 15	Oct. 21
Boise	ID	153	May 8	Oct. 9	Portland	OR	217	Apr. 3	Nov. 7
Chicago	IL	187	Apr. 22	Oct. 26	Carlisle	PA	182	Apr. 20	Oct. 20
Springfield	IL	185	Apr. 17	Oct. 19	Williamsport	PA	168	Apr. 29	Oct. 15
Indianapolis	IN	180	Apr. 22	Oct. 20	Kingston	RI	144	May 8	Sept. 30
South Bend	IN	169	May 1	Oct. 18	Charleston	SC	253	Mar. 11	Nov. 20
Atlantic	IA	141	May 9	Sept. 28	Columbia	SC	211	Apr. 4	Nov. 2
Cedar Rapids	IA	161	Apr. 29	Oct. 7	Rapid City	SD	145	May 7	Sept. 29
Topeka	KS	175	Apr. 21	Oct. 14	Memphis	TN	228	Mar. 23	Nov. 7
Lexington	KY	190	Apr. 17	Oct. 25	Nashville	TN	207	Apr. 5	Oct. 29
Monroe	LA	242	Mar. 9	Nov. 7	Amarillo	TX	197	Apr. 14	Oct. 29
New Orleans	LA	288	Feb. 20	Dec. 5	Denton	TX	231	Mar. 25	Nov. 12
Portland	ME	143	May 10	Sept. 30	San Antonio	TX	265	Mar. 3	Nov. 24
Baltimore	MD	231	Mar. 26	Nov. 13	Cedar City	UT	134	May 20	Oct. 2
Worcester	MA	172	Apr. 27	Oct. 17	Spanish Fork	UT	156	May 8	Oct. 12
Lansing	MI	140	May 13	Sept. 30	Burlington	VT	142	May 11	Oct. 1
Marquette	MI	159	May 12	Oct. 19	Norfolk	VA	239	Mar. 23	Nov. 17
Duluth	MN	122	May 21	Sept. 21	Richmond	VA	198	Apr. 10	Oct. 26
Willmar	MN	152	May 4	Oct. 4	Seattle	WA	232	Mar. 24	Nov. 11
Columbus	MS	215	Mar. 27	Oct. 29	Spokane	WA	153	May 4	Oct. 5
Vicksburg	MS	250	Mar. 13	Nov. 18	Parkersburg	WV	175	Apr. 25	Oct. 18
Jefferson City	MO	173	Apr. 26	Oct. 16	Green Bay	WI	143	May 12	Oct. 2
Fort Peck	MT	146	May 5	Sept. 28	Janesville	WI	164	Apr. 28	Oct. 10
Helena	MT	122	May 18	Sept. 18	Casper	WY	123	May 22	Sept. 22
Blair	NE	165	Apr. 27	Oct. 10	*Frosts do not occur every year.				

Outdoor Planting Table
2 0 0 3

The best time to plant flowers and vegetables that bear crops *above ground* is during the *light* of the Moon; that is, from the day the Moon is new to the day it is full. Flowering bulbs and vegetables that bear crops *below ground* should be planted during the *dark* of the Moon; that is, from the day after it is full to the day before it is new again. The Moon Favorable columns at right give these days, which are based on the Moon's phases for 2003 and the safe periods for planting in areas that receive frost. Consult **page 113** for dates of frosts and lengths of growing seasons. See the **Left-Hand Calendar Pages 44–70** for the exact days of the new and full Moons.

Aboveground Crops Marked (*)
(E) means Early   (L) means Late
Map shading corresponds to shading of date columns.

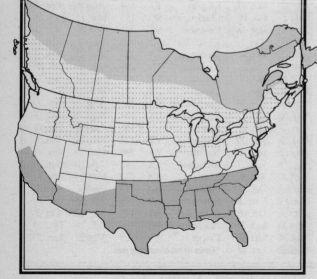

* Barley	
* Beans	(E)
	(L)
Beets	(E)
	(L)
* Broccoli plants	(E)
	(L)
* Brussels sprouts	
* Cabbage plants	
Carrots	(E)
	(L)
* Cauliflower plants	(E)
	(L)
* Celery plants	(E)
	(L)
* Collards	(E)
	(L)
* Corn, sweet	(E)
	(L)
* Cucumbers	
* Eggplant plants	
* Endive	(E)
	(L)
* Flowers	
* Kale	(E)
	(L)
Leek plants	
* Lettuce	
* Muskmelons	
Onion sets	
* Parsley	
Parsnips	
* Peas	(E)
	(L)
* Pepper plants	
Potatoes	
* Pumpkins	
Radishes	(E)
	(L)
* Spinach	(E)
	(L)
* Squashes	
Sweet potatoes	
* Swiss chard	
* Tomato plants	
Turnips	(E)
	(L)
* Watermelons	
* Wheat, spring	
* Wheat, winter	

Planting Dates	Moon Favorable	Planting Dates	Moon Favorable	Planting Dates	Moon Favorable	Planting Dates	Moon Favorable
2/15-3/7	2/15-16, 3/2-7	3/15-4/7	3/15-18, 4/1-7	5/15-6/21	5/15, 5/31-6/14	6/1-30	6/1-14, 6/29-30
3/15-4/7	3/15-18, 4/1-7	4/15-30	4/15-16	5/7-6/21	5/7-15, 5/31-6/14	5/30-6/15	5/31-6/14
8/7-31	8/27-31	7/1-21	7/1-13	6/15-7/15	6/29-7/13	—	—
2/7-28	2/17-28	3/15-4/3	3/19-31	5/1-15	—	5/25-6/10	5/25-30
9/1-30	9/11-24	8/15-31	8/15-26	7/15-8/15	7/15-28, 8/13-15	6/15-7/8	6/15-28
2/15-3/15	2/15-16, 3/2-15	3/7-31	3/7-18	5/15-31	5/31	6/1-25	6/1-14
9/7-30	9/25-30	8/1-20	8/1-12	6/15-7/7	6/29-7/7	—	—
2/11-3/20	2/11-16, 3/2-18	3/7-4/15	3/7-18, 4/1-15	5/15-31	5/31	6/1-25	6/1-14
2/11-3/20	2/11-16, 3/2-18	3/7-4/15	3/7-18, 4/1-15	5/15-31	5/31	6/1-25	6/1-14
2/15-3/7	2/17-3/1	3/7-31	3/19-31	5/15-31	5/16-30	5/25-6/10	5/25-30
8/1-9/7	8/13-26	7/7-31	7/14-28	6/15-7/21	6/15-28, 7/14-21	6/15-7/8	6/15-28
2/15-3/7	2/15-16, 3/2-7	3/15-4/7	3/15-18, 4/1-7	5/15-31	5/31	6/1-25	6/1-14
8/7-31	8/27-31	7/1-8/7	7/1-13, 7/29-8/7	6/15-7/21	6/29-7/13	—	—
2/15-28	2/15-16	3/7-31	3/7-18	5/15-6/30	5/31-6/14, 6/29-30	6/1-30	6/1-14, 6/29-30
9/15-30	9/25-30	8/15-9/7	8/27-9/7	7/15-8/15	7/29-8/12	—	—
2/11-3/20	2/11-16, 3/2-18	3/7-4/7	3/7-18, 4/1-7	5/15-31	5/31	6/1-25	6/1-14
9/7-30	9/25-30	8/15-31	8/27-31	7/1-8/7	7/29-8/7	—	—
3/15-31	3/15-18	4/1-17	4/1-16	5/10-6/15	5/10-15, 5/31-6/14	5/30-6/20	5/31-6/14
8/7-31	8/27-31	7/7-21	7/7-13	6/15-30	6/29-30		
3/7-4/15	3/7-18, 4/1-15	4/7-5/15	4/7-16, 5/1-15	5/7-6/20	5/7-15, 5/31-6/14	5/30-6/15	5/31-6/14
3/7-4/15	3/7-18, 4/1-15	4/7-5/15	4/7-16, 5/1-15	6/1-30	6/1-14, 6/29-30	6/15-30	6/29-30
2/15-3/20	2/15-16, 3/2-18	4/7-5/15	4/7-16, 5/1-15	5/15-31	5/31	6/1-25	6/1-14
8/15-9/7	8/27-9/7	7/15-8/15	7/29-8/12	6/7-30	6/7-14, 6/29-30		
3/15-4/7	3/15-18, 4/1-7	4/15-30	4/15-16	5/7-6/21	5/7-15, 5/31-6/14	6/1-30	6/1-14, 6/29-30
2/11-3/20	2/11-16, 3/2-18	3/7-4/7	3/7-18, 4/1-7	5/15-31	5/31	6/1-15	6/1-14
9/7-30	9/25-30	8/15-31	8/27-31	7/1-8/7	7/1-13, 7/29-8/7	6/25-7/15	6/29-7/13
2/15-4/15	2/17-3/1, 3/19-31	3/7-4/7	3/19-31	5/15-31	5/16-30	6/1-25	6/15-25
2/15-3/7	2/15-16, 3/2-7	3/1-31	3/2-18	5/15-6/30	5/31-6/14, 6/29-30	6/1-30	6/1-14, 6/29-30
3/15-4/7	3/15-18, 4/1-7	4/15-5/7	4/15-16, 5/1-7	5/15-6/30	5/31-6/14, 6/29-30	6/1-30	6/1-14, 6/29-30
2/1-28	2/17-28	3/1-31	3/19-31	5/15-6/7	5/16-30	6/1-25	6/15-25
2/20-3/15	3/2-15	3/1-31	3/2-18	5/15-31	5/31	6/1-15	6/1-14
1/15-2/4	1/19-31	3/7-31	3/19-31	4/1-30	4/17-30	5/10-31	5/16-30
1/15-2/7	1/15-18, 2/1-7	3/7-31	3/7-18	4/15-5/7	4/15-16, 5/1-7	5/15-31	5/31
9/15-30	9/25-30	8/7-31	8/7-12, 8/27-31	7/15-31	7/29-31	7/10-25	7/10-13
3/1-20	3/2-18	4/1-30	4/1-16	5/15-6/30	5/31-6/14, 6/29-30	6/1-30	6/1-14, 6/29-30
2/10-28	2/17-28	4/1-30	4/17-30	5/1-31	5/16-30	6/1-25	6/15-25
3/7-20	3/7-18	4/23-5/15	5/1-15	5/15-31	5/31	6/1-30	6/1-14, 6/29-30
1/21-3/1	1/21-31, 2/17-3/1	3/7-31	3/19-31	4/15-30	4/17-30	5/15-6/5	5/16-30
10/1-21	10/11-21	9/7-30	9/11-24	8/15-31	8/15-26	7/10-31	7/14-28
2/7-3/15	2/7-16, 3/2-15	3/15-4/20	3/15-18, 4/1-16	5/15-31	5/31	6/1-25	6/1-14
10/1-21	10/1-10	8/1-9/15	8/1-12, 8/27-9/10	7/17-9/7	7/29-8/12, 8/27-9/7	7/20-8/5	7/29-8/5
3/15-4/15	3/15-18, 4/1-15	4/15-30	4/15-16	5/15-6/15	5/31-6/14	6/1-30	6/1-14, 6/29-30
3/23-4/6	3/23-31	4/21-5/2	4/21-30	5/15-6/15	5/16-30, 6/15	6/1-30	6/15-28
2/7-3/15	2/7-16, 3/2-15	3/15-4/15	3/15-18, 4/1-15	5/1-31	5/1-15, 5/31	5/15-31	5/31
3/7-20	3/7-18	4/7-30	4/7-16	5/15-31	5/31	6/1-15	6/1-14
1/20-2/15	1/20-31	3/15-31	3/19-31	4/7-30	4/17-30	5/10-31	5/16-30
9/1-10/15	9/11-24, 10/11-15	8/1-20	8/13-20	7/1-8/15	7/14-28, 8/13-15	—	—
3/15-4/7	3/15-18, 4/1-7	4/15-5/7	4/15-16, 5/1-7	5/15-6/30	5/31-6/14, 6/29-30	6/1-30	6/1-14, 6/29-30
2/15-28	2/15-16	3/1-20	3/2-18	4/7-30	4/7-16	5/15-6/10	5/31-6/10
10/15-12/7	10/25-11/8, 11/23-12/7	9/15-10/20	9/25-10/10	8/11-9/15	8/27-9/10	8/5-30	8/5-12, 8/27-30

The Man Who
Invented
PARKS

For many 19th-century city dwellers, there were no public parks—no places to stroll, to play, or to enjoy nature. Urban planners laid out America's rapidly growing cities in grids for industrial and economic efficiency. Recreational green space was a low priority. One man changed all that.

by George Homsy

Frederick Law Olmsted, who died 100 years ago, became America's first and greatest landscape architect—almost by accident. For years, he led a self-described "vagabondish and somewhat poetical" life as a surveyor, a bookkeeper, a sailor, a farmer, a mine superintendent, and a journalist. He wandered throughout the pre–Civil War South and wrote extensively for the *New York Times* about the devastating economics of slavery. Later, he co-founded *The Nation* magazine.

Wanting to settle down, and in debt from failed business ventures, Olmsted landed the superintendent's position in 1857 for an undeveloped site that was designated to become New York's Central Park. At the age of 35, he never envisioned actually designing the 700-acre park (later expanded to 843 acres), but an architect named Calvert Vaux convinced him to be his partner for the park's 1858 landscape-design competition. Although the selection of their entry, called

> Olmsted believed that parks preserved health, nurtured democracy, and built community.

Greensward, was a largely political accomplishment, the result was brilliant. The partners' creation—Olmsted's first and most famous—set the standard for public parks throughout the nation.

Olmsted correctly predicted to Central Park's commissioners that "the time [would] come when New York [would] be built up . . . and when the picturesquely varied, rocky formations of [Manhattan] Island [would] have been converted into foundations for rows of monotonous straight streets, and piles of erect, angular buildings." He believed that the lack

CENTRAL PARK.

of space, sunshine, and fresh air would compromise the health of city residents. As a remedy, he wanted to create a haven for "unrestricted movement, the most exhilarating contrast to the walled-in floors or pavements," which the city dwellers were ordinarily confined to, he said, by their homes and businesses.

In Central Park, Olmsted immersed people in scenery. He constructed long pastoral pathways; secluded, picturesque valleys; and dramatic vistas. When officials stipulated that city traffic must pass through the park, he sank the boulevards to hide the vehicles. Just two years after construction began, as many as 100,000 people a day enjoyed Central Park. In 1876, four years before the park was done, property values around it had already jumped ninefold.

Olmsted, c. 1860 *(above)*; an undated architectural drawing of Central Park and an 1872 engraving of the Terrace *(left)*.

-National Park Service, Frederick Law Olmsted National Historic Site

Park commissioners coined the term "landscape architect" for Olmsted. Together, he and Vaux created numerous other projects. After 14 years, the pair amicably dissolved their partnership, though Vaux was reportedly upset over the amount of credit Olmsted received for Central Park.

In addition to preserving the health of city dwellers, Olmsted considered parks a way to nurture democracy and build community. He believed neighborliness "to be a distinct requirement of all human beings, and appropriately provided for." He urged the public to "plant spacious parks in [its] cities, and unloose

[its] gates as wide as the gates of morning to the whole people." Despite this vision, he was often frustrated by designs that took years to grow.

In 1895, Olmsted's failing memory forced him to retire. Three years later, at the age of 76, he was committed to McLean Hospital in Belmont, Massachusetts, for what today would probably be diagnosed as senile dementia. He spent his last days at McLean, whose grounds he had designed three decades before.

Olmsted at Home

While public parks promoted democracy, Olmsted believed that home landscapes "were to facilitate family," says Alan Banks, the supervising park ranger at the Frederick Law Olmsted National Historic Site in Brookline, Massachusetts. "Olmsted believed that people always needed to be surrounded by nature, even in their own home."

Fairsted, Olmsted's home, landscaped to "facilitate family."

In 1883, Olmsted moved his home to Brookline, Massachusetts, to be near friends and his work on Boston's Emerald Necklace chain of parks. His 1.76-acre property, renamed Fairsted after his ancestral home, was probably the only landscape where he had a truly free hand, unencumbered by client demands, funding constraints, and political maneuverings. It is also the best example of how Olmsted translated his large-park concepts into a smaller plot. These are some of the design principles he executed there:

■ **IMITATE NATURE'S UNORDERLY GROWTH HABIT.** "Less wildness and disorder I object to," Olmsted wrote to his son, John Charles. The elder Olmsted hated flower boxes, hedgerows, or any straight lines that he felt merely imitated a city grid. His Brookline landscape looks almost accidental.

■ **COLOR WITH NATURE'S PALETTE.** Olmsted biographer Witold Rybczynski says that "Olmsted actually disliked flowers. His idea of a landscape was really shades of green."

■ **ENHANCE NATURE.** Olmsted liked to embellish nature's design while hiding its shortcomings. At Fairsted, he deepened a natural depression at the front of the house to create a lush grotto, which he named the Hollow.

■ **HIDE THE HOUSE.** Landscapes are often designed to draw attention to a building. Olmsted wanted just the opposite. He strung a wire trellis along the south and east walls of his house and allowed the structure to be swallowed by a thick blanket of vines and creepers.

–photo above: National Park Service, Frederick Law Olmsted National Historic Site

■ **LOOK BEYOND THE LANDSCAPE.** Olmsted always tried to borrow distant views. In an 1888 essay evaluating a suburban parcel, he wrote that "the only valuable landscape resource of the property lies in the distant view eastward from it."

■ **DESIGN FOR SURPRISE.** Winding paths that keep their end points secret were common design elements for Olmsted. At Fairsted, a tightly curving path through the Rock Garden provides a brief passage of scenery as it unwinds unexpectedly into a small meadow, the South Lawn.

A Walk in His Parks

Frederick Law Olmsted designed hundreds of public parks, private estates, college campuses, and suburban developments. Here are ten; to learn more about how these projects illustrate his concepts and influence, go to www.almanac.com and click on Article Links 2003.

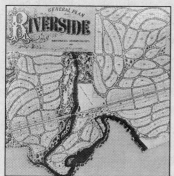 

–illustrations: National Park Service, Frederick Law Olmsted National Historic Site

MOUNTAIN VIEW CEMETERY
Oakland, California, 1864–1865

RIVERSIDE SUBDIVISION (*illustration above, left*)
Riverside, Illinois, 1868–1887

NIAGARA FALLS PARK
Buffalo, New York, 1869–1885

MOUNT ROYAL
Montreal, Quebec, 1873–1893

U.S. CAPITOL GROUNDS
Washington, D.C., 1875–1894

EMERALD NECKLACE (*illustration above, right*)
Boston, Massachusetts, 1880–1896

STANFORD UNIVERSITY
Palo Alto, California, 1886–1914

CHICAGO'S WORLD COLUMBIAN EXPOSITION
Chicago, Illinois, 1888–1893

THE BILTMORE ESTATE
Asheville, North Carolina, 1891–1909

DRUID HILLS SUBDIVISION
Atlanta, Georgia, 1892–1905

□ □

George Homsy writes about the environment, science, and gardening from his home in Canandaigua, New York.

BEWARE *the* WHISPERING WILLOWS

C alled "the whispering one" by the Seneca Indians of North America, and "the tree of enchantment" by the Druids, willows are well known for their beautiful, ground-sweeping branches and the soft rustling of their leaves. From the family Salicaceae, willow species range from the majestic white willow tree, *Salix alba,* named for the white undersides of its leaves and growing to 75 feet, to the humble, swamp-dwelling pussy-willow shrub, *S. discolor,* growing 10 to 18 feet. In northern climates, the catkins (scale-covered furry buds) of the pussy willow are harbingers of spring.

Most willow varieties will grow virtually anywhere in the United States and Canada, from Zone 2 southward. Willows prefer moist or wet soils. If you've got a nice spot by a pond or stream, or you decide to try one of the smaller, shrub-size willows in a wet spot in your yard, you can expect fast and vigorous growth and a life span of 30 to 80 years, depending on the willow variety. Because willows are so shallow-rooted, however, think twice before planting

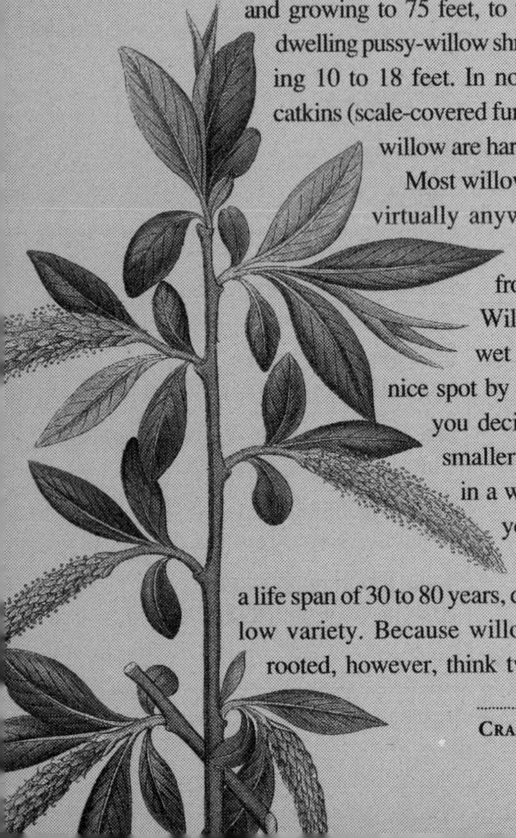

Perhaps you have a small pond or stream on your property and you are picturing a graceful willow grove there. Before you go any further, consider these words of care and caution.

by Martha White

CRACK WILLOW, *S. fragilis*

them in a grassy lawn where you'll want to mow.

Dwarf varieties need no pruning. Those grown for the color of their stems—used in basketry, wicker, and wreaths—should be cut to ground level every second or third year in late winter. Ornamentals such as the weeping willow can be pruned after the catkins go by in the spring. Be as severe as you like, taking at least a third of the old wood. **(continued)**

Thirsty willows not only dry the soil in soggy gardens, but they protect riverbanks from erosion.

BRANCHING OUT

**Lovely to look at, graceful and grand,
but if you're not careful, they'll get out of hand.**

–Anonymous

Ask an arborist how to cultivate a willow and you're apt to hear the word *foolproof*. Any twig or branch of a willow will root easily in moist soil. As long as you avoid dry locations and sandy soils, you can't go wrong.

In a wet spring, you may be able to prune your willows and stick the shoots into the ground to start new trees or shrubs. Alternatively, cut shoots as big around as your thumb, about ten inches long, and root them in a starter medium indoors. Because of a natural rooting hormone produced by willows (and also by dogwoods, poplars, and others), the green twigs and branches can be cut into small pieces and soaked overnight in a gallon or more of water to make a starter liquid for transplanting. Water young seedlings well with this tea one day or so before planting them outside. (This tea also helps other plant cuttings to start rooting.)

Plant willows outside in the fall (Zone 5 and southward) or spring (Zones 2 to 4), once the new roots are strong. Choose a moist, loamy spot with good sun and plenty of room for the roots to wander.

WEEPING
WILLOW,
S. babylonica

THE ROOT OF THE MATTER

Willows are weak, yet they bind other wood.

–George Herbert, priest and poet (1593–1633)

Regarding the proper location for a willow, there are as many opinions as there are landscapers. When we asked Greg Wilkerson, co-owner of Taylor's Stump & Tree Service, Inc., in Huntley, Illinois, he said, "Willows are a beautiful tree to have next door, in your neighbor's yard, or off by the stream or pond, but not

THE WIDE WORLD OF WILLOWS

By one count, there are more than 400 types of willow trees or shrubs found worldwide, except in Australia.

Here are some common large willows:

☐ Black willow *(S. nigra)* is primarily a lowland tree and is susceptible to storm damage, although even damaged trees grow back quickly. With its nearly black bark, it is often used for baskets or lightweight berry boxes. The Ojibwe Indians used it for fishnets, pouches, and bags.

☐ Weeping willow *(S. babylonica)* is planted ornamentally, but it is being replaced in many parks by golden weeping willow *(S. niobe)*, a similar tree more resistant to blight. Weeping willow is marketed for Zones 6 to 8, but it has succeeded in northern spots up to and including Zone 2.

☐ Crack willow *(S. fragilis)* gets its name from its brittle branches. Some experts say that this is an adaptation to flooding, allowing the tree to release its branches but keep itself rooted during high winds and rain.

These are among the common small willows:

☐ Purple osier *(S. purpurea)* is a popular dwarf shrub, also called basket willow. Osier is the common name for willow wood, prized for fence posts and wattle-and-daub woven fences in the British Isles because of its resistance to rot.

☐ Several other shrub willows, grown for their colorful foliage or bark, are popular as ornamentals. Shining willow *(S. lucida)*, with shiny green foliage, and scarlet willow *(S. alba chermesina)*, with bright orange-red bark, are examples.

☐ Rosemary willow *(S. elaeagnos)* is a shrub-size plant found in Zone 4 and southward, with silvery leaves that resemble rosemary.

☐ Flame willow *(S. 'Flame')* grows up to 20 feet tall and has bright orange-red bark that adds winter interest.

☐ Tricolor willow *(S. cinerea 'Tricolor')* shows variegated leaves of green, white, and yellow.

TRICOLOR WILLOW, *S. cinerea* 'Tricolor'

anywhere near your house, pool, or septic system." Clearly a man who has seen the hazards that this tree can pose, Wilkerson continued, "You don't want [a willow] outside your bedroom window on a windy night. They're prone to blow over. They're brittle, and their limbs break easily." In general, he says, "They grow rapidly. Ice can accumulate on their long leaves. They grow big limbs that sometimes come out perpendicularly; you don't want that near your house. And they're messy, with their leaves and catkins."

WILLOW
WONDERS

☐ Medicinally, willows were prized for the salicin content in their bark (now synthesized as aspirin) as early as the first century A.D.

☐ Dowsers prefer willow branches for finding underground water.

☐ The wood of willows is used to build harps because it gives the best sound.

☐ Forceps made of split willow were used by native tribes in eastern Canada to remove arrowheads embedded in the skin.

☐ Willow-leaf sachets were once traditional "love tokens," a symbol of affection.

☐ The words and music for "Willow Weep for Me" were written by Ann Ronell in 1932.

Joseph O'Brien, a forester and plant pathologist with the USDA Forest Service in St. Paul, Minnesota, dispels a couple of myths about willows and location. On the subject of their propensity to blow over, he disagrees: "Their shallow root system would seem to make them at risk for windthrow, but because they root so prolifically, I don't think that willows pose an inordinately high risk of falling at the ground line. In fact, they probably suffer much less windthrow than many other shallow-rooted species such as the blue spruce."

As for keeping willows at least 100 feet from the house, water system, or septic system because of invasive roots, O'Brien says, "Willows will not damage

COMMON PUSSY WILLOW, *S. discolor*

pipes or foundations that are not already compromised with cracks. The roots of willows, like most other trees, will grow more prolifically where there is water. If your sewer pipes are leaking and there is a willow nearby, the willow will exploit the pipe as a resource for obtaining water, to the detriment of your plumbing budget. Foundations with cracks are also candidates for invasion by the roots of any tree, not just willows. I think that the willow gets a bad reputation. However, it is prudent to avoid planting a willow tree too close to such things, if you don't know for certain that you don't have structural flaws." If you already have a willow close to your water system and everything seems to be fine, it's probably safe to assume you can leave it alone.

On the other hand, if you want to remove a willow, grind the stump to a depth of a foot below the ground surface, then cover what remains with dirt so it doesn't sprout anew. Burn or bury any logs or pruned branches. Otherwise, you'll find your compost pile sprouting with willows, and you may be the one who's weeping. □□

Martha White, author of *Traditional Home Remedies*, has been a contributor to *Old Farmer's Almanac* publications since 1991.

WILLOW WOES

A problem with a willow tree can bring tears to your eyes. To learn how to avoid pests and minimize problems, go to **www.almanac.com** and click on **Article Links 2003.**

The SCARY TRUTH ABOUT
EARWIGS

They've been around for more than 200 million years, so we'd better get used to them.

Have you noticed those three-quarter-inch-long, reddish-brown bugs with tails that look like forceps? Earwigs seem to be wriggling their way in increasing numbers throughout our lawns, gardens, and sometimes even our homes.

Some people think there are more earwigs than ever. "Two things are happening," says Jack DeAngelis, an entomologist at the Oregon State University Extension Service. "First, we're moving into wilderness areas that are the earwig's natural habitat. Second, people aren't always prepared to deal with the critters, especially in the spring when they haven't seen bugs for a while."

Tom Ellis, an entomologist at Michigan State University, has another theory. "Our backyards are ecosystems, and we've altered them by adding decks and mulched beds full of organic matter. These environments are tailor-made for earwigs, so it stands to reason we see more."

If earwigs are bugging you, read on. And remember: Neither you—nor they—are alone.

This Bug's Life

Earwigs are the sole members of the insect order Dermaptera, ancient bugs who began crawling around Earth about 208 million years ago. Today, some 1,100 species are scattered everywhere but in Earth's polar regions. In North America, we're most familiar with *Forficula auricularia,* a European variety thought to have arrived with our immigrant ancestors. According to Donald Lewis, an entomologist at Iowa State University, *F. auricularia* has been with us since at least 1907, when it was reported in Seattle, Washington. This invader has now spread to most of the United States and parts of Canada.

(continued)

by VICTORIA DOUDERA

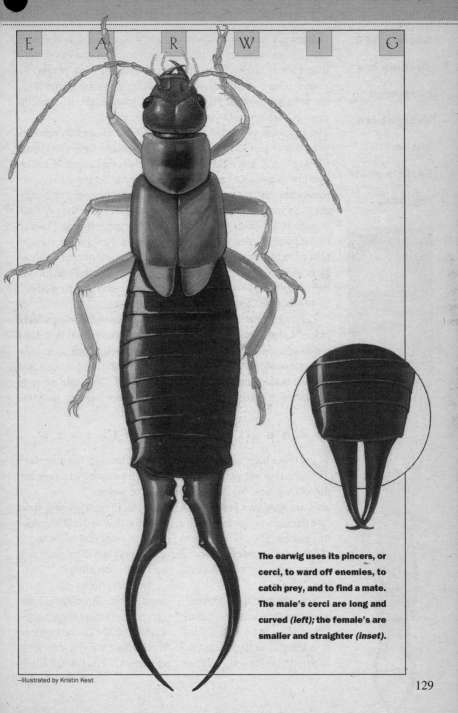

E A R W I G

The earwig uses its pincers, or cerci, to ward off enemies, to catch prey, and to find a mate. The male's cerci are long and curved *(left);* the female's are smaller and straighter *(inset).*

−illustrated by Kristin Kest

Some 1,100 species are scattered everywhere but in Earth's polar regions.

Entomologist Tom Ellis

-courtesy Tom Ellis

Earwigs mate indiscriminately in the summer but often live monogamously in the winter. Once spring arrives, the females lay 40 to 50 shiny eggs in underground tunnels. The eggs are protected from predators—including Papa Earwig—and are licked frequently to prevent fungal infestations. About a week later, the eggs hatch into miniature versions of their parents, called nymphs. Ten weeks and several skins later, the youngsters reach adulthood, with their whole lives—ten months or so—before them.

Earwigs crave close, moist places and are found primarily outdoors, especially under logs, leaves, boards, and stones or in organic matter such as mulch. Nocturnal by nature, an ear-wig's main meal is decaying plant material and wood, but it will attack living plants, including vegetables, fruit trees, and ornamentals, if given the opportunity.

When earwigs aren't chomping on plants, they're enjoying a lively social scene. "Earwigs congregate during the day, not really on purpose, but coincidentally, because they're finding the same hiding places," says Ellis. Nests of earwigs can sometimes number in the thousands. "They aren't territorial, so they tend to group together," he explains.

Fortunately, earwigs have two redeeming qualities: They dine on pests such as aphids, maggots, and army worms, and they work the night shift to break down organic material.

About Those Pincers

Few other bugs have a set of scary-looking pincers like the earwig has. So recognizable are they that some folks call the insects "pincer bugs" or "pinching bugs." Attached at the insect's abdomen, these appendages are called cerci (SER-sye).

Some people think that earwigs use their cerci to pinch. "Physically, they can do it," says Ellis. "But they won't really hurt you. You'd feel their cerci squeezing, but there isn't enough pressure to cause any kind of wound."

In fact, earwigs use their pincers to ward off enemies such as toads and birds and to catch prey such as plant lice and fruit caterpillars.

The cerci also play a romantic role. "An earwig's pincers are important for mating," explains Ellis. "Like tusks on an elephant, they're indicators of gender." You can tell a lady from a gent just by looking at the pincers: A male earwig's are long and curved; a female's are smaller and straighter. That's if you can catch one! Earwigs are rapid runners that can also fly, although they rarely—if ever—take the time to do this. But they certainly can, and with four wings. (That's right, two sets.) The front set is leathery and protects the hind wings. The pincers even aid the earwig in unfolding all its wings.

Home, Sweet Habitat

Experts say that earwigs are accidental home invaders. They arrive unintentionally, often with your help. Check for bugs on everything you bring in, especially laundry, lawn furniture, flowers, vegetables, and firewood.

Catching and squishing earwigs requires speed and, some say, a strong stomach. "They can produce a noticeable foul odor when disturbed," says Lewis. According to Ellis, the distinctive scent they emit is due to their diet. "You are what you eat," he says. "If you devour dead and dying stuff, you start to smell like it."

You can vacuum up the intruders if squishing them makes you squirm, but it's better to keep them out of the house in the first place. Most important, say experts, is to move mulch and other moist material away from your house's foundation. Establish a zone of bare soil that will dry out, and seal any cracks in the foundation.

As If That's Not Enough . . .

Here's an Earful

The creepy name *earwig* derives from the old English *earwicga,* with *wicga* meaning "wiggle"—thus, "ear wiggler." Other cultures have fearsome-sounding names, too: In France they're called ear piercers, and in Germany, ear worms. These chilling appellations arose from the terrifying but false notion that an earwig could crawl into a sleeping person's ear and bore into his or her brain with its pincers.

"It's folklore, of course," says entomologist Ellis. "Earwigs don't lay eggs in people's brains or anything like that."

Nonetheless, this ear fear gave rise to one of the most memorable episodes of Rod Serling's *Night Gallery,* a TV program that originally ran from 1969 until 1973. Episode number 28 was called "The Caterpillar," and it aired on March 1, 1972. Based on the short story "Boomerang," by Oscar Cook (1888–1952), it tells of a man who nearly dies when an earwig crawls into his ear, wiggles through his brain, and finally emerges out the other ear. Miraculously, the poor guy (convincingly played by Laurence Harvey) survives, only to realize that the insect is an egg-laying female.

Anyone for earplugs? □□

Master gardener **Victoria Doudera** fights earwigs, deer, and other garden pests along the coast of Maine and regularly contributes to *The Old Farmer's Almanac Gardener's Companion.*

BUG OFF!
Feeling outnumbered? For tips on reducing earwigs in your backyard, go to **www.almanac.com** and click on **Article Links 2003.**

A Spicy Account of

(QUITE POSSIBLY)

the Worst Day in

Gunung Api, or the "fire mountain," and
the nearby island and town of Neira (a
drawing by Francois Valentijn, c. 1680,
from *Oud en Nieuw Oost-Indien*, vol. 3)

by James Rodger Fleming

Weather History

In eastern Indonesia, there lies an archipelago called the Banda Islands, which are part of the Moluccas, or Spice Islands. The tiny and isolated Banda Islands are famous for two things: first, for being the only naturally occurring source of the *Myristica fragrans* tree that produces nutmeg and mace, and second, for a series of disastrous events that took place there 225 years ago.

A combination of a planar (two-dimensional) and profile view of the Banda Islands, from the log book of the Dutch ship *Gelderland*, 1602.

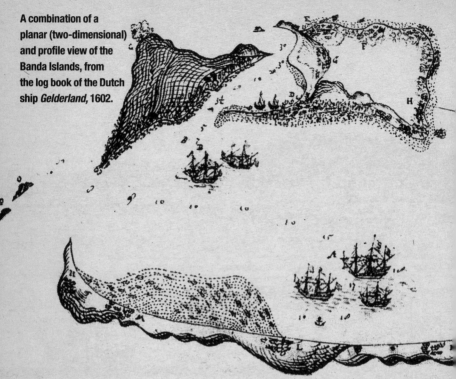

Traders from China and South Asia had long valued the islands' spices. In the 11th century, Arabian traders first brought them to Europe. By the 17th century, the Dutch monopolized the Banda nutmeg trade.

Banda islanders, however, were unwilling to cooperate with the Dutch colonial regime and were nearly exterminated in a 1621 war. Of approximately 15,000 original Bandanese, only a few hundred survived. They were replaced by foreign workers (or *perkeniers*) and slaves. European demand for spices kept the Dutch East-India Company busy protecting their holdings from the English and expanding their monopoly through plantation-style cultivation of the nutmeg trees. In 1667, the Treaty of Breda guaranteed the Dutch full rights to the Banda spice trade.

All this island activity took place in the shadow of the active volcano Gunung Api (literally "fire mountain"), which towers 2,100 feet (640 m) above the town and island of Neira—one of the Banda Islands.

There is an oft-repeated tale of how the people of Banda lost their homes and their livelihood in a quadruple natural disaster on one fateful day in 1778, described by Willard A. Hanna in his book *Indonesian Banda: Colonialism and Its Aftermath in the Nutmeg Islands* (Philadelphia Institute for the Study of Human Issues, 1978): "During one awful

Indonesia has more active volcanoes than any other region of the world—76, including Gunung Api.

hour in midmorning of April 2, 1778, there occurred, simultaneously, an especially destructive volcanic eruption, an earthquake, a tidal wave, and a hurricane. This manifestation of nature's malevolence worked devastation in the towns and in the *perken* [plantation] and even in the stoutly built fortifications. The damage in the nutmeg gardens was so extensive that one tree out of every two was uprooted or badly splintered. The harvest during the next twelve months dropped to a mere 30,000 pounds (14,000 kg) of nutmeg and 10,000 pounds (4,500 kg) of mace, as compared with 800,000 pounds (365,000 kg) and 200,000 pounds (90,000 kg), respectively, in 1777."

Giles Milton repeats and condenses this story in *Nathaniel's Nutmeg* (Penguin, 2000): "In 1778, the twin forces of an eruption and earthquake, followed by a hurricane and an immense tidal wave, all but wrecked the Banda Islands' nutmeg groves. One out of every two trees

was felled and production of nutmeg plummeted." John Seabrook gives the event an even briefer mention in a recent article in *New Yorker* magazine: ". . . on a single day—April 2, 1778—the Bandas suffered an earthquake, a tidal wave, a volcanic eruption, and a hurricane."

How did such a combination of natural disasters occur?

Indonesia has more active volcanoes than any other region of the world—76, including Gunung Api. The Sunda Arc of volcanoes stretches from northwest Sumatra to the Banda Sea, more than 1,850 miles (3,000 km). In the terminology of plate tectonics, this is where the floor of the Indian Ocean is being subducted (or crushed) beneath the Asian Plate. Historically, these steep, conical volcanoes have set records for the most fatalities and the greatest devastation to agriculture. Collectively, the volcanoes are known to erupt explosively, collapse catastrophically, and produce deadly tsunamis and pyroclastic flows of ash, rock, and hot gases. The Indonesians even have a special term, *lahar,* for violent mud and debris flowing down the side of a volcano—a deadly river of cementlike material that can be hundreds of yards/meters wide and tens of yards/

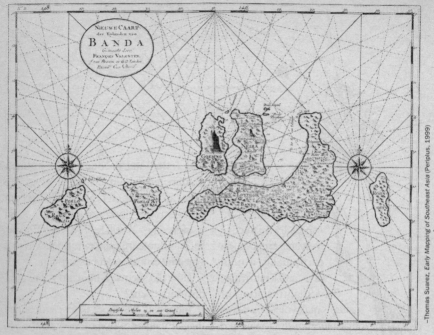

Map of Banda by Valentijn, c. 1680. Banda Api is in the center of the map; the island of Banda Neira lies to the east; Lonthor is to the southeast. These three islands form the rim of a submerged caldera of a much larger ancient volcano.

meters deep, traveling at up to 60 feet (18 m) per second.

Mountainous Banda Api, with its conical volcanic Gunung Api, is in reality just the tip of a tectonic iceberg. It sits on the western edge of a submerged caldera (or volcanic crater) formed by the collapse of a much larger ancient volcano. The rim of this caldera includes the nearby islands of Banda Neira and Lonthor and is some 6 miles (10 km) in diameter. Historical eruptions have been recorded there since 1586, mostly consisting of eruptions of smoke and ash from the summit crater, but larger explosive eruptions have occurred and occasional lava flows have reached the coast.

It is tempting to assume that the earthquake, the tsunami, and even the "hurricane" of 1778 were related to the eruption of Gunung Api. An underground rock slide in the Banda harbor could have caused extremely high waves in the narrow harbors that appeared to be a tsunami. The volcano could have produced a pyroclastic surge—a turbulent cloud of rock debris charging down the volcano's slopes that would have destroyed structures and vegetation. The eruption could have covered the entire area with a layer of ash and debris several feet/meters thick. The ash cloud could have generated lightning, thunder, torrential rains, and even tornadoes, possibly explaining the simultaneous occurrence of a "hurricane."

But is that what actually happened? Did a tropical cyclone or typhoon hit the island on the day of the eruption? Possibly, although the phenomenon was not yet named in 1778. Typically, these storms originate over warm water between the latitudes of 8° and 20° (north and south) and move away from the equator. The rotation of a tropical cyclone depends on the Coriolis force, which is zero at the equator. Banda, at latitude 4.5°S, would not be expected to lie in the path of such storms, but evidently it did—and does. Looking back again, Henry Piddington, the 19th-century British official in the port of Calcutta who coined the term *cyclone,* noted that "Banda is visited at times by severe cyclones, one of which in 1778 destroyed 85 percent of all the nutmeg trees." Early in the 20th century, Cornelis Braak, a Dutch meteorologist, mentioned in his book on the climate of the Netherlands Indies that nearly all the houses on Banda Island lost their roofs in the space of four hours when the storm of 1778 passed just south of the island.

More recently, researchers have identified a phenomenon known as a low-latitude tropical cyclone caused by the seasonal passage of the monsoon trough. In November 1967, tropical cyclone Annie developed near 6°S, resulting in widespread damage and loss of life in the maritime provinces of Papua New Guinea. Typhoons Hannah (May 1972) and Adel (May 1993) both developed near 5.5°S. Typhoon Kate (October 1970) reached its greatest strength at 4.5°N and caused over 600 deaths in a region considered to be typhoon-free. And on December 27, 2001, a typhoon was reported at 1.6°N, 32°W. Although this is not near the Banda Islands, it shows that such storms do form very near the equator.

So if it happened again, how bad could it be? A Javanese text called the *Pustaka Raja (The Book of Kings),* dating to A.D. 416, describes an island that disappeared beneath the waves in the Sunda Straits: "The whole world was greatly shaken, and violent thundering, accompanied by heavy rain and storms . . . [only fed] the fire of the mountain Kapi; . . . the noise was fearful; at last, the mountain Kapi, with a tremendous roar, burst into pieces and sank. . . . The water of the sea rose and inundated the land; . . . the inhabitants of the northern part of the Sunda country . . . were drowned and swept away with all property."

Fourteen centuries later, Krakatau blew its top. The Banda Islands may have been lucky that they lost only 85 percent of their nutmeg trees in the quadruple whammy of 1778. They could disappear beneath the waves tomorrow in a fiery eruption. □□

James Rodger Fleming is a professor of science, technology, and society at Colby College in Waterville, Maine, and founder and first president of the International Commission on the History of Meteorology (www.meteohistory.org). He would like to thank Jeff Callaghan, Kerry Emanuel, and Robert Nelson for their valuable geophysical insights. Peter Lape provided advice, encouragement, and historical images.

BLASTS FROM THE PAST
To learn about three of the deadliest volcanic eruptions since A.D. 1500, visit **www.almanac.com** and click on **Article Links 2003.**

General Weather Forecast
2002 – 2003

(For detailed regional forecasts, see pages 140–155.)

This year will not be as warm as recent years in most of the country, and February and March will be particularly cold. Abundant precipitation will ease concerns in most drought-stricken areas. Snowfall will be well above normal in the northeast but below normal in most other areas.

November through March will start relatively mild, with above-normal temperatures in most of the country, on average, through much of January. February will be colder than normal everywhere except the extreme west, and March will be colder than normal in most areas. Overall, temperatures will be much above normal from the Rockies to the Pacific Northwest and in the northern Great Plains, and a bit above normal in New England and the western Great Lakes regions. Temperatures will be much below normal in the southeast, especially in Florida, which may see damaging freezes, and below normal in the Ohio and Mississippi Valleys, Texas, and the southern Great Plains. Elsewhere, temperatures will be near normal.

Precipitation will be below normal in the Ohio Valley, central and western Great Lakes, parts of the central Great Plains, and the western portion of the Desert Southwest. Precipitation will be above normal in the rest of the country, especially in southeastern New England, the area bordering the Gulf of Mexico, and most of California.

Snowfall will be much above normal from Washington, D.C., northeastward through most of New England and in the lee of the Great Lakes in New York State, and above normal near the Gulf of Mexico, in the southeast, in the Central Rockies, in the Cascades, and from New Mexico to Kansas City. Snowfall will be much below normal in the western and central Great Lakes, the northern Great Plains, the Ohio Valley, and low elevations of the Pacific Northwest. Elsewhere, snowfall will be near or slightly below normal.

April and May will be warmer than normal in most of the western half of the nation, with near-normal temperatures in the east. Rainfall will be above normal in the southeast and in the western Desert Southwest, below normal in the western Great Lakes, and near normal elsewhere.

June through August will be hotter than normal from the Rockies and Desert Southwest westward to the Pacific Coast. Temperatures will be below normal from New England westward through the Great Lakes and Ohio Valley and into the northern and central Great Plains. Temperatures will be near normal, on average, from the mid-Atlantic and southeastern states westward into Texas and Oklahoma.

Rainfall will be above normal in the mid-Atlantic states, Ohio Valley, Mississippi Valley, central Great Plains, and Oklahoma. Rainfall will be below normal in Florida and most of the Desert Southwest. Elsewhere, rainfall will be close to normal.

September through October will be much warmer than normal in southern and central California, and above normal from the western Great Lakes westward to the Pacific Northwest, in the western Desert Southwest, and from the western Great Plains through most of the Rockies. Temperatures will be below normal from Texas and Oklahoma into the eastern Desert Southwest. Elsewhere, temperatures will be near normal, on average. Rainfall will be much above normal in southern Texas and above normal in the northeast and Desert Southwest. Rainfall will be below normal from the mid-Atlantic states southward through Florida and from the western Great Lakes into the central and northern Great Plains. Elsewhere, rainfall will be near normal.

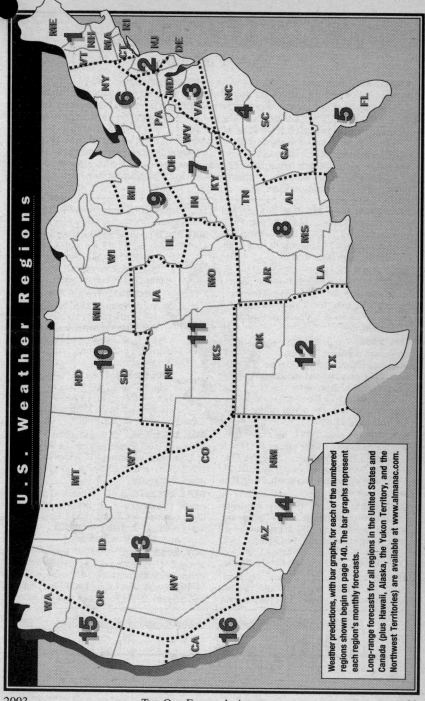

U.S. Weather Regions

ME
VT NH
MA
RI
CT
NJ
DE
NY
MD
PA
WV
VA
NC
SC
FL
GA
OH
KY
TN
AL
MI
IN
MS
WI
IL
AR
LA
IA
MO
MN
KS
OK
TX
ND
SD
NE
CO
WY
NM
MT
UT
AZ
ID
NV
WA
OR
CA

1
2
3
4
5
6
7
8
9
10
11
12
13
14
15
16

Weather predictions, with bar graphs, for each of the numbered regions shown begin on page 140. The bar graphs represent each region's monthly forecasts.

Long-range forecasts for all regions in the United States and Canada (plus Hawaii, Alaska, the Yukon Territory, and the Northwest Territories) are available at www.almanac.com.

New England

SUMMARY: In some ways, this winter will be like the last one, with above-normal temperatures through most of the season. But storms that missed us last winter will hit us this winter, bringing above-normal precipitation and snowfall. Expect the heaviest snow in January and February across the north and in February and March across the south. Watch for a major blizzard in the second week of February.

April and May will be wetter than normal but with many days suitable for outdoor activities.

Summer temperatures will be slightly cooler than normal, on average, with above-normal rainfall. The hottest temperatures will be in late June, early July, and late August. Don't expect any prolonged heat waves. June and July will be drier than normal, followed by several downpours in the first half of August.

September will be cool, with plenty of sunshine in the first half of the month but heavy rain in midmonth. October will be near normal in temperature.

NOV. 2002: Temp. 45° (2° above avg.); precip. 4" (avg.). 1-3 Rain, mild. 4-7 Cold, dry. 8-14 Rain, mild. 15-18 Sprinkles and flurries. 19-21 Cold, flurries. 22-24 Snow north, rain south. 25-30 Cold, snow, then sunny.

DEC. 2002: Temp. 40° (7° above avg.); precip. 5.5" (2" above avg.). 1-6 Snow north, heavy rain south. 7-12 Sprinkles and flurries. 13-15 Warm, rain. 16-19 Mild, dry. 20-22 Stormy. 23-26 Snow north, showers south. 27-31 Cold, dry.

JAN. 2003: Temp. 30.5° (8° above avg. northeast; 1° above southwest); precip. 5" (2" above avg.). 1-3 Heavy rain and snow. 4-8 Cold, dry. 9-12 Nor'easter. 13-14 Sunny, cold. 15-23 Rain and snow showers. 24-26 Snow north, sunny south. 27-31 Cold, dry.

FEB. 2003: Temp. 25° (2° below avg.; 3° above north); precip. 4" (1" above avg.). 1-5 Snow, then sunny. 6-8 Flurries, cold. 9-13 Blizzard. 14-20 Dry, mild. 21-23 Snow north, heavy rain south. 24-28 Rain and snow showers.

MAR. 2003: Temp. 40° (5° above avg. north; 0.5° below south); precip. 2.5" (1" below avg. north; 3" above south). 1-7 Sunny, mild. 8-10 Snowstorm; rain southeast. 11-13 Sunny. 14-17 Nor'easter. 18-21 Mild. 22-24 Sunny, cool. 25-27 Cool, showers. 28-31 Sunny, then heavy rain.

APR. 2003: Temp. 51° (2° above avg.); precip. 4.5" (1" above avg.). 1-7 Cold, rain and snow showers. 8-12 Sunny. 13-17 Warm, rain.

18-20 Sunny. 21-23 Heavy rain. 24-30 Sunny, then showers.

MAY 2003: Temp. 56° (1° below avg.); precip. 4" (0.5" above avg.). 1-2 Rain, cool. 3-7 Showers. 8-10 Chilly, rain. 11-17 Showers. 18-23 Cool, showers. 24-25 Sunny, warm. 26-31 Cool, showers.

JUNE 2003: Temp. 62° (3° below avg.); precip. 3" (0.5" below avg.). 1-7 Partly sunny, showers. 8-12 Cool; showers north, sunny south. 13-17 Cool, rain. 18-21 Warm, t-storms. 22-26 Sunny, hot. 27-30 Cooler, showers.

JULY 2003: Temp. 71° (avg.); precip. 3.5" (avg.). 1-4 Warm, dry. 5-10 Hot, t-storms. 11-15 Sunny. 16-19 Rain, then sunny. 20-25 Showers. 26-31 Partly sunny, t-storms.

AUG. 2003: Temp. 70° (avg.); precip. 5" (1.5" above avg.). 1-3 Severe t-storms. 4-6 Sunny. 7-13 Cool; heavy t-storms. 14-17 Warm, showers. 18-22 Cool, rain. 23-25 Sunny, hot. 26-31 T-storm, then cooler.

SEPT. 2003: Temp. 62° (1° below avg.); precip. 5" (2" above avg.; 1" below north). 1-4 Cool, t-storms. 5-9 Sunny. 10-16 Cool; rain, heavy south. 17-20 Sunny, hot. 21-24 T-storm, then sunny. 25-30 Rain, then sunny.

OCT. 2003: Temp. 53.5° (0.5° below avg.); precip. 5" (1.5" above avg.). 1-3 Sunny. 4-8 T-storm, then sunny and cool. 9-10 Sunny, warm. 11-16 Showers, then sunny. 17-23 Heavy rain. 24-26 Sunny. 27-31 Rain, then sunny.

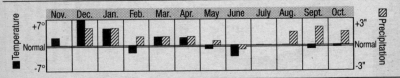

Greater New York–New Jersey

SUMMARY: Winter will be milder than normal, on average, but cooler than last winter. Precipitation and snowfall will be greater than normal. Expect snow accumulations in late November, around the New Year, in late January, in the first half of February, and in the second week of March. The coldest temperatures will occur in the first half of February.

April and May will bring prolonged sunny periods, with the usual spring showers. Overall, the period will be near normal in temperature and precipitation.

June through August will be cooler than normal, on average. The hottest temperatures will occur in late June and early August, but there will not be any prolonged heat waves. Rainfall will be below normal in the northwest, but heavy thunderstorms will add up to above-normal rainfall in the southeast.

September and October will be cooler and wetter than normal, with unseasonably cold temperatures in late September.

NOV. 2002: Temp. 46° (1° above avg.); precip. 3.5" (1" above avg. east; 1" below west). 1-6 Rain; then sunny, chilly. 7-13 Mild, showers. 14-21 Seasonable, mainly dry. 22-25 Rain, mild. 26-30 Windy, colder, rain to snow.

DEC. 2002: Temp. 39° (4° above avg.); precip. 5" (1.5" above avg.). 1-4 Rain, mild. 5-9 Colder, snow, then sunny. 10-12 Sunny, mild. 13-20 Warm, showers. 21-25 Mild, mainly dry. 26-31 Showers, then sunny and much colder.

JAN. 2003: Temp. 29° (1° above avg. north; 1° below south.); precip. 4" (1" above avg.). 1-7 Snowstorm, then sunny and cold. 8-12 Rain and snow, seasonable. 13-20 Mild, showers. 21-24 Cloudy, seasonable. 25-31 Cold, snow.

FEB. 2003: Temp. 28° (3° below avg.); precip. 4.5" (1" above avg.). 1-8 Snow, then sunny and very cold. 9-13 Snow, then bitter cold. 14-20 Sunny, becoming mild. 21-28 Mild, rainy periods.

MAR. 2003: Temp. 38° (1° below avg. north; 3° below south); precip. 5.5" (2" above avg.). 1-6 Sunny, seasonable. 7-15 Cold, periods of snow. 16-21 Seasonable, sunny, then showers. 22-28 Seasonable, mainly dry. 29-31 Rain.

APR. 2003: Temp. 52° (2° above avg.); precip. 5.5" (2" above avg.). 1-6 Chilly, periods of rain and snow. 7-13 Sunny, becoming warm. 14-19 Showers, mild. 20-23 Rain, seasonable. 24-30 Sunny, then rain and cold.

MAY 2003: Temp. 58° (2° below avg.); precip. 3" (1" below avg.). 1-2 Chilly, rain. 3-7 Sunny, seasonable. 8-14 Showers, chilly, then warmer. 15-19 Seasonable, showers. 20-31 Sunny, seasonable.

JUNE 2003: Temp. 67° (3° below avg.); precip. 3.5" (avg.; 2" above southeast). 1-8 Seasonable, t-storms. 9-11 Sunny, cool. 12-16 Cool, showers. 17-21 Seasonable, sunny, then rain. 22-27 Sunny, hot. 28-30 T-storms, seasonable.

JULY 2003: Temp. 75° (avg.); precip. 4.5" (1.5" below avg. northwest; 3" above southeast). 1-10 Seasonable, partly sunny, t-storms. 11-15 Sunny, pleasant. 16-25 T-storms, warm. 26-31 Sunny, very warm.

AUG. 2003: Temp. 73° (0.5° above avg. north; 0.5° below south); precip. 4" (1.5" below avg. north; 1.5" above south). 1-5 Sunny, hot. 6-10 T-storms, hot. 11-17 Sunny, seasonable. 18-20 Heavy t-storms. 21-25 Sunny, very warm. 26-31 Sunny, cool, then very warm.

SEPT. 2003: Temp. 64.5° (1.5° below avg.); precip. 5" (1.5" above avg.). 1-4 Showers, seasonable. 5-10 Sunny, becoming very warm. 11-15 Rain, cool. 16-19 Sunny, warm. 20-25 Rain, turning cooler. 26-30 Sunny, cold.

OCT. 2003: Temp. 54.5° (0.5 below avg.); precip. 5" (2" above avg.). 1-6 Sunny, warm, then cooler. 7-11 Showers, cool, then warm. 12-15 Sunny, seasonable. 16-22 Rain, cool. 23-26 Sunny, seasonable. 27-28 Rain, cool. 29-31 Sunny, mild.

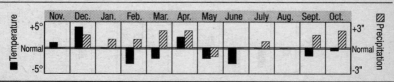

Middle Atlantic Coast

SUMMARY: November through March will be wetter, snowier, and colder than normal, on average. Unlike last winter, the heaviest snow will be across the northern part of the region, with snowfalls in late November, early December, early and late January, and the second week of February. November and most of December will be milder than normal, on average, but cold weather will predominate thereafter, with the coldest temperatures in late December, early January, and early February.

April and May will be a bit warmer and wetter than normal.

Summer will be hotter and wetter than normal. The hottest temperatures will occur in late June and late July, but there will not be any prolonged periods with excessive heat and humidity. Rain in mid-August will be heavy in much of the region. Other heavy rain will be from more-localized thunderstorms.

September will be cooler than normal, with near-normal rainfall. October will be mild and dry.

NOV. 2002: Temp. 49.5° (0.5° above avg.); precip. 4" (1" above avg.). 1-7 Rain, then sunny and unseasonably cold. 8-13 Warm, showers. 14-21 Seasonable, showers, then sunny. 22-24 Mild, showers. 25-30 Snowstorm, cold.

DEC. 2002: Temp. 41° (2° above avg.); precip. 4" (2" above avg. east; 0.5" below west). 1-4 Mild, rain. 5-7 Snow, then sunny and cold. 8-12 Sunny, mild. 13-15 Warm, rain. 16-18 Sunny, warm. 19-25 Mild, showers. 26-31 Sunny, very cold.

JAN. 2003: Temp. 32.5° (1° below avg. north; 2.5° below south); precip. 3.5" (0.5" above avg.). 1-7 Snow, then sunny and cold. 8-12 Mild, then colder, rain to snow. 13-19 Turning milder, sunny, then rain. 20-25 Sunny, mild. 26-31 Cold, rain and snow.

FEB. 2003: Temp. 33° (4° below avg.); precip. 3.5" (0.5" above avg.). 1-7 Rain, then sunny and very cold. 8-13 Blizzard, then sunny and bitter cold. 14-19 Sunny, turning milder. 20-22 Rain, mild. 23-28 Mild, mainly dry.

MAR. 2003: Temp. 41° (5° below avg.); precip. 5.5" (2" above avg.). 1-6 Snow, then sunny and seasonable. 7-12 Snow, then sunny and cold. 13-15 Cold, snow and rain. 16-21 Cold, sunny, then showers. 22-25 Chilly, sunny, then rain. 26-29 Sunny, seasonable. 30-31 Rain.

APR. 2003: Temp. 58° (2° above avg.); precip. 5.5" (2" above avg.). 1-5 Chilly, showers. 6-13 Sunny, becoming very warm. 14-23 Mild,

showers. 24-26 Showers, seasonable. 27-30 Rain, turning colder.

MAY 2003: Temp. 65° (avg.); precip. 3" (1" below avg.). 1-10 Rain, chilly, then sunny and turning warm. 11-14 Warm, t-storms. 15-22 Showers, seasonable. 23-25 Sunny, warm. 26-31 T-storm, then sunny and cooler.

JUNE 2003: Temp. 74° (avg.); precip. 4.5" (0.5" above avg.). 1-7 Warm, t-storms. 8-11 Sunny, cool. 12-20 Cool, showers. 21-24 Sunny, seasonable. 25-30 Hot, sunny, then t-storms.

JULY 2003: Temp. 79° (1° above avg.); precip. 6" (1.5" above avg.). 1-10 T-storms, seasonable. 11-15 Comfortable, mainly dry. 16-21 Warm, t-storms. 22-25 Sunny, hot. 26-31 T-storms, cooler.

AUG. 2003: Temp. 76.5° (0.5° above avg.); precip. 4.5" (1" above avg. east; 1" below west). 1-5 Sunny, warm. 6-11 Seasonable, t-storms. 12-14 Sunny, cool. 15-19 Heavy rain. 20-31 Sunny, seasonable.

SEPT. 2003: Temp. 68° (2° below avg.); precip. 3.5" (avg.). 1-8 Sunny, cool. 9-15 Showers, warm, then cooler. 16-19 Sunny, nice. 20-30 Warm, then rain and cool.

OCT. 2003: Temp. 60° (1° above avg.); precip. 2" (1" below avg.). 1-4 Sunny, turning warmer. 5-8 Sunny, cool. 9-14 Sunny, warm, then cool. 15-19 Rain, then sunny and warm. 20-28 Showers, cool. 29-31 Sunny, seasonable.

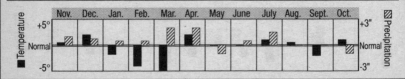

Piedmont and Southeast Coast

SUMMARY: Although temperatures in November and December will be normal or slightly above, on average, an early cold spell in the first part of November will presage colder-than-normal weather from late December through March. The coldest temperatures will occur in late January and early February, with record cold in mid-February. November through March will be wetter than normal, with snow or ice in early December, around New Year's Eve, and in early February.

Above-normal rainfall will continue in April and May, with temperatures near normal.

June will be cooler than normal, July will be hot, and August temperatures will be near normal, on average. The hottest temperatures will occur in mid- and late July and mid-August. Rainfall from June through August will be above normal in the north and near normal in the south.

September and October will be cooler than normal, on average. September will bring near-normal rainfall, followed by a dry October.

NOV. 2002: Temp. 55.5° (0.5° above avg.); precip. 6" (3" above avg.). 1-6 Rain, then sunny and unseasonably cold. 7-13 Rain, mild. 14-19 Cool, sunny, then rain. 20-24 Mild, sunny, then rain. 25-30 Sunny, cold.

DEC. 2002: Temp. 46° (avg.); precip. 4" (avg.). 1-3 Rain, mild. 4-7 Very cold, snow showers, then sunny. 8-14 Mild, showers. 15-18 Sunny, warm. 19-22 Showers, cooler. 23-30 Sunny, turning very cold. 31 Cold; rain south.

JAN. 2003: Temp. 38° (4° below avg.); precip. 5.5" (1.5" above avg.). 1-6 Snow north, rain south; then sunny and very cold. 7-14 Rain, then sunny and cold. 15-18 Heavy rain, cool. 19-22 Sunny. 23-26 Rain showers; snow showers north. 27-29 Sunny, cold. 30-31 Rain, milder.

FEB. 2003: Temp. 38° (6° below avg.); precip. 3.5" (avg.). 1-5 Rain, then sunny and very cold. 6-9 Cold, snow. 10-15 Sunny, record cold. 16-21 Turning warmer, sunny, then heavy rain. 22-28 Sunny north, rain south.

MAR. 2003: Temp. 50° (4° below avg.); precip. 6.5" (2" above avg.). 1-3 Rain, seasonable. 4-6 Sunny, cool. 7-10 Rain, then sunny and cool. 11-17 Chilly, rain, then sunny. 18-31 Cool, showers.

APR. 2003: Temp. 63.5° (1.5° above avg.); precip. 5.5" (2" above avg.). 1-5 Cool, sunny, then rain. 6-8 Sunny. 9-14 Showers, then sunny and warm. 15-19 Warm, showers. 20-30 Seasonable; scattered t-storms.

MAY 2003: Temp. 69° (1° below avg.); precip. 4.5" (1" above avg.). 1-4 Sunny, cool. 5-12 T-storm, then sunny and warm. 13-22 Seasonable; scattered t-storms. 23-31 Sunny, warm.

JUNE 2003: Temp. 74.5° (1.5° below avg.); precip. 5" (1" above avg.). 1-6 Sunny, hot; t-storms north. 7-15 Warm; scattered t-storms. 16-21 T-storms, cooler. 22-26 Sunny, warm. 27-30 Humid, t-storms.

JULY 2003: Temp. 81° (1° above avg.); precip. 4.5" (avg.). 1-8 Warm, partly sunny, t-storms. 9-13 Sunny, hot. 14-22 Very warm; scattered t-storms. 23-26 Sunny, hot. 27-31 Warm, t-storms, then sunny.

AUG. 2003: Temp. 78° (avg.); precip. 3.5" (1" above avg. north; 1" below south). 1-7 Hot; scattered t-storms. 8-11 Sunny, hot. 12-16 Cooler; t-storms south. 17-20 Seasonable, showers. 21-28 Sunny, comfortable. 29-31 Sunny north, t-storms south.

SEPT. 2003: Temp. 73° (1° below avg.); precip. 3.5" (avg.). 1-5 Sunny, warm. 6-10 Showers, cool, then warm. 11-14 Sunny, warm. 15-20 T-storms, then sunny and warm. 21-24 Cooler; showers north, sunny south. 25-30 Rain; chilly north.

OCT. 2003: Temp. 63.5° (0.5° below avg.); precip. 1.5" (1" below avg.). 1-4 Sunny, warm. 5-7 Sunny, cool. 8-12 Sunny, warm; showers south. 13-16 Showers, cool. 17-26 Sunny, cool. 27-31 Warmer, showers.

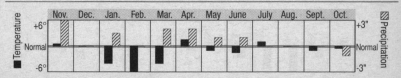

Florida

SUMMARY: November through March will be cooler and wetter than normal. Temperatures will be three to five degrees cooler than normal, on average, with freezes as far south as central Florida in late November, early December, early January, and mid-February. Although there will be many sunny days during the period, rainfall will be about 50 percent above normal.

Wet weather will continue in April and May, with near-normal temperatures. The heaviest rain will occur in early and late April and mid-May.

Summer will be a bit hotter and drier than normal. The hottest weather will be in mid-June, late July, and mid-August. We can't rule out a hurricane or tropical storm, but the number of tropical storms will be below average.

Despite a hot spell in mid-September, the month will be only slightly warmer than normal, followed by a cool October. Rainfall will be below normal.

NOV. 2002: Temp. 69.5° (1.5° above avg.); precip. 2" (avg.). 1-5 Sunny, warm, then cooler. 6-8 Warm, showers. 9-12 Sunny, very warm. 13-15 Showers, cooler. 16-23 Warm, showers. 24-30 Showers, then sunny and much colder.

DEC. 2002: Temp. 60° (3° below avg.); precip. 4.5" (2" above avg.). 1-4 Showers, cool. 5-8 Sunny, cold. 9-16 Sunny, seasonable. 17-22 Showers, warm. 23-26 Sunny, warm. 27-31 Chilly, showers.

JAN. 2003: Temp. 54° (7° below avg.); precip. 4.5" (1.5" above avg.). 1-6 Rain, then sunny and cold. 7-10 Showers, cool. 11-14 Sunny, cool. 15-23 Showers, cool. 24-31 Sunny, chilly.

FEB. 2003: Temp. 57° (6° below avg.); precip. 5" (2" above avg.). 1-4 Showers, then sunny and cool. 5-9 Rain, chilly. 10-16 Sunny, cold. 17-25 Mild, showers. 26-28 Sunny, seasonable.

MAR. 2003: Temp. 64° (3° below avg.); precip. 3.5" (1" above avg.). 1-8 Seasonable, partly sunny, showers. 9-11 Sunny, cool. 12-17 Rain, then sunny and cool. 18-24 Showers, cool. 25-28 Seasonable. 29-31 Warm, showers.

APR. 2003: Temp. 72° (avg.); precip. 5" (2" above avg.). 1-2 Sunny, cool. 3-9 Rain, seasonable. 10-14 Sunny, nice. 15-22 Showers, then sunny and warm. 23-28 T-storms, then sunny and warm. 29-30 T-storms, warm.

MAY 2003: Temp. 74° (1° below avg.); pre-

cip. 6" (2" above avg.). 1-4 Sunny, cool. 5-13 T-storms, then sunny and nice. 14-19 Rain, seasonable. 20-23 Sunny north, showers south. 24-31 Sunny, warm.

JUNE 2003: Temp. 80° (avg.); precip. 6" (avg.). 1-6 Sunny, hot north; t-storms south. 7-14 T-storms north; sunny, hot south. 15-23 Partly sunny, daily t-storms. 24-30 Seasonable; scattered t-storms.

JULY 2003: Temp. 82.5° (0.5° above avg.); precip. 6" (1" below avg.). 1-4 Sunny, warm. 5-14 Partly sunny, scattered t-storms. 15-22 Very warm; t-storms north and central. 23-27 Sunny, hot. 28-31 Very warm, t-storms.

AUG. 2003: Temp. 82° (avg.); precip. 6.5" (0.5" below avg.). 1-6 Seasonable; scattered t-storms. 7-11 Hot; sunny north, t-storms south. 12-20 Hot; scattered t-storms. 21-23 Cool north, t-storms south. 24-26 Sunny, very warm. 27-31 T-storms, seasonable.

SEPT. 2003: Temp. 80.5° (0.5° above avg.); precip. 4" (2" below avg.). 1-5 Sunny, hot. 6-9 T-storms, seasonable. 10-13 Sunny, hot. 14-19 Warm; scattered t-storms. 20-24 Sunny, warm north; t-storms south. 25-30 T-storms, turning cooler.

OCT. 2003: Temp. 73.5° (1.5° below avg.); precip. 6" (avg.). 1-8 Sunny, warm. 9-13 Rain, seasonable. 14-17 Sunny, nice. 18-23 Sunny, mild, then cooler. 24-26 Rain, warm. 27-31 Sunny, then rain.

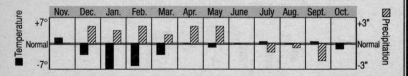

Upstate New York

SUMMARY: November through March will be wetter and snowier than normal, with slightly above-normal temperatures, on average. After a mild start, cold weather will predominate from late December through mid-February. The coldest temperatures will occur in mid-February, with other cold periods in late December and early February. Heavy lake snows will occur in mid-November, early and late December, and early February, with more-widespread snowstorms in early and late January and mid-February.

After a cold start, April will be warmer than usual, with above-normal rainfall. May will be cool and dry.

Summer will be a degree or two cooler than normal, with a cool June and July and a near-normal August. The hottest temperatures will occur in early to mid-July and late August. Although it will be cloudier, with more showers than normal, total rainfall for the period will be near or slightly below normal.

September and October will be cooler and wetter than normal.

NOV. 2002: Temp. 39° (avg.); precip. 2.5" (1" below avg.; 2" above west). 1-4 Cold, rain, then snow. 5-6 Sunny. 7-13 Mild, showers. 14-20 Colder, lake snows. 21-23 Rain, mild. 24-30 Cold, flurries.

DEC. 2002: Temp. 32° (5° above avg.); precip. 4" (1" above avg.). 1-7 Cold, lake snows. 8-15 Unseasonably warm; rainy periods. 16-26 Mild, showers. 27-31 Very cold, lake snows.

JAN. 2003: Temp. 20.5° (0.5° below avg.); precip. 3.5" (1" above avg.). 1-8 Flurries, cold. 9-12 Cold, snow. 13-17 Milder, rain and snow showers. 18-23 Rain, then snow showers. 24-31 Snow, cold.

FEB. 2003: Temp. 19° (4° below avg.); precip. 4.5" (2" above avg.). 1-8 Very cold, lake snows. 9-13 Heavy snow, bitter cold. 14-17 Seasonable, flurries. 18-20 Sunny, mild. 21-22 Rain to snow. 23-28 Mild, rain and snow showers.

MAR. 2003: Temp. 33° (avg.); precip. 2" (1" below avg.). 1-7 Cold, mainly dry. 8-16 Seasonable, snow showers. 17-28 Sunny, mild. 29-31 Rain.

APR. 2003: Temp. 47° (2° above avg.); precip. 4" (1" above avg.). 1-4 Cold, snow, then sunny. 5-8 Showers, then sunny. 9-13 Sunny, warm. 14-18 Mild, t-storms. 19-21 Sunny, cool. 22-26 Rain, then sunny. 27-30 Rain, cool.

MAY 2003: Temp. 54° (2° below avg.); precip. 3" (0.5" below avg.). 1-2 Showers, cool. 3-7 Seasonable, mainly dry. 8-10 Cool, showers. 11-12 Sunny, warm. 13-16 Cool, showers. 17-20 Sunny, cool. 21-31 T-storms, warm, then cooler.

JUNE 2003: Temp. 62° (3° below avg.); precip. 3" (0.5" below avg.). 1-7 T-storms, cool. 8-16 Sunny, cool. 17-20 Seasonable, t-storms. 21-25 Sunny, very warm. 26-30 Warm, t-storms.

JULY 2003: Temp. 71° (avg.); precip. 3" (0.5" below avg.). 1-6 Warm, showers. 7-9 Hot, t-storms. 10-17 Cool, showers. 18-21 Sunny, hot. 22-25 Warm, t-storms. 26-31 Sunny, very warm.

AUG. 2003: Temp. 67° (1° below avg.); precip. 4.5" (0.5" above avg.). 1-4 Warm, t-storms. 5-10 Sunny, warm. 11-19 Cool; scattered t-storms. 20-23 Sunny, becoming hot. 24-28 T-storms, then sunny and cooler. 29-31 Warm, t-storms.

SEPT. 2003: Temp. 59° (2° below avg.); precip. 4.5" (1" above avg.). 1-4 Cool, rain. 5-9 Sunny, turning warmer. 10-15 Seasonable, rain. 16-18 Sunny, warm. 19-23 T-storms, then sunny and cool. 24-30 Rain, then sunny and cool.

OCT. 2003: Temp. 49° (1° below avg.; 1° above west); precip. 3" (avg.). 1-3 Sunny, warm. 4-8 Cooler, showers. 9-11 Warm, t-storms. 12-15 Sunny, nice. 16-23 Showers, mild, then cooler. 24-31 Seasonable, mainly dry.

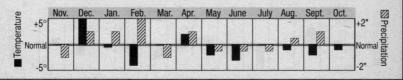

Greater Ohio Valley

SUMMARY: November through March will be colder and drier than normal, with below-normal snowfall in most of the region. A widespread heavy snowstorm is unlikely, despite snowy periods in late November, mid- to late January, mid-February, and early to mid-March. Temperatures through early January will be milder than normal, on average, with cold weather from mid-January into mid-March. The coldest periods will be in early and late December and the first half of February.

April will be wetter and May drier than normal, with temperatures close to normal, on average.

June through August will be cooler and wetter than normal, with the heaviest rains in July. There will not be any prolonged heat waves, despite some hot temperatures in late June and early and late August.

Although mid-September will be warm, the month will be cooler than normal, on average, with normal rainfall. Temperatures in October will be above normal, with below-normal precipitation.

NOV. 2002: Temp. 45.5° (0.5° above avg.); precip. 4.5" (1" above avg.). 1-6 Rain, then sunny and cold. 7-12 Rain, mild. 13-21 Sunny, cool, then warmer. 22-24 Showers, then flurries and colder. 25-28 Sunny, then rain and snow. 29-30 Rain, warm.

DEC. 2002: Temp. 38° (3° above avg.); precip. 4" (1" above avg.). 1-3 Rain, then sunny. 4-6 Very cold, snow showers. 7-9 Sunny, mild. 10-20 Warm, showers. 21-25 Mild, showers. 26-31 Very cold, snow showers, then sunny.

JAN. 2003: Temp. 29° (avg.); precip. 2.5" (0.5" above avg. east; 1" below west). 1-6 Flurries, then sunny and seasonable. 7-9 Showers. 10-13 Cold, flurries. 14-17 Rain, then colder with showers. 18-24 Seasonable, periods of snow. 25-29 Cold, snow showers. 30-31 Milder.

FEB. 2003: Temp. 27° (5° below avg.); precip. 1.5" (1.5" below avg.). 1-7 Very cold, flurries. 8-13 Bitter cold, snow showers. 14-19 Sunny, turning warm. 20-23 Rain, mild. 24-28 Flurries and showers.

MAR. 2003: Temp. 40° (3° below avg.); precip. 2.5" (1.5" below avg.). 1-6 Cold, flurries. 7-9 Cold, snow. 10-16 Cold, flurries. 17-19 Rain, chilly. 20-28 Turning milder, mainly dry. 29-31 T-storms.

APR. 2003: Temp. 54° (1° above avg.); precip. 5" (2" above avg. east; avg. west). 1-6 Chilly, showers. 7-12 Sunny, becoming warm. 13-23 Showers, turning cooler. 24-30 T-storms, warm, then cooler.

MAY 2003: Temp. 62° (1° below avg.); precip. 3.5" (0.5" below avg.). 1-3 Rain east, sunny west. 4-12 Warm, partly sunny, t-storms. 13-21 Seasonable; scattered t-storms. 22-24 Sunny, cool. 25-31 Warm, mainly dry.

JUNE 2003: Temp. 69° (3° below avg.); precip. 3.5" (avg.). 1-8 T-storms, warm. 9-12 Sunny, cool. 13-20 Cool, t-storms. 21-28 Sunny, turning hot. 29-30 T-storms.

JULY 2003: Temp. 75° (1° below avg.); precip. 8" (4" above avg.). 1-12 Warm, partly sunny, t-storms. 13-15 Cooler, showers. 16-23 Warm, mainly dry. 24-28 T-storms, warm. 29-31 Sunny, warm.

AUG. 2003: Temp. 73° (1° below avg.); precip. 4" (2" above avg. east; 1" below west). 1-7 Hot; scattered t-storms. 8-14 T-storms, then sunny and comfortable. 15-19 Seasonable, showers. 20-24 Sunny, cool, then hot. 25-27 T-storm, then cooler. 28-31 Warm; scattered t-storms.

SEPT. 2003: Temp. 66° (2° below avg.); precip. 3" (avg.). 1-8 Sunny, cool, then warmer. 9-14 Showers, turning cooler. 15-19 Sunny, warm. 20-23 T-storms, then sunny and cooler. 24-30 Rain, then sunny and cool.

OCT. 2003: Temp. 57° (1° above avg.); precip. 1.5" (1" below avg.). 1-4 Warm; sunny east, showers west. 5-10 Sunny, cool, then warm. 11-15 Showers, then sunny. 16-21 Seasonable, showers. 22-25 Sunny, cool. 26-31 Showers, seasonable.

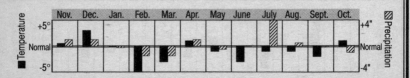

Deep South

SUMMARY: Winter will be wet and chilly, with temperatures averaging two to three degrees cooler than normal and rainfall four to eight inches above normal. The coolest periods will occur from late December into early January and from late January through the first half of February. Snow is likely in northern parts of the region in mid-November and late January. Snow in early February may reach all the way to the Gulf Coast.

Expect above-normal rainfall in April. May will be quite pleasant, with relatively warm and dry weather predominating.

June through August will be near normal in temperature and rainfall, on average. The hottest periods will be in early June and early to mid-July.

September and October will be slightly cooler than normal. After a wet September, October will be dry.

NOV. 2002: Temp. 55° (1° above avg.); precip. 6" (2" above avg.). 1-6 T-storms, then sunny and cool. 7-12 Warm, t-storms. 13-16 Sunny, then snow north, rain south. 17-19 Rain, cool. 20-23 Warmer, sunny, then showers. 24-30 Sunny, cool.

DEC. 2002: Temp. 45.5° (3° above avg. north; 2° below south); precip. 6" (1" above avg.). 1-6 Cool, rain, then sunny. 7-12 Showers, then sunny and warm. 13-18 Warm, t-storms, then sunny. 19-24 Showers, then sunny and cool. 25-31 Showers, then sunny and cold.

JAN. 2003: Temp. 36° (3° below avg.); precip. 5.5" (1" above avg.). 1-3 Sunny, cold. 4-9 Showers. 10-13 Sunny, cold. 14-18 Cool, rain. 19-22 Sunny. 23-29 Snow north, rain south; then sunny and cold. 30-31 Rain.

FEB. 2003: Temp. 36° (7° below avg.); precip. 4.5" (2" below avg. north; 2" above south). 1-3 Sunny, cold. 4-7 Very cold, sunny north; rain and snow south. 8-9 Snow north, rain south. 10-15 Sunny, cold. 16-21 Turning warmer, rain. 22-25 Sunny, seasonable. 26-28 Showers.

MAR. 2003: Temp. 48° (4° below avg.); precip. 6" (2" above avg.). 1-5 Rain, then sunny. 6-10 Cool, rain, then sunny. 11-16 Rain, then sunny and cool. 17-24 Cool, rain. 25-31 Turning warmer; t-storms north.

APR. 2003: Temp. 62.5° (2° below avg. north; 1° above south); precip. 7.5" (3" above avg.). 1-4 Cool, showers. 5-7 Sunny. 8-13 Rain, then sunny and warm. 14-20 Partly sunny, showers, warm. 21-30 T-storms, warm, then sunny and cooler.

MAY 2003: Temp. 72.5° (1.5° above avg.); precip. 3.5" (1" below avg.). 1-4 Showers, turning warmer. 5-11 Sunny, warm. 12-14 T-storms. 15-31 Mostly sunny; scattered t-storms, very warm.

JUNE 2003: Temp. 77° (2° below avg. north; avg. south); precip. 4" (2" above avg. north; 1" below south). 1-7 Sunny, hot. 8-17 Warm, partly sunny; scattered t-storms. 18-21 T-storms, turning cooler. 22-26 Sunny, warm. 27-30 T-storms.

JULY 2003: Temp. 80.5° (0.5° above avg.); precip. 5.5" (2" above avg.). 1-8 Seasonable, t-storms. 9-13 Sunny, hot. 14-20 Warm, t-storms. 21-31 T-storms north; sunny, hot south.

AUG. 2003: Temp. 80° (avg.); precip. 4" (1" below avg.). 1-7 Seasonable; scattered t-storms. 8-15 Sunny, very warm. 16-20 T-storms, turning cooler. 21-27 Sunny, seasonable. 28-31 Warm, t-storms.

SEPT. 2003: Temp. 72.5° (3° below avg. north; avg. south); precip. 4.5" (1" above avg.). 1-3 Sunny. 4-9 Cool, t-storms. 10-13 Warm, t-storms. 14-16 Heavy rain. 17-23 Sunny, warm, then cooler. 24-30 T-storms, then sunny.

OCT. 2003: Temp. 63.5° (1° above avg. north; 2° below south); precip. 1" (2" below avg.). 1-9 Sunny, seasonable. 10-17 Warm; scattered showers. 18-23 Sunny, cool. 24-31 Showers, cool.

Nashville
Little Rock
Montgomery
Shreveport
Mobile
New Orleans

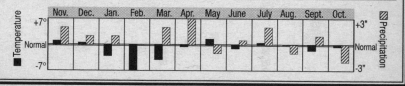

Chicago and Southern Great Lakes

SUMMARY: November through March will be a bit milder and drier than normal, with much less snow than normal. Most of the region will get less than half its normal snowfall, with the best chances for significant accumulation in early December, late December, mid-January, and mid-February. Overall, February will be the coldest month, with the season's coldest temperatures in the first half of the month. Other cold spells will occur in early December and from late December into early January.

Temperatures in April and May will be above normal, with below-normal precipitation.

Summer will be a bit cooler than normal, with near-normal rainfall. Hottest temperatures will occur in late June, mid- and late July, and early August, but there will not be any prolonged periods of excessive heat.

September will be cooler and drier than normal. October will be milder and drier than normal.

NOV. 2002: Temp. 41° (1° above avg.); precip. 3" (0.5" above avg.). 1-4 Showers, then cold with flurries. 5-13 Mild, rain. 14-19 Chilly, flurries. 20-24 Warm, then colder; rain to snow. 25-28 Flurries. 29-30 Rain, warm.

DEC. 2002: Temp. 32° (4° above avg.); precip. 3.5" (1" above avg.). 1-3 Rain, then cool. 4-6 Very cold, snow showers. 7-10 Sunny, mild. 11-14 Warm, showers. 15-19 Warm, sunny, then rain. 20-25 Cool, rain and snow showers. 26-31 Cold, flurries.

JAN. 2003: Temp. 24° (2° above avg.); precip. 0.5" (1" below avg.). 1-2 Cold, flurries. 3-7 Sunny, mild. 8-13 Cloudy, mild. 14-16 Rain and snow. 17-23 Cool, snow showers. 24-28 Cold, sunny. 29-31 Flurries, mild.

FEB. 2003: Temp. 21° (4° below avg.); precip. 0.5" (1" below avg.). 1-13 Very cold, partly sunny, lake snows. 14-20 Sunny, becoming mild. 21-28 Cold, rain and snow showers.

MAR. 2003: Temp. 37° (avg.); precip. 0.5" (2" below avg.). 1-15 Seasonable, mostly cloudy, sprinkles and flurries. 16-19 Sunny north, rain and snow south. 20-25 Sunny, mild. 26-31 Mild, showers.

APR. 2003: Temp. 51° (2° above avg.); precip. 2" (1" below avg.). 1-6 Cool, showers. 7-12 Sunny, becoming warm. 13-23 Showers, warm, then cooler. 24-26 Sunny. 27-30 Showers, cool.

MAY 2003: Temp. 60° (1° above avg.); precip. 3" (1" below avg.). 1-8 Sunny, becoming warm. 9-12 T-storms, warm. 13-15 Sunny. 16-21 Cool; scattered t-storms. 22-24 Sunny, seasonable. 25-31 T-storms, warm, then sunny.

JUNE 2003: Temp. 67° (3° below avg.); precip. 5" (1" below avg. east; 3" above west). 1-7 T-storms, seasonable. 8-10 Sunny, cool. 11-19 Showers, cool. 20-25 Sunny, turning hot. 26-30 T-storms, hot.

JULY 2003: Temp. 73° (1° below avg.); precip. 4" (avg.). 1-9 Warm, partly sunny, showers. 10-17 Cool; partly sunny, showers east. 18-21 Hot, sunny east; t-storms west. 22-25 T-storms, cooler. 26-30 Sunny, hot. 31 T-storms.

AUG. 2003: Temp. 72° (avg.); precip. 3.5" (avg.). 1-5 T-storms, hot. 6-8 Sunny, hot. 9-13 T-storms, then sunny and cooler. 14-18 Showers, cool. 19-23 Sunny, turning warmer. 24-27 T-storm, then sunny and cool. 28-31 Warm, showers.

SEPT. 2003: Temp. 63° (1° below avg.); precip. 3" (avg. east; 1" below west). 1-3 Showers. 4-8 Sunny, cool, then warm. 9-11 T-storms. 12-15 Seasonable, showers. 16-19 Sunny, warm. 20-24 Showers, cool. 25-30 Sunny, cool.

OCT. 2003: Temp. 55.5° (3.5° above avg.); precip. 2" (1" below avg.). 1-3 T-storms, warm. 4-9 Sunny, cool, then warm. 10-15 Warm, showers, then sunny. 16-21 Showers. 22-31 Sunny, seasonable.

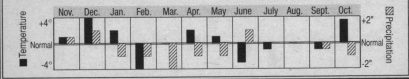

Northern Great Plains–Great Lakes

SUMMARY: Temperatures this winter will be about four degrees above normal, on average. Most of December and January will be mild, with cold weather in late December and the first half of February. Precipitation will be below normal in the east and near normal in the west, with well below-normal snowfall throughout. The snowiest periods will occur in mid-November, mid- to late January, late February, mid-March, and mid-April, but there will not be any big snowstorms.

April will be a bit milder than normal, followed by a warm May. Both months will be drier than normal.

June through August will be cooler and a bit drier than normal, on average. The hottest temperatures will occur in mid- to late June, late July, and early August.

September and October will be milder than normal, with very warm temperatures in early and mid-September. Flurries later in September will remind us that winter is on the way.

NOV. 2002: Temp. 33.5° (avg. east; 3° above west); precip. 1" (0.5" below avg,). 1-6 Flurries, then sunny and mild. 7-9 Showers. 10-14 Cold, snow. 15-20 Sunny, mild. 21-23 Snow showers. 24-30 Sunny, mild.

DEC. 2002: Temp. 26° (7° above avg.); precip. 0.5" (0.5" below avg.). 1-6 Sunny, seasonable. 7-11 Sunny, mild. 12-13 Flurries. 14-18 Sunny, mild. 19-21 Flurries. 22-27 Cold, flurries. 28-31 Sunny, mild.

JAN. 2003: Temp. 22° (10° above avg.); precip. 1" (avg.). 1-6 Sunny, mild. 7-15 Mild, flurries. 16-24 Turning colder, snow showers. 25-31 Seasonable, flurries.

FEB. 2003: Temp. 14° (2° below avg.); precip. 1" (0.5" below avg. east; 0.5" above west). 1-8 Cold, flurries. 9-12 Sunny, very cold. 13-19 Sunny, becoming warm. 20-24 Cold, snow. 25-28 Flurries.

MAR. 2003: Temp. 30° (2° above avg.); precip. 1.5" (0.5" below avg. east; 0.5" above west). 1-6 Sunny, seasonable; cold, flurries west. 7-12 Flurries, cold. 13-19 Snow north, sunny south. 20-22 Sunny east, snow showers west. 23-27 Sunny, then showers. 28-31 Rain and wet snow.

APR. 2003: Temp. 44.5° (0.5° above avg.); precip. 1.5" (0.5" below avg.). 1-7 Sunny, seasonable. 8-12 Sunny, warm. 13-19 Colder; sunny north, rain east, snow west. 20-23 Chilly, showers. 24-30 Mostly sunny; scattered showers.

MAY 2003: Temp. 60° (4° above avg.); precip. 1" (0.5" below avg.). 1-6 Sunny, becoming very warm. 7-13 T-storms, then sunny. 14-22 Seasonable; scattered t-storms. 23-31 Seasonable, t-storms.

JUNE 2003: Temp. 61° (4° below avg.); precip. 3" (1" below avg.). 1-18 Scattered t-storms, cool. 19-24 Sunny, hot. 25-30 T-storms, cooler.

JULY 2003: Temp. 70° (3° below avg.); precip. 4.5" (1" above avg.). 1-8 Cool, t-storms. 9-13 Cool, sunny east; t-storms west. 14-17 Warm; scattered t-storms. 18-25 Seasonable; scattered t-storms. 26-31 Mostly sunny, hot; t-storms east.

AUG. 2003: Temp. 72° (1° below avg. east; 3° above west); precip. 2.5" (1" below avg.). 1-5 Sunny, hot. 6-9 Seasonable; t-storms east. 10-13 Hot; scattered t-storms. 14-19 Showers, cool east; sunny, warm west. 20-23 Sunny, warm. 24-26 Rain, cool east; sunny west. 27-31 Showers.

SEPT. 2003: Temp. 61° (2° above avg.); precip. 1.5" (1.5" below avg.). 1-7 Sunny, warm. 8-15 Sunny, seasonable. 16-22 Hot, t-storms, then sunny and cooler. 23-25 Cold, flurries. 26-30 Sunny, turning warmer.

OCT. 2003: Temp. 49° (3° above avg.); precip. 2" (avg.). 1-4 Chilly, sprinkles and flurries. 5-13 Sunny, warm. 14-20 Cooler, showers. 21-28 Sunny, mild. 29-31 Cool, flurries and sprinkles.

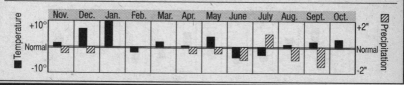

Central Great Plains

SUMMARY: Temperatures will be milder than normal in the first half of the winter but colder than normal in the second half. Precipitation and snowfall will be below normal in the northeast, above normal in the southeast, and near normal elsewhere. The heaviest snowfalls will occur in mid- and late January, late February, and early March. The coldest temperatures will occur in late December, mid- and late January, and early February.

April will be cooler than normal, followed by a warm May. The east will be dry; precipitation in the west will be above normal.

Summer will be cooler and wetter than normal. Widespread heavy thunderstorms will occur in early June and mid-July. The hottest temperatures will occur in mid- to late August, with other hot spells in late June and late July.

September and October will be warm, with rainfall below normal in the east and near normal in the west.

NOV. 2002: Temp. 41° (1° below avg. north; 0.5° above south); precip. 2" (0.5" below avg.). 1-2 Rain and snow. 3-12 Sunny, then rain and snow. 13-20 Sunny, cool, then warm. 21-27 Showers, then sunny. 28-30 Rain, mild.

DEC. 2002: Temp. 33° (4° above avg.); precip. 2" (0.5" above avg.; 0.5" below west). 1-6 Rain, snow, then sunny and cold. 7-9 Sunny. 10-14 Mild; rain east. 15-17 Sunny. 18-23 Rain and snow. 24-29 Snow, then sunny and cold. 30-31 Sunny.

JAN. 2003: Temp. 26° (2° above avg.); precip. 1" (0.5" below avg. north; 1" above south). 1-5 Sunny, mild. 6-11 Mild, rain and snow showers. 12-16 Snowstorm. 17-22 Flurries. 23-31 Snow then sunny; cold east, mild west.

FEB. 2003: Temp. 26.5° (7° below avg. east; 2° above west); precip. 1.5" (1" below avg. east; 0.5" above west). 1-6 Cold, sunny east; snow west. 7-14 Flurries. 15-19 Sunny, mild. 20-22 Rain east, snow west. 23-28 Snow north; rain south.

MAR. 2003: Temp. 37° (3° below avg.); precip. 2" (1" below avg. north; 1" above south). 1-4 Snowstorm. 5-7 Sunny, cold. 8-15 Cold, rain and snow showers. 16-23 Rainy periods. 24-31 Warm, t-storms.

APR. 2003: Temp. 50° (2° below avg.); precip. 2.5" (0.5" below avg.). 1-5 Sunny east, snow west. 6-8 Showers. 9-12 Sunny, warm.

13-16 Showers. 17-23 Chilly; showers east, snow west. 24-30 T-storms east, sunny west.

MAY 2003: Temp. 65° (3° above avg.); precip. 4" (2" below avg. east; 2" above west). 1-7 T-storms, then sunny and warm. 8-18 Partly sunny, t-storms. 19-31 Sunny, warm.

JUNE 2003: Temp. 70° (2° below avg.); precip. 5.5" (1.5" above avg.). 1-3 T-storms north, hot south. 4-9 T-storms. 10-11 Sunny. 12-19 Cool, t-storms. 20-25 Sunny, hot. 26-30 T-storms.

JULY 2003: Temp. 75° (3° below avg.); precip. 5.5" (2" above avg.). 1-3 Sunny. 4-10 Partly sunny, t-storms. 11-13 Heavy t-storms. 14-16 Sunny, cool. 17-24 T-storms. 25-31 Sunny, hot.

AUG. 2003: Temp. 75.5° (0.5° above avg.); precip. 3" (0.5" below avg.). 1-4 Sunny. 5-9 Hot; scattered t-storms. 10-16 T-storms, cool. 17-20 Sunny, cool. 21-24 Sunny, hot. 25-31 T-storms.

SEPT. 2003: Temp. 66° (2° below avg. east; 2° above west); precip. 3" (1" below avg. east; 1" above west). 1-6 Sunny, warm. 7-11 Rain. 12-14 Sunny. 15-17 T-storms. 18-22 Sunny, cool. 23-24 Chilly, rain. 25-30 Sunny, turning warmer.

OCT. 2003: Temp. 57° (2° above avg.); precip. 2" (1" below avg.). 1-3 Warm, t-storms. 4-14 Sunny, mild. 15-19 Showers, then sunny and cool. 20-24 Cool; sunny east, snow showers west. 25-31 Showers, then sunny and mild.

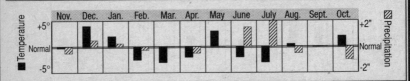

Texas–Oklahoma

SUMMARY: Winter will be cool and wet, especially across the south. Snowfall will be below normal from eastern Oklahoma into the Metroplex but above normal in most other areas. Snow in early February may whiten the ground all the way to the Gulf Coast. Other snowfalls will be limited to the north. Expect the coldest temperatures in early December, with a freeze even in parts of the Valley. Other cold periods will be in late November and early February.

April, early May, and mid-May will be a bit cooler and drier than normal.

Summer will be a bit hotter and wetter than normal. Expect hot temperatures in early June and most of July and August.

September and October will be a bit cooler than normal, with near-normal rainfall across the north but unusually heavy rain in the south.

NOV. 2002: Temp. 54° (2° below avg.); precip. 4" (avg. north; 4" above south). 1-5 Chilly, rain. 6-8 T-storms. 9-10 Sunny, warm. 11-14 T-storms. 15-18 Cold; rain, snow north. 19-26 Sunny, cold. 27-30 Cloudy, mild.

DEC. 2002: Temp. 52° (3° above avg.); precip. 2.5" (1" below north; 3" above south). 1-6 Sunny, cold. 7-13 Mild; sunny north, drizzle south. 14-17 Sunny, warm. 18-21 Rain. 22-23 Sunny, mild. 24-31 Chilly; sunny northeast, rain south.

JAN. 2003: Temp. 45° (3° above avg. northwest; 1° below southeast); precip. 1.5" (avg.). 1-4 Sunny; mild north, cool south. 5-7 Rain, mild. 8-11 Sunny. 12-17 Chilly; snow north, rain south. 18-21 Sunny, mild. 22-28 Rain, then sunny and mild. 29-31 Rain; snow northwest.

FEB. 2003: Temp. 45° (5° below avg.); precip. 4" (avg. north; 5" above south). 1-6 Turning much colder, rain to snow. 7-11 Sunny, cold. 12-17 Cloudy north; heavy rain, chilly south. 18-22 Sunny. 23-28 Rain; snow northwest.

MAR. 2003: Temp. 53° (4° above avg.); precip. 3.5" (1" above avg.). 1-6 Snow north, rain south. 7-10 Rain north, sunny south. 11-15 Sunny north, rain south. 16-19 Chilly; sprinkles, flurries north. 20-22 Sunny. 23-31 T-storms, then sunny and warm.

APR. 2003: Temp. 64° (4° below avg. north; avg. south); precip. 3" (avg.). 1-8 Cool, t-storms. 9-15 Mild, t-storms. 16-24 Sunny, warm. 25-30 T-storms.

MAY 2003: Temp. 73.5° (4° above avg. north; 1° below south); precip. 3" (1.5" below avg.). 1-6 Sunny, warm. 7-13 T-storms. 14-23 Sunny, hot; scattered t-storms east. 24-31 Sunny, hot.

JUNE 2003: Temp. 80° (avg.); precip. 5" (3" above avg. north; avg. south). 1-7 Sunny, hot. 8-12 Scattered t-storms. 13-17 Heavy t-storms. 18-23 Sunny. 24-30 Scattered t-storms.

JULY 2003: Temp. 84.5° (2° above avg.; 1° below north); precip. 2.5" (avg.). 1-4 T-storms. 5-12 Sunny, hot. 13-16 Hot; t-storms north. 17-23 Hot; scattered t-storms. 24-31 Sunny, hot.

AUG. 2003: Temp. 83° (avg.); precip. 3" (avg.). 1-10 Hot; scattered t-storms. 11-18 Seasonable; scattered t-storms. 19-23 Sunny, hot. 24-31 Seasonable; scattered t-storms.

SEPT. 2003: Temp. 74° (2° below avg.); precip. 7" (1" above avg. north; 5" above south). 1-3 T-storms. 4-5 Sunny. 6-21 Seasonable, t-storms. 22-24 Sunny. 25-27 Rain, cool. 28-30 Sunny.

OCT. 2003: Temp. 66° (1° below avg.); precip. 4.5" (2" below avg. north; 5" above south). 1-3 Sunny, warm. 4-11 Sunny north, rain south. 12-18 Sunny, warm. 19-23 Chilly; rain south. 24-26 Sunny. 27-31 Sunny north, showers south.

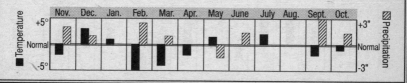

Rocky Mountains

SUMMARY: Winter will be milder than normal, with midwinter temperatures averaging five degrees above normal. The coldest temperatures will occur in mid-November and mid-January, but extreme cold is unlikely. Although precipitation will be above normal, most of the region will have below-normal snowfall. Most snow will be localized, with more-widespread snow in early and late February.

After a chilly April, May will be warmer than normal, with a heat wave in mid-May. Precipitation will be near normal in both months, with snow in mid-April.

June through August will be hotter than normal, on average, with the usual amount of rain. The last third of June will be cool across the north, with an unusually late-season freeze in some parts. Hot temperatures are likely in mid-June, early and late July, and early and mid-August.

September will be a bit wetter than normal, with a cool first half of the month and milder-than-normal temperatures in the second half. October will be warmer and drier than normal.

NOV. 2002: Temp. 40° (2° below avg.); precip. 0.5" (0.5" below avg.). 1-4 Sunny, seasonable. 5-13 Rain and snow showers. 14-17 Sunny, cold. 18-28 Sunny, seasonable. 29-30 Flurries.

DEC. 2002: Temp. 31° (3° above avg.); precip. 1.5" (0.5" above avg.). 1-8 Sunny, seasonable. 9-12 Rain and snow showers. 13-15 Sunny, mild. 16-24 Snow showers. 25-31 Sunny, seasonable.

JAN. 2003: Temp. 31° (5° above avg.); precip. 1" (avg.). 1-7 Rain and snow showers, seasonable. 8-11 Sunny, mild. 12-16 Cold, snow showers. 17-24 Mild, rain and snow. 25-27 Sunny, mild. 28-31 Rain and snow showers, cooler.

FEB. 2003: Temp. 37° (5° above avg.); precip. 1.5" (0.5" above avg.). 1-9 Periods of rain and snow. 10-16 Sunny, mild. 17-22 Colder, rain to snow. 23-28 Sunny.

MAR. 2003: Temp. 36° (3° below avg.); precip. 2.5" (avg. east; 1" above west). 1-10 Cold, snow showers. 11-13 Sunny. 14-19 Mild, showers. 20-30 Cold, periods of rain and snow.

APR. 2003: Temp. 47° (1° below avg.); precip. 2" (avg.). 1-4 Rain. 5-10 Sunny, warm. 11-16 Chilly, showers. 17-19 Cold, snow. 20-

25 Sunny, cool. 26-30 Showers, then sunny and warm.

MAY 2003: Temp. 61° (4° above avg.); precip. 2" (avg.). 1-6 Showers. 7-10 Sunny, cool. 11-15 Sunny, very warm. 16-22 T-storms, then sunny and hot. 23-31 Showers, warm.

JUNE 2003: Temp. 67.5° (3° above avg. east; avg. west); precip. 1.5" (avg.). 1-3 Sunny, warm. 4-7 T-storms. 8-11 Sunny. 12-16 Sunny, hot. 17-19 T-storms. 20-30 Sunny; cool north, warm south.

JULY 2003: Temp. 74° (avg.); precip. 1" (avg.). 1-7 Sunny, hot. 8-12 Showers, seasonable. 13-17 Sunny, warm. 18-24 T-storms. 25-31 Sunny, hot.

AUG. 2003: Temp. 75° (3° above avg.); precip. 1" (avg.). 1-8 Sunny, hot. 9-16 T-storms, warm. 17-21 Sunny, hot. 22-31 Warm; scattered t-storms.

SEPT. 2003: Temp. 63° (avg.); precip. 1.5" (0.5" above avg.). 1-7 Showers, turning cooler. 8-16 Sunny, cool. 17-18 Showers, seasonable. 19-30 Sunny, mild.

OCT. 2003: Temp. 55.5° (2.5° above avg.); precip. 0.5" (0.5" below avg.). 1-12 Sunny, warm. 13-18 Showers, then cooler. 19-28 Showers, then sunny and mild. 29-31 Showers, mild.

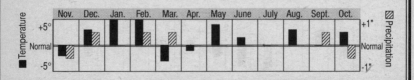

Desert Southwest

SUMMARY: Winter will bring above-normal precipitation and snowfall to the east but will be drier than normal in the west. Snow is likely in the east in mid-November, late December, late February, and early March. Temperatures will be near normal, on average, with a relatively cool November and March and relatively mild temperatures in between. The coldest temperatures will occur in mid-November and early March.

April and May will be warmer than normal, with near-normal rainfall in the east and above-normal rainfall in the west.

Summer will be hotter than normal, with record heat in early July. Other very hot periods will occur in the second half of June, mid- and late July, and early and late August. Rainfall will be near normal in the east and below normal in the west.

September and October will be wetter than normal, with relatively cool temperatures in the east and above-normal temperatures in the west.

NOV. 2002: Temp. 54° (3° below avg.); precip. 0.6" (0.2" above avg. east; 0.2" below west). 1-3 Sunny, cool. 4-9 Showers, then sunny. 10-14 Showers, then sunny. 15-18 Cold; snow east, sunny west. 19-27 Sunny, cool. 28-30 Showers.

DEC. 2002: Temp. 51° (3° above avg.); precip. 0.5" (0.5" below avg.). 1-8 Sunny, warm. 9-17 Showers, then sunny and mild. 18-24 Snow showers, then sunny and mild. 25-27 Sunny. 28-31 Snow east, sunny west.

JAN. 2003: Temp. 49° (2° above avg.); precip. 0.8" (avg. east; 0.4" above west). 1-11 Sunny, mild. 12-17 Snow east, then sunny and cold. 18-21 Showers. 22-27 Sunny, mild. 28-31 T-storms, then sunny.

FEB. 2003: Temp. 53° (1° above avg.); precip. 1.1" (1.5" above avg. east; 0.5" below west). 1-4 Sunny, mild. 5-7 Showers and flurries. 8-13 Sunny, mild. 14-20 Showers, turning cooler. 21-24 Sunny, cool. 25-28 Rain, mountain snow.

MAR. 2003: Temp. 55° (3° below avg.); precip. 1.6" (1" above avg.). 1-6 Cold; rain, snow east. 7-18 Partly sunny, showers. 19-25 Sunny, cool. 26-31 Showers, then sunny and cool.

APR. 2003: Temp. 66.5° (1° below avg. north; 2° above south); precip. 0.7" (avg. east; 0.6" above west). 1-11 Chilly, partly sunny, showers.

12-16 Sunny, warm. 17-25 Sunny. 26-30 Showers, then sunny and warm.

MAY 2003: Temp. 78° (4° above avg.); precip. 0.3" (avg.). 1-5 Warm, showers. 6-11 T-storms east, sunny west. 12-18 Sunny, warm. 19-24 Hot; t-storms east, sunny west. 25-31 Sunny, warm.

JUNE 2003: Temp. 86.5° (2.5° above avg.); precip. 0.7" (1" above avg. east; 0.2" below west). 1-5 Sunny. 6-13 Hot; t-storms east, sunny west. 14-16 T-storms. 17-30 Sunny, hot.

JULY 2003: Temp. 90.5° (2.5° above avg.); precip. 0.5" (0.5" below avg.). 1-6 Sunny, record heat. 7-13 Partly sunny; scattered t-storms. 14-21 Sunny, hot. 22-31 Hot; scattered t-storms.

AUG. 2003: Temp. 90° (3° above avg.); precip. 1.1" (0.4" below avg.). 1-8 Hot; scattered t-storms. 9-19 Partly sunny; scattered t-storms. 20-24 Sunny, hot. 25-31 T-storms, then sunny and hot.

SEPT. 2003: Temp. 81° (2° below avg. east; 2° above west); precip. 3" (2" above avg.). 1-7 T-storms. 8-15 Sunny, warm. 16-22 T-storms, cool. 23-27 Sunny. 28-30 Showers.

OCT. 2003: Temp. 69.5° (1° below avg. east; 4° above west); precip. 1.2" (0.4" above avg.). 1-6 Sunny, warm. 7-17 Showers, then sunny and warm. 18-24 Showers, turning cooler. 25-31 Sunny, warmer.

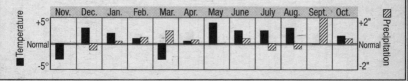

Pacific Northwest

SUMMARY: Winter will be milder than normal, with above-normal rainfall, especially in the south. There will be little or no snow outside of the higher elevations, with the best chances for widespread snow in mid-December, late February, and early March. The coldest temperatures will occur in mid-November, late February, and early March. The stormiest periods will be in early November, mid-December, early and mid-January, and mid-February.

The first half of April will be rainy, but the second half will be dry. The coolest temperatures will occur in mid-month. May will be warmer than normal, with near-normal rainfall. The warmest temperatures will occur in midmonth.

Summer will be hotter and drier than normal. The hottest temperatures will occur in mid-August, with other hot periods around mid-June and mid-July.

September will be relatively warm and dry, but October will be rainier than normal, with near- or slightly above-normal temperatures.

NOV. 2002: Temp. 46° (1° above avg. north; 1° below south); precip. 5.5" (0.5" below avg.). 1-12 Rain. 13-17 Partly sunny, mild. 18-24 Showers. 25-30 Light rain.

DEC. 2002: Temp. 45° (3° above avg.); precip. 6" (2" below avg. north; 2" above south). 1-5 Partly sunny, mild. 6-10 Showers, seasonable. 11-15 Heavy rain; heavy snow in the passes. 16-23 Rain, mild. 24-31 Partly sunny, scattered showers, mild.

JAN. 2003: Temp. 48° (7° above avg.); precip. 9" (3" above avg.). 1-6 Rain. 7-11 Rain, heavy north. 12-16 Partly sunny, showers. 17-24 Rain, heavy at times. 25-31 Mild, showers.

FEB. 2003: Temp. 48° (4° above avg.); precip. 5.5" (1" above avg. north; 3" above south). 1-11 Rain, mild. 12-15 Cloudy, showers. 16-19 Rain. 20-24 Partly sunny, cool. 25-28 Showers; snow showers inland.

MAR. 2003: Temp. 46.5° (avg. north; 1° below south); precip. 2.5" (1" below avg.). 1-3 Rain and snow showers. 4-9 Partly sunny. 10-19 Light rain. 20-22 Partly sunny. 23-27 Showers. 28-31 Partly sunny.

APR. 2003: Temp. 50° (avg.); precip. 2.5" (1" above avg. north; 0.5 below south). 1-7 Mild, showers. 8-17 Rain, cool. 18-30 Partly sunny, mild.

MAY 2003: Temp. 60° (4° above avg.); precip. 2" (1" above avg.; 0.5" below north). 1-6 Sunny. 7-12 Sunny, warm. 13-25 Partly sunny, showers. 26-31 Partly sunny; scattered t-storms.

JUNE 2003: Temp. 66° (3° above avg.); precip. 1" (0.5" below avg.). 1-5 Showers. 6-9 Partly sunny. 10-16 Sunny, hot. 17-24 Partly sunny, t-storms. 25-30 Sunny, hot.

JULY 2003: Temp. 71° (3° above avg.); precip. 0.5" (0.5" below avg.). 1-7 Sunny. 8-10 Sunny, hot. 11-16 Partly sunny. 17-22 Sunny, hot. 23-27 Partly sunny. 28-31 Partly sunny, showers.

AUG. 2003: Temp. 72° (3° above avg.); precip. 0.5" (0.5" below avg.). 1-9 Showers, then sunny and warm. 10-13 Sunny, warm. 14-18 Partly sunny, hot. 19-26 Cooler, showers. 27-31 Sunny, warm.

SEPT. 2003: Temp. 66° (2° above avg.); precip. 2" (0.5" below avg.). 1-3 Partly sunny, showers. 4-7 Partly sunny. 8-13 Rain. 14-19 Showers. 20-30 Sunny.

OCT. 2003: Temp. 57° (1° above avg.); precip. 5.5" (2" above avg.). 1-9 Showers, mainly north; mild. 10-16 Rain, seasonable. 17-24 Partly sunny, mild. 25-31 Rain, cool.

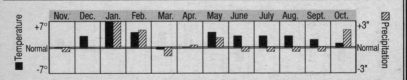

California

SUMMARY: Winter will be much wetter than normal, with temperatures one to three degrees above normal, on average. There will not be any very cold weather, but the coolest temperatures will be in mid-December and mid-January. The heaviest rains will occur in mid-December, late January, mid-February, and just about any time in March.

April and May will be drier and warmer than normal, on average.

June through August will be warmer than normal, on average, with near-normal sunshine. Hottest temperatures in the Valley will be in early July, late July, and early August. In other parts of the region, hot weather will hold off until late August.

Santa Ana winds will bring hot temperatures to the coast in early September, late September, and the second week of October. Rainfall in September and October will be below normal.

NOV. 2002: Temp. 56° (1° below avg. northeast; 1° above southwest); precip. 3" (0.5" above avg.). 1-5 Showers north, sunny south. 6-12 Showers, cool. 13-19 Sunny, warm. 20-27 Sunny, seasonable. 28-30 T-storms.

DEC. 2002: Temp. 52.5° (avg. north; 5° above south); precip. 2.5" (1" above avg. north; 1" below south). 1-5 Sunny, warm coast; Valley fog, cool. 6-7 Low clouds, fog. 8-12 Heavy rain. 13-20 Showers north, sunny south. 21-25 Mostly cloudy, mild. 26-31 Showers north, sunny south.

JAN. 2003: Temp. 53° (4° above avg.); precip. 5.5" (2" above avg.). 1-6 Showers, mainly north. 7-16 Mild, sunny; Valley fog. 17-24 Rain, cool. 25-31 Windy, heavy rain, t-storms.

FEB. 2003: Temp. 54° (1° above avg. east; 3° above west); precip. 5" (2" above avg.). 1-6 Showers. 7-11 Mild, partly sunny. 12-14 T-storms. 15-17 Sunny. 18-20 Windy, heavy rain, t-storms. 21-23 Sunny, cool. 24-28 Showers.

MAR. 2003: Temp. 54° (1° below avg.); precip. 7.5" (5" above avg.). 1-6 Showers. 7-11 Heavy rain. 12-13 Sunny. 14-18 Heavy rain. 19-20 Sunny. 21-24 Rain. 25-31 Windy, heavy rain, t-storms.

APR. 2003: Temp. 60.5° (avg. east; 5° above west); precip. 0.5" (1" below avg.). 1-6 Showers,

then sunny and warm. 7-14 Partly sunny, warm. 15-20 Sunny, seasonable. 21-30 Partly sunny.

MAY 2003: Temp. 64.5° (avg. east; 3° above west); precip. 0.6" (avg.). 1-6 Scattered t-storms. 7-12 Sunny, very warm. 13-22 Showers, then sunny and warm. 23-27 Cloudy; showers north. 28-31 Sunny.

JUNE 2003: Temp. 67° (3° below avg. east; 3° above west); precip. 0" (0.1" below avg.). 1-7 Sunny, cool. 8-14 Sunny, warm. 15-20 Warm; scattered showers north. 21-30 Sunny, warm.

JULY 2003: Temp. 73° (3° above avg.); precip. 0" (avg.). 1-7 Coastal fog; sunny, hot inland. 8-12 Sunny, cool. 13-19 Sunny, warm. 20-22 Partly sunny; scattered t-storms north. 23-31 Sunny, warm.

AUG. 2003: Temp. 74° (4° above avg.); precip. 0" (avg.). 1-6 Sunny, warm. 7-10 Hot; scattered t-storms. 11-28 Sunny, warm. 29-31 Sunny, hot.

SEPT. 2003: Temp. 71° (4° above avg.); precip. 0.4" (0.1" above avg.). 1-3 Hot; scattered t-storms. 4-14 Sunny, very warm. 15-18 T-storms. 19-30 Sunny, hot.

OCT. 2003: Temp. 67° (5° above avg.); precip. 0.3" (0.5" below avg.). 1-7 Sunny, warm. 8-11 Sunny; hot south. 12-19 Showers, seasonable. 20-31 Sunny, warm.

San Francisco

Fresno

Los Angeles

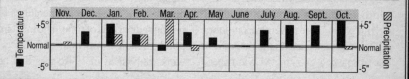

Does It Feel Warmer?

The new windchill index says it's so.

BY TOM KONVICKA

It's not as cold as it used to be—at least according to the new windchill index from the National Weather Service. Although the windchill index has been a fixture in weather reports since the National Weather Service (NWS) began using it in 1973, it was revised on November 1, 2001. (Canada started using the new formula on October 1, 2001.) The change came about when critics charged that the venerable index was based on flawed science.

The windchill index is a popular way to measure what the temperature really feels like in windy conditions. Millions of people expect the windchill reading to help them decide how much to bundle up and if it is even safe to venture outdoors.

The index is based on the rate of heat loss from exposed skin. As wind speed increases, more heat is carried away from the body. In temperatures that would otherwise not pose a risk, wind adds enough of a chill factor such that unprotected skin can freeze (resulting in frostbite) or internal body temperature can be reduced (resulting in hypothermia).

The original windchill index was based on the research of Paul Siple and Charles Passel, members of the U.S. Antarctic Service Expedition, in Antarctica during the winter of 1940–41. They suspended plastic cylinders of water from a tall pole and measured the time it took for the water to freeze. Their goal was to help the Army develop appropriate clothing for soldiers who were exposed to wind and low temperatures for prolonged periods of time. The most important result from Siple and Passel's work, published in 1945, was that not only air temperature—but air temperature coupled with wind speed—determined the rate of heat loss from the container.

Antarctica seems like the ideal place to carry out such a study, but modern technology enabled another team of scientists to do its research indoors. Randall Osczevski, of the Defence and Civil Institute of Environmental Medicine (DCIEM) in Toronto (renamed Defence R&D Canada–Toronto in April 2002), and Maurice Bluestein, associate professor of mechanical engineering technology at Indiana University–Purdue University in Indianapolis, used a refrigerated wind tunnel at the DCIEM.

The pair conducted clinical trials with six men and six women in May and June of 2001, exposing them to a variety of temperatures and wind speeds. Each person walked four times, at 3 miles (4.8 km) per hour, on a treadmill in the wind tunnel. Each walk lasted for 90 minutes, three in temperatures of 14°F (–10°C), 32°F (0°C), and 50°F (10°C), and one, a "wet trial" walk, at 50°F (10°C) with a light splash of water on the face every 15 seconds. The volunteers walked facing wind speeds that changed every 30 minutes, from 5 to 11 to 18 miles (7 to 18 to 28 km) per hour. The wind speed was measured at a height of 5 feet (1.5 m) instead of the standard wind-measurement height of 33 feet (10 m), because the face is the part of the body most exposed to the environment.

Skin temperature and heat loss were measured with sensors attached to the volunteers' forehead, cheeks, chin, and nose. A computer model predicted the onset of frostbite when the temperature fell below freezing. As a result, a new formula has been devised that incorporates modern theories of body movement, body-temperature maintenance, wind flow around the natural contours of the body, and skin-tissue heat loss.

According to Osczevski and Bluestein, the old index had several problems: The methods that Siple and Passel used (waiting for water to freeze) are not considered good scientific practice by today's standards. Heat loss from a pan of water is not applicable to human beings; we are much more complex. Also, each person responds differently to the stress of cold weather, depending on age, size, physical fitness, and gender, as well as attitude toward cold.

The old index exaggerates how cold it feels. For example, if the temperature is 45°F (7°C) and the wind speed is 20 miles (32 km) per hour, the old index gives a windchill of 25°F (–4°C); the new formula arrives at 37°F (3°C). Even with temperatures well above freezing, the old index reads well below freezing. To see the new windchill index, go to www.almanac.com/weathercenter/windchill.html.

Are you still cold? In the coming year, the effect of the Sun will be factored in. Expect a new windchill index soon.

☐ ☐

Tom Konvicka is a meteorologist and writer in Pineville, Louisiana.

The Art of Reading

At least once, the message in the cup could have changed the course of history! Could it change your life?

by Anastasia Kusterbeck

Here's a revolutionary thought: If, on the cold morning of December 16, 1773, the tea-loving British had read the tea leaves in their cups, they might have foreseen images of colonists disguised as Native Americans dumping boatloads of taxed tea into Boston Harbor!

No one knows for sure when tea-leaf reading actually started, but it was practiced in ancient China. The custom is believed to have been introduced to Europeans by nomadic Gypsies sometime around the 18th century.

The English poet Alexander Pope wrote in his 1734 work, *An Essay on Man:* "Matrons, who toss the cup, and see / The grounds of fate in grounds of tea."

Although Pope was probably referring to Victorian women with an abundance of leisure time for playing parlor games, he could very well be describing some of today's professional fortune-tellers. Unlike other antiquated practices that have gone the way of Victrolas, such as phrenology (the divining of a person's character through the inspection of head bumps) or haruspication (using animal entrails to predict the future), tea-leaf reading is alive and well in modern times. Indeed, this unscientific-seeming practice boasts a contemporary, even technical-sounding

Tea Leaves

term: tasseography, meaning "the reading of a map in the teacup."

Today, one place that many people travel to for a tasseography session is New Orleans' famed Bottom of the Cup Tea Room, which opened its doors in that city's French Quarter in 1929. That's where Adele Mullen has read tea leaves for countless devoted enthusiasts over the past four decades, and she steadfastly rejects notions that tea-leaf reading is a lost or vanishing art. "People come from all over the country and all over the world to have their leaves read," she asserts. "We have some people who won't make a decision until I give them a tea-leaf reading."

At first glance, the ritual may seem complicated, and the uninitiated may have to confront mixed feelings about basing life decisions on the task of "reading" brown muck that belongs in a compost heap. Proponents say that these challenges give rise to thought-provoking creativity and wholesome entertainment. "I always tell people it's like a road map. Tea-leaf reading is not going to cure your ills, but maybe it can show you a viewpoint you didn't see before," says Mullen.

How to Conduct a Reading

Opinions vary somewhat as to how readings should be done. The following tips are based on suggestions from *The Tea Book,* by Dawn L. Campbell (Pelican Publishing Company, Inc., 1995):

1

Set the Mood

■ Make a "tea party" reading whimsical, with tea sandwiches and dainty plates, cups, and utensils. If you host a Halloween reading, create an eerie ambience with spooky music and candlelight.

2

Use Loose Tea

■ Tea bags and strainers are not acceptable, but you can use whatever flavor of loose tea you fancy.

CONTINUED

Tea-leaf reading is not going to cure your ills, but maybe it can show you a viewpoint you didn't see before.

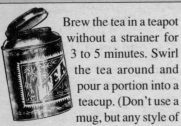

Brew the tea in a teapot without a strainer for 3 to 5 minutes. Swirl the tea around and pour a portion into a teacup. (Don't use a mug, but any style of teacup will do, as long as the inside is plain white so you can see the leaves clearly.)

Drink the Tea

■ Have the fate seeker drink the

cup of tea, leaving only ⅛ to ¼ teaspoon of liquid and tea leaves. Then you turn the teacup three times in a counter-clockwise direction, using your left hand. Ask the fate seeker to turn the cup over onto a saucer, place his or her left hand on the upside-down cup, and turn it again three times in a counter-clockwise direction. The teacup handle should end up facing you.

Turn Over the Cup

■ Next, carefully turn the cup upright. Avoid the temptation to make any dramatic flourishes; you don't want to shake the cup and move the tea leaves.

Begin the Reading

■ Look carefully at what you see in the cup. Any loose clumps of leaves are fodder for your fortune-telling skills.

Don't be afraid to be specific. If a clump of leaves reminds you of a peony tree, say so. When Wendy Gillespie, a devoted tea-leaf reader who practices the art on her Web site, "Madame G's Tea Room" (www.madamegstearoom.com), was reading the leaves for a colleague during their lunch break, she spotted a leaf formation in the shape of a Dustbuster. "It was in the location for the month of October," she recalls. "My friend laughed, saying that she always does her spring cleaning in the fall!"

Deciphering the Code in the Bottom of the Cup

Here are some clues for interpreting tea leaves, followed by a sample:

When Will "Something" Happen?

■ If tea settles near the brim, something will happen in the near future.

■ If tea settles near the bottom, something will happen in the distant future.

To gauge a more precise time frame for events to happen within the current year, use points along the circumference of the cup. The area nearest where the tea leaves settle determines when the predicted event will occur. Starting at the left side of the handle and moving clockwise, the 90-degree point from the left of the handle signifies three months; the 180-degree point opposite the handle signifies six months; the 270-degree point signifies nine months; and the 360-degree point, just to the right side of the handle, signifies one year.

Good News? Bad News?

■ Tea leaves that settle near the rim of the cup foretell happy events.

■ Tea leaves that settle near the bottom of the cup foretell sad events.

Who's Involved?

■ Tea leaves that settle closest to the handle suggest home and family.

■ Tea leaves that settle farthest from the handle suggest strangers.

■ Tea leaves that settle to the right of the handle suggest events or people coming into your life.

■ Tea leaves that settle to the left of the handle suggest events or people leaving your life.

Look for Meaning

Search for images in the leaves. If you're the type of person who, as a child, could while away hours staring at images in the clouds, you will enjoy this part of the ritual. Let your imagination run wild. "Everyone has intuition," Adele Mullen insists. "It's like an artist with a paintbrush: Your talent improves only if you practice. Above all, make it fun."

What If You See a Palm Tree?

Here's a sample prediction:

If the tea leaves are opposite the handle, near the rim, and slightly to the right of the handle, and you see the shape of a man and a palm tree, your reading might sound something like this: In six months, a strange man will come into your life and take you on a trip to an exotic island, which will be cause for celebration. ☐ ☐

Anastasia Kusterbeck, an avid tea drinker and a teapot collector, has more than 30 kinds of tea in her cupboard.

$\mathcal{T}$HE Far-Out Idea

Talking turkey with the man behind the first TV dinner.

BY KEITH WAGNER

n 1951, Swanson was the largest turkey grower in the world," says Gerry Thomas. Now 80 years old and living in Arizona, Thomas was a salesman at Swanson at that time. "On company-owned farms and through contracts with farmers throughout the West and Midwest, Swanson grew and processed more turkeys

When Swanson brothers Clarke (below) and Gilbert (right) directed their sales staff to find ways to sell turkeys, Gerry Thomas (opposite) came up with a plan.

–photos courtesy Gerry Thomas

162

TURKEY

QUICK F

TURKEY D

WITH GIBLET GRAVY, DRESSING, SWEE

JUST HEAT AND

INSPECTED

That Fed a Nation

than anyone else." Growing turkeys, he explains, is a commodity business in which growers try to anticipate the market—to determine in April, when turkeys are poults, what the consumer demand will be at the end-of-year holidays.

That year, for unknown reasons, the turkey attrition rate was uncommonly low; 20 to 25 percent is normal, says Thomas. "Turkeys are panic-prone. They often kill each other." That outcome is built into inventory expectations. But they all got along in 1951, so the company found itself with an abundance of birds.

As happened every year, by October, the entire crop of turkeys had been processed for sale to the market. But in 1951, they weren't selling. The eastern United States was experiencing unusually warm weather (brought about by the phenomenon we now know as El Niño), and when the

Fifty years ago, C. A. Swanson & Sons in Omaha, Nebraska, began selling TV dinners nationwide. Mealtime hasn't been the same since.

Thomas (left) *with Swanson plant manager Pat Murray* (second from left) *at the TV dinner assembly line in Omaha in 1998.*

weather is warm, says Thomas, people aren't interested in cooking, especially not roasting turkeys. Lacking sufficient warehouse space to store 260 unsold tons of turkey, Swanson leased ten refrigerated boxcars to hold them. Because the refrigeration systems worked only when the trains were in motion, the company contracted the railroad to haul the turkeys between Omaha and the East Coast until they could find a market for them—a costly move.

All in all, the experience knocked some of the stuffing out of Swanson.

FROM SKETCH PAD TO TEST KITCHEN

■ In early 1952, owners Clarke and Gilbert Swanson called the sales staff together for a meeting. The immediate assignment was clear, recalls Thomas: "We needed customers for the turkeys." A secondary goal was to find ways to use any extra inventory in the future.

Soon after that, while on a routine sales trip to a food distributor in Pitts-

burgh, Thomas saw aluminum-wrapped packages and asked for one. On the flight home, he opened it and discovered beef, potatoes, and gravy. (He learned later that it was an experiment in hot-food service for Pan Am Airways.)

Gerry Thomas was inspired. He envisioned a complete turkey dinner in one package. He began sketching trays—square, rectangular, round—with separate compartments for the food. He asked a colleague's wife to help develop the menu, and they came up with sliced turkey and corn-bread dressing with gravy; sweet potatoes; and buttered peas.

When Thomas presented his plan to his coworkers, the reaction was lukewarm. "Most of them thought I had a far-out idea." However, Clarke Swanson, who was in charge of sales, thought Thomas's idea was better than any others that had been suggested, including selling turkey parts in cans.

From February to July 1952, the Swanson staff worked out production,

ecalls: "I was looking for something memorable."

distribution, and display problems for the turkey dinner. A nearby wheelbarrow maker was contacted to produce aluminum trays. Using a die press, the company stamped Thomas's three-compartment design from rolls of sheet aluminum, creating a wrinkle-free tray that resembled pewter in appearance. (Later, a thinner-gauge, less-costly aluminum was used, allowing the edges of the trays to be rolled for more rigidity.)

In August, a team of Swanson employees prepared 8,000 dinners, using some of the turkey that had been stored in the boxcars. They worked in secret after business hours and behind canvas tarps "so no one would know," says Thomas—including Gilbert Swanson, who was among those not convinced of the frozen-dinner idea and who was vacationing in Hawaii at the time.

The food for the dinners was prepared from scratch. Each component was blanched at a different rate so that when the meal was finally cooked to eat, it would all be ready at the same time. A team of about 20 women standing alongside 50-foot rollers used ice-cream scoops to fill the food compartments as the trays slid by. "It was all a very experimental procedure," says Thomas.

When it came time to name the product, Gerry Thomas looked around. "TVs were making their way into homes around the country," he recalls. "I was looking for something memorable." Hoping to capitalize on the popularity of this new form of entertainment, he suggested calling the meal a "TV dinner." To complete the theme, the packaging was designed to resemble a console television (down to the simulated wood-grain cabinet with knobs) with an image of the prepared dinner on the screen.

FROM GROCERY STORE TO DINNER TABLE

■ In September 1952, the turkey TV dinner made its debut in grocery stores in six cities between Omaha

–Gerry Thomas

For his contribution to culinary history, Gerry Thomas was inducted into the American Frozen Food Institute's Frozen Food Hall of Fame in October 1998.

WHAT'S FOR DINNER?

As TV dinners grew in popularity, Swanson introduced new menus:

■ fried chicken
  (October 1953)

■ sliced pot roast of
  beef (March 1954)

■ fillet of haddock
  (January 1955)

Cranberry sauce, and a fourth tray compartment to hold it, was added to the turkey dinner in 1960.

and Chicago, selling for $ .98 to $1.29—a whopping amount, considering that a McDonald's hamburger was only 15 cents.

The dinners were not an instant success. Some people objected to the sweet potatoes and corn-bread stuffing. (By the end of 1953, these items were replaced by conventional white-bread dressing and Idaho white mashed potatoes.) Acceptance was also hindered by the fact that most people ate turkey only on Thanksgiving Day, says Thomas; plus heat-and-eat convenience food was a new phenomenon, and people didn't know how to handle it. What's more, few grocery stores had frozen-food cabinets, making it difficult for storekeepers to display the dinners. At least one storeowner expected women to buy the dinner only once—so that they would have the tray to use as a button box.

Swanson, however, recognized that the problems could be overcome with experience, and when the dinner was offered in grocery stores across the country in 1953, that hunch proved correct: In the first 12 months, Americans bought 10 million turkey TV dinners.

WHY America Was

Following World War II, America was a changed place. More than 11 million veterans had returned

home from the war, and the nation began to turn its considerable industrial might toward creating new ways of doing things and enjoying life.

■ **In 1946, the** U.S. birthrate jumped almost 20 percent over the previous year, a trend reflected in the demand for baby food: By 1948, a potential Gerber customer was born every nine seconds. By 1953, the U.S. population had grown to 160 million, up from 152 million in 1950 and 141 million in 1946.

■ **In 1947, William Levitt introduced the first of his** prefabricated neighborhoods. In all, 17,000 near-identical houses were built in a former potato

field on Long Island, New York. Each home came complete with a refrigerator, a washing machine, and a TV and sold, in 1949, for $7,990—this at a time when two-bedroom

So Hungry for the TV Dinner

homes typically cost $10,000. A second, similarly sized Levittown was built in 1951 in Bucks County, Pennsylvania. Following the success of the Levittowns, other developers eagerly copied the idea, and similar housing developments sprouted across the country.

■ **The new suburbs were far-flung, with few** convenient amenities, so driving became a necessity. In 1950, more than 8 million cars were manufactured. Americans owned a total of 40 million cars, up from fewer than 33 million in 1941. By the late 1950s, nearly 12 million families, mostly suburbanites, had two cars.

Technology and its application to everyday products helped propel these social changes. "People were looking for modern things, modern ways of doing things," says Thomas Hine, author of *Populuxe* (Fine Communications, 1999), a study of the consumer culture of the 1950s. The country was obsessed by what Hine calls a "mania for new appliances."

■ **Although electric washing machines had** been around since the turn of the century, in 1947 the company that became Whirlpool introduced the first top-loading automatic clothes washer.

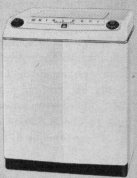

■ **The dual-temperature refrigerator, with** separate compartments for frozen and chilled foods, arrived in 1947. By the 1950s, the day of the freestanding deep freeze had come and gone.

■ **The country's burgeoning car culture** received its own conveniences. Power steering first appeared in the Chrysler Crown Imperial in 1951, the same year that drivers could coast into garages equipped with the first electric garage doors.

■ **In 1952, the mechanical** lawn mower made its debut and became a necessity in suburban developments

$\mathscr{B}$Y THE end of 1952, a number of fast foods were gaining popularity.

like the Levittowns, where residents mowed their lawns at least once a week.

■ **By the end of 1952, there were more than** 15 million TV sets in American homes, up from an estimated 4 million just two years earlier, and up from just 7,000 sets in 1946. There was more to watch, too, with upwards of 108 stations across the country, a jump from just 17 in 1947.

At this same time, an increasing variety of fast foods were gaining popularity.

■ **In 1946, the modern orange-juice busi-**ness was born when the first shipments of Minute Maid frozen concentrated orange juice were sold in the United States.

■ **In 1947, General Mills, Inc., introduced** the first boxed cake mix—Betty Crocker Ginger Cake. Minute Rice appeared on store shelves the following year.

In the midst of these lifestyle changes, Gerry Thomas's TV dinner idea contributed to and reflected the times. He aided convenience and launched an industry (frozen meals) that helped

—Gerry Thomas

change the character of household life. "The TV dinner was the equivalent of having a maid in the house. There were no dishes to wash, no pans to scrub, no oven to scour," says Sara Little Turnbull, director of the Process of Change Laboratory at Stanford University. "The truth of the matter is that these TV dinners were a miracle."

—courtesy General Mills, Inc.

Keith Wagner covers contemporary culture topics for print media and the Internet.

WHAT'S COOKING?
Turkey dinner! To find three prizewinning recipes for a beautiful bird with all the fixings, go to our Web site, **www.almanac.com,** and click on **Article Links 2003.**

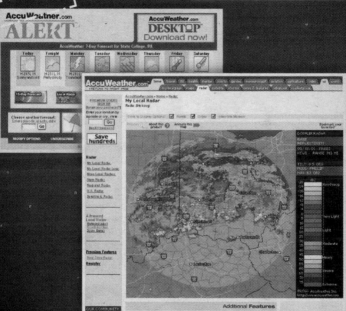

Jackson *(left)*, Crocker, and Bud sitting on the 20-horsepower Winton. Jackson insisted that mud from every state along their route remain on the vehicle until the end.

ACROSS THE COUNTRY IN 90 DAYS (OR LESS)

BY DAYTON DUNCAN

WHEN HORATIO NELSON JACKSON STOPPED IN AT SAN Francisco's exclusive University Club on May 19, 1903, he had no intention of making history. Jackson, 31 years old, was a Vermont physician who had recently given up his medical practice after a bout with tuberculosis, but he was still full of youthful enthusiasm and dreams and—thanks to a wealthy wife—had the means to pursue them. An interest in mining had brought him to the West Coast, but the discussion at the club that fateful night centered on his latest passion: the newfangled horseless carriage.

Almost everyone else in the room, Jackson later remembered, was disparaging the automobile as an "unreliable novelty" with no real future, "a passing mechanical fancy [that] thinking men could do no other than discard." But Jackson argued otherwise.

(continued)

—photos: University of Vermont

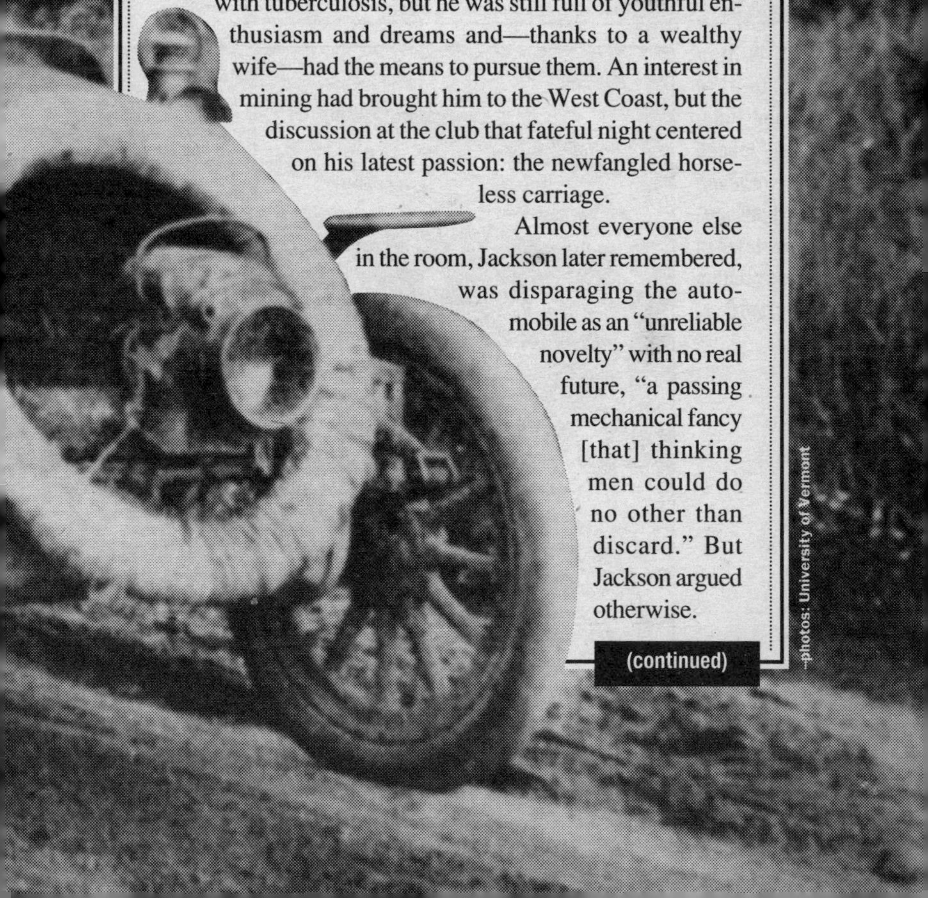

The Vermont was the first car to make an appearance throughout much of the West, and it created quite a sensation.

The 1903 Winton two-seat touring car, number 1684, not yet fully loaded and intact *(above)*; the car and passengers weeks later in Omaha, less pristine but proud *(right)*.

Then someone wagered $50 that a car could not be driven from San Francisco to New York in less than 90 days, and Jackson impulsively accepted. It turned out to be the most expensive—and adventurous—bet he'd ever made.

He began by buying a slightly used 1903 Winton touring car (paying the owner $500 more than the $2,500 list price) and hiring Sewall K. Crocker, a young mechanic, to accompany him. They removed the car's rear seat and loaded the back end with supplies: sleeping bags and cooking gear; a set of tools, including a spade and a fireman's ax; a block and tackle with 150 feet of hemp rope; a shotgun, a rifle, pistols, and am-

munition; and an extra 12-gallon can for emergency gasoline. (There were no gas stations in 1903, but general stores carried small supplies of gas for stoves, pumps, and farm equipment.)

Four days after making his bet, Jackson headed east. The two-cylinder, 20-horsepower Winton, which he had christened the *Vermont,* was capable of speeds up to 30 miles per hour, and he and Crocker made good time at first. Their pace slowed a bit on the bumpy roads north of Sacramento, where the cooking gear bounced off without anyone noticing. To avoid the deserts of Nevada, Jackson steered toward southeastern Oregon, a detour that took him nearly a thousand miles out of his way through a region that even the railroads had not reached. When the car's tires were shredded by rocky mountain roads and its batteries began to fail, the two men had to wait several days in Lakeview, Oregon, while replacements from San Francisco were shipped to them via stagecoach.

The *Vermont* was the first car to make an appearance throughout much of the West, and it created quite a sensation. From town to town, people often telegraphed ahead to announce the impending arrival of what a local newspaper called "one of the wonders of the century." Crowds gathered on the streets; schools let out; and ranch wives traded home-cooked meals for a ride in the contraption that one cowboy dubbed the "Go-Like-Hell Machine." At one isolated intersection, a woman deliberately gave Jackson wrong directions, sending him miles down a path that dead-ended at a farmhouse because, she confessed

The bulldog was "the one member of [our] trio who used no profanity on the entire trip," bragged Jackson.

Crocker, presumed to be tightening one of the clutches *(above)*; preparing to winch the Winton up a riverbank *(right, standing alone)* with three unidentified assistants; and the Winton on display in New York City *(opposite)*.

when he returned, "I wanted Paw and Maw and my husband to see you. They've never seen an automobile."

In Caldwell, Idaho, a new member joined the expedition—Bud, a small bulldog who rode in front (wearing goggles, just like his master) and braced himself for every bump and turn in the road. "Bud soon became an enthusiast for motoring," Jackson bragged, adding that the bulldog was "the one member of [our] trio who used no profanity on the entire trip."

Following dusty trails, Jackson and his passengers encountered emigrants in covered wagons and once had to be

towed a few miles by a cowboy who strung his lariat from his saddle horn to the *Vermont*'s front axle. Where bridges weren't available, they forded small streams, sometimes having to use their block and tackle to get the car through. Occasionally, they wheeled the auto onto railroad tracks and crossed rivers on Union Pacific trestles. More belongings bounced off and disappeared: eyeglasses, Jackson's favorite pen, three cyclometers used to keep track of mileage, and even a jacket with $200 cash in it. In western Wyoming, they got totally lost for a day and a half, zigging and zagging from one

impassable gully to the next and going without food for 36 hours until they happened upon a lonely sheepherder who fed them roasted lamb and boiled corn—and pointed them back in the right direction.

Delays for mechanical problems became common. The front wheel bearings wore out and had to be replaced by bearings from a farmer's mowing machine. A front spring broke, then the front axle—both were fixed by blacksmiths who never sensed, Jackson said, "that our strange vehicle was a symbol of doom to [their] profession." Twice in Wyoming, the connecting rod of the crankshaft sheared off, forcing Jackson to wait for days while new parts were shipped by rail from the Winton factory in Cleveland.

They ran out of gas only once (requiring Crocker to walk 26 miles to the nearest town), but in several small villages, merchants gouged Jackson, charging him in one instance an outrageous $1.05 per gallon—about three times the going rate. Being taken advantage of in this way so angered Jackson that he complained about it for the rest of the trip to every newspaper reporter he encountered.

PROOF THAT THE THIRD TIME IS THE CHARM

Two previous attempts to drive across the country had failed miserably. One car's progress had been so slow that a one-armed bicyclist passed it. The other had covered a mere 530 miles before being abandoned.

First Across the Con[t]

(continued)

Rain pelted the open-seated car throughout the Great Plains and Corn Belt, turning the roads into quagmires in which the *Vermont* frequently got stuck. On the worst day, Jackson and Crocker deployed the block and tackle 17 times to pull themselves out of the mud. Farther east, the roads gradually improved, though the rain did not stop. ("If it continues, will ask you to send paddles for the wheels and rudder for the rear of car," Jackson jokingly telegraphed home. "May have to take out navigation papers.")

Spurred by news reports that had begun to chronicle his groundbreaking passage, admiring crowds turned out in Chicago, Toledo, Cleveland, and Rochester to cheer Jackson on. In one last push, he and Crocker drove 230 miles without stopping, reaching New York City at 4:30 in the morning on July 26, exactly 63½ days after departing from San Francisco.

The next day's papers heralded the "daring automobilist" and his "bold chauffeur" (and, of course, Bud—now a celebrity dog) for their feat. The *Vermont* was proudly displayed on 58th Street, still covered with mud but now bedecked with American flags.

And the $50 bet that had started it all? Horatio Nelson Jackson spent $8,000 of his own money—the price of the car, a salary for Crocker, food and lodging, new tires and replacement parts, 800 gallons of gasoline, and the $15 purchase price for Bud—to win that bet. But he never collected his winnings, a fact he enjoyed telling people for the rest of his life, almost as much as he loved to show off a clipping from his hometown newspaper that appeared shortly after his triumphant return:

October 3, 1903. Dr. H. N. Jackson, first man to cross the continent in an automobile, was arrested in Burlington, Vermont, and fined five dollars, plus court costs, for driving the machine more than six miles an hour.

WHY THE ROADS WERE LESS TRAVELED A CENTURY AGO

When Jackson set out, no one had ever driven across the country in an automobile—and for good reason:

■ Of the 2.3 million miles of road in the United States, fewer than 150 miles were paved.

■ Most roads were essentially dirt paths, suitable at best for horses, cows, and slow-moving wagons.

■ Road signs were virtually nonexistent.

■ Dealers, parts, and mechanics were available only in big cities; if you broke down out on the road, you had to fend for yourself. □□

Dayton Duncan is an author, filmmaker, and longtime collaborator with Ken Burns. Their film, *Horatio's Drive*, based on Jackson's trip, airs on PBS in 2003.

WAS THIS MAN WRONGED BY THE WRIGHT BROTHERS?

Wilbur and Orville Wright were hailed as aviation pioneers when they successfully flew a brilliantly conceived, powered contraption of wood, wire, and canvas over a sandy shore near Kitty Hawk, North Carolina, on December 17, 1903. Some would say, however, that the fame they claimed belongs to someone else.

BY HARRY MANNING

As a boy in his native Germany, Gustav Albin Weisskopf had a fascination with manned flight that earned him the nickname among his schoolmates of "The Flyer." As he grew older, this hobby consumed him. In 1894, when he was 20 years old, Weisskopf came to the United States and soon after anglicized his name to Gustave Whitehead. An inventor and machinist, he worked as a manual laborer in a series of jobs he held from Boston to Pittsburgh. As a rule, he stayed in each job just until he had earned enough money to stop working for a while and pursue his avocation—designing and building light steam engines and constructing gliders. He took inspiration for some of his concepts from aviation pioneer and fellow German Otto Lilienthal, who designed and successfully flew gliders in the early 1890s, and under whom Whitehead is believed to have studied for a short period.

In 1897, the Boston Aeronautical Society commissioned the 23-year-old Whitehead to build a glider, but the undertaking proved disappointing. The glider didn't fly. Undeterred by the setback, he continued to experiment with different designs for engines and gliders, aiming for the ultimate goal of powered flight. (So convinced was Whitehead of his vocational calling that he listed his occupation as "aeronaut" on his marriage license that same year.)

In early 1899, nearly five years

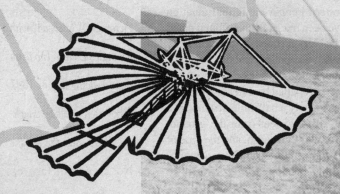

The wings on *No. 21* folded so that it could be pushed through the streets to a field.

before the Wright brothers' flight, Whitehead and his wife moved to Pittsburgh. There he met Louis Darvarich, a blacksmith who began helping him with his aeronautical experiments.

It was in western Pennsylvania that aviation history may have been made. In an affidavit dated July 19, 1934, Darvarich stated, "Approximately April or May 1899, I was present and flew with Mr. Whitehead on the occasion when he succeeded in flying his machine propelled by a steam motor, on a flight of approximately a half-mile distance at a height of about 20 to 25 feet from the ground. This flight occurred in Pittsburgh, and the type of machine used by Mr. Whitehead was a monoplane. We were unable to rise high enough to

Aeronaut Whitehead, with his bride, Louisa Tuba, on their wedding day in 1897 (above left); with his daughter, Rose, and the batlike No. 21, c. 1901 (above).

avoid a three-story building in our path, and when the machine fell, I was scalded severely by . . . steam, for I had been firing the boiler. I was obliged to spend several weeks in the hospital, and I recall the incident of the flight very clearly. Mr. Whitehead was not injured, as he had been in the front part of the machine steering it."

In 1900, Whitehead and his wife moved to Bridgeport, Connecticut, where, according to historical accounts, he continued to build flying machines. One of the most notable was *No. 21,* an airplane with wings that spanned 36 feet and were shaped like those of a bat and designed to fold up so the airplane could be pushed through the streets to a field where it could be safely tested. A four-cylinder, two-cycle engine powered *No. 21.* In the summer of 1901, eyewitnesses recalled seeing Whitehead fly along the edge of property belonging to the

TWO AGAINST ONE

■ Unlike Gustave Whitehead, the Wright brothers had the independent means to pursue their dream of powered flight.

■ With the Wright brothers at the controls, the *Kitty Hawk* remained aloft for 59 seconds and flew 852 feet.

■ The crucial difference between what Gustave Whitehead and the Wright brothers did about their achievements was that the brothers were the first to secure a patent for control of a flying machine.

As exhilarating as the early demonstrations must have been, Whitehead, a perfectionist, was never satisfied.

No. 20, *which survived many short hops, crash-landed in 1900.*

Bridgeport Gas Company, landing without damage or injury, and piloting it back to the original starting point.

Even more remarkable was a flight Whitehead claimed he made in *No. 22* on January 17, 1902. A group of men helped him move that airplane, which was kerosene-powered, to a beach on the outskirts of Bridgeport, where he hoped to complete a series of short flights over Long Island Sound. On the first one, according to eyewitness accounts, the airplane performed so well that Whitehead extended his flight along the shoreline for a distance of about two miles. Emboldened by his success, he planned to cross the Sound. At an altitude of about 200 feet and partway across, Whitehead decided to test his ability and that of the airplane to alter the course in midflight. Turning the rudder slowly and changing the speed of one of two propellers, he succeeded in making a 180-degree turn. Eyewitnesses estimated that he covered a total distance of about seven miles. In so doing, he demonstrated sustained, mechanical flight.

As exhilarating as these early demonstrations must have been, Whitehead, a perfectionist, was never satisfied. He was obsessed with improving upon each design. After each landing, he routinely disassembled his airplane and experimented with new and different wing configurations. In fact, he believed that powered flight would never be practical until an airplane could rise vertically from the ground—a concept he was unable to demonstrate successfully.

Despite his perseverance, Whitehead was constantly in need of funds to continue his aeronautical experiments. He lacked business instinct, and much of what he earned was used to pay for materials to build engines and airplanes. Fortunately for him, several people (including Stanley Beach, whose father was editor of *Scientific American*) took an interest in his work and provided some financial assistance over the years. Others offered moral support and encouragement. One of the most compelling testimonials to Whitehead's contributions to early powered flight comes from aviation pioneer Charles R. Wittemann, who built airplanes from 1906 into the 1920s— some of which used Whitehead engines. Asked his opinion of the absorbed Bavarian inventor, Wittemann stated, "I'd say he was a genius. All around."

Today, many aviation buffs are quick to recognize the name Gustav Weisskopf (or Whitehead) as that of the first person to demonstrate powered flight—but without the credit. Perhaps if he had had a sense of self-promotion to match his passion for aviation, it might have elevated him from relative obscurity. He died penniless in 1927 at the age of 53 and was buried in a pauper's grave.

FLIGHTS OF FACT—OR FANCY?

■ Assuming that the 1899 flight actually occurred, how is it that Whitehead never received the acclaim he deserved? Foremost is that he made no effort to document basic information, such as the precise distance he flew or his speed and altitude. For that matter, Whitehead didn't even record the flight in any type of log or journal. In *Lost Flights of Gustave Whitehead* (Places, Inc., 1937), aviation historian Stella Randolph writes, "He believed he could repeat such demonstrations whenever he chose. . . . He appeared to experience a boyish delight in the sensation of flight." The fact that Louis Darvarich was the only eyewitness didn't help, either, although according to Randolph, several people re-

called hearing about the crash.

The fact that Gustave Whitehead's achievements failed to win widespread recognition says more about journalism of that era than it does about the man himself. As historian Randolph points out in her book, "The nation did not acclaim Whitehead when accounts of his flights appeared in the papers; [but] neither did the nation immediately honor the Wrights after their flights on December 17, 1903. In fact, the news failed to make the first pages of some metropolitan papers. The *New York Herald* and *Boston Transcript* gave the Wrights little more space in December 1903 than they gave Whitehead in August 1901." ◻◻

Harry Manning works for an internationally recognized aviation magazine and speaks often on aviation and aerospace topics.

READY FOR TAKEOFF
To learn more about this controversy and both Whitehead and the Wright brothers, go to **www.almanac.com** and click on **Article Links 2003**.

The Towns That Hosted the World

A story of unexpected generosity and friendship among strangers.

by Shawn Woodford

High over the Atlantic Ocean in the midmorning hours of Tuesday, September 11, 2001, passengers on hundreds of aircraft were told of a minor problem on board and the need to land. Only the flight crews and those on the ground knew the real reason for the change in flight plan: The U.S. Federal Aviation Administration had ordered the airspace over North America closed down. The order followed the attacks by terrorists who had commandeered four commercial jets. They had flown two of them into the World Trade Center towers in New York City and one into the Pentagon in Washington, D.C. The fourth plane had crashed in Pennsylvania.

Following the FAA announcement, air-traffic

184

controllers at Gander International Airport, in the province of Newfoundland and Labrador, began diverting some 200 flights heading toward the continent to Gander and other Canadian airports.

Every four minutes, a plane landed in Gander—more than three dozen in 2 hours and 39 minutes. "Thirty-nine planes were accommodated on Gander's tarmac, with a total of 6,495 passengers and crew," says Gary Vey, president and CEO of the Gander International Airport Authority. "We have had that number of aircraft at times but never coming as fast as that with as many crew and passengers."

Once on the ground, the crews of each flight were briefed by airport authorities on the situation in the United States, and passengers were informed of the terrorist attacks. Like others around

Gander International Airport, September 12, 2001, with all planes grounded *(bottom)*; a map of the area *(below)*.

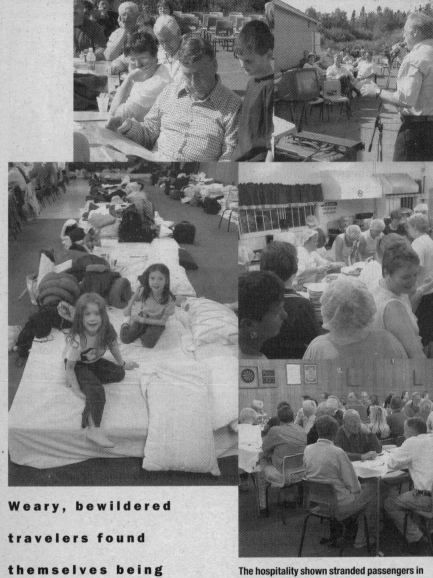

Weary, bewildered travelers found themselves being treated like special guests.

The hospitality shown stranded passengers in Lewisporte typified that of communities in the area. Residents entertained and prepared and served meals to passengers, who ate and slept in makeshift quarters. Mayor Hooper *(opposite page)* enlisted many volunteers.

186

the world, they were shocked by the news. In the silence that followed, they wondered, "What do we do now?"

For hours, the answer to that question was, "Nothing." Passengers were not immediately allowed off the planes. For security reasons, all passenger manifest lists were scrutinized, and background checks were completed on a number of travelers. Because of the unique circumstances, the deplaning process, which now involved passenger registration, didn't begin until late in the afternoon. Despite the aid of Red Cross workers, Salvation Army members, and police and customs authorities, it continued for 30 hours.

At the start of deplaning, authorities from towns within a 40-mile radius of Gander were contacted and asked to make preparations to accommodate passengers. One of those was William Hooper, mayor of Lewisporte, a Newfoundland town of 4,500 people, located about 35 miles from Gander. He received a call at approximately 2 P.M. Newfoundland time (12:30 P.M. EDT).

Like the authorities in each of the enlisted communities, Hooper immediately began phoning churches, community organizations, schools, and service groups in the town asking for support. Bedding materials, accommodations, and food for upwards of 1,000 people were needed.

By 8 P.M., Lewisporte was ready. Local volunteers were notified that passengers would be arriving "at any time," so many stayed up through the night, waiting.

The townspeople needn't have lost sleep. Because of the tedious deplaning process, the first busload of passengers did not arrive at Lewisporte's St. Matthew's United Church until 1:30 P.M. on September 12. Busloads continued to arrive for the next four to five hours. By day's end, weary, bewildered travelers from four flights—773 people of all ages from more than a dozen countries, toting only their carry-on bags—found themselves being treated like special guests in makeshift quarters set up in churches, service-organization buildings, and schools. (Passengers on the same flight were kept together in each town to more easily round them up when the airspace was cleared and planes were again permitted to fly.) For many, telephones and televisions were priorities—the first, to contact family and friends and assure them of their safety; the second, to view for the first time images of the attacks.

With the risk of additional terrorist attacks real, no one knew how long the planes would be grounded. As the hours became days, volunteers in Lewisporte

The Point You Won't Find on a Map

On September 11, 2001, transatlantic planes that had passed the "point of no return" continued to North America and were diverted to the closest available Canadian airport. The "point of no return" refers to the point at which an airplane traveling across an ocean no longer has enough fuel to return to its airport of origin and must continue to the closest airport on the next landfall. It is different for different types of aircraft. Transatlantic planes that had not passed that point were directed to turn around and land at the closest European airport.

and the other communities—physicians, students, even office and business workers who used personal vacation leave in order to be available—made the travelers feel welcome and comfortable. They fed them thousands of hot meals, supplied hundreds of toiletries, and provided friendship and support—all at no charge—until the skies reopened on Saturday, September 15.

Returning the Kindness of Strangers

Since returning home, many of the stranded travelers have been finding ways of repaying the townspeople for their kindness. Mayor Hooper and community leaders from Lewisporte, as well as the surrounding communities, have said that a simple thank-you was enough, but the passengers have thought otherwise. Here are

two examples; there are many others.

■ Shirley Brooks-Jones, from Columbus, Ohio, was one of 218 passengers on Delta Airlines flight 15. She was housed at the Lions Club while in Lewisporte. "When we got back on the plane," she recalls, "I was talking with a physician, a native of Canada who now lives in the United States, about what we could do to let the people know that we really appreciated what they had done."

They decided on a scholarship fund for students at Lewisporte Collegiate, the local high school. With permission from the captain to use the plane's public address system, Mrs. Brooks-Jones proposed the idea to all aboard. Before landing, she collected more than $15,000 from the passengers and crew.

The scholarship is now coordinated through the Columbus Foundation, a nonprofit organization in Ohio. A $15,000 matching donation was made, and the scholarship continues to grow.

■ Passengers from Continental Airlines flight 45 were housed at the Philadelphia Pentecostal Tabernacle, across the street from the Lewisporte Middle School. During their stay, several travelers, including five from the Rockefeller Foundation in New York, used the school's computers.

When the five returned to New York, the Foundation surprised the school with a grant of $52,500 to upgrade its computers. □ □

Shawn Woodford is the Lewisporte, Newfoundland, town manager and the former manager/editor of *The Pilot*, a community newspaper based in Lewisporte.

Kill Foot Pain Dead!

Total Relief Guaranteed– Risk-Free.

Don't blame foot pain on your shoes! Most foot pain comes from misalignment of the bones in your feet.

Foot pain begins when your foot's balance and natural elasticity is gone. Corns, calluses, bunions, even hammertoes can develop, as well as toe cramps, fallen arches, burning skin, tender blisters, flaking and chafing. Ankle, leg, knee, hip - even lower back pain, can result from improper foot alignment. And when your feet hurt, you hurt all over.

Now! No More Foot Pain. Guaranteed!

Featherspring® Foot Supports, a remarkable discovery from Europe are unlike anything you have ever tried. First, they are *custom-formed* for your feet and your feet only! Secondly, they help restore and maintain the elastic support you had when you were younger. They actually help realign your feet, while absorbing shock and relieving pain.

© Featherspring, 712 N. 34th Street, Seattle, WA 98103-8881

For over 40 years, Feathersprings have brought blessed relief to more than 3,000,000 foot pain sufferers world wide. No other foot support has ever given so much relief to so many people.

It doesn't matter whether you are a woman or man, whether your feet are size 4 or 14, what width your foot is, how low or high your arches are, how old you are or how long you've had foot pain... we know Feathersprings will work for you.

Visit our web site at www.featherspring.com

Guaranteed To Kill Your Foot Pain Dead! We'll Prove It To You Risk Free!

If you are bothered by aches and pains of the feet, legs, or lower back, we state without reservation that Feathersprings will bring you relief or *you risk nothing*.

Send today for FREE Fact Kit.

Cut out and mail in the coupon below TODAY for FREE information, including details of our risk-free money back guarantee.

Custom–Formed Feathersprings end foot pain... once and for all!

A FOREST OF FACTS ABOUT
ARBOR DAY
BY ALICE CARY

—USDA

■ **Celebrated throughout the United States, Arbor Day exists because of a zealous tree lover named Julius Sterling Morton.** J. Sterling Morton was born in Adams, New York, in 1832, but his life took a decisive turn on his wedding day in October 1854. After he and his bride, Caroline Joy French, were married in Detroit, they headed west for adventure in the wilds of the Nebraska Territory. Soon Morton became editor of the *Nebraska City News,* Nebraska's first newspaper, and the couple settled on 160 treeless acres. The keyword here is *treeless.* Despite the barren landscape, Morton believed that Nebraska could become a great agricultural and horticultural state. Calling orchards "missionaries of culture and refinement," he stated that not only do they provide shade, shelter, fruit, fuel, and beauty, but failure to plant fruit trees could "delay [the] settlement and improvement" of Nebraska.

■ **Morton did more than just admire and plant trees; they became part of his work.** Despite having a busy career and four sons, the Ne-braska settler planted thousands of trees on the homestead he called the Morton "Ranche." He planted an apple orchard, as well as peach, plum, and pear trees, plus cottonwoods, evergreens, beeches, and more. He also worked as a journalist and a politician, becoming secretary and acting governor of the Nebraska Territory from 1858 to 1861. In 1893, President Grover Cleveland appointed him U.S. secretary of agriculture. He also served on the Nebraska State Board of Agriculture and the State Horticultural Society.

■ **Morton took every opportunity to spread the word.** He gave speeches and filled his newspaper with agricultural advice, urging Nebraskans to plant trees and try new crops. Morton was the main speaker at the first "territorial fair" in 1859, a precursor to the Nebraska State Fair (Nebraska became a state in 1867). Just getting to the fair posed a challenge for many people because the local steamboats weren't running—one was stuck on a sandbar and the other had sunk. In spite of such troubles, the fair was a success, and Morton even won three prizes (two for his stallion and one for his boar).

■ **Arbor Day was almost called Sylvan Day.** In 1872, Morton declared: "If I had the power, I would compel every man in the State who had a home of his own to plant out and cultivate fruit trees." He began to implement his dream by suggesting that April 10, 1872, be declared Arbor Day in Nebraska and that awards be given to the individual and to the agricultural society that planted the most trees on that day. Folks liked his idea, but several members of the Nebraska State Board of Agriculture favored the name Sylvan Day (*sylvan* means "wooded"). Morton argued that *sylvan* refers only to forest trees and that the name Arbor Day was more inclusive, covering forest trees *and* fruit trees.

■ **Morton's own first celebration of Arbor Day was something of a failure.** He had ordered 800 trees to plant on April 10, 1872, but they didn't arrive in time. Morton noted in his diary: "But they will come soon & [sic] then I will put them out." The statewide ceremony was more successful, with over 1 million trees planted. Two years later, he wrote: "Arbor Day, an invention of mine, now [is] a public holiday, destined to become a blessing to posterity as well as to ourselves."

■ **Morton's seed of an idea kept growing.** By 1885, Arbor Day became a legal holiday in Nebraska, and April 22, Morton's birthday, was selected as its date. On that day, thousands of Nebraska City citizens turned out for one big party, including 1,000 schoolchildren who formed a parade. Within 20 years of its creation, the holiday was celebrated in every American state except Delaware, which eventually joined in. Par-

ticularly pleasing to Morton was the fact that schools across the country began celebrating Arbor Day by dedicating the trees they planted to special people. He liked to say, "Other holidays repose upon the past; Arbor Day proposes for the future."

■ **The Morton family motto was "Plant trees," and the family sank deep roots.** Today, the family home, Arbor Lodge, is a state park in Nebraska City, Nebraska. Over the years, it grew from four rooms into a 52-room mansion, complete with a terraced garden, a pine grove, and 65 acres with more than 250 varieties of trees and shrubs.

J. Sterling Morton died at age 70 on April 27, 1902, writing just a month earlier that he hoped to plant trees as soon as the weather turned warm. A statue of him stands in the National Hall of Fame in Washington, D.C. Morton's oldest son, Joy (who founded the Morton Salt Company), created the Morton Arboretum, located in Lisle, Illinois.

□□

Alice Cary is a contributing editor at *Biography Magazine*. Her books include biographies of children's authors Jean Craighead George and Katherine Paterson.

WHEN IS ARBOR DAY?

National Arbor Day is celebrated on the last Friday in April, although some states observe it on different dates to coincide with the local area's best planting times. For instance, Hawaii celebrates it on the first Friday in November, and Alaskans celebrate it on the third Monday in May.

BRANCH OUT

To learn more about Arbor Day and the Morton family, go to **www.almanac.com** and click on **Article Links 2003.**

UNCANNY
FACTS
ABOUT

GOATS

Goats don't eat tin cans and they're not gruff. In fact,

many owners say they're charming and smart.

by Martha White

Looking back 10,000 years, it may have been the goat, not the dog, that was man's best friend. Called the "poor-man's cow" for its ability to live in dry climates on meager pasture, the goat was the portable milk, meat, and trading supply that enabled early nomads, explorers, and colonists to travel. Today, goats continue to provide a wide range of products: Worldwide, more people drink goat milk than any other variety; it is more easily digestible than cow milk. In farmers' markets from Maine to California, and north into Canada, you're apt to find goat cheese (also called chèvre, fromage, feta, crottin, and others), goat-milk soaps, and skeins of mohair and cashmere yarn. You may also find that goats are charming, whimsical, unpredictable, and—yes—endearing.

Cashmere-producing goats *(left)* **are bred for their luxurious undercoat, or down.**

"Goats are friendly. You can talk with them. . . . [G]oats come up very quickly and brush against you, as if to say, 'Isn't life good?'"

–Carl Sandburg, American poet and goatkeeper (1878–1967)

Barnyard Basics

If you've lost your heart to a cute little kid, or baby goat, and have decided to raise one (or two or . . .?), find a mentor, preferably a goat breeder. Whether it's a neighboring goatherd or your local 4-H or extension service agent, you'll want someone with experience in housing, feeding, breeding, kidding, and milking goats.

Expect to provide a shelter. Goats hate to get wet, and even the Swiss breeds need protection from the cold. Plan to keep the stalls clean and draft-free, or you'll pay the cost in vet bills. Trimming hooves, dehorning, castrating, shots, grooming equipment, feed, and fencing are other chores and expenses.

Veteran goatkeeper Linda Meadows, who started with three goats and now keeps 75 to 100 goats on her Quarter Acre Farm in Asotin, Washington, says, "Feed and health care, or veterinary costs, are certainly the highest. Costs will vary from herd to herd and state to state, and between types of goats being raised. Intensively managed dairy goats will have a higher cost per head than will meat goats maintained on pasture in a mild climate for most of the year."

Fence 'Em In

If there's one thing goats have in common with pigs, it's a reputation for escaping to greener pastures. If you have an orchard or garden, be sure your fence is high (six feet) and secure. "Well-fed, content goats with good fencing will stay contained," Meadows

193

says. "Poorly fed, poorly fenced animals will find a way out, especially if they need feed or water. Goats are very smart."

An old proverb suggests "the goat must browse where she is tied," but a tied goat is rarely a healthy goat. Tethered goats are more prone to internal parasites.

Milkers, breeders, and kids need a balanced grain ration. Corl A. Leach (1907–1960), the late editor of *Dairy Goat Journal* and author of the goatkeeper's "bible," *Aids to Goatkeeping* (Dairy Goat Publishing, 1983), recommended that goats be fed from two to six times a day for high-yield production. With decent browsing available, however, the goat will do some of that work for you.

The myth that goats eat anything, from tin cans to noxious weeds, is false; goats are notoriously persnickety. Anything spoiled or soiled repels them, so if your free-range chickens nest in their stall, you'll waste a lot of hay. Goats have been kept by fire departments and ranchers to keep down the brush in fire-prone areas, but they shun certain weeds (including alders and sumacs) and go crazy for fruit trees. They feed from the top down and along perimeters, so they make poor substitutes for a lawn mower. For curiosity, affection, and fun, however, they've got the mowers beat.

Don't approach a goat from the front, a horse from the back, or a fool from any side.

–Yiddish proverb

(continued)

The Best of Breeds

A purebred goat costs more than a mixed breed, sometimes called a common goat. Of the major breeds in North America, you'll find:

ALPINE: This breed originated in the Alps. They are also known as French-Alpine and Alpine dairy goats and are chosen for their excellent milk production.

ANGORA: Originating in the district of Angora in Asia Minor, this is one of the oldest-known breeds and is used predominantly for its wool.

BOER: Introduced into North America in the 1990s, the Boer is a meat breed from South Africa. It shows a variety of colors.

LAMANCHA: A Spanish Murciana, with Swiss and Nubian crosses, the LaMancha breed was developed in Oregon by Eula Frey and has no external ear. These goats are milk producers.

NUBIAN: Also called Anglo-Nubian and developed in England, the Nubian is bred for milk, meat, and hide production. It is the most popular breed in North America.

OBERHASLI: A dairy goat of medium size, this Swiss breed is vigorous and alert in appearance.

PYGMY: Originally called the Cameroon Dwarf, from the former French Cameroon area, this breed is generally chosen as a pet.

SAANEN: From the Saanen Valley in Switzerland, this is a predominantly white goat and a superior milk producer.

TOGGENBURG: Called Tog, this is the oldest-known dairy goat, mostly brown with white stripes on the face, ears, and legs. (Poet Carl Sandburg and his wife kept Togs.)

ALPINE

OBERHASLI

LAMANCHA

TOGGENBURG

NUBIAN

PYGMY
—courtesy National
Pygmy Goat Association

SAANEN

—Illustrations courtesy American Dairy Goat Association, except as noted

A Bite of Cud and a Bit of Culture

Goats have long enjoyed a spotted reputation:

■ **They belong to the genus *Capra*, an offshoot of the cattle family, and like cows, camels, and giraffes, they are ruminants, which means that they are cud-chewing and hoofed.**

■ **The Egyptians worshipped goats, and the Greeks sacrificed them, making them "scapegoats" that took on the sins of the community.**

■ **During the Middle Ages, Christians feared that goats were Satan's associates because of their cloven hooves and their lecherous ways when in heat.**

■ **In the traditional zodiac, the sign of Capricorn, represented by the goat, is noted for creativity.**

■ **In Latin, the word for goat, *capre*, gives us *capricious*, for "lighthearted" or "impulsive."**

Solving the Mystery of Fainting Goats

Identified in 1880 on a farm in Tennessee, fainting goats are also called Tennessee stiff-leg goats. These goats are myotonic, which means that their leg muscles lock up whenever they are startled. Although they do not lose consciousness, their leg muscles may go into a spasm so suddenly that they fall over, which makes it look as though they are fainting. The temporary paralysis passes as they relax, but, oddly, it has the result of making them better meat goats because the repeated stiffening and relaxing of those muscles gives them a superior muscle tone. Some say that their meat is more tender and that they have a greater quantity of meat in proportion to bone.

You can tell whether a goat is a fainter by its ears. Fainting goats have "airplane ears." They do not stand erect but, instead, stick out horizontally.

-photos courtesy Randall Carter/Hollywood Acres Farm

Who Are You Calling an Old Goat?

Most people think that an old goat is discerned by its lascivious reputation. In fact, an old goat can be appraised by its teeth. Young goats lose their milk teeth progressively in their first five years. After that, their permanent teeth are evident and, over time, show signs of wear. ☐ ☐

Martha White, a frequent contributor to *The Old Farmer's Almanac,* has kept ants, gerbils, fish, chickens, cats, rabbits, and dogs and is working up to kids of the four-legged variety.

GET YOUR GOAT
For a nutritional comparison of goat, cow, and human milk; goat cheese recipes; and other fun facts, as well as books for goat care and feeding, go to **www.almanac.com** and click on **Article Links 2003.**

Gestation and Mating Table

	Proper Age for First Mating	Period of Fertility (years)	Number of Females for One Male	Period of Gestation (days) AVERAGE	RANGE
Ewe	90 lb. or 1 yr.	6		147 / 151[8]	142–154
Ram	12–14 mo., well matured	7	50–75[2] / 35–40[3]		
Mare	3 yr.	10–12		336	310–370
Stallion	3 yr.	12–15	40–45[4] / Record 252[5]		
Cow	15–18 mo.[1]	10–14		283	279–290[6] 262–300[7]
Bull	1 yr., well matured	10–12	50[4] / Thousands[5]		
Sow	5–6 mo. or 250 lb.	6		115	110–120
Boar	250–300 lb.	6	50[2] / 35–40[3]		
Doe goat	10 mo. or 85–90 lb.	6		150	145–155
Buck goat	Well matured	5	30		
Bitch	16–18 mo.	8		63	58–67
Male dog	12–16 mo.	8			
She cat	12 mo.	6		63	60–68
Doe rabbit	6 mo.	5–6		31	30–32
Buck rabbit	6 mo.	5–6	30		

[1]Holstein and beef: 750 lb.; Jersey: 500 lb. [2]Hand-mated. [3]Pasture. [4]Natural. [5]Artificial. [6]Beef; 8–10 days shorter for Angus. [7]Dairy. [8]For fine wool breeds.

Maximum Life Spans of Animals in Captivity (years)

Ant (queen) ...... 18+
Badger 26
Beaver .... 15+
Box turtle (Eastern) 138
Camel .... 35+
Cat (domestic) 34
Chicken (domestic) . 25
Chimpanzee 51
Coyote .... 21+
Dog (domestic) 29
Dolphin.......... 25
Duck (domestic)... 23
Eagle........... 55
Elephant 75
Giraffe 36
Goat (domestic) ... 20
Goldfish 41
Goose (domestic).. 20
Gorilla .... 50+
Horse 62
Housefly...... 17 days
Kangaroo 30
Lion............ 29
Monarch butterfly . 1+
Mouse (house) .. 6
Mussel
  (freshwater)... 70–80
Octopus 2–3
Quahog.......... 150
Rabbit.......... 18+
Squirrel, gray 23
Tiger............ 26
Toad 40
Tortoise (Marion's)152+
Turkey (domestic)...16

Incubation Periods of Birds and Poultry (days)

Canary 14–15
Chicken 21
Duck 26–32
Goose......30–34
Guinea.....26–28
Parakeet....18–20
Pheasant....22–24
Swan 42
Turkey 28

Gestation Periods of Wild Animals (days)

Black bear 210
Hippo...225–250
Moose ...240–250
Otter.....270–300
Reindeer .210–240
Seal 330
Squirrel, gray...44
Whale, sperm. .480
Wolf.......60–63

	Estral (estrous) Cycle Including Heat Period AVERAGE	RANGE	Length of Heat (estrus) AVERAGE	RANGE	Usual Time of Ovulation	When Cycle Recurs if Not Bred
Mare	21 days	10–37 days	5–6 days	2–11 days	24–48 hours before end of estrus	21 days
Sow	21 days	18–24 days	2–3 days	1–5 days	30–36 hours after start of estrus	21 days
Ewe	16½ days	14–19 days	30 hours	24–32 hours	12–24 hours before end of estrus	16½ days
Goat	21 days	18–24 days	2–3 days	1–4 days	Near end of estrus	21 days
Cow	21 days	18–24 days	18 hours	10–24 hours	10–12 hours after end of estrus	21 days
Bitch	24 days		7 days	5–9 days	1–3 days after first acceptance	Pseudo-pregnancy
Cat		15–21 days	3–4 days, if mated	9–10 days, in absence of male	24–56 hours after coitus	Pseudo-pregnancy

The MOST

Ethelda at the peak of her career, on the block at the Olympics in Antwerp, Belgium *(this page);* **and as a teenager with the Women's Swimming Association of New York City** *(opposite, in circle).*

I F IT HADN'T BEEN FOR A CASE OF polio, a basement swimming pool, and a water-polo player with a radical idea, Ethelda Bleibtrey's life might have been unremarkable.

In 1918, when she was 16 years old, Ethelda, the daughter of a mortician, left her hometown of Waterford, New York, to attend Erasmus Hall High School, a private school in Brooklyn. While there, she fell victim to polio. To strengthen her weakened limbs, she joined the newly formed Women's Swimming Association of New York City.

The swimmers, who took their exercise in a small heated pool in the basement of a nearby hotel, had attracted the attention of Louis deBreda Handley, a world-class

The first American woman to win a gold medal

at the Olympics died 25 years ago. Who knew?

BY MEL ALLEN

PERFECT SWIMMER

swimmer and water-polo player. Handley volunteered to coach them. He had analyzed the swimming strokes of the day and thought he knew a more efficient way to move through water. The girls provided an opportunity for him to test his theories.

Handley taught the girls a stroke he called the six-beat-double-trudgen crawl. (It soon became known simply as the American crawl.) It required three leg kicks to each powerful arm stroke—a radical departure from the practice of the day. He also taught them to breathe by turning the head slightly to the side, instead of the rolling motion employed by the Australians, the elite swimmers of the period. None of the girls learned the stroke quicker or swam faster than the blond, blue-eyed Ethelda.

Handley ended each swim practice with a game of water polo. This improved the girls' endurance and, combined with their streamlined stroke, gave them speed and stamina never before seen in women swimmers.

Her First Big Race

■ On August 16, 1919, over 5,000 spectators surrounded the swimming pool on Manhattan Beach, just beyond Coney Island. They had come to watch a quarter-mile race between Ethelda,

Wearing a new style of suit, Ethelda poses with swimmers Burt Kelly and Ludy Langer for a photo promoting swimming exhibitions.

country," reported the *New York Times*. "Spectators slapped one another on the back, jumped into the air with glee; women . . . hugged one another, and sometimes in mistake or out of pure, unexalted joy—the man nearest them." With the victory, Ethleda assured herself a spot on the American Olympic team for the following summer.

Her Golden Opportunity

■ In August 1920, the U.S. Olympic team set sail on a transport ship for Antwerp, Belgium. They were over 200 strong, including—for the first time in Olympic competition—more than a dozen women swimmers. Many believed that Ethelda was the brightest star among the female athletes onboard.

The two-week voyage became a test of endurance. The ship reeked of formaldehyde because the caskets of 1,800 American soldiers killed in the European battlefields had just been unloaded. During the trip, the athletes tried to stay in shape. The swimmers swam in a makeshift eight-foot-long canvas pool erected on the deck, taking turns swimming in place while strapped to the side of the pool. The runners jogged around the deck. The javelin throwers attached a rope to their javelins and aimed them out to sea.

The team arrived in a country torn apart by the war, yet chosen to host the Olympic games to help in its recovery. Lodging was scarce, so the Americans slept eight to a room on folding cots and got by with no hot water. Having no suitable competition pools in Antwerp, city officials used boards to fashion a makeshift pool in a frigid tidal estuary. The water was so dark

who had only a year of competitive experience, and Australian Fanny Durack, who held 11 world records. The race generated unprecedented excitement because women athletes were still a curiosity.

Though Fanny was considered unbeatable, Ethelda led from start to finish, astonishing onlookers. When it was over, the crowd erupted with "a spontaneous volley of applause which has seldom been surpassed at a swimming meet in this

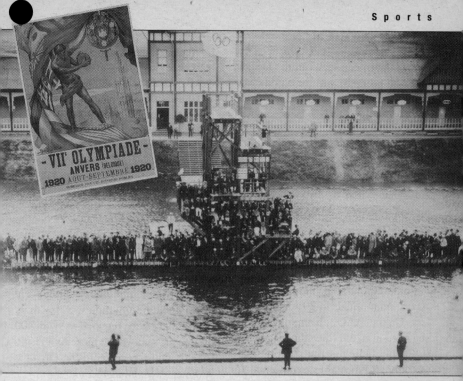

The official poster of the 1920 Olympics *(inset, above)* and the estuary in Antwerp where the Olympic swimming events were held. Members of the 1920 women's Olympic swim team, all in uniform, surround Ethelda *(right)*.

that swimmers could not see below the surface, and one diver suffered nightmares about striking the murky mud bottom, getting stuck, and not being found. The water was so cold—50°F—that several water-polo players collapsed from hypothermia, causing officials to declare a winner after only half a game had been completed.

Despite these conditions, 18-year-old Ethelda, outfitted in a black silk racing suit, excelled. She set world records in every event in which she swam: the individual 100-meter and 300-meter races, and the 400-meter relay.

She returned to New York a national heroine. In Waterford, townspeople lined the riverbanks and filled canoes and rowboats to watch her perform her now-famous American crawl in the Hudson. The next year, she was the world champion in every event she entered.

Officials in New Zealand and Australia, where swimming was extremely popular, begged her to visit and compete against their fastest women. She did, and caused a sensation. After watching her, an Australian writer described her as "the most perfect swimmer, [female] or male, ever developed." Ethelda typically responded modestly to such praise: "Records are like bubbles," she said. "They don't last very long."

For three years, she never lost a race. At one point, she held 20 Amateur Athletic Union (AAU) championships, yet she lived in an era when the president of the AAU believed that "sport was a morally questionable experience for women."

Her Last Laps

■ In 1922, Ethelda retired from competition. She became a swimming teacher and swam in exhibitions, popularizing the notion that women could swim fast and long. She made news again in 1925 while vacationing in Rhode Island. There she saw a mother and her two children in a boat about to capsize. She swam out to the boat and held it steady until rescuers arrived.

Ethelda married twice and had a daughter, who became a champion swimmer. When Ethelda's second husband died, she moved to Florida. In 1967, she and Louis deBreda Handley were inducted into the International Swimming Hall of Fame in Fort Lauderdale. Later, she donated all her medals and trophies to a church for a fund drive. Years passed quietly before her death on May 7, 1978.

Today, Ethelda Bleibtrey is a footnote in history, the answer to the trivia question, Who was the first American woman to win an Olympic gold medal? She won three, about which an Olympic teammate said, "She would have won more, but there were only three races."

One Unbeatable Record

■ At the 1920 Olympics, Ethelda was so strong at the finish of the 300-meter race, a distance believed to favor female swimmers, that organizers eliminated the event from all future Olympics. Since then, women have been required to swim 400 meters, the same as the men. As a result, Ethelda will forever hold the Olympic 300-meter swimming record.

WHERE IT ALL BEGAN

Today, thanks to the efforts of Sister Joyce Gadoua of Waterford, New York, a plaque honoring Ethelda Bleibtrey's achievements is displayed in Knickerbocker Park, near the river where she learned to swim.

□□

Mel Allen, executive editor of *Yankee* Magazine, frequently writes about sports for *The Old Farmer's Almanac*.

READY, SET, GO!
To learn more about Ethelda Bleibtrey's daring exploits, go to www.almanac.com and click on **Article Links 2003.**

Best Fishing Days, 2003

The best fishing times are when the ocean tides are restless before their turn and in the first hour of ebbing. All fish in all waters, salt and fresh, feed most heavily at those times.

The best temperatures for different fish species vary widely, of course, and are important mainly if you are going to have your own fishpond. The best temperatures for brook trout are 45° to 65°F. Brown trout and rainbow trout are more tolerant of higher temperatures. Smallmouth black bass do best in cool water. Horned pout take any temperature.

Most of us go fishing when we can get time off, not because it is the best time. But there *are* best times, according to fishing lore:

■ One hour before and one hour after high tides, and one hour before and one hour after low tides. (The times of high tides for Boston are given on pages 44–70 and corrected for your locality on pages 232–233. Inland, the times for high tides correspond with the times the Moon is due south. Low tides are halfway between high tides.)

■ During the "morning rise" (after sunup for a spell) and the "evening rise" (just before sundown and the hour or so after).

■ When the barometer is steady or on the rise. (But, of course, even in a three-day driving northeaster, the fish aren't going to give up feeding. Their hunger clock keeps right on working, and the smart fisherman will find just the right bait.)

■ When there is a hatch of flies—caddis flies or mayflies, commonly. (The fisherman will have to match the hatching flies with *his* fly or go fishless.)

■ When the breeze is from a westerly quarter rather than from the north or east.

■ When the water is still or rippled, rather than during a wind.

■ Starting on the day the Moon is new and continuing through the day it is full.

Moon Between New and Full, 2003

- January 2–18
- February 1–16
- March 2–18
- April 1–16
- May 1–15
- May 31–June 14
- June 29–July 13
- July 29–August 12
- August 27–September 10
- September 25–October 10
- October 25–November 8
- November 23–December 8
- December 23–January 7

What People Fish For (freshwater)

Bass	35%
Trout	18%
Catfish	11%
All species	9%
Bream	6%
Crappie	6%
Carp/muskie/panfish/ pike/shad/steelhead/ striper	5%
Walleye	5%
Perch	3%
Salmon	2%

–courtesy American Sportfishing Association

Mr. Smith's MADDENING Mind-Manglers

Test your math and logic skills with these puzzles, compiled for *The Old Farmer's Almanac* by RAYNOR R. SMITH SR., mathematics teacher at Keene High School, Keene, New Hampshire.

Answers appear on page 225.

WORDPLAY

1 Eric challenged Ray to take the letters of the expression "nor do we" and make them into one word. Ray surprised him with a quick answer. What was it?

2 Miss Thomson told her students, "I am going to try to 'stump' you. What can you place in a corner so it will never move from the corner, but it can travel around the world? You'll get an 'A' for the correct answer!" Did you get an "A"?

3 Jordan asked Cassidy why a nautical mile was nearly one-seventh longer than a mile on land. Cassidy gave Jordan an absorbing answer, but it wasn't what he expected. Can you guess Cassidy's answer?

NUMBER CRUNCHERS

4 Rob went into a store that advertised a sale with successive discounts of 15%, 10%, and 5% off. Customers could take the discounts in any order they wanted. Which order would give Rob the best deal?

5 Joseph had to sell at least 20 candy bars for the youth league. So starting with 20, the first night he sold a certain number of bars. He took the number of bars that remained and doubled it to sell on the second night. He sold the same number of bars on the second night as on the first. He then took what remained and tripled them and sold the same number of bars as on each of the first two nights, this time with none remaining. How many bars did he sell each night?

6 Clark told Lois that five screwdrivers and two wrenches weigh the same as three hammers. He then said that one hammer weighs the same as one screwdriver and one wrench. If so, how many screwdrivers weigh as much as one hammer?

7 Jesse went shopping with a wallet full of money. She told her dad, "I spent one-third of my money in the first store, one-fourth of my money in the second store, and one-fifth of my money in the last store, and I have $13 left!" How much money did she start with?

MATCH GAME
Bones and Muscles

Below are the names of 20 bones or muscles in the human body. Can you match them with where they're found?

–Rob Simbeck

1. biceps	A. ankle
2. carpus	B. arm (2)
3. clavicle	C. chest (3)
4. deltoid	D. ear
5. femur	E. fingers/toes
6. fibula	F. foot
7. humerus	G. hand
8. mandible	H. head (2)
9. metacarpal	I. jaw
10. metatarsal	J. leg (2)
11. occipital	K. shoulder (2)
12. pectoral	L. thigh (2)
13. phalanges	M. wrist
14. quadriceps	
15. scapula	
16. stapes	
17. sternum	
18. talus	
19. temporal	
20. tibia	

How to Tell When Someone's Lying

"I'll tell you God's truth." His right hand suddenly ordered divine retribution to stand by. "I am the son of some wealthy people in the middle-west—all dead now. I was brought up in America but educated at Oxford because all my ancestors have been educated there for many years. It is a family tradition."

He looked at me sideways—and I knew why Jordan Baker had believed he was lying. He hurried the phrase "educated at Oxford," or swallowed it or choked on it as though it had bothered him before. And with this doubt his whole statement fell to pieces and I wondered if there wasn't something sinister about him after all.

"What part of the middle-west?" I inquired casually.

"San Francisco."

–The Great Gatsby,
F. Scott Fitzgerald (1896–1940)

According to a recent study conducted by the University of Connecticut, the average American tells 26 lies every day. So if you have the feeling someone's not being entirely honest with you, you're probably right. But how can you tell for sure?

As the philosopher G. J. Warnock puts it, "Even looking sincere, though perhaps slightly more difficult than simply saying that one is, is an art that can be learned." And although lie detectors have been in use for more than a century, many courts still refuse to admit their findings as evidence, because a coolheaded liar can learn to fool the machine.

I consulted several sources and talked with a number of people whose jobs require them to sift fact from fiction. The subtle signs of lying they rely on are all present in

by Tim Clark

the passage from F. Scott Fitzgerald's *The Great Gatsby* quoted here—sworn oaths, peculiar body language, unverifiable facts, shifty eyes, verbal stumbling, and absurd claims.

SWORN OATHS

■ "A liar is always lavish of oaths," said the 17th-century French playwright Pierre Corneille. Like Gatsby, the liar often begins his prevarication by swearing to God that he's telling the truth, the whole truth, and nothing but the truth. "Sociopaths are especially elegant at this," says a psychologist I consulted. "And addicts are often so adept at lying to themselves that they actually believe the lies they are telling you." So be on your guard if a person swears—on his mother's grave, on his children's lives, in any exaggerated and overemotional way—that he's not lying.

"Once, I had a girl swear to me she hadn't eaten some candy belonging to another kid," says the dean of discipline at a middle school. "Several kids had seen her do it, but she wouldn't admit it. So I said, 'Well, I guess we'll have to use the stomach pump!' And I went to the closet and got out a little length of rubber hose that attached to the sink, and that was all I needed to do. When she saw that hose, the truth came out."

PECULIAR BODY LANGUAGE

■ Experts on body language contend that when people touch their face, especially the area between the nose and the upper lip, they are being untruthful. It may be that they are unconsciously trying to cover their mouth to prevent the lie from being told or to prevent you from "seeing" it being told. Many liars involuntarily smirk when they are being deceptive. There is a story told of a psychiatrist in a mental institution who was surprised to find a group of his autistic patients laughing uproariously while watching a television with the sound turned off. He checked to see what was on and found that it was a speech by the President of the United States. The

Would I lie to you?

I never seen that before in my life, copper!

patients had no idea what he was saying, but they could tell just by looking at him that he was lying.

A police officer with long experience as an interrogator says, "People will cooperate right up to the point where they know you know they're lying. Then there's a big physical change. They'll take an extremely defensive posture—suddenly straighten up in the chair, cross their arms, tighten their muscles, start tapping their fingers on the table. If you were innocent, you wouldn't do that."

UNVERIFIABLE FACTS

■ Gatsby was careful to say that his parents were dead. When a person gives you information that's impossible to check easily, watch out. A banker told me he gets suspicious when a loan applicant claims expensive assets such as furniture or paintings instead of stocks and bonds or real estate: "Eighty thousand dollars worth of furniture? I can't check that in the *Wall Street Journal*. That makes me nervous."

In the same way, a district court judge says he watches for inconsistencies in what a defendant remembers. "If he or she remembers exactly

what words someone used in a private conversation three months ago but is vague about things you can check, like whether it was raining that day, I get suspicious. Something doesn't add up. That's when I look for a baseline of truth, something everyone can agree happened."

SHIFTY EYES

■ Everyone I talked with mentioned eye contact. In fact, most people would probably agree that the "shifty-eyed" have always been considered untrustworthy. Some experts believe that when you are asked a question, the direction in which you roll your eyes is revealing. A person trying to remember a fact, they say, will unconsciously roll the eyes up and to his or her right. The right side of the body, including the face, is controlled by the left hemisphere of the brain, which deals with facts, figures, and logical thought. A liar will roll his or her eyes up and to the left, the side controlled by the right hemisphere, the source of imaginative stories. "If you watch politicians, they look to the left," says my police interrogator. "I know a detective who was trained in this stuff, and they showed him a tape of President Clinton when he

Lipstick? Don't be silly, dear. I cut myself shaving!

said he hadn't slept with that woman. He looked to the left!"

Some people will go to great lengths to keep you from seeing their eyes. "The first time I interviewed chefs for a new restaurant," a human-resources specialist told me, "one guy had sunglasses on and wouldn't take them off. That made me suspicious. He said he'd graduated from Johnson & Wales University, but when I checked, he'd taken only one course there. The funny thing is, I hired him anyway because my gut told me he'd be the best chef, and he was!"

VERBAL STUMBLING

■ A former private-school headmaster says he became suspicious of students who talked too fast when called on to explain their behavior. "Rather than directly confront them, I found it best to just remain silent," he explains. "They were uncomfortable with silence. They'd try to fill it up with words. If I just sat there looking at them, not saying anything, eventually the truth would come out."

The police interrogator says, "If you ask, 'Were you there on Friday night?' an innocent person will say, 'No, I wasn't.' Guilty people will ask you a question to buy some time: 'Which Friday night?' If they're trying to hide something, they'll ask another question."

Sometimes, a liar will say more than he or she intends to. "When you ask a kid a question, don't give away what you already know," says the middle-school dean. "If you have a note you think the kid wrote, don't ask him, 'Did you write this note?' Just hand it to him and say, 'Read this.' I've had kids get to the bad part and say, 'Well, I didn't mean that!'"

ABSURD CLAIMS

■ San Francisco isn't in the "middle-west," and a cornered liar will occasionally say something so completely absurd that it's obvious he or she is hiding the truth. This happens frequently with very small children. "My mother went in to get my brother after his nap, and every piece of paper had been torn off the wall above his crib and torn into pieces," recalls the headmaster. "She asked him what happened, and with perfect candor he explained that a huge rat had come in and torn up all the papers."

"Moms are the best interrogators," the police officer agreed. □□

Munch, munch

Tim Clark, author of *A Millennium Primer: Timeless Truths and Delightful Diversions,* has written dozens of articles for *The Old Farmer's Almanac.*

Winning Essays

in the 2002 Essay Contest

MY BRUSH WITH FAME

It was April 1946. World War II had recently ended and the automobile plants were working overtime to produce enough cars for eager buyers. People put their names on car dealers' lists in hopes of having the chance to buy a new car. Our family was planning the cross-country trip of a lifetime, and our name was on one of those lists.

One day, my father was notified that there was a new car waiting at the dealer. Suddenly, it was in the driveway! We stood in awe of the most beautiful car my eight-year-old eyes had ever beheld, an aquamarine 1946 Ford deluxe sedan.

After a thrilling trip "back East," my father decided to stop at Dearborn, Michigan, to tell the Ford people how much pleasure their product had provided us. Arrangements were made for him to meet a company official, and he took me along. After I shook hands with the representative, my father said, "Remember this day, son, because you've just shaken hands with the greatest man in the world, Mr. Henry Ford."

There will always be a special place in my memory for the white-haired old gentleman who chuckled and replied, "Don't you believe it, lad. The greatest man in the world is your father."

–Russell Duke, Portland, Oregon

SECOND PRIZE

In kindergarten, I loved to read and write so much that I decided I would be an author when I grew up. One day, my teacher began reading a book called *A Chair for My Mother*. It was the first time I had ever heard it. I fell in love with the story. I knew I wanted to write like that.

About a year ago, my mom had a dentist appointment. My sister and I went with her. While we were waiting for Mom, I decided to write a story. A nice woman came in and sat in the empty chair between my sister and me. She asked me what I was doing. I told her I was writing a story because I wanted to become an author. She said her name was Vera B. Williams, the author of *A Chair for My Mother*! I told her it was one of my favorite books. Then she went in. My mom came out and we told her everything.

We rushed out and got two copies of the book and went back. Vera signed mine: "To the future author."

We sent stories to each other, and I now have the two sequels to her book.

–Kimberly Condoulis, age 10, Brick, New Jersey

THIRD PRIZE

I was eight years old, growing up in sun-washed Cuba. We lived in poverty, so my siblings and I had to sacrifice a playful youth for one of work and responsibility.

My mother worked for a dollar a day at a local cigar factory. She was considered the best tobacco roller, for she had the "hand" that was necessary for a well-shaped cigar. Eventually, the factory assigned her to work from home, where I became her assistant.

At night, under dim candlelight, we would go about our work. I would first check the tobacco fillings for quality. I would then tightly press the fillings all night. Finally, my mother would carefully roll the pressed fillings with whole tobacco leaves so that they would taper from one end to the other in a style called a bell.

We made those cigars for three years. It wasn't until ten years later that I discovered they were for the prime minister of England. Little did I know that we were creating the most famous cigars to date: "Churchill's Bells"!

–*Julio Valdes, Petaluma, California*

HONORABLE MENTION

Several years ago, I attended a family barbecue at a friend's house. Their teenage son had invited his guitar teacher and a friend to come over and provide some music.

After the meal, we had a sing-along. Although the songs we adults requested were not exactly the kind of tunes the boys regularly played, they were generous enough to accommodate us, and everyone had a good time.

Some years later, the guitar teacher and friend formed a rock group that quickly gained in popularity. Although their music isn't exactly my cup of tea, I can brag that at one time, I sang with (some of) the Barenaked Ladies.

–*Diane Hall, Havelock, Ontario*

EDITOR'S NOTE: *We received dozens of essays describing encounters with famous people. Some of those with whom readers "brushed" include Steve Allen, Leroy Anderson, Neil Armstrong, Lucille Ball, George Bush, Johnny Cash, Linda Evans, Eddie Giacomin, Mark Grace, Wade Hayes, Dustin Hoffman, Mick Jagger, Bob Keeshan, Stephen King, the Dalai Lama, Billy Martin, Walter Mondale, Oliver North, Tip O'Neill, Arnold Palmer, Ronald Reagan, Elizabeth Taylor, Bobby Vinton, and John Wayne. Thank you and congratulations to everyone!*

**Announcing the 2003
Essay Contest**

My Most Memorable Weather Event

Have you ever been caught in a blizzard? Lost in a fog? Spared by a tornado? Kissed by morning dew? Tell us a story about a specific weather event or condition and how it affected your life. Please describe your experience in 200 words or less. See page 213 for prizes, rules, and submission information.

Winning Recipes

in the 2002 Recipe Contest

CASEROLES

Thanks to everyone who sent recipes.
To see some of the other submissions, go to
www.almanac.com.

Cheesy Chicken Crunch Casserole

3 cups cubed cooked chicken or turkey
2 cups diced celery
1/2 cup grated American cheese
1/4 cup grated Swiss cheese
1/3 cup slivered almonds
3/4 cup mayonnaise
1/2 teaspoon salt
2 teaspoons onion juice
2 teaspoons lemon juice
2 cups crushed potato chips

■ PREHEAT OVEN TO 400°F. OIL A 13x9-inch or equivalent casserole dish or glass cake pan. In a large bowl, combine all ingredients except potato chips. Fill pan with chicken mixture. Sprinkle mixture with potato chips. Bake for 15 to 20 minutes. **Serves 6 to 8.**

–*Marcia Puri, Rockford, Illinois*

Forgotten Chicken and Baby Limas

1 pound dry baby lima beans
cold water
6 slices bacon, diced
1 cup flour
2 teaspoons poultry seasoning
4-1/2 to 5 pounds chicken, cut into
    serving pieces
4 sweet onions, sliced
2 cloves garlic, minced
1-1/2 teaspoons dried thyme
1 quart chicken broth, boiling hot
2 teaspoons salt
1/2 teaspoon pepper

■ PUT THE BEANS INTO A LARGE STOVE-top-to-oven-safe casserole dish or a large Dutch oven, and add enough water to cover, plus an inch. Soak for at least an hour. Drain the beans in a colander and set aside. Preheat oven to 275°F. In the same casserole dish or pot, cook the bacon until it curls (don't cook until crisp). Remove and set aside, leaving bacon drippings in the casserole dish or pot. In a 1-gallon plastic or brown bag, mix the flour and poultry seasoning. Put the chicken into the bag, and shake several times until all pieces are lightly coated. Brown the chicken in the bacon drippings. Remove and set aside. In the remaining drippings, cook the onion and garlic until translucent (not brown). Remove and set aside. Pour off any excess bacon drippings, leaving just enough to grease the casserole dish or pot. Add chicken pieces. In a bowl, toss together the beans, bacon, onions, garlic, and thyme, and spoon the mixture over the chicken. Add the hot broth, salt, and pepper. Bake for 5½ hours, or until the beans are tender and the liquid is absorbed; this should be moist but not soupy. **Serves 6 to 8.**

–Jamie Parchman, Ogden, Utah

THIRD PRIZE

Ham-and-Pineapple Casserole

1/4 cup (1/2 stick) margarine, softened
1/2 cup granulated sugar
5 large eggs
1-1/2 cups cubed cooked ham
1 can (20 ounces) cubed pineapple, drained
2 tablespoons fresh lemon juice
8 to 10 slices slightly stale white bread,
    crust removed and cubed

■ COAT AN OVEN-TO-TABLE 13x9-INCH casserole dish with nonstick spray. Preheat oven to 325°F. In a large bowl, cream together margarine and sugar. Beat in eggs, one at a time, until well mixed. Stir in ham, pineapple, and lemon juice; fold in bread cubes. Pour mixture into prepared casserole dish and smooth the top. Bake, uncovered,

for 30 to 35 minutes, or until custard is set and top is golden. **Serves 6 to 8.**

–Marilou Robinson, Portland, Oregon

Special thanks to our friends at Cook's Illustrated *magazine for sorting through the entries, identifying and testing 14 finalists, and providing taste-test results. Thanks, also, to the staff of* The Old Farmer's Almanac, *who cooked, tasted, and chose the winning recipes.*

Announcing the 2003 Recipe Contest

Potato Dishes

One potato, two potato, three potato— more? How many ways can you cook potatoes? Send us your best recipes using any type of "white" potatoes as the main ingredient in appetizers, main dishes, salads, side dishes, or desserts. (Save your yam and sweet potato recipes for another time.)

□ □

Essay and Recipe Contest Rules

Cash prizes (first prize, $100; second prize, $75; third prize, $50) will be awarded for the best original essays on the subject "My Most Memorable Weather Event" and the best recipes for potato dishes (amateur cooks only, please). All entries become the property of Yankee Publishing Inc., which reserves all rights to the material. Winners will be announced in the 2004 edition of *The Old Farmer's Almanac* and posted on our Web site: www.almanac.com. The deadline is January 31, 2003. Please type all essays and recipes. Label "Essay Contest" or "Recipe Contest" and send to: The Old Farmer's Almanac, P.O. Box 520, Dublin, NH 03444; or e-mail (subject: Essay Contest or Recipe Contest) to almanac@yankeepub.com.

NORTH AMERICA'S
ONLY NATIVE GRAIN

I t's not corn or wheat. North America's only native grain is wild rice. Wild rice *(Zizania palustris)*—not a true rice in the sense of the common cultivated white and brown rices but an edible grain of a perennial aquatic grass species—was harvested and processed as far back as 3,000 years ago in the western Great Lakes region of the United States and Canada. People of that time used it primarily as a food staple, although it was used as a trade item as well.

Knowledge of wild-rice harvesting traditions comes to us today primarily from Native American Ojibwe (also known as Ojibwa, Ojibway, Anishinabe, and Chippewa). They handed down tales of the origin and discovery of wild rice. They also passed on the traditional ways of harvesting it.

BY SUSAN CAROL HAUSER

–Monroe Killy/Minnesota Historical Society

Grace Rogers and Joe Aitken harvesting wild rice near Walker, Minnesota, in 1939. As he guides the canoe, she knocks ripe rice into it.

–rice illustration: Jacolyn A. Morrison

IT'S ALL IN THE KNOCK

NATURALLY OCCURRING WILD rice grows along river channels and backwaters, in beds that range from a few feet to maybe 100 feet wide. The only way it can be harvested is by boat. A canoe propelled by a forked pole (not paddles) is the perfect vessel because it can slide through the thick grasses that sometimes stand four feet above water. Motorboats would ruin the beds.

Every autumn for centuries, women riced while men hunted. Then and now, it takes two people and skillful action to harvest wild rice: a poler, who stands in the canoe and

■ The Full Wild Rice Moon, called *manoo-minike-giizis* by the Native American Ojibwe people, usually occurs in late August or early September and coincides with the harvest.

215

guides it by pushing the end of a wooden pole that's about 15 feet long into the mucky ground, and a knocker, who "knocks" the ripe rice loose.

The knocker's tools, called knockers, are sticks made of poplar or other lightweight wood that are no more than 30 inches long and weigh up to one pound each. The knocker kneels in the middle of the canoe, reaches into the tall rice grass with one stick, and pulls a bunch of stalks so that they overhang the canoe. With the other stick, the knocker gently and deftly strikes the heads of the stalks, knocking the rice into the canoe. During the harvesting season, a pass is made through the rice beds every four or five days.

■ **The Ojibwe people call wild rice** *manoomin,* **which means "good, kernel-like berry." Early French explorers used the term** *folles avoines,* **which translates as "crazy oats." Early European settlers assigned it the term** *rice,* **comparing it with common white rice.**

FROM CANOE

To be made edible, all harvested wild rice must go through four processing steps. The traditional methods, though rarely practiced today, were common up to the 1960s. They were performed in the rice camp, near the harvesting site. Today, most rice is sold to processing companies that have mechanized these steps.

First, the rice must be dried. The grains are spread 6 to 12 inches deep on tarps and dried (or cured) in the sun for a day or so.

Next, it is parched, or scorched, to loosen the husks. Today, this is done in large metal barrels heated by a wood or a propane fire, but traditionally, this second step was done in cast-iron kettles over a fire. The rice was stirred continually for about an hour. It was determined to be "done"

FOR THE BIRDS

Zizania aquatica, another species of wild rice, once grew in many places east of the Mississippi River, from Louisiana to Maine. Although not suitable for human food (the grain is too thin and meager for processing), it was a major source of food for

wildlife, especially birds. Some *Z. aquatica* still grows along the eastern seaboard, including a major bed in Patuxent River Park, a wild marsh preserve in Maryland, where it is an important food for migrating waterfowl.

Z. texana grows only in

the San Marcos River in Texas. It grows like seaweed, attaining lengths of up to 15 feet, with only a foot or so of the flowering heads rising above the water. Though it could potentially still be a meaningful food for wildlife, it competes in the San

TO TABLE

when it went from soft white to crystalline white inside.

In the third step, called hulling (or jigging), the grain's crisp hulls are separated from the kernels. Today, mechanized equipment does much of this work, but the traditional jigging method was like dancing lightly. A person wearing newly made mocassins stood in or astride a large bucket or in a jig pit (a shallow hole dug in the ground and lined with clay or hides) and tread on the rice.

Finally, the rice is winnowed to remove the dust and broken hulls. Traditionally, this was done by placing the rice in a shallow basket or tray and tossing the rice gently into the air. The chaff blew away, and the rice was finished. Today, this too is done by machine.

Marcos River with recreational traffic and is an endangered species.

CULTIVATING AN APPETITE

In the first half of the 20th century, wild rice began to show up in gourmet restaurants and in grocery and gift stores. It was expensive ($9 to $12 per pound) because of labor-intensive hand-harvesting and a limited supply.

In the 1960s, cultivated wild-rice paddies were developed—first in Minnesota, then in California—thus dramatically changing the availability of wild rice. The ensuing drop in price, to around $4 a pound, affected many western Great Lakes–area families that harvested and processed rice using traditional methods and relied on rice for seasonal income. They eventually responded to the competition by marketing lake and river wild rice as a specialty item, promoting hand-harvesting by canoe. (Cultivated rice is harvested by machine.) Today, about 80 percent of the wild rice grown in the United States is cultivated. In fact, by law, packages of wild rice sold in Minnesota must state the origin of the rice and the method of harvesting.

Some wild rice comes from Canada. Most of it is a variety of *Z. palustris* that has a longer grain than either cultivated wild rice or naturally occurring U.S. rice. Airboats modified as combines are used to harvest the Canadian grain. Because the Canadian beds are frequently in wilderness areas, the rice must be bagged on-site and flown out, making it more expensive than U.S. wild rice.

AN ACQUIRED TASTE

Z. latifolia, sometimes called Manchurian wild rice, is the only *Zizania* that grows naturally outside of North America. Its bulb harbors a fungus that is used as a human food delicacy in Manchuria, Korea, Japan, Burma, and northeastern India.

c o n t i n u e

HOW TO COOK
WILD RICE

Hand-harvested wild rice is usually processed to remove more of the bran, resulting in a light-brown color, a thin kernel, and a mild taste. It cooks in 30 to 45 minutes. Cultivated and Canadian wild rice is usually processed to retain more of the bran, resulting in its darker color, plumper kernel, and stronger flavor. It cooks in 45 to 60 minutes.

Remember that one cup of raw wild rice yields three to four cups of cooked rice.

3 parts water or broth
1 part wild rice
1/2 teaspoon salt per cup of rice
(optional)

■ Rinse the rice in a strainer. In a large pan, bring water, rice, and salt to a boil. Reduce heat, cover, and simmer. Stir, if desired. Add more liquid, if necessary. Wild rice is done when most of the kernels have butterflied, or opened out. (Overcooked rice falls apart; undercooked rice is tough or woody.) When done, allow it to sit for 10 to 15 minutes, then stir or fluff up with a fork before serving.

Savory Meal
in a
Muffin

FROM THE KITCHEN OF
Carol Jessen-Klixbull

2 cups flour
1 tablespoon baking
** powder**
1 cup buttermilk
1/2 cup vegetable oil
2 large eggs
1 cup cooked wild rice
3/4 cup shredded cheese
1 cup diced cooked ham,
** or 1/4 pound of bacon,**
** crisply fried and**
** crumbled**
1/2 medium onion, finely
** chopped**
2 tablespoons finely
** chopped fresh cilantro**
** or parsley**

Preheat oven to 400°F. Grease 18 muffin-tin cups (2½-inch size), or line with paper baking cups. Combine flour and baking powder in a large bowl. In a small bowl, whisk together the buttermilk, oil, and eggs. Stir liquid ingredients into dry ingredients just until combined. Fold in the rice, cheese, ham or bacon, onion, and cilantro or parsley.

Spoon into prepared muffin cups, filling each about three-quarters full. Bake for 15 to 20 minutes, or until toothpick inserted into center of muffin comes out clean. Cool in pans on wire racks for 5 minutes. Remove from tin and serve warm.

Makes 18 muffins.

Karen's Overnight Cream of Wild-Rice Soup

FROM THE KITCHEN OF
Karen Skoog

- 1 tablespoon minced onion
- 2 tablespoons butter
- 1/4 cup flour
- 4 cups chicken broth
- 2 cups cooked wild rice
- 1/2 teaspoon salt
- 1 cup half-and-half
- 1/2 cup thinly diced carrots
- 1/2 cup finely diced celery
- 1/2 cup tiny pieces of cooked ham (optional)
- 1/2 cup slivered almonds

Sauté onion in butter until tender. Blend in flour and gradually add the broth. Cook, stirring constantly, until it thickens slightly. Stir in rice and salt, and simmer for 5 minutes. Blend in half-and-half, and add carrots, celery, ham (if using), and almonds. Bring to a low simmer and cook for 5 minutes. Refrigerate overnight to bring out the flavors, and reheat the next day.

Serves 6 to 8.

Curried Chicken or Shrimp Wild-Rice Salad

FROM THE KITCHEN OF
Gretchen Pinsonneault

- 4 cups cooked wild rice
- 2 cups diced cooked chicken breasts or diced cooked shrimp
- 1 can (8 ounces) sliced water chestnuts
- 1 can (8 ounces) artichoke hearts in water
- 2 cups grapes, or 2 cans (8 ounces each) mandarin oranges
- 1 cup pecans
- 5 green onions, chopped

DRESSING:
- 1 cup mayonnaise
- 1/2 cup sour cream
- 1-1/2 teaspoons curry powder
- 1 tablespoon lime juice

Dice, slice, or halve main ingredients so they are of a uniform size—about that of half a grape. Mix main ingredients in a large bowl. In a separate smaller bowl, stir dressing ingredients together until well blended. Add dressing to main ingredients and toss gently. Cover and chill.

Serves 10 to 12.

□□

Susan Carol Hauser is the author of *Wild Rice Cooking: History, Natural History, Harvesting, and Lore* (The Lyons Press, 2000). She once went "ricing" in a canoe with her husband and found it to be an exhausting and exhilarating experience.

GO WILD!
For additional recipes and more information about wild rice, go to **www.almanac.com** and click on **Article Links 2003.**

The Case of the Fluky Fruit

Or how 'Bing' cherries got named.

BY GEORGIA ORCUTT

The story of the sweet 'Bing' cherry has all the makings of a sexy, historical thriller: a violent political climate; two brothers turning a profit from a graft; a tall, strapping Manchurian man seen carrying a knife; a dark-fleshed beauty; and telltale stains on hands and clothing. But in truth, it's just the delicious tale of a fluke of nature that was discovered about 130 years ago.

In 1847, pioneer nurseryman Henderson Luelling from Iowa traveled west on the Oregon Trail, accompanied by his wife, eight children, and an oxcart filled with 700 young plants—apples, peaches, pears, plums, grapes, nuts, and cherries. After a seven-month journey, he stopped in Milwaukie, Oregon, planted his stock, and set to work grafting trees. His brother Seth (Lewelling) arrived in 1853, and the two brothers started a business, offering 100,000 trees to orchardists at $1 to $1.50 each.

When Henderson left the business a year later and moved to California, Seth expanded the nursery to 100 acres. He employed a number of Chinese immigrants. Among them was Ah Sit Bing, who had come to America from Manchuria. Hired under a 35-year contract, the tall and reliable Bing became Seth Lewelling's friend and his foreman, in charge of 30 workers. One day, while tending the test rows, Bing discovered a heart-shaped cherry much darker and larger than the others. It also had a great taste. He and Lewelling took cuttings from the tree and cultivated a new variety in 1875. To honor his friend's work at the nursery and to make a political statement concerning the strained relations between whites and Chinese workers in the Pacific Northwest at the time, Lewelling named the cherry 'Bing'. The rest is history.

Just Don't Spit the Pits

Etiquette mavens affirm that it's positively OK to remove cherry pits from your mouth—discreetly, with your fingers, even in polite society. (You can do whatever you like in impolite society.)

Baking with Cherries

A fresh 'Bing' cherry is hard to beat for juiciness, sweet taste, and long shelf life. But the cherry season is only two months long, and cooks who love sweet cherries rely on dried, canned, and frozen cherries to get them through the other ten months. Supermarkets sell 15-ounce cans labeled "Dark Sweet Cherries"; these are 90 percent 'Bing', but they don't hold up well in baking. Use them in dessert sauces, or drain and substitute for pineapple in an upside-down cake. Dried 'Bing' cherries hold their own in cakes and cookies; dice and use as a substitute for raisins. Trader Joe's supermarkets sell dried 'Bing' cherries in eight-ounce bags. The following mail-order source also sells dried 'Bing' cherries: **Chukar Cherry Company, 320 Wine Country Rd., P.O. Box 510, Prosser, WA 99350; 800-624-9544; www.chukar.com.**

Chocolate Cherry Pecan Cake

Good enough for a holiday dessert,
this festive cake keeps well if stored in an airtight container.

1/2 cup cocoa
1-1/2 cups flour
1 teaspoon baking powder
1/2 cup (1 stick) unsalted butter, softened
3/4 cup sugar
3 eggs
1 teaspoon vanilla extract
1 cup milk
1 cup (8 ounces) dried whole 'Bing' cherries
1 cup chopped pecans

Preheat oven to 325°F. Grease a 10-inch tube pan, line it with waxed paper, and grease the waxed paper. Sift together the cocoa, flour, and baking powder and set aside. Cream the butter and sugar in a mixing bowl. Add the eggs one at a time and beat well. Beat in the vanilla. Gradually add the sifted flour mixture, alternating with the milk, until the batter is smooth. By hand, stir in the cherries and nuts. Spoon the batter into the prepared pan and bake for 30 to 40 minutes, just until the top is springy. Let cool slightly and turn out onto a rack. Remove the waxed paper while the cake is still warm. Frost generously with Chocolate Glaze (below).

Serves 8 to 10.

Chocolate Glaze

3 tablespoons butter
1 cup semisweet chocolate chips or bits
1 cup confectioners' sugar
1/4 cup milk

Melt the butter over low heat in a heavy saucepan. Add the chocolate and stir until melted. Stir in the confectioners' sugar and gradually add the milk, stirring to form a thick, smooth frosting. Immediately pour over the cake, circling several times to cover it completely.

□□

Georgia Orcutt, a cookbook writer and editor of *The Old Farmer's Almanac Gardener's Companion,* spent several summers picking cherries in Dunkirk, New York.

A LITTLE PIT MORE

For more cherry recipes, places to buy dried 'Bing' cherries, and advice on growing 'Bing' cherries in your backyard, visit **www.almanac.com** and click on **Article Links 2003.**

Secrets of the Zodiac

Ancient astrologers associated each of the signs with a part of the body over which they believed the sign held some influence. The first sign of the zodiac—Aries—was attributed to the head, with the rest of the signs moving down the body, ending with Pisces at the feet.

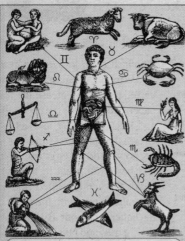

The Man of Signs

♈	Aries, head	**ARI**	*Mar. 21–Apr. 20*
♉	Taurus, neck	**TAU**	*Apr. 21–May 20*
♊	Gemini, arms	**GEM**	*May 21–June 20*
♋	Cancer, breast	**CAN**	*June 21–July 22*
♌	Leo, heart	**LEO**	*July 23–Aug. 22*
♍	Virgo, belly	**VIR**	*Aug. 23–Sept. 22*
♎	Libra, reins	**LIB**	*Sept. 23–Oct. 22*
♏	Scorpio, secrets	**SCO**	*Oct. 23–Nov. 22*
♐	Sagittarius, thighs . . .	**SAG**	*Nov. 23–Dec. 21*
♑	Capricorn, knees	**CAP**	*Dec. 22–Jan. 19*
♒	Aquarius, legs	**AQU**	*Jan. 20–Feb. 19*
♓	Pisces, feet	**PSC**	*Feb. 20–Mar. 20*

Astrology and Astronomy

■ Astrology is a tool we use to time events according to the *astrological* placement of the two luminaries (the Sun and the Moon) and eight planets in the 12 signs of the zodiac. Astronomy, on the other hand, is the charting of the *actual* placement of the known planets and constellations, taking into account precession of the equinoxes. As a result, the placement of the planets in the signs of the zodiac is not the same astrologically and astronomically. (The Moon's astronomical place is given in the **Left-Hand Calendar Pages 44–70**, and its astrological place is given in **Gardening by the Moon's Sign, page 223.**)

Modern astrology is a study of synchronicities. The planetary movements do not cause events. Rather, they explain the "flow," or trajectory, that events tend to follow. Because of free will, you can choose to plan a schedule in harmony with the flow, or you can choose to swim against the current.

The dates given in the **Astrological Timetable (page 224)** have been chosen with particular care to the astrological passage of the Moon. However, because other planets also influence us, it's best to take a look at all indicators before seeking advice on major life decisions. An astrologer can study the current relationship of the planets and your own personal birth chart to assist you in the best possible timing for carrying out your plans.

When Mercury Is Retrograde

■ Sometimes when we look out from our perspective here on Earth, the other planets appear to be traveling backward through the zodiac. (All heavenly bodies move forward. An optical illusion makes them seem as if they are moving backward.) We call this *retrograde motion*.

Mercury's retrograde periods, which occur three or four times a year, can cause travel delays and misconstrued communications. Plans have a way of unraveling, too. However, this is an excellent time to research or look into the past. Intuition is high during these periods, and coincidences can be extraordinary.

When Mercury is retrograde, astrologers advise us to keep plans flexible, allow extra time for travel, and avoid signing contracts. It's OK and even useful to look over projects and plans, because we may see them with different eyes. However, our normal system of checks and balances might not be active, so it's best to wait until Mercury is direct again to make any final decisions. In 2003, Mercury will be retrograde from January 2 to 23, April 26 to May 20, August 28 to September 20, and December 17 to January 4, 2004. –*Celeste Longacre*

Gardening by the Moon's Sign

■ It is important to note that the placement of the planets through the signs of the zodiac is not the same in astronomy and astrology. The *astrological* placement of the Moon, by sign, is given in the table below. (Its *astronomical,* or actual, placement is given in the **Left-Hand Calendar Pages 44–70.**)

For planting, the most-fertile Moon signs are the three water signs: Cancer, Scorpio, and Pisces. Good second choices are Taurus, Virgo, and Capricorn. Weeding and plowing are best done when the Moon occupies Aries, Gemini, Leo, Sagittarius, or Aquarius. Insect pests can also be handled at these times. Transplanting and grafting are best done under a Cancer, Scorpio, or Pisces Moon. Pruning is best done under an Aries, Leo, or Sagittarius Moon, with growth encouraged during waxing (from the day of new to the day of full Moon) and discouraged during waning (from the day after full to the day before new Moon). (For the dates of the Moon's phases, see **pages 44–70.**)

Clean out the garden shed when the Moon occupies Virgo. Fences and permanent beds can be built or mended when Capricorn predominates. Avoid indecision when under the Libra Moon.

Moon's Place in the Astrological Zodiac

	NOV. 2002	DEC. 2002	JAN. 2003	FEB. 2003	MAR. 2003	APR. 2003	MAY 2003	JUNE 2003	JULY 2003	AUG. 2003	SEPT. 2003	OCT. 2003	NOV. 2003	DEC. 2003
1	VIR	SCO	SAG	AQU	AQU	ARI	TAU	GEM	LEO	VIR	SCO	SAG	AQU	PSC
2	LIB	SCO	CAP	AQU	PSC	ARI	TAU	CAN	LEO	LIB	SCO	CAP	AQU	ARI
3	LIB	SAG	CAP	PSC	PSC	TAU	GEM	CAN	LEO	LIB	SAG	CAP	PSC	ARI
4	SCO	SAG	AQU	PSC	ARI	TAU	GEM	LEO	VIR	SCO	SAG	AQU	PSC	ARI
5	SCO	CAP	AQU	ARI	ARI	TAU	CAN	LEO	VIR	SCO	CAP	AQU	ARI	TAU
6	SAG	CAP	AQU	ARI	ARI	GEM	CAN	VIR	LIB	SAG	CAP	PSC	ARI	TAU
7	SAG	CAP	PSC	TAU	TAU	GEM	CAN	VIR	LIB	SAG	AQU	PSC	TAU	GEM
8	CAP	AQU	PSC	TAU	TAU	CAN	LEO	VIR	SCO	SAG	AQU	PSC	TAU	GEM
9	CAP	AQU	ARI	TAU	GEM	CAN	LEO	LIB	SCO	CAP	PSC	ARI	TAU	GEM
10	AQU	PSC	ARI	GEM	GEM	CAN	VIR	LIB	SAG	CAP	PSC	ARI	GEM	CAN
11	AQU	PSC	ARI	GEM	GEM	LEO	VIR	SCO	SAG	AQU	ARI	TAU	GEM	CAN
12	PSC	ARI	TAU	CAN	CAN	LEO	LIB	SCO	CAP	AQU	ARI	TAU	GEM	LEO
13	PSC	ARI	TAU	CAN	CAN	VIR	LIB	SAG	CAP	PSC	ARI	TAU	CAN	LEO
14	PSC	ARI	GEM	CAN	LEO	VIR	SCO	SAG	AQU	PSC	TAU	GEM	CAN	LEO
15	ARI	TAU	GEM	LEO	LEO	LIB	SCO	CAP	AQU	ARI	TAU	GEM	LEO	VIR
16	ARI	TAU	GEM	LEO	VIR	LIB	SAG	CAP	PSC	ARI	GEM	CAN	LEO	VIR
17	ARI	GEM	CAN	VIR	VIR	SCO	SAG	AQU	PSC	ARI	GEM	CAN	VIR	LIB
18	TAU	GEM	CAN	VIR	LIB	SCO	CAP	AQU	PSC	TAU	GEM	CAN	VIR	LIB
19	TAU	GEM	LEO	LIB	LIB	SAG	CAP	PSC	ARI	TAU	CAN	LEO	VIR	SCO
20	GEM	CAN	LEO	LIB	SCO	SAG	AQU	PSC	ARI	GEM	CAN	LEO	LIB	SCO
21	GEM	CAN	VIR	SCO	SCO	CAP	AQU	ARI	TAU	GEM	LEO	VIR	LIB	SAG
22	CAN	LEO	VIR	SCO	SAG	CAP	AQU	ARI	TAU	GEM	LEO	VIR	SCO	SAG
23	CAN	LEO	LIB	SAG	SAG	AQU	PSC	ARI	TAU	CAN	LEO	LIB	SCO	CAP
24	CAN	VIR	LIB	SAG	SAG	AQU	PSC	TAU	GEM	CAN	VIR	LIB	SAG	CAP
25	LEO	VIR	SCO	CAP	CAP	PSC	ARI	TAU	GEM	LEO	VIR	SCO	SAG	AQU
26	LEO	LIB	SCO	CAP	CAP	PSC	ARI	GEM	CAN	LEO	LIB	SCO	CAP	AQU
27	VIR	LIB	SCO	CAP	AQU	PSC	ARI	GEM	CAN	VIR	LIB	SAG	CAP	PSC
28	VIR	LIB	SAG	AQU	AQU	ARI	TAU	GEM	CAN	VIR	SCO	SAG	AQU	PSC
29	LIB	SCO	SAG	—	PSC	ARI	TAU	CAN	LEO	LIB	SCO	CAP	AQU	ARI
30	LIB	SCO	CAP	—	PSC	TAU	GEM	CAN	LEO	LIB	SAG	CAP	PSC	ARI
31	—	SAG	CAP	—	PSC	—	GEM	—	VIR	LIB	—	AQU	—	ARI

Astrological Timetable, 2003

■ The following month-by-month chart is based on the Moon's sign and shows the most-favorable times each month for certain activities.

—Celeste Longacre

	JAN.	FEB.	MAR.	APR.	MAY	JUNE	JULY	AUG.	SEPT.	OCT.	NOV.	DEC.
Give up smoking	22, 23	20, 21, 28	1, 19, 27, 28	23, 24, 28, 29	8, 9, 12, 13	17, 18, 22, 23	14, 15, 19, 20	15, 16, 25, 26	12, 13, 22, 23	19, 20, 23, 24	15, 16, 20, 21	12, 13, 17, 18
Begin diet to lose weight	22, 23	20, 21, 28	1, 19, 27, 28	23, 24, 28, 29	8, 9, 12, 13	17, 18, 22, 23	14, 15, 19, 20	15, 16, 25, 26	12, 13, 22, 23	19, 20, 23, 24	15, 16, 20, 21	12, 13, 17, 18
Begin diet to gain weight	5, 6, 10, 11	2, 5, 6	5, 6, 14, 15	1, 2, 11, 12	21, 22, 25, 26	4, 5, 9, 10	2, 3, 6, 7	2, 3, 11	7, 8, 27	4, 5, 9	5, 6, 28, 29	2, 3, 30, 31
Cut hair to encourage growth	12, 13	8, 9	7, 8	4, 15	2, 12, 13	9, 10	6, 7	2, 3	9, 27	7, 8	2, 3, 30	5, 6, 28
Cut hair to discourage growth	23, 24	19, 20	19, 29	25, 26	28, 29	24, 25	21, 22	25, 26, 29, 30	14, 15	11, 12, 23	20, 21	17, 18
Have dental care	21, 22	17, 18	16, 17	13, 14	10, 11	7, 8	4, 5, 31	1, 27, 28	24, 25	22, 23	18, 19	15, 16
End old projects	1, 2	1, 28	1, 2	1, 30	1, 31	27, 28	27, 28	25, 26	24, 25	23, 24	21, 22	21, 22
Start new projects	3, 4	2, 3	4, 5	2, 3	2, 3	1, 30	30, 31	28, 29	27, 28	26, 27	24, 25	24, 25
Entertain	19, 20	15, 16	14, 15	11, 12	8, 9	4, 5	2, 3, 29, 30	25, 26	22, 23	19, 20	15, 16	12, 13, 14
Go camping	1, 27, 28	23, 24	23, 24	19, 20	16, 17	13, 14	10, 11	6, 7	3, 4, 30	1, 27, 28	24, 25	21, 22
Plant aboveground crops	7, 8	3, 4, 13, 14	12, 13	8, 9	6, 7	2, 3	9, 10	4, 5	1, 2, 9, 28	7, 8, 26	3, 4, 30	1, 27, 28
Plant belowground crops	25, 26	21, 22	20, 21, 29, 30	17, 18	11, 12, 23, 24	19, 20, 29, 30	17, 18, 26, 27	13, 14, 23, 24	19, 20	16, 17	13, 14, 22	10, 11, 19, 20
Destroy pests and weeds	9, 10	5, 6	5, 6	1, 2, 28, 29	25, 26	22, 23	19, 20, 21	15, 16	12, 13	9, 10	5, 6	3, 4, 30, 31
Graft or pollinate	16, 17	13, 14	12, 13	8, 9	6, 7	2, 3, 29, 30	26, 27, 28	23, 24	19, 20	16, 17, 18	13, 14	10, 11
Prune to encourage growth	1, 8, 9	5, 6	5, 6	1, 2, 11, 12	8, 9	4, 5, 13	2, 3, 10	6, 7	3, 4	1, 9, 28	5, 6, 25	2, 3, 4
Prune to discourage growth	28, 29	23, 24	23, 24	28, 29	17, 26, 27	22, 23	17, 18, 26, 27	13, 14, 23, 24	22, 23	19, 20	15, 16	12, 13, 14
Harvest above-ground crops	12, 13	8, 9	7, 8	3, 4	10, 11	7, 8	4, 5	1, 9, 10	5, 6	2, 3, 29, 30	8, 9, 26, 27	5, 6, 24
Harvest below-ground crops	21, 22	18, 26, 27	25, 26	21, 22	28, 29	24, 25	21, 22, 23	18, 19	14, 15, 24, 25	11, 12, 21, 22	18, 19	15, 16
Cut hay	9, 10	5, 6	5, 6	1, 2, 28, 29	25, 26	22, 23	19, 20, 21	15, 16	12, 13	9, 10	5, 6	3, 4, 30, 31
Begin logging	2, 3, 29, 30	26, 27	25, 26	21, 22	18, 19	15, 16	12, 13	9, 10	5, 6	2, 3, 30, 31	26, 27	23, 24
Set posts or pour concrete	2, 3, 29, 30	26, 27	25, 26	21, 22	18, 19	15, 16	12, 13	9, 10	5, 6	2, 3, 30	26, 27	23, 24
Breed	25, 26	21, 22	20, 21	17, 18	14, 15	11, 12	8, 9	4, 5	1, 2, 28, 29	25, 26	22, 23	19, 20
Wean	22, 23	20, 21, 28	1, 19, 27, 28	23, 24, 28, 29	8, 9, 12, 13	17, 18, 22, 23	14, 15, 19, 20	15, 16, 25, 26	12, 13, 22, 23	19, 20, 23, 24	15, 16, 20, 21	12, 13, 17, 18
Castrate animals	4, 5, 31	1, 2, 28	1, 27, 28	23, 24	21, 22	17, 18	14, 15	11, 12	7, 8	4, 5, 31	1, 2, 28, 29	25, 26
Slaughter	25, 26	21, 22	20, 21	17, 18	14, 15	11, 12	8, 9	4, 5	1, 2, 28, 29	25, 26	22, 23	19, 20

SOLUTIONS TO

Mr. Smith's MADDENING Mind-Manglers

From pages 204–205.

1. Ray simply rearranged those letters into "one word."

2. A stamp. From "stUmp" to "stAmp" is where you get your "A"!

3. Cassidy said, "Because everything swells up in water."

4. Any order! No matter what order Rob uses to take the percentages off, he always saves 27.325%!

5. 12 bars.
Start with 20, sell x, have 20 − x remaining. Double that: 2(20 − x), sell x, have 2(20 − x) − x remaining. [Completing this calculation: 40 − 2x − x = 40 − 3x]. Triple that: 3(40 − 3x), sell x, have 0 remaining. Now you can set up a formula:
3(40 − 3x) − x = 0
120 − 9x − x = 0
120 − 10x = 0
10x = 120
x = 12

6. 3 screwdrivers.
We know that 5 screwdrivers (S) + 2 wrenches (W) = 3 hammers (H), and that 1S + 1W = 1H. Set up the problem as a simple subtraction from both sides of an equation, like a balance. Subtract what you know (do this twice) to eliminate all the wrenches and get a result for the relationship between the screwdrivers and one hammer:

$$5S + 2W = 3H \quad \text{start with this}$$
$$- (1S + 1W = 1H) \quad \text{subtract this}$$
$$4S + 1W = 2H \quad \text{result}$$
$$- (1S + 1W = 1H) \quad \text{subtract again}$$
$$3S \quad\quad\quad = 1H$$

7. $60.
x = the amount she started with
$$\tfrac{1}{3}(x) + \tfrac{1}{4}(x) + \tfrac{1}{5}(x) = x - 13$$
$$\tfrac{x}{3} + \tfrac{x}{4} + \tfrac{x}{5} = x - 13$$
$$\tfrac{20x}{60} + \tfrac{15x}{60} + \tfrac{12x}{60} = x - 13$$
$$\tfrac{47x}{60} = x - 13$$
$$47x = 60x - 780$$
$$13x = 780$$
$$x = 60$$

BONES AND MUSCLES SOLUTION:
1. B; 2. M; 3. C; 4. K; 5. L; 6. J; 7. B; 8. I; 9. G; 10. F; 11. H; 12. C; 13. E; 14. L; 15. K; 16. D; 17. C; 18. A; 19. H; 20. J.

□□

Time Corrections

■ Times of sunrise/sunset and moonrise/moonset, and selected times for transit of the bright stars and for observing the visible planets are given for Boston **on pages 44–70, 84, and 90–91.** Use the Key Letter shown to the right of each time on those pages with this table to find the number of minutes, already adjusted for different time zones, that you must add to or subtract from Boston time to get the correct time for your city. (Because of complex calculations for different locales, times may not be precise to the minute.) If your city is not listed, find the city closest to you in latitude and longitude and use those figures. Boston's latitude is 42° 22' and its longitude is 71° 03'. Canadian cities appear at the end of the table. For further information on the use of Key Letters and this table, see **How to Use This Almanac, page 39.**

Time Zone Code: Codes represent *standard time*. Atlantic is –1, Eastern is 0, Central is 1, Mountain is 2, Pacific is 3, Alaska is 4, and Hawaii-Aleutian is 5.

City	North Latitude ° '	West Longitude ° '	Time Zone Code	A (min.)	B (min.)	C (min.)	D (min.)	E (min.)
Aberdeen, SD	45 28	98 29	1	+37	+44	+49	+54	+59
Akron, OH	41 5	81 31	0	+46	+43	+41	+39	+37
Albany, NY	42 39	73 45	0	+ 9	+10	+10	+11	+11
Albert Lea, MN	43 39	93 22	1	+24	+26	+28	+31	+33
Albuquerque, NM	35 5	106 39	2	+45	+32	+22	+11	+ 2
Alexandria, LA	31 18	92 27	1	+58	+40	+26	+ 9	– 3
Allentown–Bethlehem, PA	40 36	75 28	0	+23	+20	+17	+14	+12
Amarillo, TX	35 12	101 50	1	+85	+73	+63	+52	+43
Anchorage, AK	61 10	149 59	4	–46	+27	+71	+122	+171
Asheville, NC	35 36	82 33	0	+67	+55	+46	+35	+27
Atlanta, GA	33 45	84 24	0	+79	+65	+53	+40	+30
Atlantic City, NJ	39 22	74 26	0	+23	+17	+13	+ 8	+ 4
Augusta, GA	33 28	81 58	0	+70	+55	+44	+30	+19
Augusta, ME	44 19	69 46	0	–12	– 8	– 5	– 1	0
Austin, TX	30 16	97 45	1	+82	+62	+47	+29	+15
Bakersfield, CA	35 23	119 1	3	+33	+21	+12	+ 1	– 7
Baltimore, MD	39 17	76 37	0	+32	+26	+22	+17	+13
Bangor, ME	44 48	68 46	0	–18	–13	– 9	– 5	– 1
Barstow, CA	34 54	117 1	3	+27	+14	+ 4	– 7	–16
Baton Rouge, LA	30 27	91 11	1	+55	+36	+21	+ 3	–10
Beaumont, TX	30 5	94 6	1	+67	+48	+32	+14	0
Bellingham, WA	48 45	122 29	3	0	+13	+24	+37	+47
Bemidji, MN	47 28	94 53	1	+14	+26	+34	+44	+52
Berlin, NH	44 28	71 11	0	– 7	– 3	0	+ 3	+ 7
Billings, MT	45 47	108 30	2	+16	+23	+29	+35	+40
Biloxi, MS	30 24	88 53	1	+46	+27	+11	– 5	–19
Binghamton, NY	42 6	75 55	0	+20	+19	+19	+18	+18
Birmingham, AL	33 31	86 49	1	+30	+15	+ 3	–10	–20
Bismarck, ND	46 48	100 47	1	+41	+50	+58	+66	+73
Boise, ID	43 37	116 12	2	+55	+58	+60	+62	+64
Brattleboro, VT	42 51	72 34	0	+ 4	+ 5	+ 5	+ 6	+ 7
Bridgeport, CT	41 11	73 11	0	+12	+10	+ 8	+ 6	+ 4
Brockton, MA	42 5	71 1	0	0	0	0	0	– 1
Brownsville, TX	25 54	97 30	1	+91	+66	+46	+23	+ 5
Buffalo, NY	42 53	78 52	0	+29	+30	+30	+31	+32
Burlington, VT	44 29	73 13	0	0	+ 4	+ 8	+12	+15
Butte, MT	46 1	112 32	2	+31	+39	+45	+52	+57
Cairo, IL	37 0	89 11	1	+29	+20	+12	+ 4	– 2
Camden, NJ	39 57	75 7	0	+24	+19	+16	+12	+ 9
Canton, OH	40 48	81 23	0	+46	+43	+41	+38	+36
Cape May, NJ	38 56	74 56	0	+26	+20	+15	+ 9	+ 5
Carson City–Reno, NV	39 10	119 46	3	+25	+19	+14	+ 9	+ 5

City	North Latitude °	'	West Longitude °	'	Time Zone Code	A (min.)	B (min.)	C (min.)	D (min.)	E (min.)
Casper, WY	42	51	106	19	2	+19	+19	+20	+21	+22
Charleston, SC	32	47	79	56	0	+64	+48	+36	+21	+10
Charleston, WV	38	21	81	38	0	+55	+48	+42	+35	+30
Charlotte, NC	35	14	80	51	0	+61	+49	+39	+28	+19
Charlottesville, VA	38	2	78	30	0	+43	+35	+29	+22	+17
Chattanooga, TN	35	3	85	19	0	+79	+67	+57	+45	+36
Cheboygan, MI	45	39	84	29	0	+40	+47	+53	+59	+64
Cheyenne, WY	41	8	104	49	2	+19	+16	+14	+12	+11
Chicago–Oak Park, IL	41	52	87	38	1	+ 7	+ 6	+ 6	+ 5	+ 4
Cincinnati–Hamilton, OH	39	6	84	31	0	+64	+58	+53	+48	+44
Cleveland–Lakewood, OH	41	30	81	42	0	+45	+43	+42	+40	+39
Columbia, SC	34	0	81	2	0	+65	+51	+40	+27	+17
Columbus, OH	39	57	83	1	0	+55	+51	+47	+43	+40
Cordova, AK	60	33	145	45	4	−55	+13	+55	+103	+149
Corpus Christi, TX	27	48	97	24	1	+86	+64	+46	+25	+ 9
Craig, CO	40	31	107	33	2	+32	+28	+25	+22	+20
Dallas–Fort Worth, TX	32	47	96	48	1	+71	+55	+43	+28	+17
Danville, IL	40	8	87	37	1	+13	+ 9	+ 6	+ 2	0
Danville, VA	36	36	79	23	0	+51	+41	+33	+24	+17
Davenport, IA	41	32	90	35	1	+20	+19	+17	+16	+15
Dayton, OH	39	45	84	10	0	+61	+56	+52	+48	+44
Decatur, AL	34	36	86	59	1	+27	+14	+ 4	− 7	−17
Decatur, IL	39	51	88	57	1	+19	+15	+11	+ 7	+ 4
Denver–Boulder, CO	39	44	104	59	2	+24	+19	+15	+11	+ 7
Des Moines, IA	41	35	93	37	1	+32	+31	+30	+28	+27
Detroit–Dearborn, MI	42	20	83	3	0	+47	+47	+47	+47	+47
Dubuque, IA	42	30	90	41	1	+17	+18	+18	+18	+18
Duluth, MN	46	47	92	6	1	+ 6	+16	+23	+31	+38
Durham, NC	36	0	78	55	0	+51	+40	+31	+21	+13
Eastport, ME	44	54	67	0	0	−26	−20	−16	−11	− 8
Eau Claire, WI	44	49	91	30	1	+12	+17	+21	+25	+29
Elko, NV	40	50	115	46	3	+ 3	0	− 1	− 3	− 5
Ellsworth, ME	44	33	68	25	0	−18	−14	−10	− 6	− 3
El Paso, TX	31	45	106	29	2	+53	+35	+22	+ 6	− 6
Erie, PA	42	7	80	5	0	+36	+36	+35	+35	+35
Eugene, OR	44	3	123	6	3	+21	+24	+27	+30	+33
Fairbanks, AK	64	48	147	51	4	−127	+ 2	+61	+131	+205
Fall River– New Bedford, MA	41	42	71	9	0	+ 2	+ 1	0	0	− 1
Fargo, ND	46	53	96	47	1	+24	+34	+42	+50	+57
Flagstaff, AZ	35	12	111	39	2	+64	+52	+42	+31	+22
Flint, MI	43	1	83	41	0	+47	+49	+50	+51	+52
Fort Myers, FL	26	38	81	52	0	+87	+63	+44	+21	+ 4
Fort Scott, KS	37	50	94	42	1	+49	+41	+34	+27	+21
Fort Smith, AR	35	23	94	25	1	+55	+43	+33	+22	+14
Fort Wayne, IN	41	4	85	9	0	+60	+58	+56	+54	+52
Fresno, CA	36	44	119	47	3	+32	+22	+15	+ 6	0
Gallup, NM	35	32	108	45	2	+52	+40	+31	+20	+11
Galveston, TX	29	18	94	48	1	+72	+52	+35	+16	+ 1
Gary, IN	41	36	87	20	1	+ 7	+ 6	+ 4	+ 3	+ 2
Glasgow, MT	48	12	106	38	2	− 1	+11	+21	+32	+42
Grand Forks, ND	47	55	97	3	1	+21	+33	+43	+53	+62
Grand Island, NE	40	55	98	21	1	+53	+51	+49	+46	+44
Grand Junction, CO	39	4	108	33	2	+40	+34	+29	+24	+20
Great Falls, MT	47	30	111	17	2	+20	+31	+39	+49	+58
Green Bay, WI	44	31	88	0	1	0	+ 3	+ 7	+11	+14
Greensboro, NC	36	4	79	47	0	+54	+43	+35	+25	+17

City	North Latitude ° '	West Longitude ° '	Time Zone Code	Key Letters A (min.)	B (min.)	C (min.)	D (min.)	E (min.)
Hagerstown, MD	39 39	77 43	0	+35	+30	+26	+22	+18
Harrisburg, PA	40 16	76 53	0	+30	+26	+23	+19	+16
Hartford–New Britain, CT...	41 46	72 41	0	+ 8	+ 7	+ 6	+ 5	+ 4
Helena, MT...............	46 36	112 2	2	+27	+36	+43	+51	+57
Hilo, HI	19 44	155 5	5	+94	+62	+37	+ 7	−15
Honolulu, HI.............	21 18	157 52	5	+102	+72	+48	+19	− 1
Houston, TX	29 45	95 22	1	+73	+53	+37	+19	+ 5
Indianapolis, IN	39 46	86 10	0	+69	+64	+60	+56	+52
Ironwood, MI	46 27	90 9	1	0	+ 9	+15	+23	+29
Jackson, MI..............	42 15	84 24	0	+53	+53	+53	+52	+52
Jackson, MS	32 18	90 11	1	+46	+30	+17	+ 1	−10
Jacksonville, FL	30 20	81 40	0	+77	+58	+43	+25	+11
Jefferson City, MO	38 34	92 10	1	+36	+29	+24	+18	+13
Joplin, MO	37 6	94 30	1	+50	+41	+33	+25	+18
Juneau, AK	58 18	134 25	4	−76	−23	+10	+49	+86
Kalamazoo, MI............	42 17	85 35	0	+58	+57	+57	+57	+57
Kanab, UT...............	37 3	112 32	2	+62	+53	+46	+37	+30
Kansas City, MO	39 1	94 20	1	+44	+37	+33	+27	+23
Keene, NH................	42 56	72 17	0	+ 2	+ 3	+ 4	+ 5	+ 6
Ketchikan, AK	55 21	131 39	4	−62	−25	0	+29	+56
Knoxville, TN	35 58	83 55	0	+71	+60	+51	+41	+33
Kodiak, AK..............	57 47	152 24	4	0	+49	+82	+120	+154
LaCrosse, WI	43 48	91 15	1	+15	+18	+20	+22	+25
Lake Charles, LA	30 14	93 13	1	+64	+44	+29	+11	− 2
Lanai City, HI............	20 50	156 55	5	+99	+69	+44	+15	− 6
Lancaster, PA	40 2	76 18	0	+28	+24	+20	+17	+13
Lansing, MI..............	42 44	84 33	0	+52	+53	+53	+54	+54
Las Cruces, NM	32 19	106 47	2	+53	+36	+23	+ 8	− 3
Las Vegas, NV	36 10	115 9	3	+16	+ 4	− 3	−13	−20
Lawrence–Lowell, MA	42 42	71 10	0	0	0	0	0	+ 1
Lewiston, ID	46 25	117 1	3	−12	− 3	+ 2	+10	+17
Lexington–Frankfort, KY ...	38 3	84 30	0	+67	+59	+53	+46	+41
Liberal, KS	37 3	100 55	1	+76	+66	+59	+51	+44
Lihue, HI................	21 59	159 23	5	+107	+77	+54	+26	+ 5
Lincoln, NE..............	40 49	96 41	1	+47	+44	+42	+39	+37
Little Rock, AR	34 45	92 17	1	+48	+35	+25	+13	+ 4
Los Angeles–Pasadena– Santa Monica, CA	34 3	118 14	3	+34	+20	+ 9	− 3	−13
Louisville, KY	38 15	85 46	0	+72	+64	+58	+52	+46
Macon, GA	32 50	83 38	0	+79	+63	+50	+36	+24
Madison, WI.............	43 4	89 23	1	+10	+11	+12	+14	+15
Manchester–Concord, NH...	42 59	71 28	0	0	0	+ 1	+ 2	+ 3
McAllen, TX..............	26 12	98 14	1	+93	+69	+49	+26	+ 9
Memphis, TN	35 9	90 3	1	+38	+26	+16	+ 5	− 3
Meridian, MS	32 22	88 42	1	+40	+24	+11	− 4	−15
Miami, FL................	25 47	80 12	0	+88	+57	+37	+14	− 3
Miles City, MT	46 25	105 51	2	+ 3	+11	+18	+26	+32
Milwaukee, WI...........	43 2	87 54	1	+ 4	+ 6	+ 7	+ 8	+ 9
Minneapolis–St. Paul, MN...	44 59	93 16	1	+18	+24	+28	+33	+37
Minot, ND...............	48 14	101 18	1	+36	+50	+59	+71	+81
Moab, UT	38 35	109 33	2	+46	+39	+33	+27	+22
Mobile, AL...............	30 42	88 3	1	+42	+23	+ 8	− 8	−22
Monroe, LA..............	32 30	92 7	1	+53	+37	+24	+ 9	− 1
Montgomery, AL	32 23	86 19	1	+31	+14	+ 1	−13	−25
Muncie, IN	40 12	85 23	0	+64	+60	+57	+53	+50
Nashville, TN	36 10	86 47	1	+22	+11	+ 3	− 6	−14
Newark–East Orange, NJ....	40 44	74 10	0	+17	+14	+12	+ 9	+ 7

City	North Latitude °	'	West Longitude °	'	Time Zone Code	Key Letters				
						A (min.)	B (min.)	C (min.)	D (min.)	E (min.)
New Haven, CT 41		18	72	56	0	+11	+ 8	+ 7	+ 5	+ 4
New London, CT 41		22	72	6	0	+ 7	+ 5	+ 4	+ 2	+ 1
New Orleans, LA 29		57	90	4	1	+52	+32	+16	− 1	−15
New York, NY 40		45	74	0	0	+17	+14	+11	+ 9	+ 6
Norfolk, VA 36		51	76	17	0	+38	+28	+21	+12	+ 5
North Platte, NE 41		8	100	46	1	+62	+60	+58	+56	+54
Norwalk–Stamford, CT 41		7	73	22	0	+13	+10	+ 9	+ 7	+ 5
Oakley, KS 39		8	100	51	1	+69	+63	+59	+53	+49
Ogden, UT............... 41		13	111	58	2	+47	+45	+43	+41	+40
Ogdensburg, NY.......... 44		42	75	30	0	+ 8	+13	+17	+21	+25
Oklahoma City, OK 35		28	97	31	1	+67	+55	+46	+35	+26
Omaha, NE 41		16	95	56	1	+43	+40	+39	+37	+36
Orlando, FL.............. 28		32	81	22	0	+80	+59	+42	+22	+ 6
Ortonville, MN 45		19	96	27	1	+30	+36	+40	+46	+51
Oshkosh, WI 44		1	88	33	1	+ 3	+ 6	+ 9	+12	+15
Palm Springs, CA 33		49	116	32	3	+28	+13	+ 1	−12	−22
Parkersburg, WV 39		16	81	34	0	+52	+46	+42	+36	+32
Paterson, NJ 40		55	74	10	0	+17	+14	+12	+ 9	+ 7
Pendleton, OR............ 45		40	118	47	3	− 1	+ 4	+10	+16	+21
Pensacola, FL 30		25	87	13	1	+39	+20	+ 5	−12	−26
Peoria, IL............... 40		42	89	36	1	+19	+16	+14	+11	+ 9
Philadelphia–Chester, PA ...39		57	75	9	0	+24	+19	+16	+12	+ 9
Phoenix, AZ 33		27	112	4	2	+71	+56	+44	+30	+20
Pierre, SD 44		22	100	21	1	+49	+53	+56	+60	+63
Pittsburgh–McKeesport, PA 40		26	80	0	0	+42	+38	+35	+32	+29
Pittsfield, MA 42		27	73	15	0	+ 8	+ 8	+ 8	+ 8	+ 8
Pocatello, ID 42		52	112	27	2	+43	+44	+45	+46	+46
Poplar Bluff, MO 36		46	90	24	1	+35	+25	+17	+ 8	+ 1
Portland, ME............. 43		40	70	15	0	− 8	− 5	− 3	− 1	0
Portland, OR 45		31	122	41	3	+14	+20	+25	+31	+36
Portsmouth, NH 43		5	70	45	0	− 4	− 2	− 1	0	0
Presque Isle, ME.......... 46		41	68	1	0	−29	−19	−12	− 4	+ 2
Providence, RI 41		50	71	25	0	+ 3	+ 2	+ 1	0	0
Pueblo, CO 38		16	104	37	2	+27	+20	+14	+ 7	+ 2
Raleigh, NC.............. 35		47	78	38	0	+51	+39	+30	+20	+12
Rapid City, SD 44		5	103	14	2	+ 2	+ 5	+ 8	+11	+13
Reading, PA 40		20	75	56	0	+26	+22	+19	+16	+13
Redding, CA 40		35	122	24	3	+31	+27	+25	+22	+19
Richmond, VA 37		32	77	26	0	+41	+32	+25	+17	+11
Roanoke, VA 37		16	79	57	0	+51	+42	+35	+27	+21
Roswell, NM............. 33		24	104	32	2	+41	+26	+14	0	−10
Rutland, VT.............. 43		37	72	58	0	+ 2	+ 5	+ 7	+ 9	+11
Sacramento, CA 38		35	121	30	3	+34	+27	+21	+15	+10
St. Johnsbury, VT......... 44		25	72	1	0	− 4	0	+ 3	+ 7	+10
St. Joseph, MI 42		5	86	26	0	+61	+61	+60	+60	+59
St. Joseph, MO 39		46	94	50	1	+43	+38	+35	+30	+27
St. Louis, MO 38		37	90	12	1	+28	+21	+16	+10	+ 5
St. Petersburg, FL......... 27		46	82	39	0	+87	+65	+47	+26	+10
Salem, OR............... 44		57	123	1	3	+17	+23	+27	+31	+35
Salina, KS 38		50	97	37	1	+57	+51	+46	+40	+35
Salisbury, MD............ 38		22	75	36	0	+31	+23	+18	+11	+ 6
Salt Lake City, UT 40		45	111	53	2	+48	+45	+43	+40	+38
San Antonio, TX.......... 29		25	98	30	1	+87	+66	+50	+31	+16
San Diego, CA 32		43	117	9	3	+33	+17	+ 4	− 9	−21
San Francisco–Oakland–										
San Jose, CA 37		47	122	25	3	+40	+31	+25	+18	+12
Santa Fe, NM 35		41	105	56	2	+40	+28	+19	+ 9	0

City	North Latitude ° '	West Longitude ° '	Time Zone Code	Key Letters A (min.)	B (min.)	C (min.)	D (min.)	E (min.)
Savannah, GA	32 5	81 6	0	+70	+54	+40	+25	+13
Scranton–Wilkes-Barre, PA	41 25	75 40	0	+21	+19	+18	+16	+15
Seattle–Tacoma– Olympia, WA	47 37	122 20	3	+ 3	+15	+24	+34	+42
Sheridan, WY	44 48	106 58	2	+14	+19	+23	+27	+31
Shreveport, LA	32 31	93 45	1	+60	+44	+31	+16	+ 4
Sioux Falls, SD	43 33	96 44	1	+38	+40	+42	+44	+46
South Bend, IN	41 41	86 15	0	+62	+61	+60	+59	+58
Spartanburg, SC	34 56	81 57	0	+66	+53	+43	+32	+23
Spokane, WA	47 40	117 24	3	−16	− 4	+ 4	+14	+23
Springfield, IL	39 48	89 39	1	+22	+18	+14	+10	+ 6
Springfield–Holyoke, MA	42 6	72 36	0	+ 6	+ 6	+ 6	+ 5	+ 5
Springfield, MO	37 13	93 18	1	+45	+36	+29	+20	+14
Syracuse, NY	43 3	76 9	0	+17	+19	+20	+21	+22
Tallahassee, FL	30 27	84 17	0	+87	+68	+53	+35	+22
Tampa, FL	27 57	82 27	0	+86	+64	+46	+25	+ 9
Terre Haute, IN	39 28	87 24	0	+74	+69	+65	+60	+56
Texarkana, AR	33 26	94 3	1	+59	+44	+32	+18	+ 8
Toledo, OH	41 39	83 33	0	+52	+50	+49	+48	+47
Topeka, KS	39 3	95 40	1	+49	+43	+38	+32	+28
Traverse City, MI	44 46	85 38	0	+49	+54	+57	+62	+65
Trenton, NJ	40 13	74 46	0	+21	+17	+14	+11	+ 8
Trinidad, CO	37 10	104 31	2	+30	+21	+13	+ 5	0
Tucson, AZ	32 13	110 58	2	+70	+53	+40	+24	+12
Tulsa, OK	36 9	95 60	1	+59	+48	+40	+30	+22
Tupelo, MS	34 16	88 34	1	+35	+21	+10	− 2	−11
Vernal, UT	40 27	109 32	2	+40	+36	+33	+30	+28
Walla Walla, WA	46 4	118 20	3	− 5	+ 2	+ 8	+15	+21
Washington, DC	38 54	77 1	0	+35	+28	+23	+18	+13
Waterbury–Meriden, CT	41 33	73 3	0	+10	+ 9	+ 7	+ 6	+ 5
Waterloo, IA	42 30	92 20	1	+24	+24	+24	+25	+25
Wausau, WI	44 58	89 38	1	+ 4	+ 9	+13	+18	+22
West Palm Beach, FL	26 43	80 3	0	+79	+55	+36	+14	− 2
Wichita, KS	37 42	97 20	1	+60	+51	+45	+37	+31
Williston, ND	48 9	103 37	1	+46	+59	+69	+80	+90
Wilmington, DE	39 45	75 33	0	+26	+21	+18	+13	+10
Wilmington, NC	34 14	77 55	0	+52	+38	+27	+15	+ 5
Winchester, VA	39 11	78 10	0	+38	+33	+28	+23	+19
Worcester, MA	42 16	71 48	0	+ 3	+ 2	+ 2	+ 2	+ 2
York, PA	39 58	76 43	0	+30	+26	+22	+18	+15
Youngstown, OH	41 6	80 39	0	+42	40	+38	+36	+34
Yuma, AZ	32 43	114 37	2	+83	+67	+54	+40	+28

CANADA

City								
Calgary, AB	51 5	114 5	2	+13	+35	+50	+68	+84
Edmonton, AB	53 34	113 25	2	− 3	+26	+47	+72	+93
Halifax, NS	44 38	63 35	−1	+21	+26	+29	+33	+37
Montreal, QC	45 28	73 39	0	− 1	+ 4	+ 9	+15	+20
Ottawa, ON	45 25	75 43	0	+ 6	+13	+18	+23	+28
Peterborough, ON	44 18	78 19	0	+21	+25	+28	+32	+35
Saint John, NB	45 16	66 3	−1	+28	+34	+39	+44	+49
Saskatoon, SK	52 10	106 40	1	+37	+63	+80	+101	+119
Sydney, NS	46 10	60 10	−1	+ 1	+ 9	+15	+23	+28
Thunder Bay, ON	48 27	89 12	0	+47	+61	+71	+83	+93
Toronto, ON	43 39	79 23	0	+28	+30	+32	+35	+37
Vancouver, BC	49 13	123 6	3	0	+15	+26	+40	+52
Winnipeg, MB	49 53	97 10	1	+12	+30	+43	+58	+71

ARTERY 90% CLOGGED BY PLAQUE

ARTERY 50% CLOGGED BY PLAQUE

CLEAN ARTERY

HIGH BLOOD PRESSURE? The artery-cleaning vegetable that helps clean arteries like a scrub brush!

OVERWEIGHT? Try these 8 foods that "force" your body to shed weight!

"High Blood Pressure Lowered Naturally — Your Arteries Can Clean Themselves"

(By Frank K. Wood)

FC&A, a Peachtree City, Georgia, publisher, announced today the release of a new book for the general public, *"High Blood Pressure Lowered Naturally — Your Arteries Can Clean Themselves."* The authors provide many health tips with full explanations.

▶ If you want a slim, attractive waistline, these 20 tasty, heart-healthy foods are perfect for helping to dissolve the inches.

▶ The #1 weight-loss food! Eliminates snacking by "turning off" your body's internal hunger switch while lowering your cholesterol and blood pressure.

▶ Save your heart and help guard against cancer, too. In a four-year study, scientists found that those eating these foods had over 60% fewer deaths from cancer.

▶ The heart-healthy elixir you should be drinking every day. Contains a mineral that helps lower high blood pressure and tastes yummy, too.

▶ Studies show that people who take this vitamin daily significantly reduce their risk of suffering a heart attack or stroke. This same vitamin may also heal stroke damage.

▶ 6 signs of heart attack that must never be ignored ... and the simple, little-known step that dramatically increases your chances of survival. This life-saving secret alone makes this book indispensable.

▶ Test your own cholesterol in just 15 minutes. Easy and accurate.

▶ Perfect anti-stress exercise! No running, no sweating, no heavy weights. Yet, scientifically proven to relieve tension, reduce your cholesterol, and lower your blood pressure.

▶ Healthiest herb for diabetics. Studies show this herb not only helps control blood sugar but also lowers dangerous triglycerides.

▶ How to control your temptations and successfully resist fattening foods — even your favorite desserts.

▶ What never to drink if you're taking high blood pressure medicine. This fruit juice may drive your blood pressure to toxic levels.

Learn all these natural healing secrets. Book includes over 1,001 ways to perfect health. To order a copy, just return this notice with your name and address and a check for $9.99 plus $3.00 shipping and handling to: **FC&A, Dept. 2OF-03**, 103 Clover Green, Peachtree City, GA 30269. We will send you a copy of *"High Blood Pressure Lowered Naturally — Your Arteries Can Clean Themselves."*

Sorry, only one copy per customer.

You get a no-time-limit guarantee of satisfaction or your money back.

You must cut out and return this notice with your order. Copies will not be accepted!

IMPORTANT — FREE GIFT OFFER EXPIRES IN 30 DAYS

All orders mailed within 30 days will receive a free gift, *"Take Off 20 Pounds and 20 Years in 20 Weeks or Less, Naturally"* guaranteed. Order right away! © FC&A 2002

Tide Corrections

■ Many factors affect the times and heights of the tides: the coastal configuration, the time of the Moon's southing (crossing the meridian), and the Moon's phase. The High Tide column on the **Left-Hand Calendar Pages 44–70** lists the times of high tide at Commonwealth Pier in Boston Harbor. The heights of some of these tides, reckoned from Mean Lower Low Water, are given on the **Right-Hand Calendar Pages 45–71.** Use this table to calculate the approximate times and heights of high water at the places shown. Apply the time difference to the times of high tide at Boston **(pages 44–70)** and the height difference to the heights at Boston **(pages 45–71).**

Estimations derived from this table are *not* meant to be used for navigation. *The Old Farmer's Almanac* accepts no responsibility for errors or any consequences ensuing from the use of this table.

Predictions for many other stations can be found on our Web site, www.almanac .com/tides/predictions.

Coastal Site	Difference: Time (h. m.)	Height (ft.)
Canada		
Alberton, PE	−5 45**	−7.5
Charlottetown, PE	−0 45**	−3.5
Halifax, NS	−3 23	−4.5
North Sydney, NS	−3 15	−6.5
Saint John, NB	+0 30	+15.0
St. John's, NF	−4 00	−6.5
Yarmouth, NS	−0 40	+3.0
Maine		
Bar Harbor	−0 34	+0.9
Belfast	−0 20	+0.4
Boothbay Harbor	−0 18	−0.8
Chebeague Island	−0 16	−0.6
Eastport	−0 28	+8.4
Kennebunkport	+0 04	−1.0
Machias	−0 28	+2.8
Monhegan Island	−0 25	−0.8
Old Orchard	0 00	−0.8
Portland	−0 12	−0.6
Rockland	−0 28	+0.1
Stonington	−0 30	+0.1
York	−0 09	−1.0

Coastal Site	Difference: Time (h. m.)	Height (ft.)
New Hampshire		
Hampton	+0 02	−1.3
Portsmouth	+0 11	−1.5
Rye Beach	−0 09	−0.9
Massachusetts		
Annisquam	−0 02	−1.1
Beverly Farms	0 00	−0.5
Boston	0 00	0.0
Cape Cod Canal		
East Entrance	−0 01	−0.8
West Entrance	−2 16	−5.9
Chatham Outer Coast	+0 30	−2.8
Inside	+1 54	*0.4
Cohasset	+0 02	−0.07
Cotuit Highlands	+1 15	*0.3
Dennis Port	+1 01	*0.4
Duxbury–Gurnet Point	+0 02	−0.3
Fall River	−3 03	−5.0
Gloucester	−0 03	−0.8
Hingham	+0 07	0.0
Hull	+0 03	−0.2
Hyannis Port	+1 01	*0.3
Magnolia–Manchester	−0 02	−0.7
Marblehead	−0 02	−0.4
Marion	−3 22	−5.4
Monument Beach	−3 08	−5.4
Nahant	−0 01	−0.5
Nantasket	+0 04	−0.1
Nantucket	+0 56	*0.3
Nauset Beach	+0 30	*0.6
New Bedford	−3 24	−5.7
Newburyport	+0 19	−1.8
Oak Bluffs	+0 30	*0.2
Onset–R.R. Bridge	−2 16	−5.9
Plymouth	+0 05	0.0
Provincetown	+0 14	−0.4
Revere Beach	−0 01	−0.3
Rockport	−0 08	−1.0
Salem	0 00	−0.5
Scituate	−0 05	−0.7
Wareham	−3 09	−5.3
Wellfleet	+0 12	+0.5
West Falmouth	−3 10	−5.4
Westport Harbor	−3 22	−6.4
Woods Hole		
Little Harbor	−2 50	*0.2
Oceanographic Institute	−3 07	*0.2
Rhode Island		
Bristol	−3 24	−5.3
Narragansett Pier	−3 42	−6.2

Coastal Site	Difference: Time (h. m.)	Height (ft.)	Coastal Site	Difference: Time (h. m.)	Height (ft.)
Newport	−3 34	−5.9	Hampton Roads	−2 02	−6.9
Point Judith	−3 41	−6.3	Norfolk	−2 06	−6.6
Providence	−3 20	−4.8	Virginia Beach	−4 00	−6.0
Sakonnet	−3 44	−5.6	Yorktown	−2 13	−7.0
Watch Hill	−2 50	−6.8	**North Carolina**		
Connecticut			Cape Fear	−3 55	−5.0
Bridgeport	+0 01	−2.6	Cape Lookout	−4 28	−5.7
Madison	−0 22	−2.3	Currituck	−4 10	−5.8
New Haven	−0 11	−3.2	Hatteras		
New London	−1 54	−6.7	Inlet	−4 03	−7.4
Norwalk	+0 01	−2.2	Kitty Hawk	−4 14	−6.2
Old Lyme			Ocean	−4 26	−6.0
Highway Bridge	−0 30	−6.2	**South Carolina**		
Stamford	+0 01	−2.2	Charleston	−3 22	−4.3
Stonington	−2 27	−6.6	Georgetown	−1 48	*0.36
New York			Hilton Head	−3 22	−2.9
Coney Island	−3 33	−4.9	Myrtle Beach	−3 49	−4.4
Fire Island Light	−2 43	*0.1	St. Helena		
Long Beach	−3 11	−5.7	Harbor Entrance	−3 15	−3.4
Montauk Harbor	−2 19	−7.4	**Georgia**		
New York City–Battery	−2 43	−5.0	Jekyll Island	−3 46	−2.9
Oyster Bay	+0 04	−1.8	St. Simon's Island	−2 50	−2.9
Port Chester	−0 09	−2.2	Savannah Beach		
Port Washington	−0 01	−2.1	River Entrance	−3 14	−5.5
Sag Harbor	−0 55	−6.8	Tybee Light	−3 22	−2.7
Southampton			**Florida**		
Shinnecock Inlet	−4 20	*0.2	Cape Canaveral	−3 59	−6.0
Willets Point	0 00	−2.3	Daytona Beach	−3 28	−5.3
New Jersey			Fort Lauderdale	−2 50	−7.2
Asbury Park	−4 04	−5.3	Fort Pierce Inlet	−3 32	−6.9
Atlantic City	−3 56	−5.5	Jacksonville		
Bay Head–Sea Girt	−4 04	−5.3	Railroad Bridge	−6 55	*0.1
Beach Haven	−1 43	*0.24	Miami Harbor Entrance	−3 18	−7.0
Cape May	−3 28	−5.3	St. Augustine	−2 55	−4.9
Ocean City	−3 06	−5.9			
Sandy Hook	−3 30	−5.0			
Seaside Park	−4 03	−5.4			
Pennsylvania					
Philadelphia	+2 40	−3.5			
Delaware					
Cape Henlopen	−2 48	−5.3			
Rehoboth Beach	−3 37	−5.7			
Wilmington	+1 56	−3.8			
Maryland					
Annapolis	+6 23	−8.5			
Baltimore	+7 59	−8.3			
Cambridge	+5 05	−7.8			
Havre de Grace	+11 21	−7.7			
Point No Point	+2 28	−8.1			
Prince Frederick					
Plum Point	+4 25	−8.5			
Virginia					
Cape Charles	−2 20	−7.0			

*Where the difference in the Height column is so marked, height at Boston should be multiplied by this ratio.

**Varies widely; accurate within only 1½ hours. Consult local tide tables for precise times and heights.

Example: The conversion of the times and heights of the tides at Boston to those at Cape Fear, North Carolina, is given below:

Sample tide calculation July 4, 2003:

High tide at Boston (p. 60)	3:45 P.M.	EDT
Correction for Cape Fear	−3:55 hrs.	
High tide at Cape Fear	11:50 A.M.	EDT
Tide height at Boston (p. 61)	9.5 ft.	
Correction for Cape Fear	−5.0 ft.	
Tide height at Cape Fear	4.5 ft.	

The **Old Farmer's**

General Store

A special section featuring unique mail order products for all our readers who shop by mail.

Classified Advertising

What flowers are always under a person's nose?

Answer: Tulips (two lips).

...LE WITCH. Psychic readings and counseling. Casting and removal of spells. Contact with spirits. Call 24/7. Tom 800-419-3346. Credit/debit cards. Get your lover back.

HELP WANTED

EASY WORK! Excellent pay! Assemble products at home. Call toll-free 800-467-5566 ext. 12627.

Why is a weathercock like ambition?

Answer: Because it is often vain (vane) to aspire (a spire).

WARNING! Don't fall for homeworking scams. Free consumer newsletter helps you find legitimate home employment and business opportunities. 800-519-3607 (doc. 502).

HERBS

HERB PLANTS. Free catalog. Possum Creek Herb Farm. www.possumcreekherb.com. 423-332-0347. E-mail: poscreek@bellsouth.net.

INSECT REPELLENT

BUZZ-OFF. Powerful insect repellent. Deet free. All insects away. $10/4 oz. Lewey's, 176 Amsden Rd., Corrina ME 04928; or 866-539-3971; or www.4u2buzzoff.com.

KITCHEN SUPPLIES

TUPPERWARE! www.getproducts.com. 866-887-7371. E-mail mytupperware@juno.com. Sales/service! Quality products affordably priced.

LANDSCAPING

GROW INCREDIBLE LAWNS and gardens. Discover what the professionals know. Get proven results! Visit www.agropro.com.

MAINE RESORTS

BAR HARBOR AND ACADIA National Park. 153 ocean-view rooms. Atlantic-Oakes-By-The-Sea. Open year-round. 800-33-MAINE (62463). www.barharbor.com.

MISCELLANEOUS

CASH FOR 78-RPM RECORDS! Send $2 (refundable) for 72-page illustrated booklet with thousands of specific prices I pay, shipping instructions, etc. Docks, Box 691035(FA), San Antonio TX 78269-1035.

What beverage will surely change our pain?

Answer: A little tea (t) will change pain into paint.

$7,000 REWARD for proof that the Savior's name was originally "Jesus." Read "The Mistaken J" on-line at www.YNCA.com.

NEED SOME GREAT-LOOKING OLD-STYLE pine or cedar sawhorses? Check out our Web site at www.old-style-sawhorses.com.

NEW PRODUCTS

BALL-CAP LINER adds hidden warmth to favorite hat. Simple and cheap. Great gift. Web site: www.gerrycraft.com.

NURSERY STOCK

TREE/SHRUB SEEDLINGS direct from grower. Plants for landscaping, wildlife food and cover, timber, and Christmas tree production. Free color catalog. Carino Nurseries. 800-223-7075. Web site: www.carinonurseries.com.

OF INTEREST TO ALL

PHOTOGRAPHS COPIED, restored. Send SASE to Big Foto, Box 521, Cataula GA 31804.

TWO-HOUR WEDDING-PLANNING VIDEO. $19.95. Learn from the professionals! Free coupon and discounts. www.idoinfo.com.

BEAUTIFUL HAND-PAINTED MAILBOXES. Great gifts! Florals, birds, baskets, more. www.countrymailboxes.com. 603-899-2146.

AMAZING HI-TECH CDs. Secret info. Free energy, cable, satellite, computers, phone, health, and more. www.hi-techstuff.com.

FREE MONEY AVAILABLE! Wealthy foundations unload billions in grants! Blessing, Box 47-44FA, Springfield MO 65801.

ORGANIZATIONS

UNMARRIED CATHOLICS. Nationwide club. Huge membership. Newsletter. Free information. Sparks, Box 872-FA, Troy NY 12181.

PERSONALS

MEET LATIN WOMEN! Beautiful Mexican-South American ladies seeking marriage! All ages, free brochures! TLC, PO Box 924994, Houston TX 77292-4994. 713-896-9224. Web site: www.tlcworldwide.com.

How do rabbits travel?

Answer: By hareplane!

MOTHER ISABELL tells past, present, and future. Gifted healer. 404-755-1301. 1214 Gordon St., Atlanta GA 30310. Write or call.

POWERFUL SPELLS PERFORMED. Dominique reunites lovers immediately. Reveals future love, finance. One free reading. 423-472-3035.

IT'S FREE! Ladies talk to local guys. It's new, fun, and exciting! Call 800-485-4047. 18+.

DIAL-A-MATE LIVE TALK and voice personals. 10,000 singles call every day! Try it free! 800-234-5558. 18+.

BEAUTIFUL ASIAN LADIES overseas seek love, marriage. Lowest rates! Free brochure: PR, Box 1245 FA, Benicia CA 94510. 707-747-6906.

MEET NICE SINGLES. Christian values. All ages. Free catalog. Box 310-OFA, Allardt TN 38504. 931-879-4625.

PET SUPPLIES

REMOVE PET HAIR from carpet like magic. Universal Rug Rake! Free information. Call 877-784-7253. www.rugrake.com.

POULTRY

GOSLINGS, DUCKLINGS, chicks, turkeys, guineas, books. Picture catalog $1. Pilgrim Goose Hatchery, GC-20, Williamsfield OH 44093.

REAL ESTATE

LET THE GOVERNMENT PAY for your new or existing home. Hundreds of programs. Web site: www.usgovernmentinformation.com. Free recorded message: 707-448-3210 (9KE1).

GOVERNMENT LAND now available for claim. 160 acres/person. Free recorded message: 707-448-1887 (4KE1). www.usgovernmentinformation.com.

RECIPES

ORIGINAL HUNGARIAN RECIPES, $3 each. Specialty cookware available at our Web site www.gaborsgourmet.com or write to: Gabor's Gourmet, PO Box 561, Stayton OR 97383.

AUTHENTIC CORNISH RECIPES to discover and enjoy. $5 American, $8 Canadian by money order to: Gorda Hilton, PO Box 61507, Langley BC V3A 8C8.

FULL-COLOR LABELS for soaps, jams, jellies, honey, lotions, creams. Small quantities available. Free samples. 877-901-4989.

RELIGION

OLD RELIGIOUS LP RECORD ALBUMS wanted: Robert Beckendorf, Alton Beale, De Vern Mullen, Dick Goodwin, Hilding Halvarson, Paul Carson, Mary Ross, Mary Steed, Marilyn Jones, Musical Betts, Hetrick family, Payne family, Doerksen sisters, Jones sisters, Lang sisters, Leppien sisters, Delphia Lawrence, Singing Leichtys/3001/03, Church in the barn/1001, Kenny Walker Bailey, Lloyd Orrell/6080-8229, Palmetto State/LP222, Mariners/CL609. Also harp, vibraharp, marimba/xylophone albums. Excellent prices for good clean copies. Check thrift stores; mint copies abound. Your efforts compensated, shipping reimbursed. This is an ongoing offer. Write: Songtime, PO Box 1625, Bloomington IN 47402.

HOW TO STUDY THE BIBLE and have it make sense. Free booklet. Clearwater Bible Students, PO Box 8216, Clearwater FL 33758.

READ "WHAT HAPPENED with Christianity?" on-line at www.YNCA.com, or write for your free booklet: YNCA, Dept. F, PO Box 50, Kingdom City MO 65262.

RESEARCH

WANTED: DIVORCED COUPLES to share their experiences for research project/book. 877-684-8991 toll-free. www.divorce-stories.com.

RESORTS/TRAVEL/VACATIONS

HUNTING/GOLFING. Coastal Georgia, Sapelo River. Marsh and river views. Sleeps 4-7. Fully equipped, includes a public boat ramp. Guided fishing available. 10 miles from Sapelo Hammock Golf Course. Call 888-547-1223 or send e-mail to tlingerfelt@mindspring.com.

What did the sock say to the foot?

Answer: You are putting me on!

NEED SUNSHINE? Great prices to Mexico, Hawaii, Las Vegas, Florida, Europe. Packages or cruises. Great Connections Travel, toll-free 888-574-0311.

SEEDS & PLANTS

THE ORIGINAL "Grow Your Own" seed company. Tobacco, medicinal plants, tropicals, and more. Free catalog. E.O.N.S., Dept./FA, PO Box 4604, Hallandale FL 33008. 954-455-0229. www.eonseed.com.

FREE CATALOG. Top-quality vegetable, flower, and herb seeds since 1900. Burrell, Box 150-GC, Rock Ford CO 81067.

RARE HILARIOUS PETER, FEMALE, and squash pepper seeds. $3 per package. Any two $5, all three $8, over 100 others. Seeds, 2119 Hauss Nursery Rd., Atmore AL 36502.

SPIRITUALISTS

SAVANNAH MILLS. 100% accurate. Master psychic, soul mate advisor. Solves all problems. Reunites lovers. Immediate results guaranteed. Call 24 hours. Phone: 334-702-8853. Web site: www.psychicsavannah.com.

ANN MITCHELL. Need help? Marriage, love, personal happiness, luck. All answers found. Brings back desire. 601-271-2493.

SISTER HOPE, healing specialist. Removes bad luck. Reunites loved ones. Solves all problems. 662-844-8053.

MISS TINA, spiritual healer. Removes bad luck. Reunites lovers. Call now. Free sample reading. 662-287-0234.

DO YOU NEED HELP finding a loved one? I can help solve all your problems. Miss Hart, 2146 Celanese Rd., Rock Hill SC 29732. Telephone: 803-981-7679.

REVEREND GINGER - Indian healer - works miracles, guaranteed in hours. Specializing in re-uniting the separated. Call 504-463-3358.

FREE SAMPLE READING! Mrs. Ruth, southern-born spiritualist, removes evil, bad luck. Helps with all problems. 334-616-6363.

WEATHER VANES

WEATHER VANES AND CUPOLAS. 50% off sale. America's largest selection. Free catalog. Immediate delivery. 800-724-2548. Web site: www.weathervaneandcupola.com.

WORK CLOTHES

SUSPENDER WEARERS! Our suspenders feature a patented "no-slip clip." Free catalog. 800-700-4515. www.suspenders.com.

WORK CLOTHES. Save 80%, shirts, pants, coveralls. Free folder. Write Galco, 4004 E. 71st St., Dept. OF-3, Cleveland OH 44105.

SOMETHING FOR EVERYONE

BEAUTIFUL INTERNATIONAL WOMEN desire love and marriage. 50,000+ on Web site. New listings daily, tours, chat rooms. 800-322-3267 ext. 71. Cherry Blossoms, Box 190, Dept. 71, Kapaau HI 96755. www.blossoms.com/?adid=71.

CARRY YOUR OWN medical information on CD-ROM, for travelers, emergencies, specialists, snowbirds. Write: Technology for Life, 211 Hornbine Rd., Swansea MA 02777 or e-mail TravelMedInfo@aol.com.

FREE BOOKLETS: Life, death, soul, resurrection, pollution crisis, hell, Judgement Day, restitution. Bible Standard (OF), PO Box 67, Chester Springs PA 19425-0067. www.biblestandard.com.

SINGLE NONSMOKERS, make a date to find your health-minded mate. 603-256-8686. E-mail sniusa@hotmail.com.

The Old Farmer's Almanac classified rates: $17 per word (15-word minimum per insertion). Payment required with order: MasterCard, Visa, AmEx, and Discover/NOVUS accepted. For *Gardener's Companion* rates, Web classifieds, or additional information, contact Marie Knopp: 203-263-7171; fax 203-263-7174; or e-mail to gallagroup@aol.com. Write to: Marie Knopp, Gallagher Group, PO Box 959, Woodbury, CT 06798. *The 2004 Old Farmer's Almanac* closing date is May 13, 2003.

Discover more wit, wisdom, and weather at www.almanac.com.

Indiana Firm Discovers:

Special ^*New* cream for arthritis

(SPECIAL)–A small company in central Indiana has developed a special cream that relieves arthritis pain in minutes, even chronic arthritis pain—deep in the joints. The product which is called **PAIN-BUST-R-II,** is one of the fastest acting therapeutic formulas ever developed in the fight against arthritis. Immediately upon application it goes to work by penetrating deep to the areas most affected—the joints themselves, bringing fast relief where relief is needed most. Men and women who have suffered arthritis pain for years are reporting incredible results with this product. Even a single application seems to work remarkably well in relieving pain and bringing comfort to cramped, knotted joints. ***PAIN-BUST-R-II** was researched and formulated to be absorbed directly into the joints and muscles—where the pain originates. Long-time arthritis sufferers will be glad to know that this formula will help put an end to agonizing days and sleepless nights. It is highly recommended by users who have resumed daily activities and are enjoying life again.

Read what our users have to say:

"I use **PAIN BUST** because I suffer from tension in my back and shoulders. I can't praise your product enough, I've used other ointments, but they don't seem to work as fast nor last as long. Thank you. Thank you...Thank you!"   *C.K.F.*

"Last night when I went to sleep I rubbed some **PAIN BUST** on my sore aching knee. 15 minutes later I fell sound asleep and woke 8 hours later with absolutely no pain. I wish I knew about **PAIN BUST** long ago." *B.M.S.*

NO-RISK FREE TRIAL
We Trust You — Send No Money!

<u>TO ORDER:</u> Just write **"PAIN BUST•RII"** on a sheet of paper and send it along with your name, address and the number of tubes you wish to order. We will promptly ship you 1 large tube for $7.95, 2 large tubes for $13.90 or 3 large tubes for only $19.35 *(SAVES $4.50)*. Prices include all shipping and handling. We will enclose an invoice and if for any reason you wish to cancel your order, simply mark Cancel on the invoice and there will be no charge to you. You don't even have to bother returning the merchandise. Send for your <u>NO-RISK FREE TRIAL ORDER</u> today to:
Continental Quest/Research Corp.
220 W. Carmel Dr. - Dept. OFA-03
Carmel, IN 46032.

Anecdotes AND Pleasantries

A sampling from the hundreds of letters, clippings, and e-mails sent to us by Almanac readers from all over the United States and Canada during the past year.

How to Grow a Square Watermelon
(And why.)
Courtesy of C.H.S. of Reno, Nevada.

I recently read an article by Cara Murphy in the Manhattan Beach, California, *Beach Reporter* about a Rev. Kurt Dahlin who was growing square watermelons. I thought it was a great idea—they'd fit better in the refrigerator and slice like a loaf of bread—so now I've been growing them that way myself and thought maybe some of your readers would like to know the technique.

DIRECTIONS:

1) Buy an ordinary rectangular cinder block at a local home-and-garden store or wherever.

2) When your melon is still as small as a pea, drape its vine across the top of your cinder block, with the little melon over the hole.

3) Be sure to water occasionally, if needed.

4) When the watermelon is ripe and has grown to fill the inside of the cinder block so tightly that you can not remove it, crack the cinder block in half with a sledge hammer.

Voilà, you have a square watermelon! Slice and serve.

The Best Farmer Joke of the Year . . .
(It's reasonably clean, too.)
Courtesy of F. P. of West Caldwell, New Jersey.

When a Vermont farmer was pulled over by a state trooper for speeding, the trooper proceeded to lecture him at length, throwing his weight around and generally making the farmer uncomfortable. Finally, the trooper got around to writing out a ticket, and as he was doing so, he had to keep swatting away at some flies that were buzzing around his head.

"Having some trouble with those circle flies, are ya?" asked the farmer.

The trooper stopped writing for a moment. "Well, yeah," he said, "if that's what they are. I never heard of circle flies."

"Well, circle flies are common on farms," replied the farmer. "You see,

they're called circle flies because they're almost always found circling around the back end of a horse."

"Oh," said the trooper. Then he went back to writing the ticket. After a minute, he stopped and said, "Hey, wait a minute. Are you trying to call me a horse's rear end?"

"Oh, no, no," replied the farmer. "I have too much respect for the law and police officers to even think about calling you that."

"Good," said the trooper, as he went back to writing the ticket.

After a long pause, the farmer said, "Hard to fool them flies, though."

. . . and the Three Worst Puns

(Apologies all around.)

Courtesy of R. P. of Columbia, Tennessee.

■ **Two boll weevils grow up in South Carolina.** One goes to Hollywood and becomes a famous actor. The other stays behind in the cotton fields and never amounts to much. The second one, naturally, becomes known as the lesser of two weevils.

■ **A three-legged dog walks into a saloon in the** Old West. He slides up to the bar and announces: "I'm looking for the man who shot my paw."

■ **A woman has twins and gives them up for** adoption. One of them goes to a family in Egypt and is named Ahmal. The other goes to a family in Spain and they name him Juan. Years later, Juan sends a picture of himself to his birth mother. Upon receiving the picture, she tells her husband that she wishes she also had a picture of Ahmal. Her husband responds, "They're twins! If you've seen Juan, you've seen Ahmal."

What Color Is the Universe?

(It's not blue. No, not black. Give up?)

Courtesy of E. B. of Antrim, New Hampshire, who sent us the gist of an article by Amanda Gardner of Health Scout News.

Well, initially, researchers at Johns Hopkins University, in Baltimore, Maryland, concluded that the color was more of a greenish purple. By combining the average value of all the light in thousands of galaxies, they determined that the overall color of the universe lay somewhere between "medium aquamarine" and "pale turquoise." Then, last spring, saying that the

What Color Is the Universe?

(continued)

computer had made a "mistake," they decided that it wasn't the color after all. "It's beige," they said. (Beige?)

Of course, it should be noted that the human eye has adapted to a very limited band of the particular color spectrum of light that our star, the Sun, produces. Therefore, the color that we humans see might not even be visible to others from some alien world.

The Hopkins astronomers say that the universe probably started with a "blue period," which took its color from the preponderance of young blue stars. A "green period" ensued, as the number of older red stars increased. Upcoming is a "red period," as older, redder stars dominate the celestial canvas. (Apparently, there are some beige stars out there somewhere, too.)

American Tourists Ask the Darnedest Questions

(Especially at the Banff National Park, Banff, Alberta. And, yes, they're all questions actually heard at the information centers last year.)

Courtesy of R.C.T. of Saskatoon, Saskatchewan, who credits the weekly newsletter, Fast Facts Canada.

■ "At what elevation does an elk become a moose?"

■ Tourist: "How do you pronounce 'Elk'?"
Park staff: "Elk."
Tourist: "Oh."

■ "Are the bears with collars tame?"

■ "Is there anywhere I can see the bears pose?"

■ "Where does Alberta end and Canada begin?"

■ "Is this the part of Canada that speaks French—or is that Saskatchewan?"

■ "Which is the way to the Columbia Rice Fields?"

■ "What's the best way to see Canada in a day?"

■ "Where can I get my husband really, *really* lost?"

■ "Is that two kilometers by foot or by car?"

■ "Where do you put the animals at night?"

■ Tourist: "How do you get your lakes so blue?"
Park staff: "We take the water out in the winter and paint the bottom."
Tourist: "Oh."

Whatever Happened to Florence and Bertha?

Courtesy of R.D.S. of Knoxville, Tennessee, who credits Bill Dedman of the New York Times.

MOST POPULAR BOYS' NAMES 100 YEARS AGO (in order of popularity): John, William, James, George, Charles, Joseph, Frank, Henry, Robert, and Harry.

TODAY: Michael, Jacob, Matthew, Christopher,

Joshua, Austin, Nicholas, Tyler, Brandon, and Joseph.

MOST POPULAR GIRLS' NAMES 100 YEARS AGO (in order of popularity): Mary, Helen, Anna, Margaret, Ruth, Elizabeth, Marie, Rose, Florence, and Bertha.

TODAY: Emily, Samantha, Madison, Ashley, Sarah, Hannah, Jessica, Alyssa, Alexis, and Kayla.

Note: Florence and Bertha, numbers 9 and 10 a century ago, do not even make the top 10,000 names today!

Illustrating the Rapid Demise of Common Sense

By F. P. of West Caldwell, New Jersey.

One day last winter, I was signing the receipt for a credit card purchase I'd just made, when the clerk noticed that I had never signed my name on the back of that particular credit card. She informed me that she could not complete the transaction unless my credit card was signed. When I asked her why, she explained that it was necessary to compare the signature on the credit card with the signature on the receipt to be sure they matched.

So I signed the back of my credit card in front of her. She then carefully compared that signature with the one I'd just affixed to the receipt.

As luck would have it, they matched.

Three Scientific Questions Answered at Last

Courtesy of J.B.R. of Charlotte, North Carolina, who credits the Fortean Times *and Chet Raymo's "Science Musings" column in the* New York Times.

Can you tell which bear defecated in the woods?

ANSWER: Yes. Scientists from the Center for Wildlife Conservation in Seattle, Washington, recently developed a way to extract DNA from bear feces so that individual feces found in the woods can now be matched to specific bears. *(Editor's note: Does anyone care to hazard a guess as to why?)*

Are octopi ever capable of having a little fun?

ANSWER: Yes. Animal behaviorists at the University of Lethbridge, Lethbridge, Alberta, and at the Seattle (Washington) Aquarium gave plastic bottles to some octopi. The animals soon devised a game with them, pushing them into the water flowing into their tanks and allowing them to drift back. They did it over and over.

Is it possible to continue "gardening" after you're dead?

ANSWER: Yes. Well, probably. Swedish biologist Susanne Wiigh-Masak has recently developed a method of converting bodies into harmless—and useful—compost. Frozen cadavers are immersed in liquid nitrogen to remove water, causing them to crumble into fine organic dust, which is placed into a container where it's allowed to biodegrade for six months or so. Ms. Wiigh-Masak hopes to turn the first corpse into compost this year, provided the Swedish government changes the law to allow it.

The Inspiring Story of Esau Wood

(Go ahead, try to tell it!)

Courtesy of M.P.S. of Ashford, Washington.

Esau Wood sawed wood. Esau Wood would saw wood! Oh, the wood Wood would saw! All the wood Esau Wood saw, Esau Wood would saw. In other words, all the wood Wood saw, Esau sought to saw.

One day, Wood's wood-saw would saw no wood. Hence, all the wood Wood saw was the wood Wood would saw if Wood's wood-saw would saw wood. But because Wood could saw wood only with a wood-saw that would saw wood, Esau sought a saw that would saw wood.

Then Esau saw a saw saw as no other wood-saw would saw. In fact, of all the wood-saws Wood ever saw saw wood, Wood never saw a saw saw as the wood-saw Wood saw would saw. And even I never saw a saw saw as the wood-saw Wood saw would saw until I saw Esau saw wood with the wood-saw Wood saw saw wood. Now Wood saws wood with the wood-saw Wood saw saw wood, so the story has a happy ending.

Welcome Home, Soldier

Courtesy of R.G.H. of Burnt Hills, New York.

I'm wondering if your Almanac readers enjoy sharing memories of their military service. Well, if so, here's one of mine:

World War II had just ended, and I was home on a ten-day furlough from the army. I had so much to catch up on that I was in and out of the house all day long, always in uniform. My mother was having difficulty trying to keep up with all my comings and goings and, in fact, was beginning to get a little tired of trying.

One afternoon toward the end of my furlough, after I'd left the house for the fourth or fifth time that day, my older brother, also in his army uniform, walked through the front door unexpectedly, having been overseas in Europe for almost three years.

My mother glanced over at the uniform from the open kitchen door and greeted him with the words we've laughed about at family gatherings every since: "Oh," she said irritably, "are you back again?" (Sorry, Mom.)

(c o n t i n u e d)

Should We Be Walking—or Running—in the Rain?

(Singing is, of course, perfectly fine in either case.)

Courtesy of R.D.H., Seattle, Washington.

OK. It's raining cats and dogs and you have, say, 200 yards to cover between your car and your office. Most people would probably run because, duh, there would be less exposure time in the rain.

But wait. There's a certain amount of water between you and your destination, and no matter what, you're going to run into that water. Also, when you run, you run *into* the raindrops and therefore more water hits your horizontal areas like face, chest, and legs. So perhaps walking would be the wisest choice. Right?

Well, as reported by *Seattle Times* science reporter Eric Sorensen, this dilemma was pretty much put to rest last year by Doug Craigen, a physicist based in Winnipeg, Manitoba. Craigen tackled the problem with a calculator on his Web site (www.dctech.com/physics/features/physics_0600a.html) to factor in such things as kinematics, relative velocity, vector components, and flux.

The results: Craigen's "subject" was a six-foot-tall, practically bald, 44-year-old male. By walking those 200 yards at a speed of 1 yard per second, Craigen's calculations indicated that the man's bald spot and other surface features would be hit by 61.5 milliliters of water—about 2 ounces—in the 3 minutes and 20 seconds required to cover that specific distance.

On the other hand, by jogging at a 10-minute-mile pace, he would catch only 40 milliliters of water. Actually, he would be catching *more* water per second, but the jogging came out ahead by cutting in half the time he would be in the rain.

Did we or did we not already know that? Well, now we know *for sure*—that is, if you can trust computers.

The Four Stages of a Man's Life

Courtesy of S. T. of Hanover, New Hampshire.

You **believe in** Santa Claus.

You **don't believe in** Santa Claus.

You **are** Santa Claus.

You **look like** Santa Claus.

Share Your Anecdotes and Pleasantries

We'd love to hear from you. Send your contribution for the 2004 edition of *The Old Farmer's Almanac* by January 31, 2003, to: "A & P," The Old Farmer's Almanac, P.O. Box 520, Dublin, NH 03444; or e-mail it to almanac@yankeepub.com (subject: A & P). ☐☐

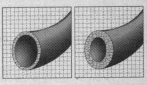

2002

January
S	M	T	W	T	F	S
		1	2	3	4	5
6	7	8	9	10	11	12
13	14	15	16	17	18	19
20	21	22	23	24	25	26
27	28	29	30	31		

February
S	M	T	W	T	F	S
					1	2
3	4	5	6	7	8	9
10	11	12	13	14	15	16
17	18	19	20	21	22	23
24	25	26	27	28		

March
S	M	T	W	T	F	S
					1	2
3	4	5	6	7	8	9
10	11	12	13	14	15	16
17	18	19	20	21	22	23
24	25	26	27	28	29	30
31						

April
S	M	T	W	T	F	S
	1	2	3	4	5	6
7	8	9	10	11	12	13
14	15	16	17	18	19	20
21	22	23	24	25	26	27
28	29	30				

May
S	M	T	W	T	F	S
			1	2	3	4
5	6	7	8	9	10	11
12	13	14	15	16	17	18
19	20	21	22	23	24	25
26	27	28	29	30	31	

June
S	M	T	W	T	F	S
						1
2	3	4	5	6	7	8
9	10	11	12	13	14	15
16	17	18	19	20	21	22
23	24	25	26	27	28	29
30						

July
S	M	T	W	T	F	S
	1	2	3	4	5	6
7	8	9	10	11	12	13
14	15	16	17	18	19	20
21	22	23	24	25	26	27
28	29	30	31			

August
S	M	T	W	T	F	S
				1	2	3
4	5	6	7	8	9	10
11	12	13	14	15	16	17
18	19	20	21	22	23	24
25	26	27	28	29	30	31

September
S	M	T	W	T	F	S
1	2	3	4	5	6	7
8	9	10	11	12	13	14
15	16	17	18	19	20	21
22	23	24	25	26	27	28
29	30					

October
S	M	T	W	T	F	S
		1	2	3	4	5
6	7	8	9	10	11	12
13	14	15	16	17	18	19
20	21	22	23	24	25	26
27	28	29	30	31		

November
S	M	T	W	T	F	S
					1	2
3	4	5	6	7	8	9
10	11	12	13	14	15	16
17	18	19	20	21	22	23
24	25	26	27	28	29	30

December
S	M	T	W	T	F	S
1	2	3	4	5	6	7
8	9	10	11	12	13	14
15	16	17	18	19	20	21
22	23	24	25	26	27	28
29	30	31				

2003

January
S	M	T	W	T	F	S
			1	2	3	4
5	6	7	8	9	10	11
12	13	14	15	16	17	18
19	20	21	22	23	24	25
26	27	28	29	30	31	

February
S	M	T	W	T	F	S
						1
2	3	4	5	6	7	8
9	10	11	12	13	14	15
16	17	18	19	20	21	22
23	24	25	26	27	28	

March
S	M	T	W	T	F	S
						1
2	3	4	5	6	7	8
9	10	11	12	13	14	15
16	17	18	19	20	21	22
23	24	25	26	27	28	29
30	31					

April
S	M	T	W	T	F	S
		1	2	3	4	5
6	7	8	9	10	11	12
13	14	15	16	17	18	19
20	21	22	23	24	25	26
27	28	29	30			

May
S	M	T	W	T	F	S
				1	2	3
4	5	6	7	8	9	10
11	12	13	14	15	16	17
18	19	20	21	22	23	24
25	26	27	28	29	30	31

June
S	M	T	W	T	F	S
1	2	3	4	5	6	7
8	9	10	11	12	13	14
15	16	17	18	19	20	21
22	23	24	25	26	27	28
29	30					

July
S	M	T	W	T	F	S
		1	2	3	4	5
6	7	8	9	10	11	12
13	14	15	16	17	18	19
20	21	22	23	24	25	26
27	28	29	30	31		

August
S	M	T	W	T	F	S
					1	2
3	4	5	6	7	8	9
10	11	12	13	14	15	16
17	18	19	20	21	22	23
24	25	26	27	28	29	30
31						

September
S	M	T	W	T	F	S
	1	2	3	4	5	6
7	8	9	10	11	12	13
14	15	16	17	18	19	20
21	22	23	24	25	26	27
28	29	30				

October
S	M	T	W	T	F	S
			1	2	3	4
5	6	7	8	9	10	11
12	13	14	15	16	17	18
19	20	21	22	23	24	25
26	27	28	29	30	31	

November
S	M	T	W	T	F	S
						1
2	3	4	5	6	7	8
9	10	11	12	13	14	15
16	17	18	19	20	21	22
23	24	25	26	27	28	29
30						

December
S	M	T	W	T	F	S
	1	2	3	4	5	6
7	8	9	10	11	12	13
14	15	16	17	18	19	20
21	22	23	24	25	26	27
28	29	30	31			

2004

January
S	M	T	W	T	F	S
				1	2	3
4	5	6	7	8	9	10
11	12	13	14	15	16	17
18	19	20	21	22	23	24
25	26	27	28	29	30	31

February
S	M	T	W	T	F	S
1	2	3	4	5	6	7
8	9	10	11	12	13	14
15	16	17	18	19	20	21
22	23	24	25	26	27	28
29						

March
S	M	T	W	T	F	S
	1	2	3	4	5	6
7	8	9	10	11	12	13
14	15	16	17	18	19	20
21	22	23	24	25	26	27
28	29	30	31			

April
S	M	T	W	T	F	S
				1	2	3
4	5	6	7	8	9	10
11	12	13	14	15	16	17
18	19	20	21	22	23	24
25	26	27	28	29	30	

May
S	M	T	W	T	F	S
						1
2	3	4	5	6	7	8
9	10	11	12	13	14	15
16	17	18	19	20	21	22
23	24	25	26	27	28	29
30	31					

June
S	M	T	W	T	F	S
		1	2	3	4	5
6	7	8	9	10	11	12
13	14	15	16	17	18	19
20	21	22	23	24	25	26
27	28	29	30			

July
S	M	T	W	T	F	S
				1	2	3
4	5	6	7	8	9	10
11	12	13	14	15	16	17
18	19	20	21	22	23	24
25	26	27	28	29	30	31

August
S	M	T	W	T	F	S
1	2	3	4	5	6	7
8	9	10	11	12	13	14
15	16	17	18	19	20	21
22	23	24	25	26	27	28
29	30	31				

September
S	M	T	W	T	F	S
			1	2	3	4
5	6	7	8	9	10	11
12	13	14	15	16	17	18
19	20	21	22	23	24	25
26	27	28	29	30		

October
S	M	T	W	T	F	S
					1	2
3	4	5	6	7	8	9
10	11	12	13	14	15	16
17	18	19	20	21	22	23
24	25	26	27	28	29	30
31						

November
S	M	T	W	T	F	S
	1	2	3	4	5	6
7	8	9	10	11	12	13
14	15	16	17	18	19	20
21	22	23	24	25	26	27
28	29	30				

December
S	M	T	W	T	F	S
			1	2	3	4
5	6	7	8	9	10	11
12	13	14	15	16	17	18
19	20	21	22	23	24	25
26	27	28	29	30	31	

A Reference Compendium

compiled by Mare-Anne Jarvela

A Table Foretelling the Weather Through All the Lunations of Each Year, or Forever

This table is the result of many years of actual observation and shows what sort of weather will probably follow the Moon's entrance into any of its quarters. For example, the table shows that the week following July 29, 2003, will be cold, with frequent showers, because the Moon becomes new that day at 2:53 A.M. EDT. (See the Left-Hand Calendar Pages 44–70 for 2003 Moon phases.)

EDITOR'S NOTE: *Although the data in this table is taken into consideration in the yearlong process of compiling the annual long-range weather forecasts for* The Old Farmer's Almanac, *we rely far more on our projections of solar activity.*

Time of Change	Summer	Winter
Midnight to 2 A.M.	Fair	Hard frost, unless wind is south or west
2 A.M. to 4 A.M.	Cold, with frequent showers	Snow and stormy
4 A.M. to 6 A.M.	Rain	Rain
6 A.M. to 8 A.M.	Wind and rain	Stormy
8 A.M. to 10 A.M.	Changeable	Cold rain if wind is west; snow if east
10 A.M. to noon	Frequent showers	Cold with high winds
Noon to 2 P.M.	Very rainy	Snow or rain
2 P.M. to 4 P.M.	Changeable	Fair and mild
4 P.M. to 6 P.M.	Fair	Fair
6 P.M. to 10 P.M.	Fair if wind is northwest; rain if wind is south or southwest	Fair and frosty if wind is north or northeast; rain or snow if wind is south or southwest
10 P.M. to midnight	Fair	Fair and frosty

This table was created more than 165 years ago by Dr. Herschell for the Boston Courier; *it first appeared in* The (Old) Farmer's Almanac *in 1834.*

Safe Ice Thickness*

Ice Thickness	Permissible Load	Ice Thickness	Permissible Load
2 inches	Single person on foot	12 inches	Heavy truck (8-ton gross)
3 inches	Group in single file	15 inches	10 tons
7½ inches	Passenger car (2-ton gross)	20 inches	25 tons
8 inches	Light truck (2½-ton gross)	30 inches	70 tons
10 inches	Medium truck (3½-ton gross)	36 inches	110 tons

Solid, clear blue/black pond and lake ice

■ Slush ice has only half the strength of blue ice.
■ The strength value of river ice is 15 percent less.

–courtesy American Pulpwood Association

Winter Weather Terms

Winter Storm Outlook
■ Issued prior to a winter storm watch. An outlook is issued when forecasters believe that storm conditions are possible, usually 48 to 60 hours before the beginning of a storm.

Winter Storm Watch
■ Indicates the possibility of a winter storm and is issued to provide 12 to 36 hours notice. A watch is announced when the specific timing, location, and path of a storm are undetermined. Be alert to changing weather conditions, and avoid unnecessary travel.

Winter Storm Warning
■ Indicates that a severe winter storm has started or is about to begin. A warning is issued when more than six inches of snow, a significant ice accumulation, a dangerous windchill, or a combination of the three is expected. Anticipated snow accumulation during a winter storm is six or more inches in 24 hours. You should stay indoors during the storm.

Heavy Snow Warning
■ Issued when snow accumulations are expected to approach or exceed six inches in 12 hours but will not be accompanied by significant wind. The warning could also be issued if eight or more inches of snow accumulation is expected in a 24-hour period. During a heavy snow warning, freezing rain and sleet are not expected.

Blizzard Warning
■ Indicates that sustained winds or frequent gusts of 35 miles per hour or greater will occur in combination with considerable falling and/or blowing snow for at least three hours. Visibility will often be reduced to less than ¼ mile.

Whiteout
■ Caused by falling and/or blowing snow that reduces visibility to zero miles—typically only a few feet. Whiteouts are most frequent during blizzards and can occur rapidly, often blinding motorists and creating chain-reaction crashes involving multiple vehicles.

Nor'easter
■ Usually produces heavy snow and rain and creates tremendous waves in Atlantic coastal regions, often causing beach erosion and structural damage. Wind gusts associated with these storms can exceed hurricane force in intensity. A nor'easter gets its name from the strong, continuous northeasterly ocean winds that blow in over coastal areas ahead of the storm.

Sleet
■ Frozen or partially frozen rain in the form of ice pellets that hit the ground so fast that they bounce and do not stick to it. However, the pellets can accumulate like snow and cause hazardous conditions for pedestrians and motorists.

Freezing Rain
■ Liquid precipitation that turns to ice on contact with a frozen surface to form a smooth ice coating called a glaze.

Ice Storm Warning
■ Issued when freezing rain results in ice accumulations measuring ½ inch thick or more. This can cause trees and utility lines to fall down, causing power outages.

Windchill Advisory
■ Issued when windchill temperatures are expected to be between –20° and –34°F.

Windchill Warning
■ Issued when windchill temperatures are expected to be below –34°F.

REFERENCE

Snowflakes

Snowflakes are made up of six-sided crystals. If you look carefully at the snowflakes during the next snowstorm, you might be able to find some of the crystal types below. The basic shape of a crystal is determined by the temperature at which it forms. Sometimes a snowflake is a combination of more than one type of crystal.

CAPPED COLUMNS
(also called tsuzumi crystals) occur when the temperature is 25°F or less.

NEEDLES
(long and thin but still six-sided crystals) occur when the temperature is 21° to 25°F.

SPATIAL DENDRITES
(irregular and feathery crystals) occur in high-moisture clouds at 3° to 10°F.

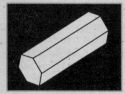

COLUMNS
(dense crystals, act like prisms) occur when the temperature is 25°F or less.

PLATES
(mirror-like crystals) occur under special weather conditions.

STELLAR CRYSTALS
(beautiful, delicate crystals) occur under special weather conditions.

Weather Phobias

Name of Fear	Object Feared	Name of Fear	Object Feared
Ancraophobia	Wind	Hygrophobia	Dampness, moisture
Antlophobia	Floods	Keraunophobia	Lightning, thunder
Astraphobia	Lightning, thunder	Lilapsophobia	Hurricanes, tornadoes
Auroraphobia	Northern lights, southern lights	Nebulaphobia	Fog
		Nephophobia	Clouds
Brontophobia	Lightning, thunder	Ombrophobia	Rain
Ceraunophobia	Thunder	Pagophobia	Frost, ice
Cheimatophobia	Cold	Phengophobia	Daylight, sunshine
Chionophobia	Snow	Pluviophobia	Rain
Cryophobia	Extreme cold, frost, ice	Psychrophobia	Cold
Frigophobia	Cold	Thermophobia	Heat
Heliophobia	Sun, sunshine	Tonitrophobia	Thunder
Homichlophobia	Fog		

Windchill

As wind speed increases, the air temperature against your body falls. The combination of cold temperature and high wind can create a cooling effect so severe that exposed flesh can freeze. (Inanimate objects, such as cars, do not experience windchill.)

To gauge wind speed: At 10 miles per hour, you can feel wind on your face; at 20, small branches move, and dust or snow is raised; at 30, large branches move and wires whistle; at 40, whole trees bend.

TEMPERATURE (°F)

Calm	35	30	25	20	15	10	5	0	–5	–10	–15	–20	–25	–30	–35
5	31	25	19	13	7	1	–5	–11	–16	–22	–28	–34	–40	–46	–52
10	27	21	15	9	3	–4	–10	–16	–22	–28	–35	–41	–47	–53	–59
15	25	19	13	6	0	–7	–13	–19	–26	–32	–39	–45	–51	–58	–64
20	24	17	11	4	–2	–9	–15	–22	–29	–35	–42	–48	–55	–61	–68
25	23	16	9	3	–4	–11	–17	–24	–31	–37	–44	–51	–58	–64	–71
30	22	15	8	1	–5	–12	–19	–26	–33	–39	–46	–53	–60	–67	–73
35	21	14	7	0	–7	–14	–21	–27	–34	–41	–48	–55	–62	–69	–76
40	20	13	6	–1	–8	–15	–22	–29	–36	–43	–50	–57	–64	–71	–78
45	19	12	5	–2	–9	–16	–23	–30	–37	–44	–51	–58	–65	–72	–79
50	19	12	4	–3	–10	–17	–24	–31	–38	–45	–52	–60	–67	–74	–81
55	18	11	4	–3	–11	–18	–25	–32	–39	–46	–54	–61	–68	–75	–82
60	17	10	3	–4	–11	–19	–26	–33	–40	–48	–55	–62	–69	–76	–84

WIND SPEED (mph)

Frostbite occurs in 15 minutes or less.

EXAMPLE: When the temperature is 15°F and the wind speed is 30 miles per hour, the windchill, or how cold it feels, is –5°F. For a Celsius version of the Windchill table, visit **www.almanac.com/weathercharts.** *–courtesy National Weather Service*

Is It Raining, Drizzling, or Misting?

	NUMBER OF DROPS (per sq. ft. per sec.)	DIAMETER OF DROPS (mm)	INTENSITY (in. per hr.)
Cloudburst	113	2.85	4.0
Excessive rain	76	2.4	1.6
Heavy rain	46	2.05	0.6
Moderate rain	46	1.6	0.15
Light rain	26	1.24	0.04
Drizzle	14	0.96	0.01
Mist	2,510	0.1	0.002
Fog	6,264,000	0.01	0.005

Cloud Definitions

High Clouds
(bases starting at an average of 20,000 feet)

CIRRUS: Thin feather-like crystal clouds.
CIRROCUMULUS: Thin clouds that appear as small "cotton patches."
CIRROSTRATUS: Thin white clouds that resemble veils.

Middle Clouds
(bases starting at about 10,000 feet)

ALTOCUMULUS: Gray or white layer or patches of solid clouds with rounded shapes.
ALTOSTRATUS: Grayish or bluish layer of clouds that can obscure the Sun.

Low Clouds
(bases starting near Earth's surface to 6,500 feet)

STRATUS: Thin, gray sheet-like clouds with low bases; may bring drizzle and snow.
STRATOCUMULUS: Rounded cloud masses that form on top of a layer.

—Weatherstock

NIMBOSTRATUS: Dark, gray shapeless cloud layers containing rain, snow, and ice pellets.

Clouds with Vertical Development
(high clouds that form at almost any altitude and reach up to 14,000 feet)

CUMULUS: Fair-weather clouds with flat bases and domeshaped tops.
CUMULONIMBUS: Large, dark, vertical clouds with bulging tops that bring showers, thunder, and lightning.

Atlantic Hurricane Names for 2003

Ana	Grace	Mindy	Teresa
Bill	Henri	Nicholas	Victor
Claudette	Isabel	Odette	Wanda
Danny	Juan	Peter	
Erika	Kate	Rose	
Fabian	Larry	Sam	

East-Pacific Hurricane Names for 2003

Andres	Guillermo	Marty	Terry
Blanca	Hilda	Nora	Vivian
Carlos	Ignacio	Olaf	Waldo
Dolores	Jimena	Patricia	Xina
Enrique	Kevin	Rick	York
Felicia	Linda	Sandra	Zelda

Retired Atlantic Hurricane Names

These storms have been some of the most destructive and costly; as a result, their names have been retired from the six-year rotating hurricane list.

NAME	YEAR RETIRED	NAME	YEAR RETIRED	NAME	YEAR RETIRED
Celia	1970	Alicia	1983	Bob	1991
Agnes	1972	Elena	1985	Andrew	1992
Carmen	1974	Gloria	1985	Opal	1995
Eloise	1975	Gilbert	1988	Roxanne	1995
Anita	1977	Joan	1988	Fran	1996
David	1979	Hugo	1989	Mitch	1998
Frederic	1979	Diana	1990	Floyd	1999
Allen	1980	Klaus	1990	Keith	2000

International Weather Symbols

Weather Conditions

،	light drizzle
،،	steady, light drizzle
؛	intermittent, moderate drizzle
∴،	steady, moderate drizzle
⋮	intermittent, heavy drizzle
∴؛	steady, heavy drizzle
•	light rain
••	steady, light rain
⦂	intermittent, moderate rain
∴•	steady, moderate rain
⋮	intermittent, heavy rain
∴••	steady, heavy rain
*	light snow
**	steady, light snow
*⋮	intermittent, moderate snow
**	steady, moderate snow
***	intermittent, heavy snow
***	steady, heavy snow
⍐	hail
∾	freezing rain
⊗	sleet
)(	tornado
§	dust devil
⭍	dust storm
≡	fog
⏚	thunderstorm
<	lightning
♀	hurricane

Sky Coverage

○	no clouds
◔	one-tenth covered
◔	two- to three-tenths covered
◔	four-tenths covered
◑	half covered
◑	six-tenths covered
◕	seven- to eight-tenths covered
◕	nine-tenths covered
●	completely overcast

High Clouds

⌓	cirrus
⌇	cirrocumulus
⌐	cirrostratus

Middle Clouds

⌣	altocumulus
∠	altostratus

Low Clouds

—	stratus
⌒	stratocumulus
⌐	nimbostratus

Vertically Developed Clouds

⌂	cumulus
⌂	cumulonimbus

Wind Speed

Symbol	(mph)	(km/h)
◎	calm	calm
—	1–2	1–3
⊥	3–8	4–13
⊿	9–14	14–23
⊿	15–20	24–33
⊿	21–25	34–40
◣	55–60	89–97
◤◣	119–123	192–198

Heat Index °F (°C)

	RELATIVE HUMIDITY (%)								
	40	45	50	55	60	65	70	75	80
100 (38)	109 (43)	114 (46)	118 (48)	124 (51)	129 (54)	136 (58)			
98 (37)	105 (41)	109 (43)	113 (45)	117 (47)	123 (51)	128 (53)	134 (57)		
96 (36)	101 (38)	104 (40)	108 (42)	112 (44)	116 (47)	121 (49)	126 (52)	132 (56)	
94 (34)	97 (36)	100 (38)	103 (39)	106 (41)	110 (43)	114 (46)	119 (48)	124 (51)	129 (54)
92 (33)	94 (34)	96 (36)	99 (37)	101 (38)	105 (41)	108 (42)	112 (44)	116 (47)	121 (49)
90 (32)	91 (33)	93 (34)	95 (35)	97 (36)	100 (38)	103 (39)	106 (41)	109 (43)	113 (45)
88 (31)	88 (31)	89 (32)	91 (33)	93 (34)	95 (35)	98 (37)	100 (38)	103 (39)	106 (41)
86 (30)	85 (29)	87 (31)	88 (31)	89 (32)	91 (33)	93 (34)	95 (35)	97 (36)	100 (38)
84 (29)	83 (28)	84 (29)	85 (29)	86 (30)	88 (31)	89 (32)	90 (32)	92 (33)	94 (34)
82 (28)	81 (27)	82 (28)	83 (28)	84 (29)	84 (29)	85 (29)	86 (30)	88 (31)	89 (32)
80 (27)	80 (27)	80 (27)	81 (27)	81 (27)	82 (28)	82 (28)	83 (28)	84 (29)	84 (29)

(Left axis: TEMPERATURE °F (°C))

EXAMPLE: When the temperature is 88°F (31°C) and the relative humidity is 60 percent, the heat index, or how hot it feels, is 95°F (35°C).

The UV Index for Measuring Ultraviolet Radiation Risk

The U.S. National Weather Service daily forecasts of ultraviolet levels use these numbers for various exposure levels:

UV Index Number	Exposure Level	Time to Burn	Actions to Take
0, 1, 2	Minimal	60 minutes	Apply SPF 15 sunscreen
3, 4	Low	45 minutes	Apply SPF 15 sunscreen; wear a hat
5, 6	Moderate	30 minutes	Apply SPF 15 sunscreen; wear a hat
7, 8, 9	High	15–25 minutes	Apply SPF 15 to 30 sunscreen; wear a hat and sunglasses
10 or higher	Very high	10 minutes	Apply SPF 30 sunscreen; wear a hat, sunglasses, and protective clothing

"Time to Burn" and "Actions to Take" apply to people with fair skin that sometimes tans but usually burns. People with lighter skin need to be more cautious. People with darker skin may be able to tolerate more exposure.

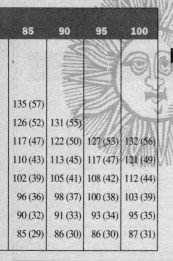

	85	90	95	100
	135 (57)			
	126 (52)	131 (55)		
	117 (47)	122 (50)	127 (53)	132 (56)
	110 (43)	113 (45)	117 (47)	121 (49)
	102 (39)	105 (41)	108 (42)	112 (44)
	96 (36)	98 (37)	100 (38)	103 (39)
	90 (32)	91 (33)	93 (34)	95 (35)
	85 (29)	86 (30)	86 (30)	87 (31)

Richter Scale for Measuring Earthquakes

Magnitude	Possible Effects
1	Detectable only by instruments
2	Barely detectable, even near the epicenter
3	Felt indoors
4	Felt by most people; slight damage
5	Felt by all; minor to moderate damage
6	Moderate destruction
7	Major damage
8	Total and major damage

–devised by American geologist Charles W. Richter in 1935 to measure the magnitude of an earthquake

Temperature Conversion Scale

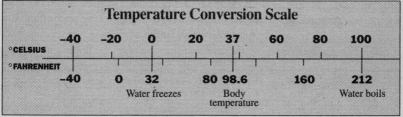

The Volcanic Explosivity Index (VEI) for Measuring Volcanic Eruptions

VEI	Description	Plume Height	Volume	Classification	Frequency
0	Nonexplosive	<100 m	$1,000 \text{ m}^3$	Hawaiian	Daily
1	Gentle	100–1,000 m	$10,000 \text{ m}^3$	Hawaiian/Strombolian	Daily
2	Explosive	1–5 km	$1,000,000 \text{ m}^3$	Strombolian/Vulcanian	Weekly
3	Severe	3–15 km	$10,000,000 \text{ m}^3$	Vulcanian	Yearly
4	Cataclysmic	10–25 km	$100,000,000 \text{ m}^3$	Vulcanian/Plinian	10 years
5	Paroxysmal	>25 km	1 km^3	Plinian	100 years
6	Colossal	>25 km	10 km^3	Plinian/Ultra-Plinian	100 years
7	Supercolossal	>25 km	100 km^3	Ultra-Plinian	1,000 years
8	Megacolossal	>25 km	$1,000 \text{ km}^3$	Ultra-Plinian	10,000 years

Beaufort Wind Force Scale

"Used Mostly at Sea but of Help to All Who Are Interested in the Weather"

Admiral Beaufort arranged the numbers 0 to 12 to indicate the strength of the wind from calm, force 0, to hurricane, force 12. Here's a scale adapted to land.

Beaufort Force	Description	When You See or Feel This Effect	Wind (mph)	(km/h)
0	Calm	Smoke goes straight up	less than 1	less than 2
1	Light air	Wind direction is shown by smoke drift but not by wind vane	1–3	2–5
2	Light breeze	Wind is felt on the face; leaves rustle; wind vanes move	4–7	6–11
3	Gentle breeze	Leaves and small twigs move steadily; wind extends small flags straight out	8–12	12–19
4	Moderate breeze	Wind raises dust and loose paper; small branches move	13–18	20–29
5	Fresh breeze	Small trees sway; waves form on lakes	19–24	30–39
6	Strong breeze	Large branches move; wires whistle; umbrellas are difficult to use	25–31	40–50
7	Moderate gale	Whole trees are in motion; walking against the wind is difficult	32–38	51–61
8	Fresh gale	Twigs break from trees; walking against the wind is very difficult	39–46	62–74
9	Strong gale	Buildings suffer minimal damage; roof shingles are removed	47–54	75–87
10	Whole gale	Trees are uprooted	55–63	88–101
11	Violent storm	Widespread damage	64–72	102–116
12	Hurricane	Widespread destruction	73+	117+

Fujita Scale (or F Scale) for Measuring Tornadoes

■ This is a system developed by Dr. Theodore Fujita to classify tornadoes based on wind damage. All tornadoes, and most other severe local windstorms, are assigned a single number from this scale according to the most intense damage caused by the storm.

F0 (weak)	40–72 mph, light damage
F1 (weak)	73–112 mph, moderate damage
F2 (strong)	113–157 mph, considerable damage
F3 (strong)	158–206 mph, severe damage
F4 (violent)	207–260 mph, devastating damage
F5 (violent)	261–318 mph (rare), incredible damage

Torro Hailstorm Intensity Scale

INTENSITY	DESCRIPTION OF DAMAGE
H0	True hail of pea size causes no damage
H1	Leaves and flower petals are punctured and torn
H2	Leaves are stripped from trees and plants
H3	Panes of glass are broken; auto bodies are dented
H4	Some house windows are broken; small tree branches are broken off; birds are killed
H5	Many windows are smashed; small animals are injured; large tree branches are broken off
H6	Shingle roofs are breached; metal roofs are scored; wooden window frames are broken away
H7	Roofs are shattered to expose rafters; cars are seriously damaged
H8	Shingle and tiled roofs are destroyed; small tree trunks are split; people are seriously injured
H9	Concrete roofs are broken; large tree trunks are split and knocked down; people are at risk of fatal injuries
H10	Brick houses are damaged; people are at risk of fatal injuries

—Weatherstock

Weather History

ON JANUARY 23, 1971, the **record-low temperature** in the United States of −79.8°F was reached at Prospect Creek Camp in Alaska.

ON FEBRUARY 8, 1891, winds peaked at 80 miles per hour in what witnesses called **"the worst blizzard ever known"** in Elkton, South Dakota.

ON MARCH 18, 1980, over nine inches of rain caused **severe flooding** in the Catskill Mountains in New York.

ON APRIL 15, 1980, temperatures soared to an early season-high of 110°F in Yuma, Arizona.

ON MAY 5, 1917, Denver, Colorado, set a record for a **May snowstorm** when it received 12 inches.

ON JUNE 16, 1984, a **flash flood** carried 64 cars a quarter-mile in Westby, Wisconsin.

ON JULY 4, 1816, New Englanders had to wear overcoats at midday despite the sunshine, in the so-called **"year without a summer."**

ON AUGUST 9, 1878, a **rare tornado** in Wallingford, Connecticut, killed 34 people.

ON SEPTEMBER 3, 1970, the **largest hailstone** on record fell near Coffeyville, Kansas. The stone was 17.5 inches in circumference.

ON OCTOBER 18, 1930, lake-effect snow fell four feet deep in the suburbs of Buffalo, New York.

ON NOVEMBER 7, 1940, the Tacoma Narrows Bridge (also known as "Galloping Gertie") in Tacoma, Washington, collapsed in **high winds.**

ON DECEMBER 16, 1835, New England experienced its famous **"Cold Wednesday":** The temperature remained steady at −15°F during the day.

PHASES OF THE MOON

New

First Quarter

Full

Last Quarter

New

W A X I N G

W A N I N G

Origin of Full-Moon Names

Historically, the Native Americans who lived in the area that is now the northern and eastern United States kept track of the seasons by giving a distinctive name to each recurring full Moon. This name was applied to the entire month in which it occurred. These names, and some variations, were used by the Algonquin tribes from New England to Lake Superior.

Name	Month	Variations
Full Wolf Moon	January	Full Old Moon
Full Snow Moon	February	Full Hunger Moon
Full Worm Moon	March	Full Crow Moon Full Crust Moon Full Sugar Moon Full Sap Moon
Full Pink Moon	April	Full Sprouting Grass Moon Full Egg Moon Full Fish Moon
Full Flower Moon	May	Full Corn Planting Moon Full Milk Moon
Full Strawberry Moon	June	Full Rose Moon Full Hot Moon
Full Buck Moon	July	Full Thunder Moon Full Hay Moon
Full Sturgeon Moon	August	Full Red Moon Full Green Corn Moon
Full Harvest Moon*	September	Full Corn Moon Full Barley Moon
Full Hunter's Moon	October	Full Travel Moon Full Dying Grass Moon
Full Beaver Moon	November	Full Frost Moon
Full Cold Moon	December	Full Long Nights Moon

The Harvest Moon is always the full Moon closest to the autumnal equinox. If the Harvest Moon occurs in October, the September full Moon is usually called the Corn Moon.

REFERENCE

When Will the Moon Rise Today?

A lunar puzzle involves the timing of moonrise. If you enjoy the out-of-doors and the wonders of nature, you may wish to commit to memory the following gem:

 The new Moon always rises at sunrise

 And the first quarter at noon.

 The full Moon always rises at sunset

 And the last quarter at midnight.

■ Moonrise occurs about 50 minutes later each day.

■ The new Moon is invisible because its illuminated side faces away from Earth, which occurs when the Moon lines up between Earth and the Sun.

■ One or two days after the date of the new Moon, you can see a thin crescent setting just after sunset in the western sky as the lunar cycle continues. (See pages 44–70 for exact moonrise times.)

Origin of Month Names

January   Named for the Roman god Janus, protector of gates and doorways. Janus is depicted with two faces, one looking into the past, the other into the future.

February   From the Latin word *februa,* "to cleanse." The Roman Februalia was a month of purification and atonement.

March   Named for the Roman god of war, Mars. This was the time of year to resume military campaigns that had been interrupted by winter.

April   From the Latin word *aperio,* "to open (bud)," because plants begin to grow in this month.

May   Named for the Roman goddess Maia, who oversaw the growth of plants. Also from the Latin word *maiores,* "elders," who were celebrated during this month.

June   Named for the Roman goddess Juno, patroness of marriage and the well-being of women. Also from the Latin word *juvenis,* "young people."

July   Named to honor Roman dictator Julius Caesar (100 B.C.–44 B.C.). In 46 B.C., Julius Caesar made one of his greatest contributions to history: With the help of Sosigenes, he developed the Julian calendar, the precursor to the Gregorian calendar we use today.

August   Named to honor the first Roman emperor (and grandnephew of Julius Caesar), Augustus Caesar (63 B.C.–A.D. 14).

September   From the Latin word *septem,* "seven," because this had been the seventh month of the early Roman calendar.

October   From the Latin word *octo,* "eight," because this had been the eighth month of the early Roman calendar.

November   From the Latin word *novem,* "nine," because this had been the ninth month of the early Roman calendar.

December   From the Latin word *decem,* "ten," because this had been the tenth month of the early Roman calendar.

Origin of Day Names

The days of the week were named by the Romans with the Latin words for the Sun, the Moon, and the five known planets. These names have survived in European languages, but English names also reflect an Anglo-Saxon influence.

English	Latin	French	Italian	Spanish	Saxon
SUNDAY	Solis (Sun)	dimanche	domenica	domingo	Sun
MONDAY	Lunae (Moon)	lundi	lunedì	lunes	Moon
TUESDAY	Martis (Mars)	mardi	martedì	martes	Tiw (the Anglo-Saxon god of war, the equivalent of the Norse Tyr or the Roman Mars)
WEDNESDAY	Mercurii (Mercury)	mercredi	mercoledì	miércoles	Woden (the Anglo-Saxon equivalent of the Norse Odin or the Roman Mercury)
THURSDAY	Jovis (Jupiter)	jeudi	giovedì	jueves	Thor (the Norse god of thunder, the equivalent of the Roman Jupiter)
FRIDAY	Veneris (Venus)	vendredi	venerdì	viernes	Frigg (the Norse god of love and fertility, the equivalent of the Roman Venus)
SATURDAY	Saturni (Saturn)	samedi	sabato	sábado	Saterne (Saturn, the Roman god of agriculture)

Solar Eclipse Dates (2003–2024)

DATE		REGIONS WITH VISIBLE TOTALITY
2003	Nov. 23	Antarctica
2005	Apr. 8	S. Pacific Ocean
2006	Mar. 29	Africa, Turkey, Russia
2008	Aug. 1	Greenland, Siberia, China
2009	July 22	India, China, S. Pacific Ocean
2010	July 11	S. Pacific Ocean, southern South America
2012	Nov. 13	Australia, S. Pacific Ocean
2013	Nov. 3	Atlantic Ocean, central Africa
2015	Mar. 20	N. Atlantic Ocean, Arctic
2016	Mar. 9	Southeast Asia, N. Pacific Ocean
2017	Aug. 17	United States
2019	July 2	S. Pacific Ocean, South America
2020	Dec. 14	S. Pacific Ocean, South America
2021	Dec. 4	Antarctica
2023	Apr. 20	Indonesia
2024	Apr. 8	Mexico, United States, Canada

How to Find the Day of the Week for Any Given Date

To compute the day of the week for any given date as far back as the mid-18th century, proceed as follows:

■ Add the last two digits of the year to one-quarter of the last two digits (discard any remainder), the day of the month, and the month key from the key box below. Divide the sum by 7; the remainder is the day of the week (1 is Sunday, 2 is Monday, and so on). If there is no remainder, the day is Saturday. If you're searching for a weekday prior to 1900, add 2 to the sum before dividing; prior to 1800, add 4. The formula doesn't work for days prior to 1753. From 2000 to 2099, subtract 1 from the sum before dividing.

Example:
The Dayton Flood was on March 25, 1913.

Last two digits of year:	13
One-quarter of these two digits:	3
Given day of month:	25
Key number for March:	4
Sum:	45

45 ÷ 7 = 6, with a remainder of 3. The flood took place on Tuesday, the third day of the week.

KEY	
January	1
leap year	0
February	4
leap year	3
March	4
April	0
May	2
June	5
July	0
August	3
September	6
October	1
November	4
December	6

Easter Dates (2003–2007)

■ Christian churches that follow the Gregorian calendar celebrate Easter on the first Sunday after the full Moon that occurs on or just after the vernal equinox.

Year	Easter
2003	April 20
2004	April 11
2005	March 27
2006	April 16
2007	April 8

■ Eastern Orthodox churches follow the Julian calendar.

Year	Easter
2003	April 27
2004	April 11
2005	May 1
2006	April 23
2007	April 8

Triskaidekaphobia Trivia

Here are a few facts about Friday the 13th:

■ Of the 14 possible configurations for the annual calendar (see any perpetual calendar), the occurrence of Friday the 13th is this:

6 of 14 years have one Friday the 13th.

6 of 14 years have two Fridays the 13th.

2 of 14 years have three Fridays the 13th.

■ There is no year without one Friday the 13th, and no year with more than three.

■ There is only one Friday the 13th in 2003. The next year to have three Fridays the 13th is 2009.

■ The reason we say "Fridays the 13th" is that no one can pronounce "Friday the 13ths."

The Animal Signs of the Chinese Zodiac

The animal designations of the Chinese zodiac follow a 12-year cycle and are always used in the same sequence. The Chinese year of 354 days begins three to seven weeks into the western 365-day year, so the animal designation changes at that time, rather than on January 1. See page 42 for the exact date.

See page 42 for the exact date.

RAT

Ambitious and sincere, you can be generous with your money. Compatible with the dragon and the monkey. Your opposite is the horse.

1900	1936	1996
1912	1948	1984
1924	1960	2008
1972		

OX OR BUFFALO

A leader, you are bright, patient, and cheerful. Compatible with the snake and the rooster. Your opposite is the sheep.

1901	1937	1985
1913	1949	1997
1925	1961	2009
1973		

TIGER

Forthright and sensitive, you possess great courage. Compatible with the horse and the dog. Your opposite is the monkey.

1902	1938	1986
1914	1950	1998
1926	1962	2010
1974		

RABBIT OR HARE

Talented and affectionate, you are a seeker of tranquility. Compatible with the sheep and the pig. Your opposite is the rooster.

1903	1939	1987
1915	1951	1999
1927	1963	2011
1975		

DRAGON

Robust and passionate, your life is filled with complexity. Compatible with the monkey and the rat. Your opposite is the dog.

1904	1940	1988
1916	1952	2000
1928	1964	2012
1976		

SNAKE

Strong-willed and intense, you display great wisdom. Compatible with the rooster and the ox. Your opposite is the pig.

1905	1941	1989
1917	1953	2001
1929	1965	2013
1977		

HORSE

Physically attractive and popular, you like the company of others. Compatible with the tiger and the dog. Your opposite is the rat.

1906	1942	1990
1918	1954	2002
1930	1966	2014
1978		

SHEEP OR GOAT

Aesthetic and stylish, you enjoy being a private person. Compatible with the pig and the rabbit. Your opposite is the ox.

1907	1943	1991
1919	1955	2003
1931	1967	2015
1979		

MONKEY

Persuasive, skillful, and intelligent, you strive to excel. Compatible with the dragon and the rat. Your opposite is the tiger.

1908	1944	1992
1920	1956	2004
1932	1968	2016
1980		

ROOSTER OR COCK

Seeking wisdom and truth, you have a pioneering spirit. Compatible with the snake and the ox. Your opposite is the rabbit.

1909	1945	1993
1921	1957	2005
1933	1969	2017
1981		

DOG

Generous and loyal, you have the ability to work well with others. Compatible with the horse and the tiger. Your opposite is the dragon.

1910	1946	1994
1922	1958	2006
1934	1970	2018
1982		

PIG OR BOAR

Gallant and noble, your friends will remain at your side. Compatible with the rabbit and the sheep. Your opposite is the snake.

1911	1947	1995
1923	1959	2007
1935	1971	2019
1983		

Traditional Foods for Feasts and Fasts

Customs and lore surrounding religious events.

January

Feast of the Circumcision: Black-eyed peas and pork (United States); oat-husk gruel or oatmeal porridge (Scotland).

Epiphany: Cake with a lucky bean baked in it; the one who finds the bean is the king or queen of the feast, in memory of the Three Wise Men (France).

Robert Burns Day: Haggis—sheep's stomach stuffed with suet, chopped organ meat (heart, lungs, liver), onions, oatmeal, and seasonings (Scotland).

February

Candlemas: Pancakes eaten today will prevent hemorrhoids for a full year (French American).

St. Agatha: Round loaves of bread blessed by a priest (southern Europe).

March

St. David: Leeks, to be worn (Wales) or eaten raw (England). Recalls a Welsh victory over the Saxons in A.D. 640; the Welsh wore leeks in their hats to distinguish them from the enemy.

Shrove Tuesday: Pancakes (England); oatcakes (Scotland); rabbit (Ireland). Rich foods are eaten to usher in the Lenten fast; pancakes use up the last of the eggs and butter.

Lent: Simnel, a large fruitcake baked so hard it has sometimes been mistaken by recipients for a hassock or footstool (Great Britain).

St. Benedict: Nettle soup (ancient monastic practice). Picking nettles, which irritate the skin, was a penance in keeping with the spirit of the monastic rule of St. Benedict.

Purim: Strong drink and three-cornered cookies flavored with poppy seeds (Jewish). These cookies, called hamantaschen, are said to represent the three-cornered hat of Haman, the enemy of the Jewish people.

April

Maundy Thursday: Green foods or foods colored green (southern Europe). The medieval liturgical observance called for green vestments; in some parts of Europe, it is still called Green Thursday.

Good Friday: Hot cross buns. If made properly on this day, they will never get moldy (England).

Easter: Lamb as a symbol of sacrifice; also ham.

Beltane, May Day Eve: Strong ale (England); oatcakes with nine knobs to be broken off one by one and offered to each of nine supernatural protectors of domestic animals (Scotland).

May

St. Dunstan: Beer. Cider pressed today will go bad (England).

Ascension Day: Fowl, or pastries molded into the shape of birds, to commemorate the taking of Jesus into the skies (medieval Europe).

June

Whitsunday (Pentecost): Dove or pigeon in honor of the Holy Spirit (southern Europe); strong ale (England).

St. Anthony of Padua: Liver, possibly based on the pre-Christian custom of eating liver on the summer solstice.

Corpus Christi: Orange peel dipped in chocolate, chicken stuffed with sauerkraut (Basque Provinces).

Feast of St. John the Baptist: First fruits of spring harvest.

July

St. Swithin: Eggs, because the saint miraculously restored intact a basket of eggs that had been broken by a poor woman taking them to market (medieval England).

(continued)

St. James: Oysters, because James was a fisherman (England).

August

Lammas Day: Oatcakes (Scotland); loaves made from new grain of the season (England). Blueberries in baskets as an offering to a sweetheart are the last vestige of this holiday as a pagan fertility festival (Ireland).

St. Lawrence of Rome: Because the saint was roasted to death on a gridiron, it is courteous to serve only cold meat today (southern Europe).

Feast of the Assumption: Onions, possibly because they have always been considered wholesome and potent against evil (Polish American).

September

St. Giles: Tea loaf with raisins (Scotland).

Nativity of Mary: Blackberries, possibly because the color is reminiscent of the depiction of the Virgin's blue cloak (Brittany).

Rosh Hashanah: Sweet foods; honey; foods colored orange or yellow to represent a bright, joyous, and sweet new year (Jewish).

Michaelmas Day: New wine (Europe); goose, originally a sacrifice to the saint (Great Britain); cake of oats, barley, and rye (Scotland); carrots (Ireland).

October

Yom Kippur: Fast day; the day before, eat kreplach (filled noodles), considered by generations of mothers to be good and filling (Jewish).

St. Luke: Oatcakes flavored with anise and cinnamon (Scotland).

Sts. Simon and Jude: Dirge cakes, simple fried buns made for distribution to the poor. Also apples or potatoes, for divination (Scotland and England).

All Hallows Eve: Apples and nuts for divination (England); buttered oat-husk gruel (Scotland); bosty, a mixture of potatoes, cabbage, and onions (Ireland).

November

All Saints' Day: Chestnuts (Italy); gingerbread and oatcakes (Scotland); milk (central Europe); doughnuts, whose round shape indicates eternity (Austria).

All Souls' Day: Skull-shaped candy (Mexico); beans, peas, and lentils, considered food of the poor, as penance for souls in purgatory (southern Europe).

St. Martin: Last religious feast day before the beginning of the Advent fast. Goose, last of fresh-killed meat before winter; blood pudding (Great Britain).

St. Andrew: Haggis, or stuffed sheep's stomach (Scotland; see Robert Burns Day, January).

December

St. Nicholas: Fruit, nuts, candy for children (Germany). Commemorates, in part, the miracle by which the saint restored to life three young boys who had been murdered by a greedy innkeeper.

St. Lucy: Cakes flavored with saffron and raisins (Sweden). The saffron imparts a yellow color representing the return of sunlight.

Chanukah: Latkes, or potato pancakes (Jewish).

Christmas Day: Boar's head or goose, plum pudding, nuts, oranges (England); turkey (United States); spiced beef (Ireland).

St. John the Evangelist: Small loaves of bread made with blessed wine (medieval Europe). On this feast, wine is ritually blessed in memory of the saint, who drank poisoned wine and miraculously survived.

Holy Innocents Day: Baby food, pablum, farina, in honor of the children killed by King Herod of Judea (monastic observance).

St. Sylvester: Strong drink (United States); haggis, oatcakes and cheese, oat-husk gruel or porridge (Scotland).

–E. Brady

Sowing Vegetable Seeds

Sow or plant in cool weather	Beets, broccoli, Brussels sprouts, cabbage, lettuce, onions, parsley, peas, radishes, spinach, Swiss chard, turnips
Sow or plant in warm weather	Beans, carrots, corn, cucumbers, eggplant, melons, okra, peppers, squash, tomatoes
Sow or plant for one crop per season	Corn, eggplant, leeks, melons, peppers, potatoes, spinach (New Zealand), squash, tomatoes
Resow for additional crops	Beans, beets, cabbage, carrots, kohlrabi, lettuce, radishes, rutabagas, spinach, turnips

A Beginner's Vegetable Garden

A good size for a beginner's vegetable garden is 10x16 feet. It should have crops that are easy to grow. A plot this size, planted as suggested below, can feed a family of four for one summer, with a little extra for canning and freezing (or giving away).

Make 11 rows, 10 feet long, with 6 inches between them. Ideally, the rows should run north and south to take full advantage of the Sun. Plant the following:

ROW
1 Zucchini (4 plants)
2 Tomatoes (5 plants, staked)
3 Peppers (6 plants)
4 Cabbage

ROW
5 Bush beans
6 Lettuce
7 Beets
8 Carrots
9 Chard
10 Radishes
11 Marigolds (to discourage rabbits!)

Traditional Planting Times

■ Plant **corn** when elm leaves are the size of a squirrel's ear, when oak leaves are the size of a mouse's ear, when apple blossoms begin to fall, or when the dogwoods are in full bloom.

■ Plant **lettuce, spinach, peas,** and other cool-weather varieties when the lilacs show their first leaves or when daffodils begin to bloom.

■ Plant **tomatoes, early corn,** and **peppers** when dogwoods are in peak bloom or when daylilies start to bloom.

■ Plant **cucumbers** and **squashes** when lilac flowers fade.

■ Plant **perennials** when maple leaves begin to unfurl.

■ Plant **morning glories** when maple trees have full-size leaves.

■ Plant **pansies, snapdragons,** and other hardy annuals after the aspen and chokecherry trees leaf out.

■ Plant **beets** and **carrots** when dandelions are blooming.

Growing Vegetables

Vegetable	Start Seeds Indoors (weeks before last spring frost)	Start Seeds Outdoors (weeks before or after last spring frost)	Minimum Soil Temperature to Germinate (°F)	Cold Hardiness
Beans		Anytime after	48–50	Tender
Beets		4 before to 4 after	39–41	Half-hardy
Broccoli	6–8	4 before	55–75	Hardy
Brussels sprouts	6–8		55–75	Hardy
Cabbage	6–8	Anytime after	38–40	Hardy
Carrots		4–6 before	39–41	Half-hardy
Cauliflower	6–8	4 before	65–75	Half-hardy
Celery	6–8		60–70	Tender
Corn		2 after	46–50	Tender
Cucumbers	3–4	1–2 after	65–70	Very tender
Lettuce	4–6	2–3 after	40–75	Half-hardy
Melons	3–4	2 after	55–60	Very tender
Onion sets		4 before	34–36	Hardy
Parsnips		2–4 before	55–70	Hardy
Peas		4–6 before	34–36	Hardy
Peppers	8–10		70–80	Very tender
Potato tubers		2–4 before	55–70	Half-hardy
Pumpkins	3–4	1 after	55–60	Tender
Radishes		4–6 before	39–41	Hardy
Spinach		4–6 before	55–65	Hardy
Squash, summer	3–4	1 after	55–60	Very tender
Squash, winter	3–4	1 after	55–60	Tender
Tomatoes	6–8		50–55	Tender

When to Fertilize	When to Water
After heavy bloom and set of pods	Regularly, from start of pod to set
At time of planting	Only during drought conditions
Three weeks after transplanting	Only during drought conditions
Three weeks after transplanting	At transplanting
Three weeks after transplanting	Two to three weeks before harvest
Preferably in the fall for the following spring	Only during drought conditions
Three weeks after transplanting	Once, three weeks before harvest
At time of transplanting	Once a week
When eight to ten inches tall, and again when first silk appears	When tassels appear and cobs start to swell
One week after bloom, and again three weeks later	Frequently, especially when fruits form
Two to three weeks after transplanting	Once a week
One week after bloom, and again three weeks later	Once a week
When bulbs begin to swell, and again when plants are one foot tall	Only during drought conditions
One year before planting	Only during drought conditions
After heavy bloom and set of pods	Regularly, from start of pod to set
After first fruit-set	Once a week
At bloom time or time of second hilling	Regularly, when tubers start to form
Just before vines start to run, when plants are about one foot tall	Only during drought conditions
Before spring planting	Once a week
When plants are one-third grown	Once a week
Just before vines start to run, when plants are about one foot tall	Only during drought conditions
Just before vines start to run, when plants are about one foot tall	Only during drought conditions
Two weeks before, and after first picking	Twice a week

Vegetable Gardening in Containers

Lack of yard space is no excuse for not gardening, because many vegetables can be readily grown in containers. In addition to providing five hours or more of full sun, you must give attention to choosing the proper container, using a good soil mix, observing planting and spacing requirements, fertilizing, watering, and selecting appropriate varieties. Here are some suggestions:

Vegetable	Type of Container	Recommended Varieties
Beans, snap	5-gallon window box	Bush 'Blue Lake', Bush 'Romano', 'Tender Crop'
Broccoli	1 plant/5-gallon pot 3 plants/15-gallon tub	'DeCicco', 'Green Comet'
Carrots	5-gallon window box at least 12 inches deep	'Danvers Half Long', 'Short 'n Sweet', 'Tiny Sweet'
Cucumbers	1 plant/1-gallon pot	'Patio Pik', 'Pot Luck', 'Spacemaster'
Eggplant	5-gallon pot	'Black Beauty', 'Ichiban', 'Slim Jim'
Lettuce	5-gallon window box	'Ruby', 'Salad Bowl'
Onions	5-gallon window box	'White Sweet Spanish', 'Yellow Sweet Spanish'
Peppers	1 plant/2-gallon pot 5 plants/15-gallon tub	'Cayenne', 'Long Red', 'Sweet Banana', 'Wonder', 'Yolo'
Radishes	5-gallon window box	'Cherry Belle', 'Icicle'
Tomatoes	Bushel basket	'Early Girl', 'Patio', 'Small Fry', 'Sweet 100', 'Tiny Tim'

TIPS

■ Clay pots are usually more attractive than plastic ones, but plastic pots retain moisture better. To get the best of both, slip a plastic pot into a slightly larger clay pot.

■ Avoid small containers. They often can't store enough water to get through hot days.

■ Add about one inch of coarse gravel in the bottom of the container to improve drainage.

■ Vegetables that can be easily transplanted are best suited for containers. Transplants can be purchased from local nurseries or started at home.

■ Feed container plants at least twice a month with liquid fertilizer, following the instructions on the label.

■ An occasional application of fish emulsion or compost will add trace elements to container soil.

■ Place containers where they will receive maximum sunlight and good ventilation. Watch for and control plant insect pests.

Fertilizer Formulas

Fertilizers are labeled to show the percentages by weight of nitrogen (N), phosphorus (P), and potassium (K). Nitrogen is needed for leaf growth. Phosphorus is associated with root growth and fruit production. Potassium helps the plant fight off diseases. A 100-pound bag of 10-5-10 contains 10 pounds of nitrogen, 5 pounds of phosphorus, and 10 pounds of potassium. The rest is filler.

Manure Guide

Type of Manure	Water Content	PRIMARY NUTRIENTS (pounds per ton)		
		Nitrogen	Phosphorus	Potassium
Cow, horse	60%–80%	12–14	5–9	9–12
Sheep, pig, goat	65%–75%	10–21	7	13–19
Chicken:				
Wet, sticky, and caked	75%	30	20	10
Moist, crumbly to sticky	50%	40	40	20
Crumbly	30%	60	55	30
Dry	15%	90	70	40
Ashed	None	None	135	100

TYPE OF GARDEN	BEST TYPE OF MANURE	BEST TIME TO APPLY
Flowers	Cow, horse	Early spring
Vegetables	Chicken, cow, horse	Fall, spring
Potatoes or root crops	Cow, horse	Fall
Acid-loving plants (blueberries, azaleas, mountain laurels, rhododendrons)	Cow, horse	Early fall or not at all

Soil Fixes

If you have . . .

CLAY SOIL: Add coarse sand (not beach sand) and compost.

SILT SOIL: Add coarse sand (not beach sand) or gravel and compost, or well-rotted horse manure mixed with fresh straw.

SANDY SOIL: Add humus or aged manure, or sawdust with some extra nitrogen. Heavy, clay-rich soil can also be added.

Soil Amendments

To improve soil, add . . .

BARK, GROUND: Made from various tree barks. Improves soil structure.

COMPOST: Excellent conditioner.

LEAF MOLD: Decomposed leaves. Adds nutrients and structure to soil.

LIME: Raises the pH of acidic soil. Helps loosen clay soil.

MANURE: Best if composted. Good conditioner.

SAND: Improves drainage in clay soil.

TOPSOIL: Usually used with another amendment. Replaces existing soil.

pH Preferences of Trees, Shrubs, Vegetables, and Flowers

Common Name	Optimum pH Range	Common Name	Optimum pH Range	Common Name	Optimum pH Range
TREES AND SHRUBS		Spruce	5.0–6.0	Bachelor's button	6.0–7.5
Apple	5.0–6.5	Walnut, black	6.0–8.0	Balloon flower	5.0–6.0
Ash	6.0–7.5	Willow	6.0–8.0	Bee balm	6.0–7.5
Azalea	4.5–6.0			Begonia	5.5–7.0
Basswood	6.0–7.5	**VEGETABLES**		Black-eyed Susan	5.5–7.0
Beautybush	6.0–7.5	Asparagus	6.0–8.0	Bleeding heart	6.0–7.5
Beech	5.0–6.7	Bean, pole	6.0–7.5	Canna	6.0–8.0
Birch	5.0–6.5	Beet	6.0–7.5	Carnation	6.0–7.0
Blackberry	5.0–6.0	Broccoli	6.0–7.0	Chrysanthemum	6.0–7.5
Blueberry	4.0–6.0	Brussels sprout	6.0–7.5	Clematis	5.5–7.0
Boxwood	6.0–7.5	Carrot	5.5–7.0	Coleus	6.0–7.0
Cherry, sour	6.0–7.0	Cauliflower	5.5–7.5	Coneflower, purple	5.0–7.5
Chestnut	5.0–6.5	Celery	5.8–7.0	Cosmos	5.0–8.0
Crab apple	6.0–7.5	Chive	6.0–7.0	Crocus	6.0–8.0
Currant, black	6.0–7.5	Cucumber	5.5–7.0	Daffodil	6.0–6.5
Currant, red	5.5–7.0	Garlic	5.5–8.0	Dahlia	6.0–7.5
Dogwood	5.0–7.0	Kale	6.0–7.5	Daisy, Shasta	6.0–8.0
Elder, box	6.0–8.0	Lettuce	6.0–7.0	Daylily	6.0–8.0
Fir, balsam	5.0–6.0	Pea, sweet	6.0–7.5	Delphinium	6.0–7.5
Fir, Douglas	6.0–7.0	Pepper, sweet	5.5–7.0	Foxglove	6.0–7.5
Gooseberry	5.0–6.5	Potato	4.8–6.5	Geranium	6.0–8.0
Hazelnut	6.0–7.0	Pumpkin	5.5–7.5	Gladiolus	5.0–7.0
Hemlock	5.0–6.0	Radish	6.0–7.0	Hibiscus	6.0–8.0
Hickory	6.0–7.0	Spinach	6.0–7.5	Hollyhock	6.0–8.0
Hydrangea, blue-flowered	4.0–5.0	Squash, crookneck	6.0–7.5	Hyacinth	6.5–7.5
Hydrangea, pink-flowered	6.0–7.0	Squash, Hubbard	5.5–7.0	Iris, blue flag	5.0–7.5
		Tomato	5.5–7.5	Lily-of-the-valley	4.5–6.0
Juniper	5.0–6.0			Lupine	5.0–6.5
Laurel, mountain	4.5–6.0	**FLOWERS**		Marigold	5.5–7.5
Lemon	6.0–7.5	Alyssum	6.0–7.5	Morning glory	6.0–7.5
Lilac	6.0–7.5	Aster, New England	6.0–8.0	Narcissus, trumpet	5.5–6.5
Maple, sugar	6.0–7.5	Baby's breath	6.0–7.0	Nasturtium	5.5–7.5
Oak, white	5.0–6.5			Pansy	5.5–6.5
Orange	6.0–7.5			Peony	6.0–7.5
Peach	6.0–7.0			Petunia	6.0–7.5
Pear	6.0–7.5			Phlox, summer	6.0–8.0
Pecan	6.4–8.0			Poppy, oriental	6.0–7.5
Pine, red	5.0–6.0			Rose, hybrid tea	5.5–7.0
Pine, white	4.5–6.0			Rose, rugosa	6.0–7.0
Plum	6.0–8.0			Snapdragon	5.5–7.0
Raspberry, red	5.5–7.0			Sunflower	6.0–7.5
Rhododendron	4.5–6.0			Tulip	6.0–7.0
				Zinnia	5.5–7.0

Lawn-Growing Tips

■ Test your soil: The pH balance should be 7.0 or more; 6.2 to 6.7 puts your lawn at risk for fungal diseases. If the pH is too low, correct it with liming, best done in the fall.

■ The best time to apply fertilizer is just before it rains.

■ If you put lime and fertilizer on your lawn, spread half of it as you walk north to south, the other half as you walk east to west to cut down on missed areas.

■ Any feeding of lawns in the fall should be done with a low-nitrogen, slow-acting fertilizer.

■ In areas of your lawn where tree roots compete with the grass, apply some extra fertilizer to benefit both.

■ Moss and sorrel in lawns usually means poor soil, poor aeration or drainage, or excessive acidity.

■ Control weeds by promoting healthy lawn growth with natural fertilizers in spring and early fall.

■ Raise the level of your lawnmower blades during the hot summer days. Taller grass better resists drought.

■ You can reduce mowing time by redesigning your lawn, reducing sharp corners and adding sweeping curves.

■ During a drought, let the grass grow longer between mowings, and reduce fertilizer.

■ Water your lawn early in the morning or in the evening.

Herbs to Plant in Lawns

C hoose plants that suit your soil and your climate. All these can withstand mowing and considerable foot traffic.

Ajuga or bugleweed *(Ajuga reptans)*

Corsican mint *(Mentha requienii)*

Dwarf cinquefoil *(Potentilla tabernaemontani)*

English pennyroyal *(Mentha pulegium)*

Green Irish moss *(Sagiona subulata)*

Pearly everlasting *(Anaphalis margaritacea)*

Roman chamomile *(Chamaemelum nobile)*

Rupturewort *(Herniaria glabra)*

Speedwell *(Veronica officinalis)*

Stonecrop *(Sedum ternatum)*

Sweet violets *(Viola odorata* or *tricolor)*

Thyme *(Thymus serpyllum)*

White clover *(Trifolium repens)*

Wild strawberries *(Fragaria virginiana)*

Wintergreen or partridgeberry *(Mitchella repens)*

A Gardener's Worst Phobias

Name of Fear	Object Feared
Alliumphobia	Garlic
Anthrophobia	Flowers
Apiphobia	Bees
Arachnophobia	Spiders
Batonophobia	Plants
Bufonophobia	Toads
Dendrophobia	Trees
Entomophobia	Insects
Lachanophobia	Vegetables
Melissophobia	Bees
Mottephobia	Moths
Myrmecophobia	Ants
Ornithophobia	Birds
Ranidaphobia	Frogs
Rupophobia	Dirt
Scoleciphobia	Worms
Spheksophobia	Wasps

Growing Herbs

Herb	Propagation Method	Start Seeds Indoors (weeks before last spring frost)	Start Seeds Outdoors (weeks before or after last spring frost)	Minimum Soil Temperature to Germinate (°F)	Height (inches)
Basil	Seeds, transplants	6–8	Anytime after	70	12–24
Borage	Seeds, division, cuttings	Not recommended	Anytime after	70	12–36
Chervil	Seeds	Not recommended	3–4 before	55	12–24
Chives	Seeds, division	8–10	3–4 before	60–70	12–18
Cilantro/ coriander	Seeds	Not recommended	Anytime after	60	12–36
Dill	Seeds	Not recommended	4–5 before	60–70	36–48
Fennel	Seeds	4–6	Anytime after	60–70	48–80
Lavender, English	Seeds, cuttings	8–12	1–2 before	70–75	18–36
Lavender, French	Transplants	Not recommended	Not recommended	—	18–36
Lemon balm	Seeds, division, cuttings	6–10	2–3 before	70	12–24
Lovage	Seeds, division	6–8	2–3 before	70	36–72
Oregano	Seeds, division, cuttings	6–10	Anytime after	70	12–24
Parsley	Seeds	10–12	3–4 before	70	18–24
Rosemary	Seeds, division, cuttings	8–10	Anytime after	70	48–72
Sage	Seeds, division, cuttings	6–10	1–2 before	60–70	12–48
Sorrel	Seeds, division	6–10	2–3 after	60–70	20–48
Spearmint	Division, cuttings	Not recommended	Not recommended	—	12–24
Summer savory	Seeds	4–6	Anytime after	60–70	4–15
Sweet cicely	Seeds, division	6–8	2–3 after	60–70	36–72
Tarragon, French	Cuttings, transplants	Not recommended	Not recommended	—	24–36
Thyme, common	Seeds, division, cuttings	6–10	2–3 before	70	2–12

* ○ = full sun   ◑ = partial shade

Spread (inches)	Blooming Season	Uses	Soil	Light*	Growth Type
12	Midsummer	Culinary	Rich, moist	○	Annual
12	Early to midsummer	Culinary	Rich, well-drained, dry	○	Annual, biennial
8	Early to midsummer	Culinary	Rich, moist	◑	Annual, biennial
18	Early summer	Culinary	Rich, moist	○	Perennial
4	Midsummer	Culinary	Light	○◑	Annual
12	Early summer	Culinary	Rich	○	Annual
18	Mid- to late summer	Culinary	Rich	○	Annual
24	Early to late summer	Ornamental, medicinal	Moderately fertile, well-drained	○	Perennial
24	Early to late summer	Ornamental, medicinal	Moderately fertile, well-drained	○	Tender perennial
18	Midsummer to early fall	Culinary, ornamental	Rich, well-drained	○◑	Perennial
36	Early to late summer	Culinary	Fertile, sandy	○◑	Perennial
18	Mid- to late summer	Culinary	Poor	○	Tender perennial
6–8	Mid- to late summer	Culinary	Medium-rich	◑	Biennial
48	Early summer	Culinary	Not too acid	○	Tender perennial
30	Early to late summer	Culinary, ornamental	Well-drained	○	Perennial
12–14	Late spring to early summer	Culinary, medicinal	Rich, organic	○	Perennial
18	Early to midsummer	Culinary, medicinal, ornamental	Rich, moist	◑	Perennial
6	Early summer	Culinary	Medium rich	○	Annual
36	Late spring	Culinary	Moderately fertile, well-drained	○◑	Perennial
12	Late summer	Culinary, medicinal	Well-drained	○◑	Perennial
7–12	Early to midsummer	Culinary	Fertile, well-drained	○◑	Perennial

Flowers and Herbs That Attract Butterflies

Allium	*Allium*	Mallow	*Malva*	
Aster	*Aster*	Mealycup sage	*Salvia farinacea*	
Bee balm	*Monarda*	Milkweed	*Asclepias*	
Butterfly bush	*Buddleia*	Mint	*Mentha*	
Catmint	*Nepeta*	Oregano	*Origanum vulgare*	
Clove pink	*Dianthus*	Pansy	*Viola*	
Cornflower	*Centaurea*	Parsley	*Petroselinum crispum*	
Creeping thyme	*Thymus serpyllum*	Phlox	*Phlox*	
Daylily	*Hemerocallis*	Privet	*Ligustrum*	
Dill	*Anethum graveolens*	Purple coneflower	*Echinacea purpurea*	
False indigo	*Baptisia*	Purple loosestrife	*Lythrum*	
Fleabane	*Erigeron*	Rock cress	*Arabis*	
Floss flower	*Ageratum*	Sea holly	*Eryngium*	
Globe thistle	*Echinops*	Shasta daisy	*Chrysanthemum*	
Goldenrod	*Solidago*	Snapdragon	*Antirrhinum*	
Helen's flower	*Helenium*	Stonecrop	*Sedum*	
Hollyhock	*Alcea*	Sweet alyssum	*Lobularia*	
Honeysuckle	*Lonicera*	Sweet marjoram	*Origanum majorana*	
Lavender	*Lavendula*	Sweet rocket	*Hesperis*	
Lilac	*Syringa*	Tickseed	*Coreopsis*	
Lupine	*Lupinus*	Zinnia	*Zinnia*	
Lychnis	*Lychnis*			

Flowers* That Attract Hummingbirds

Beard tongue	*Penstemon*	Trumpet honeysuckle	*Lonicera sempervirens*
Bee balm	*Monarda*	Verbena	*Verbena*
Butterfly bush	*Buddleia*	Weigela	*Weigela*
Catmint	*Nepeta*		
Clove pink	*Dianthus*		
Columbine	*Aquilegia*		
Coral bells	*Heuchera*		
Daylily	*Hemerocallis*		
Desert candle	*Yucca*		
Flag iris	*Iris*		
Flowering tobacco	*Nicotiana alata*		
Foxglove	*Digitalis*		
Larkspur	*Delphinium*		
Lily	*Lilium*		
Lupine	*Lupinus*		
Petunia	*Petunia*		
Pincushion flower	*Scabiosa*		
Red-hot poker	*Kniphofia*		
Scarlet sage	*Salvia splendens*		
Soapwort	*Saponaria*		
Summer phlox	*Phlox paniculata*		

* Note: Choose varieties in red and orange shades.

Bulbs to Plant in Fall

	Planting Depth (inches)	Spacing (inches)	Flower Height (inches)
FOR EARLY-SPRING BLOOMS			
Crocus	3	2–3	4–6
Glory of the snow	3	2–3	6–10
Grape hyacinth	3–4	3	8–10
Snowdrop	4	2–3	6
FOR MIDSPRING BLOOMS			
Daffodil	7	3–4	6–18
Squill	2	4–6	8
Tulip	8	3–6	6–28
Windflower	2	3–4	3–18
FOR LATE-SPRING BLOOMS			
Dutch iris	4	3–6	15–24
Hyacinth	6	6–8	4–12
Ornamental onion	6	4–6	6–24
Spanish bluebell	3	3–6	15–20

Bulbs to Plant in Spring

	Planting Depth (inches)	Spacing (inches)	Flower Height (inches)
FOR SUMMER BLOOMS			
Begonia	2	12	8–18
Blazing star	3–4	6	18
Caladium	2	8–12	12–24
Canna lily	5	16	18–72
Dahlia	4–6	16	12–60
Freesia	2	2–4	12–24
Gladiolus	5	4	24–34
Gloxinia	4	15	12–24
Lily	6–8	12	24–72

How to Force Shrubs and Trees to Bloom Indoors

R E F E R E N C E

Here is a list of some shrubs and trees that can be forced to flower indoors. (The trees tend to be stubborn, and their blossoms may not be as rewarding as those of the shrubs.) The numbers indicate the approximate number of weeks they will take to flower after you bring the branches indoors.

Buckeye 5
Cherry 4
Cornelian dogwood . . 2
Crab apple 4
Deutzia 3
Flowering almond . . 3
Flowering dogwood . . 5
Flowering quince . . . 4
Forsythia 1
Honeysuckle 3
Horse chestnut 5
Lilac 4
Magnolia 3
Pussy willow 2
Red maple 2
Redbud 2
Red-twig dogwood . . 5
Spicebush 2
Spirea 4
Wisteria 3

–courtesy Purdue University Cooperative Extension Service

Shrubs and Trees to Plant for the Birds

Bird	Ash	Birch	Blackberry/ raspberry	Blueberry	Cedar (red)/ juniper	Cherry/plum	Chokeberry	Cotoneaster	Crab apple	Cranberry	Dogwood
Blue jay	F/S	F	F/S	F/S		F	F		F		F/S
Bunting											
Cardinal						F					
Catbird						F			F/S		F/S
Cedar waxwing	F/S	F	F/S	F/S		F		F	F/S	F	
Chickadee	F/S	F		F/S							F/S
Cowbird					F/S						
Crossbill											
Duck											
Finch	F/S	F	F/S		F/S	F	F	F	F/S		
Flicker					F/S	F			F/S		F/S
Goldfinch		F				F			F		
Goose											
Grackle											
Grosbeak	F/S		F/S			F	F		F/S	F	F/S
Junco		F					F				F/S
Mockingbird			F/S		F/S	F		F	F/S	F	
Mourning dove		F	F/S								
Nuthatch											
Oriole						F			F		F/S
Pheasant							F				
Pine siskin	F/S	F									
Redpoll											
Sparrow			F/S	F/S		F	.			F	F/S
Starling											
Tanager						F					F/S
Thrasher			F/S			F	F	F			
Thrush			F/S		F/S	F				F	F/S
Titmouse		F	F/S						F		
Towhee		F	F/S						F	F	
Warbler			F/S		F/S				F		
Woodpecker						F			F/S		F/S

F=FOOD   S=SHELTER

Elderberry	Grape	Hawthorn	Holly	Honeysuckle	Maple	Oak	Pine	Rose	Spruce	Sumac	Viburnum
F/S	F	F/S	F/S	F/S		F	F			F	
F/S											
						F		F/S			
F/S			F/S	F/S					F		
F/S	F	F/S	F/S	F	F/S		F	F	F/S		F
			F/S	F		F	F	F	F/S	F	
									F/S		
F/S	F		F/S	F	F/S		F/S				
F/S		F/S	F/S			F	F			F	
						F	F	F/S			
								F/S			
F/S				F	F/S		F	F	F/S		F
			F/S				F				
F/S	F		F/S	F/S				F	F/S	F	F
F/S	F		F/S			F	S		F/S		
F/S			F/S			F	F		F/S		
		F/S				F			F/S		
									F/S		
		F/S			F/S		F		F/S		
F/S	F	F/S		F	F/S		F	S	F/S	F	F
											F
			F/S			S			F/S	F	
F/S	F	F/S	F/S	F		F	F			F	
F/S	F	F/S		F		F		F		F	F
F/S		F/S				F	F				
F/S		F/S	F/S	F		F	F	S		F	F
F/S			F/S		F/S		F			F	
F/S			F/S			F	F		F/S	F	

Food for the Bird Feeder

Bird	Sunflower seeds	Millet (white proso)	Niger (thistle seeds)	Safflower seeds	Corn, cracked	Corn, whole	Peanuts	Peanut butter	Suet	Raisins	Apples	Oranges and grapefruit
Blue jay	✓			✓	✓	✓	✓			✓		
Bunting	✓	✓	✓		✓	✓						
Cardinal	✓	✓		✓	✓					✓	✓	✓
Catbird										✓	✓	✓
Cedar waxwing											✓	✓
Chickadee	✓	✓		✓	✓		✓	✓	✓			
Cowbird												
Crossbill	✓	✓		✓				✓				
Duck		✓		✓	✓	✓						
Finch	✓	✓	✓	✓	✓		✓	✓				✓
Flicker							✓	✓	✓			
Goldfinch	✓		✓									
Goose					✓	✓						
Grackle	✓											
Grosbeak	✓	✓		✓			✓			✓	✓	✓
Junco	✓	✓	✓	✓	✓							
Mockingbird										✓	✓	
Mourning dove	✓	✓		✓	✓	✓						
Nuthatch	✓	✓		✓			✓	✓	✓			
Oriole												✓
Pheasant					✓							
Pine siskin	✓	✓	✓	✓						✓		✓
Redpoll	✓	✓	✓	✓								
Sparrow	✓	✓					✓					
Starling				✓								
Tanager												
Thrasher					✓		✓			✓	✓	
Thrush										✓	✓	
Titmouse	✓	✓		✓			✓	✓	✓			
Towhee		✓										
Warbler								✓				✓
Woodpecker							✓	✓	✓			

Plant Resources

Bulbs

American Daffodil Society
4126 Winfield Rd., Columbus, OH 43220
www.daffodilusa.org

American Dahlia Society
1 Rock Falls Ct., Rockville, MD 20854
www.dahlia.org

American Iris Society
www.irises.org

International Bulb Society (IBS)
www.bulbsociety.org

**Netherlands Flower Bulb
Information Center**
30 Midwood St., Brooklyn, NY 11225
www.bulb.com

Ferns

American Fern Society
326 West St. NW, Vienna, VA 22180
http://amerfernsoc.org

The Hardy Fern Foundation
P.O. Box 166, Medina, WA 98039
www.hardyferns.org

Flowers

American Peony Society
www.americanpeonysociety.org

American Rhododendron Society
11 Pinecrest Dr., Fortuna, CA 95540
707-725-3043 • www.rhododendron.org

American Rose Society
P.O. Box 30,000, Shreveport, LA 71130
318-938-5402 • www.ars.org

Hardy Plant Society
Mid-Atlantic Group
1380 Warner Rd., Meadowbrook, PA 19046

**International Waterlily and
Water Gardening Society**
www.iwgs.org

Lady Bird Johnson Wildflower Center
4801 La Crosse Ave., Austin, TX 78739
512-292-4200 • www.wildflower.org

Perennial Plant Association
3383 Schirtzinger Rd., Hilliard, OH 43026
614-771-8431 • www.perennialplant.org

Fruits

California Rare Fruit Growers
The Fullerton Arboretum-CSUF
P.O. Box 6850, Fullerton, CA 92834
www.crfg.org

Home Orchard Society
P.O. Box 230192, Tigard, OR 97281
www.wvi.com/~dough/hos/hos1.html

North American Fruit Explorers
1716 Apples Rd., Chapin, IL 62628
www.nafex.org

Herbs

American Herb Association
P.O. Box 1673, Nevada City, CA 95959
530-265-9552 • fax 530-274-3140

The Flower and Herb Exchange
3076 North Winn Rd., Decorah, IA 52101
319-382-5990

Herb Research Foundation
1007 Pearl St., Ste. 200, Boulder, CO 80302
800-748-2617 • 303-449-2265
www.herbs.org

Herb Society of America
9019 Kirtland Chardon Rd., Kirtland,
OH 44094
440-256-0514 • www.herbsociety.org

Cooperative Extension Services

Contact your local state cooperative extension Web site to get help with tricky insect problems, best varieties to plant in your area, or general maintenance of your garden.

Alabama
www.acenet.auburn.edu

Alaska
www.uaf.edu/coop-ext

Arizona
www.ag.arizona.edu/
extension

Arkansas
www.uaex.edu

California
www.ucnr.org

Colorado
www.ext.colostate.edu

Connecticut
www.canr.uconn.edu/ces/
index.html

Delaware
http://ag.udel.edu/
extension

Florida
www.ifas.ufl.edu/www/
extension/ces.htm

Georgia
www.ces.uga.edu

Hawaii
www2.ctahr.hawaii.edu/
extout/extout.asp

Idaho
www.uidaho.edu/ag/
extension

Illinois
www.extension.uiuc.edu/
welcome.html

Indiana
www.ces.purdue.edu

Iowa
www.exnet.iastate.edu

Kansas
www.oznet.ksu.edu

Kentucky
www.ca.uky.edu

Louisiana
www.agctr.lsu.edu/wwwac/
lces.html

Maine
www.umext.maine.edu

Maryland
www.agnr.umd.edu/MCE/
index.cfm

Massachusetts
www.umass.edu/umext

Michigan
www.msue.msu.edu/msue

Minnesota
www.extension.umn.edu

Mississippi
www.msucares.com

Missouri
www.extension.missouri
.edu

Montana
http://extn.msu.montana.edu

Nebraska
http://extension.unl.edu

Nevada
www.nce.unr.edu/nce/
extnhome.htm

New Hampshire
www.ceinfo.unh.edu

New Jersey
www.rce.rutgers.edu

New Mexico
www.cahe.nmsu.edu/ces

New York
www.cce.cornell.edu

North Carolina
www.ces.ncsu.edu

North Dakota
www.ext.nodak.edu

Ohio
www.ag.ohio-state.edu

Oklahoma
www.dasnr.okstate.edu/oces

Oregon
www.osu.orst.edu/extension

Pennsylvania
www.extension.psu.edu

Rhode Island
www.edc.uri.edu

South Carolina
www.clemson.edu/
extension

South Dakota
http://sdces.sdstate.edu

Tennessee
www.utextension.utk.edu

Texas
http://agextension.tamu.edu

Utah
www.extension.usu.edu

Vermont
www.ctr.uvm.edu/ext

Virginia
www.ext.vt.edu

Washington
http://ext.wsu.edu

West Virginia
www.wvu.edu/~exten

Wisconsin
www.uwex.edu/ces

Wyoming
www.uwyo.edu/ces/
ceshome.htm

Makeshift Measurers

When you don't have a measuring stick or tape, use what is at hand. To this list, add other items that you always (or nearly always) have handy.

Credit card . . . . 3⅜" x 2⅛"
Business card (standard) . . . . . . 3½" x 2"
Floor tile . . . . 12" square
Dollar bill . . . . 6⅛" x 2⅝"
Quarter (diameter) . . . . 1"
Penny (diameter) . . . . ¾"
Sheet of paper . . . . 8½" x 11"
     (legal size: 8½" x 14")

Your foot/shoe: _____
Your outstretched arms, fingertip
 to fingertip: _____
Your shoelace: _____
Your necktie: _____
Your belt: _____

If you don't have a scale or a measuring spoon handy, try these for size:
A piece of meat the size of your hand or a deck of cards = 3 to 4 ounces.
A piece of meat or cheese the size of a golf ball = about 1 ounce.
From the tip of your smallest finger to the first joint = about 1 teaspoon.
The tip of your thumb = about 1 tablespoon.

The idea of using available materials to measure is not new.
1 foot = the length of a person's foot.
1 yard = the distance from a person's nose to the fingertip of an outstretched arm.
1 acre = the amount of land an ox can plow in a day.

Hand Thermometer for Outdoor Cooking

■ Hold your palm close to where the food will be cooking: over the coals or in front of a reflector oven. Count "one-and-one, two-and-two," and so on (each pair is roughly equivalent to one second), for as many seconds as you can hold your hand still.

Seconds Counted	Heat	Temperature
6–8	Slow	250°–350°F
4–5	Moderate	350°–400°F
2–3	Hot	400°–450°F
1 or less	Very hot	450°–500°F

Miscellaneous Length Measures

ASTRONOMICAL UNIT (A.U.): 93,000,000 miles; the average distance from Earth to the Sun

BOLT: 40 yards; used for measuring cloth

CHAIN: 66 feet; one mile is equal to 80 chains; used in surveying

CUBIT: 18 inches; derived from distance between elbow and tip of middle finger

HAND: 4 inches; derived from the width of the hand

LEAGUE: usually estimated at 3 miles

LIGHT-YEAR: 5,880,000,000,000 miles; the distance light travels in a vacuum in a year at the rate of 186,281.7 miles per second

PICA: ⅙ inch; used in printing for measuring column width, etc.

SPAN: 9 inches; derived from the distance between the end of the thumb and the end of the little finger when both are outstretched

Body Mass Index (BMI) Formula

Here's an easy formula to figure your Body Mass Index (BMI), thought to be a fairly accurate indicator of relative body size. **W** is your weight in pounds and **H** is your height in inches.

$$BMI = \left(\frac{W}{H^2}\right) \times 703$$

■ If the result is 18.5 to 24.9, you are within a healthy weight range.

■ If it's below 18.5, you are too thin.

■ From 25 to 29.9, you are overweight and at increased risk for health problems.

■ At 30 and above, you are considered obese and at a dramatically increased risk for serious health problems.

There are exceptions to the above, including children, expectant mothers, and the elderly. Very muscular people with a high BMI generally have nothing to worry about, and extreme skinniness is generally a symptom of some other health problem, not the cause.

Tape-Measure Method

■ Here's another way to see if you are dangerously overweight. Measure your waistline. A waist measurement of more than 35 inches in women and more than 40 inches in men, regardless of height, suggests a serious risk of weight-related health problems.

Calorie-Burning Comparisons

If you hustle through your chores to get to the fitness center, relax. You're getting a great workout already. The left-hand column lists "chore" exercises, the middle column shows the number of calories burned per minute per pound of body weight, and the right-hand column lists comparable "recreational" exercises. For example, a 150-pound person forking straw bales burns 9.45 calories per minute, the same workout he or she would get playing basketball.

Chore	Cal/min/lb	Recreational
Chopping with an ax, fast	0.135	Skiing, cross country, uphill
Climbing hills, with 44-pound load	0.066	Swimming, crawl, fast
Digging trenches	0.065	Skiing, cross country, steady walk
Forking straw bales	0.063	Basketball
Chopping down trees	0.060	Football
Climbing hills, with 9-pound load	0.058	Swimming, crawl, slow
Sawing by hand	0.055	Skiing, cross country, moderate
Mowing lawns	0.051	Horseback riding, trotting
Scrubbing floors	0.049	Tennis
Shoveling coal	0.049	Aerobic dance, medium
Hoeing	0.041	Weight training, circuit training
Stacking firewood	0.040	Weight lifting, free weights
Shoveling grain	0.038	Golf
Painting houses	0.035	Walking, normal pace, asphalt road
Weeding	0.033	Table tennis
Shopping for food	0.028	Cycling, 5.5 mph
Mopping floors	0.028	Fishing
Washing windows	0.026	Croquet
Raking	0.025	Dancing, ballroom
Driving a tractor	0.016	Drawing, standing position

HOW MUCH DO YOU NEED?
Floor Tiles

Before you do anything, make a scale drawing of your room with all measurements clearly marked. Take it with you when you shop for tile flooring. Ask the salespeople to help you calculate your needs for rooms that feature bay windows, unusual jogs and turns, and special patterns or designs in the material.

Ceramic Tile

■ Ceramic tiles for floors and walls come in a range of sizes, from 1x1-inch mosaics up to 12x12-inch (or larger) squares. The most popular size is the 4¼-inch square tile, but there is a trend toward larger tiles (8x8s, 10x10s, 12x12s). Installing these larger tiles can be a challenge because the underlayment must be absolutely even and level.

■ Small 1-inch mosaic tiles are usually joined together in 12x12-inch or 12x24-inch sheets to make them easier to install. You can have a custom pattern made, or you can mix different-colored tiles to create your own mosaic borders, patterns, and pictures.

Sheet Vinyl

■ Sheet vinyl typically comes in 6- and 12-foot widths. If your floor requires two or more pieces, your estimate must include enough overlap to allow you to match the pattern.

Vinyl Tile

■ Vinyl tiles generally

come in 9- and 12-inch squares. To find the number of 12-inch tiles you need, just multiply the length of the room (in feet) by the width (rounding fractions up to the next foot). Add 5 percent extra for cutting and waste. Measure any obstructions (such as appliances and cabinets) that you will not lay tile under, and subtract that square footage from the total.

To calculate the number of 9-inch tiles, divide the room's length (in inches) by 9, then divide the room's width by 9. Multiply those two numbers together to get the number of tiles you need, then add 5 percent extra for cutting and waste.

HOW MUCH DO YOU NEED?
Asphalt Shingles

Asphalt roofing shingles usually have three sections, or "tabs," per shingle and an overall length of 3 feet. The surface area of a roof is measured in "squares" of shingles. One square covers 100 square feet. However, shingles are usually priced per bundle, with 1 square equal to 3 bundles.

■ Calculate the number of bundles you need by measuring the roof's square footage (length multiplied by width). Divide that number by 100 to get the number of squares needed. Multiply the number of squares by 3, and that will be the number of bundles you need to buy.

■ To seal out water, apply an underlayment such as builder's felt (tar paper) before shingling. Builder's felt comes in rolls, and its thickness is gauged in pounds. Typically, a roll of 15-pound felt covers about 400 square feet; a roll of 30-pound felt covers 200 square feet.

—Margo Letourneau

HOW MUCH DO YOU NEED?

Wallpaper

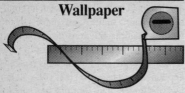

Wallpaper is sold in single, double, and triple rolls. Average coverage for a double roll, for example, is 56 square feet.

■ Measure the length of each wall, add these figures together, and multiply by the height of the walls to get the area (square footage) of the room.

■ Calculate the square footage of each door, window, or other opening in the room. Add these figures together and subtract the total from the area of the room.

■ Take that figure and multiply by 1.15, to account for a waste rate of about 15 percent in your wallpaper project.

■ Divide the coverage figure (from the label) into the total square footage of the room you're papering. Round the answer up to the nearest whole number. This is the number of rolls you need to buy.

■ Save leftover wallpaper rolls, carefully wrapped to keep them clean, or return to the store if unopened.

HOW MUCH DO YOU NEED?

Bricks

How to estimate how many nonmodular standard bricks you need for a project.

■ Multiply the length of the wall in feet by its height in feet, and that by its thickness in feet, and then multiply that result by 20. The answer will be the number of bricks in the wall.

For example, 30 feet (length) × 20 feet (height) × 1 foot (thickness) = 600 × 20 = 12,000 bricks.

HOW MUCH DO YOU NEED?

Exterior Paint

Here's how to estimate the number of gallons needed for one-coat coverage of a home that is 20 feet wide by 40 feet long, has walls that rise 16 feet to the eaves on the 40-foot sides, and has full-width gables on the 20-foot sides rising 10 feet to the peaks.

■ **First, find the area of the walls.**

Add the width to the length:
20 ft. + 40 ft. = 60 ft.

Double it for four sides:
60 ft. × 2 = 120 ft.

Multiply that by the height of the walls:
120 ft. × 16 ft. = 1,920 sq. ft.

The area of the walls is 1,920 square feet.

■ **Next, find the area of the gables.**

Take half the width of one gable at its base:
20 ft. ÷ 2 = 10 ft.

Multiply that by the height of the gable:
10 ft. × 10 ft. = 100 sq. ft.

Multiply that by the number of gables:
100 sq. ft. × 2 = 200 sq. ft.

The area of the gables is 200 square feet.

■ **Add the two figures together for the total area:**
1,920 sq. ft. + 200 sq. ft. = 2,120 sq. ft.

■ **Finally,** divide the total area by the area covered by a gallon of paint (400 square feet) to find the number of gallons needed:
2,120 sq. ft. ÷ 400 sq. ft./gal. = 5.3 gal.

Buy five gallons of paint to start with. The sixth gallon might not be necessary.

–Margo Letourneau

Lumber and Nails

The amount of lumber and nails you need will depend on your project, but these guidelines will help you determine quantities of each.

Lumber Width and Thickness (in inches)

Nominal Size	Actual Size DRY OR SEASONED	Nominal Size	Actual Size DRY OR SEASONED
1 x 3	¾ x 2½	2 x 3	1½ x 2½
1 x 4	¾ x 3½	2 x 4	1½ x 3½
1 x 6	¾ x 5½	2 x 6	1½ x 5½
1 x 8	¾ x 7¼	2 x 8	1½ x 7¼
1 x 10	¾ x 9¼	2 x 10	1½ x 9¼
1 x 12	¾ x 11¼	2 x 12	1½ x 11¼

Nail Sizes

The nail on the left is a 5d (penny) finish nail; on the right, 20d common. The numerals below the nail sizes indicate the approximate number of nails per pound.

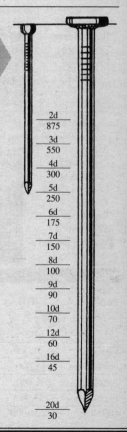

	2d
	875
	3d
	550
	4d
	300
	5d
	250
	6d
	175
	7d
	150
	8d
	100
	9d
	90
	10d
	70
	12d
	60
	16d
	45
	20d
	30

Lumber Measure in Board Feet

Size in inches	LENGTH				
	12 ft.	14 ft.	16 ft.	18 ft.	20 ft.
1 x 4	4	4⅔	5⅓	6	6⅔
1 x 6	6	7	8	9	10
1 x 8	8	9⅓	10⅔	12	13⅓
1 x 10	10	11⅔	13⅓	15	16⅔
1 x 12	12	14	16	18	20
2 x 3	6	7	8	9	10
2 x 4	8	9⅓	10⅔	12	13⅓
2 x 6	12	14	16	18	20
2 x 8	16	18⅔	21⅓	24	26⅔
2 x 10	20	23⅓	26⅔	30	33⅓
2 x 12	24	28	32	36	40
4 x 4	16	18⅔	21⅓	24	26⅔
6 x 6	36	42	48	54	60
8 x 8	64	74⅔	85⅓	96	106⅔
10 x 10	100	116⅔	133⅓	150	166⅔
12 x 12	144	168	192	216	240

R E F E R E N C E

Heat Values

Firewood

High Heat Value
1 cord = 200–250 gallons of fuel oil

American beech
Apple
Ironwood
Red oak
Shagbark hickory
Sugar maple
White ash
White oak
Yellow birch

Medium Heat Value
1 cord = 150–200 gallons of fuel oil

American elm
Black cherry
Douglas fir
Red maple
Silver maple
Tamarack
White birch

Low Heat Value
1 cord = 100–150 gallons of fuel oil

Aspen
Cottonwood
Hemlock
Lodgepole pine
Red alder
Redwood
Sitka spruce
Western red cedar
White pine

Fuels
(approximate)

Fuel	BTU	Unit of Measure
Oil	141,000	Gallon
Coal	31,000	Pound
Natural gas	1,000	Cubic foot
Steam	1,000	Cubic foot
Electricity	3,413	Kilowatt-hour
Gasoline	124,000	Gallon

How Many Trees in a Cord of Wood?

Diameter of Tree (breast high)	Number of Trees (per cord)
4	50
6	20
8	10
10	6
12	4
14	3

A Few Clues About Cords of Wood

■ A cord of wood is a pile of logs 4 feet wide by 4 feet high by 8 feet long.

■ A cord of wood may contain from 77 to 96 cubic feet of wood.

■ The larger the unsplit logs, the larger the gaps, with fewer cubic feet of wood actually in the cord.

■ A cord of air-dried, dense hardwood weighs about 2 tons (4,000 pounds).

■ From one cord of firewood, you could make 7,500,000 toothpicks, 460,000 personal checks, 30 Boston rockers, or 12 dining room tables with each table seating eight.

Freezer Storage Time

(freezer temperature 0°F or colder)

Product	Months in Freezer
Fresh meat	
Beef	6 to 12
Lamb	6 to 9
Veal	6 to 9
Pork	3 to 6
Ground beef, veal, lamb	2 to 4
Frankfurters	2
Sausage, fresh pork	2
Ground pork	1 to 2
Ready-to-serve luncheon meats	Not recommended

Product	Months in Freezer
Poultry	
Chicken or turkey (whole)	6 to 12
Chicken or turkey (parts), Rock Cornish game hens, game birds	6 to 9
Duck, cooked poultry (in gravy), chicken, turkey	6
Goose, squab	4 to 6
Cooked poultry (breaded, fried)	4
Giblets	2 to 3
Cooked poultry (plain meat)	1

Product	Months in Freezer
Fresh fruits (prepared for freezing)	
All fruits except those listed below	10 to 12
Avocados, bananas	3
Lemons, limes, plantains	Not recommended

Product	Months in Freezer
Fresh vegetables (prepared for freezing)	
Beans, beets, bok choy, broccoli, Brussels sprouts, cabbage, carrots, cauliflower, celery, corn, greens, kohlrabi, leeks, mushrooms, okra, parsnips, peas, peppers, onions, soybeans, spinach, summer squash	10 to 12
Asparagus, rutabagas, turnips	8 to 10
Artichokes, eggplant	6 to 8
Tomatoes (overripe or sliced)	2
Bamboo shoots, cucumbers, endive, lettuce, radishes, watercress	Not recommended

Product	Months in Freezer
Cheese (except those listed below)	6
Cottage cheese, cream cheese, feta, goat, fresh mozzarella, Neufchâtel, Parmesan, processed cheese (opened)	Not recommended

Product	Months in Freezer
Dairy products	
Margarine (not diet)	12
Butter	6 to 9
Cream, half-and-half	4
Milk	3
Ice cream	1 to 2
Yogurt	1 to 1½

Freezing Hints

Label foods for easy identification. Write the name of the food, number of servings, and date of freezing on containers or bags.

Freeze foods as quickly as possible by placing them directly against the sides of the freezer.

Arrange freezer into sections for each food category.

For meals, remember that a quart container holds four servings, and a pint container holds two servings.

To prevent sticking, spread the food to be frozen (berries, hamburgers, cook- ies, etc.) on a cookie sheet and freeze until solid. Then place in plastic bags and freeze.

If power is interrupted, or if the freezer is not operating normally, do not open the freezer door. Food in a loaded freezer will usually stay frozen for two days.

REFERENCE

Herb Companions in the Kitchen

Anise. Use in cookies, cakes, fruit fillings, and breads, and with cottage cheese, shellfish, and spaghetti dishes.

Basil. Use in tomato dishes, pesto, sauces, and salad dressings.

Borage. Use leaves in salads; use flowers in soups and stews.

Caraway. Use in rye breads, cheese dips and rarebits, soups, applesauce, salads, coleslaw, and over pork or sauerkraut.

Chervil. Use in soups, salads, sauces, and eggs, and with fish, veal, lamb, and pork.

Chives. Use in vegetable dishes, dressings, casseroles, rice, eggs, cheese dishes, sauces, gravies, and dips.

Dill. Use seeds for pickles and to add aroma and taste to strong vegetables like cauliflower, cabbage, and turnips. Use fresh with seafood and green beans, and in potato dishes, cheese, soups, salads, and sauces.

Fennel. Use in pastries, confectionery, sweet pickles, sausages, tomato dishes, and soups, and to flavor vinegars and oils. Gives warmth and sweetness to curries.

Garlic. Use in tomato dishes, garlic bread, soups, dips, sauces, and marinades, or with meats, poultry, fish, and vegetables.

Lovage. Use in soups, stews, and salad dressings. Goes well with potatoes. The seeds can be used on breads and biscuits.

Marjoram. Use in almost any meat, fish, dairy, or vegetable dish that isn't sweet. Add near the end of cooking.

Mint. Use in Middle Eastern dishes, salads, jellies, and teas, and with roasted lamb or fish.

Oregano. Use in any tomato dish. Try oregano with summer squash, potatoes, mushroom dishes, and beans, or in a marinade for lamb or game.

Parsley. Use fresh in soups, sauces, and salads. It lessens the need for salt in soups. You can fry parsley and use it as a side dish with meat or fish. It is, of course, the perfect garnish.

Rosemary. Use in tomato dishes, stews, and soups, and with poultry, lamb, and vegetables.

Sage. Use in salads, cheese dishes, stuffings, soups, and pickles, and with beans and peas. Excellent for salt-free cooking.

Summer Savory. Use in soups, stews, and stuffings, and with fish, chicken, green beans, and eggs.

Tarragon. Use with meat, eggs, poultry, and seafood, and in salad dressings, marinades, and sauces.

Thyme. Use in casseroles, stews, soups, and ragouts, and with eggs, potatoes, fish, and green vegetables.

Preserving Herbs

DRYING

■ Pick herbs just before they bloom, while they are still at the peak of their flavor. Harvest them in the late morning after the dew has dried and before the hot afternoon sun draws out their delicate flavors.

■ Gather the herbs in small bunches, and tie the stems together with a rubber band or piece of string.

■ Hang the herbs in a dry, well-ventilated area such as a shed or barn, making sure they are out of direct sunlight. (Basements are often too damp for drying.)

■ Use when the leaves crumble if they are rubbed between your fingers, usually within 10 to 14 days.

■ To dry herbs instantly, place them between four paper towels (two on the bottom and two on the top) in a microwave oven. Set the oven on high for two minutes and check the herbs for dryness. If they are not completely dry, rearrange them and repeat the process. This method is a good way to dry parsley. (Warning: This process requires constant attention. The paper towels in the microwave oven could catch fire.)

FREEZING

■ Strip the leaves off the stems of the herbs, and place the leaves into an airtight freezer bag or a small plastic freezer container. Many herbs freeze well, including chives, dill, fennel, lovage, and tarragon.

■ To make herb ice cubes, purée washed and stemmed herb leaves, such as basil, in a food processor with a small amount of olive oil. Pour the mixture into ice cube trays and freeze. Use in soups, stews, and sauces.

Pan Sizes and Equivalents

In the midst of cooking but without the right pan? You can substitute one size for another, keeping in mind that when you change the pan size, you must sometimes change the cooking time. For example, if a recipe calls for using an 8-inch round cake pan and baking for 25 minutes, and you substitute a 9-inch pan, the cake may bake in only 20 minutes, because the batter forms a thinner layer in the larger pan. (Use a toothpick inserted into the center of the cake to test for doneness. If it comes out clean, the cake has finished baking.) Also, specialty pans such as tube and Bundt pans distribute heat differently; you may not get the same results if you substitute a regular cake pan for a specialty one, even if the volume is the same.

Pan Size	Volume	Substitute
9-inch pie pan	4 cups	■ 8-inch round cake pan
8x4x2½-inch loaf pan	6 cups	■ Three 5x2-inch loaf pans ■ Two 3x1¼-inch muffin tins ■ 12x8x2-inch cake pan
9x5x3-inch loaf pan	8 cups	■ 8x8-inch cake pan ■ 9-inch round cake pan
15x10x1-inch jelly roll pan	10 cups	■ 9x9-inch cake pan ■ Two 8-inch round cake pans ■ 8x3-inch springform pan
10x3-inch Bundt pan	12 cups	■ Two 8x4x2½-inch loaf pans ■ 9x3-inch angel food cake pan ■ 9x3-inch springform pan
13x9x2-inch cake pan	14–15 cups	■ Two 9-inch round cake pans ■ Two 8x8-inch cake pans

■ If you are cooking a casserole and don't have the correct-size dish, here are some baking-pan substitutions. Again, think about the depth of the ingredients in the dish and lengthen or shorten the baking time accordingly.

Casserole Size	Baking-Pan Substitute
1½ quarts	9x5x3-inch loaf pan
2 quarts	8x8-inch cake pan
2½ quarts	9x9-inch cake pan
3 quarts	13x9x2-inch cake pan
4 quarts	14x10x2-inch cake pan

REFERENCE

REFERENCE

Substitutions for Common Ingredients

ITEM	QUANTITY	SUBSTITUTION
Allspice	1 teaspoon	½ teaspoon cinnamon plus ⅛ teaspoon ground cloves
Arrowroot, as thickener	1½ teaspoons	1 tablespoon flour
Baking powder	1 teaspoon	¼ teaspoon baking soda plus ⅝ teaspoon cream of tartar
Bread crumbs, dry	¼ cup	1 slice bread
Bread crumbs, soft	½ cup	1 slice bread
Buttermilk	1 cup	1 cup plain yogurt
Chocolate, unsweetened	1 ounce	3 tablespoons cocoa plus 1 tablespoon butter or fat
Cracker crumbs	¾ cup	1 cup dry bread crumbs
Cream, heavy	1 cup	¾ cup milk plus ⅓ cup melted butter (this will not whip)
Cream, light	1 cup	⅞ cup milk plus 3 tablespoons melted butter
Cream, sour	1 cup	⅞ cup buttermilk or plain yogurt plus 3 tablespoons melted butter
Cream, whipping	1 cup	⅔ cup well-chilled evaporated milk, whipped; **or** 1 cup nonfat dry milk powder whipped with 1 cup ice water
Egg	1 whole	2 yolks
Flour, all-purpose	1 cup	1⅛ cups cake flour; **or** ⅝ cup potato flour; **or** 1¼ cups rye or coarsely ground whole grain flour; **or** 1 cup cornmeal
Flour, cake	1 cup	1 cup minus 2 tablespoons sifted all-purpose flour
Flour, self-rising	1 cup	1 cup all-purpose flour plus 1¼ teaspoons baking powder plus ¼ teaspoon salt
Garlic	1 small clove	⅛ teaspoon garlic powder; **or** ½ teaspoon instant minced garlic
Herbs, dried	½ to 1 teaspoon	1 tablespoon fresh, minced and packed
Honey	1 cup	1¼ cups sugar plus ½ cup liquid
Lemon	1	1 to 3 tablespoons juice plus 1 to 1½ teaspoons grated rind

Vegetable Weights and Measures

Asparagus: 1 pound = 3 cups chopped
Beans (string): 1 pound = 4 cups chopped
Beets: 1 pound (5 medium) = 2½ cups chopped
Broccoli: ½ pound = 6 cups chopped
Cabbage: 1 pound = 4½ cups shredded
Carrots: 1 pound = 3½ cups sliced or grated
Celery: 1 pound = 4 cups chopped
Cucumbers: 1 pound (2 medium) = 4 cups sliced
Eggplant: 1 pound = 4 cups chopped (6 cups raw, cubed = 3 cups cooked)
Garlic: 1 clove = 1 teaspoon chopped
Leeks: 1 pound = 4 cups chopped (2 cups cooked)
Mushrooms: 1 pound = 5 to 6 cups sliced = 2 cups cooked
Onions: 1 pound = 4 cups sliced = 2 cups cooked
Parsnips: 1 pound unpeeled = 1½ cups cooked, puréed
Peas: 1 pound whole = 1 to 1½ cups shelled
Potatoes: 1 pound (3 medium) sliced = 2 cups mashed
Pumpkin: 1 pound = 4 cups chopped = 2 cups cooked and drained
Spinach: 1 pound = ¾ to 1 cup cooked
Squash (summer): 1 pound = 4 cups grated = 2 cups salted and drained
Squash (winter): 2 pounds = 2½ cups cooked, puréed
Sweet potatoes: 1 pound = 4 cups grated = 1 cup cooked, puréed

ITEM	QUANTITY	SUBSTITUTION
Lemon juice	1 teaspoon	½ teaspoon vinegar
Lemon rind, grated	1 teaspoon	½ teaspoon lemon extract
Milk, skim	1 cup	⅓ cup instant nonfat dry milk plus about ¾ cup water
Milk, to sour	1 cup	Add 1 tablespoon vinegar or lemon juice to 1 cup milk minus 1 tablespoon. Stir and let stand 5 minutes.
Milk, whole	1 cup	½ cup evaporated milk plus ½ cup water; **or** 1 cup skim milk plus 2 teaspoons melted butter
Molasses	1 cup	1 cup honey
Mustard, prepared	1 tablespoon	1 teaspoon dry or powdered mustard
Onion, chopped	1 small	1 tablespoon instant minced onion; **or** 1 teaspoon onion powder; **or** ¼ cup frozen chopped onion
Sugar, granulated	1 cup	1 cup firmly packed brown sugar; **or** 1¾ cups confectioners' sugar (do not substitute in baking); **or** 2 cups corn syrup; **or** 1 cup superfine sugar
Tomatoes, canned	1 cup	½ cup tomato sauce plus ½ cup water; **or** 1⅓ cups chopped fresh tomatoes, simmered
Tomato juice	1 cup	½ cup tomato sauce plus ½ cup water plus dash each salt and sugar; **or** ¼ cup tomato paste plus ¾ cup water plus salt and sugar
Tomato ketchup	½ cup	½ cup tomato sauce plus 2 tablespoons sugar, 1 tablespoon vinegar, and ⅛ teaspoon ground cloves
Tomato purée	1 cup	½ cup tomato paste plus ½ cup water
Tomato soup	1 can (10¾ oz.)	1 cup tomato sauce plus ¼ cup water
Vanilla	1-inch bean	1 teaspoon vanilla extract
Yeast	1 cake (⅗ oz.)	1 package active dried yeast (1 scant tablespoon)
Yogurt, plain	1 cup	1 cup buttermilk

Swiss chard: 1 pound = 5 to 6 cups packed leaves = 1 to 1½ cups cooked

Tomatoes: 1 pound (3 or 4 medium) = 1½ cups seeded pulp

Turnips: 1 pound = 4 cups chopped = 2 cups cooked, mashed

Orange: 1 medium = 6 to 8 tablespoons juice; 2 to 3 tablespoons grated rind

Peaches: 1 pound (4 medium) = 3 cups sliced

Pears: 1 pound (4 medium) = 2 cups sliced

Rhubarb: 1 pound = 2 cups cooked

Strawberries: 1 quart = 3 cups sliced

Fruit Weights and Measures

Apples: 1 pound (3 or 4 medium) = 3 cups sliced

Bananas: 1 pound (3 or 4 medium) = 1¾ cups mashed

Berries: 1 quart = 3½ cups

Dates: 1 pound = 2½ cups pitted

Lemon: 1 whole = 1 to 3 tablespoons juice; 1 to 1½ teaspoons grated rind

Lime: 1 whole = 1½ to 2 tablespoons juice

Substitutions for Uncommon Ingredients

ITEM	SUBSTITUTION
Balsamic vinegar, 1 tablespoon	1 tablespoon red wine vinegar plus ½ teaspoon sugar
Bamboo shoots	Asparagus (in fried dishes)
Bergamot	Mint
Chayotes	Yellow summer squash **or** zucchini
Cilantro	Parsley (for color only; flavor cannot be duplicated)
Coconut milk	2½ cups water plus 2 cups shredded, unsweetened coconut. Combine and bring to a boil. Remove from heat; cool. Mix in a blender for 2 minutes; strain. Makes about 2 cups.
Delicata squash	Butternut squash **or** sweet potato
Green mangoes	Sour, green cooking apples
Habanero peppers	5 jalapeño peppers **or** serrano peppers
Italian seasoning	Equal parts basil, marjoram, oregano, rosemary, sage, and thyme
Lemon grass	Lemon zest (zest from 1 lemon equals 2 stalks lemon grass)
Limes or lime juice	Lemons or lemon juice
Lo Mein noodles	Egg noodles
Mascarpone, 1 cup	3 tablespoons heavy cream plus ¾ cup cream cheese plus 4 tablespoons butter
Neufchâtel	Cream cheese **or** Boursin
Palm sugar	Light brown sugar
Rice wine	Pale, dry sherry **or** white vermouth
Red peppers	Equal amount pimientos
Romano cheese	Parmesan cheese
Saffron	Turmeric (for color; flavor is different)
Shallots	Red onions **or** Spanish onions
Shrimp paste	Anchovy paste
Tamarind juice	5 parts ketchup to 1 part vinegar

Can Sizes

CAN NAME	FL. OZ.	CUPS	ML
#10	103.70	12.96	3067
#5	56.00	7.00	1656
#3 cylinder	46.00	5.75	1360
#2.5	28.50	3.56	843
#2	20.00	2.50	591
#303	15.60	1.95	461
#211 cylinder	12.00	1.50	355
#1 picnic	10.50	1.30	311
8 ounces	8.30	1.04	245
6 ounces	5.75	0.72	170

The Party Planner

Cooking for a crowd? These estimates can help you determine how much food you should buy. They're based on "average" servings; adjust quantities upward for big eaters and downward if children are included.

Food	To Serve 25	To Serve 50	To Serve 100
MEATS			
Chicken or turkey breast	12½ pounds	25 pounds	50 pounds
Fish (fillets or steaks)	7½ pounds	15 pounds	30 pounds
Hamburgers	8 to 9 pounds	15 to 18 pounds	30 to 36 pounds
Ham or roast beef	10 pounds	20 pounds	40 pounds
Hot dogs	6 pounds	12½ pounds	25 pounds
Meat loaf	6 pounds	12 pounds	24 pounds
Oysters	1 gallon	2 gallons	4 gallons
Pork	10 pounds	20 pounds	40 pounds
SIDE DISHES			
Baked beans	5 quarts	2½ gallons	5 gallons
Beets	7½ pounds	15 pounds	30 pounds
Cabbage for cole slaw	5 pounds	10 pounds	20 pounds
Carrots	7½ pounds	15 pounds	30 pounds
Lettuce for salad (heads)	5	10	20
Peas (fresh)	12 pounds	25 pounds	50 pounds
Potatoes	9 pounds	18 pounds	36 pounds
Potato salad	3 quarts	1½ gallons	3 gallons
Salad dressing	3 cups	1½ quarts	3 quarts
DESSERTS			
Cakes	2	4	8
Ice cream	1 gallon	2 gallons	4 gallons
Pies	4	9	18
Whipping cream	1 pint	2 pints	4 pints
MISCELLANEOUS			
Bread (loaves)	3	5	10
Butter	¾ pound	1½ pounds	3 pounds
Cheese	¾ pound	1½ pounds	3 pounds
Coffee	¾ pound	1½ pounds	3 pounds
Milk	1½ gallons	3 gallons	6 gallons
Nuts	¾ pound	1½ pounds	3 pounds
Olives	½ pound	1 pound	2 pounds
Pickles	½ quart	1 quart	2 quarts
Rolls	50	100	200
Soup	5 quarts	2½ gallons	5 gallons

The Golden Rule
(It's true in all faiths.)

Brahmanism:
This is the sum of duty: Do naught unto others which would cause you pain if done to you.
Mahabharata 5:1517

Buddhism:
Hurt not others in ways that you yourself would find hurtful.
Udana-Varga 5:18

Christianity:
All things whatsoever ye would that men should do to you, do ye even so to them; for this is the law and the prophets.
Matthew 7:12

Confucianism:
Surely it is the maxim of loving-kindness: Do not unto others what you would not have them do unto you.   *Analects 15:23*

Islam:
No one of you is a believer until he desires for his brother that which he desires for himself.
Sunnah

Judaism:
What is hateful to you, do not to your fellowman. That is the entire Law; all the rest is commentary. *Talmud, Shabbat 31a*

Taoism:
Regard your neighbor's gain as your own gain and your neighbor's loss as your own loss.
T'ai Shang Kan Ying P'ien

Zoroastrianism:
That nature alone is good which refrains from doing unto another whatsoever is not good for itself.   *Dadistan-i-dinik 94:5*

—courtesy Elizabeth Pool

Famous Last Words

■ **Waiting are they? Waiting are they? Well— let 'em wait.**
(In response to an attending doctor who attempted to comfort him by saying, "General, I fear the angels are waiting for you.")
—Ethan Allen, American Revolutionary general, d. February 12, 1789

■ **A dying man can do nothing easy.**
—Benjamin Franklin, American statesman, d. April 17, 1790

■ **Now I shall go to sleep. Good night.**
—Lord George Byron, British writer, d. April 19, 1824

■ **Is it the Fourth?**
—Thomas Jefferson, 3rd U.S. president, d. July 4, 1826

■ **Thomas Jefferson—still survives . . .**
(Actually, Jefferson had died earlier that same day.)
—John Adams, 2nd U.S. president, d. July 4, 1826

■ **Friends applaud, the comedy is finished.**
—Ludwig van Beethoven, German-Austrian composer, d. March 26, 1827

■ **Moose . . . Indian . . .**
—Henry David Thoreau, American writer, d. May 6, 1862

■ **Go on, get out—last words are for fools who haven't said enough.**
(To his housekeeper, who urged him to tell her his last words so she could write them down for posterity.)
—Karl Marx, German political philosopher, d. March 14, 1883

■ **Is it not meningitis?**
—Louisa M. Alcott, American writer, d. March 6, 1888

■ **How were the receipts today at Madison Square Garden?**
—P. T. Barnum, American entrepreneur, d. April 7, 1891

■ **Turn up the lights, I don't want to go home in the dark.**
—O. Henry (William Sidney Porter), American writer, d. June 4, 1910

■ **Get my swan costume ready.**
—Anna Pavlova, Russian ballerina, d. January 23, 1931

■ **I should never have switched from Scotch to martinis.**
—Humphrey Bogart, American actor, d. January 14, 1957

■ **Is everybody happy? I want everybody to be happy. I know I'm happy.**
—Ethel Barrymore, American actress, d. June 18, 1959

■ **I'm bored with it all.**
(Before slipping into a coma. He died nine days later.)
—Winston Churchill, British statesman, d. January 24, 1965